TECHNOLOGY AND POLITICS

D1320461

DAUGHTERS

TECHNOLOGY AND POLITICS

Edited by Michael E. Kraft and Norman J. Vig

Duke University Press   *Durham and London* 1988

© 1988 Duke University Press
All rights reserved
Printed in the United States of America
on acid-free paper ∞
Library of Congress Cataloging-in-Publication Data
appear on the last printed page of this book.

To Salley J. Vig

and the memory of Louis and Pearl Kraft

CONTENTS

TABLES AND FIGURES

TABLES

FIGURES

PREFACE

We set sail on this new sea because there is new knowledge to be gained and new rights to be won, and they must be won and used for the progress of all people. For space science, like nuclear science and technology, has no conscience of its own. Whether it will become a force for good or ill depends on man, and only if the United States occupies a position of pre-eminence can we help decide whether this new ocean will be a sea of peace or a new terrifying theater of war.

Rarely has the idealism inspired by scientific and technological progress been expressed more simply and eloquently than by President Kennedy in this passage from his Rice University speech of September 12, 1962. The imperative is clear: we must push ahead in science and technology because new knowledge holds the key to political freedom as well as material betterment for all mankind. But whether these benefits are actually realized depends on a second order of things: man's ability to govern the use of technology by supplying the "conscience" which science and technology itself lacks.

Today, more than a quarter of a century after Kennedy launched the program to go to the moon, the contingency of the latter condition is far more evident than in the optimistic days of Apollo. Space is rapidly being militarized and the risks of many civilian technologies have been demonstrated. The manned space program that succeeded so brilliantly in the 1960s came to a sudden halt with the horrifying explosion of the Challenger Space Shuttle in January 1986, killing all seven astronauts aboard. The world's worst nuclear power plant accident at Chernobyl, USSR, occurred in April 1986; the radioactivity spewed across Europe is expected to cause thousands of cancer deaths into the next century. In October 1986 a fire at a Sandoz chemical warehouse in Basel, Switzerland, sent tons of pesticides and other toxic substances into the Rhine River, causing massive fish kills and serious water contamination as far north as The Netherlands. These disasters followed others in 1984–85: a gas pipeline fire in Cubatão, Brazil, and a liquefied gas tank explosion in Mexico City, each of which killed some 500 people; the leak at the Union Carbide chemical plant in Bhopal, India, which killed at least 2,500 and injured as many as 200,000; and the worst single plane crash in history, in Japan, which took 520 lives.

Each of these catastrophes could be viewed as isolated incidents caused by human error as much as by failures of technical design. But spread across different continents and cultures as they were, they could not but raise new questions about the growing interdependence of humanity and technology throughout the planet. This was a theme that a group of philosophers and social scientists had raised since the mid-1960s as they began to study the practice of science and technology. They pointed out that how technical artifacts are designed, and what purposes they serve, can no longer be taken for granted. Human interests, values, and politics infuse the processes by which choices are made on which lines of research to pursue, who is to benefit from technological development, and which types of risk are considered acceptable to society. The decisions made on such matters as nuclear power and the uses of space may threaten our natural life-support systems and the survival of future generations. At the same time, as technology rushes ahead and pervades all aspects of daily life, it becomes an increasingly important determinant of human character itself. In adapting to technological systems, we lose older human attachments and values that underlie our social structures and moral codes. Thus technological change raises profound philosophical as well as practical questions.

Such issues come together in politics, which is the reason for this book. We have increasingly come to believe that most of the political and social crises of the past two decades are linked to the role of technology. The arms race, the extension of military conflict and terrorism in Third World countries, the population explosion, environmental degradation, energy shortages, the decay of community and family life, the decline of literacy and educational standards, the internationalization of drug trafficking, and most recently economic stagnation and loss of competitiveness—all have been exacerbated if not caused by accelerating technological change. To be sure, many technological advancements have brought undeniable gains of the kind envisaged by Kennedy. The "green revolution" has produced food surpluses in much of the world for the first time in history (while bankrupting many American farmers). The many improvements in medical technology and health care eliminate needless suffering. The communication of knowledge raises living standards and can undermine the power of tyrants and dictators. Technologies which once gave advantage to the few are now being diffused to the many, with immense implications for world political order.

We do not attempt to deal with all of these issues in this volume, but we have tried to take a broad approach to the question of governing technology in the human interest. The first section of the book raises questions of an explicitly philosophical nature: what is the relationship between technology and human purpose? Should technology be understood as an instrument for problem solving or as a determining force in society? Do apparently neutral technologies in fact embody political values and imperatives? Does technology affect the democratic process or only reflect its tides?

A second set of questions focuses on "governing capacity," or the adequacy of institutional means for making public decisions on the introduction and use of technologies. How in our system is technology promoted and regulated? What is the role of the president and the Congress? How do economic and political incentives interact to determine which technologies are developed and which are not? Does government have a coherent policy on technology? If not, who exercises foresight on behalf of the public? How do the communications media handle technological controversies and educate the public on such issues?

A third set of questions focuses more sharply on the means for assessing and regulating technologies. How and to what extent should technological innovation be regulated? What are the economic and social costs of such regulation? Who should bear the burden of proof in judging the safety of new technologies? And what specific methodologies should be used in assessing such risks? Are quantitative scientific techniques appropriate, or must broader "social" assessments be made? Are we in fact anticipating and mitigating long-term risks such as depletion of the ozone layer and the buildup of carbon dioxide and other gases that may cause a greenhouse effect in the atmosphere?

Finally, we examine several case studies involving the evaluation of specific technologies. Who should make decisions about use of controversial technologies for human reproduction and genetic alteration? What role should citizens play in evaluating technologies such as nuclear waste disposal? Are new forms of public participation needed to legitimize technological policies? What other methods are available for resolving disputes over the feasibility of such contentious matters as the Strategic Defense Initiative? Can technical issues be separated from political value judgments in such cases?

We have decided to concentrate on questions concerning technology rather than science, but the two cannot always be separated. Policies for research and development (R&D) inevitably affect basic and applied scientific research as well as technological development, and in some areas (such as recombinant DNA research) the line between science and technology is virtually impossible to draw. But we have tried to avoid some of the ground normally covered in "science policy" discussions—such as R&D priorities, the role of scientists in politics, and the dangers of political restraints on the freedom of research—to focus on some of the distinctive questions that have come to the fore in the current debate over technology. Even so, the role of technology is so vast and complex a subject that many aspects are necessarily neglected here. We cannot, for example, address in detail the momentous restructuring of international political economy currently in progress due to accelerated technology transfer. Nor do we attempt to evaluate the experience of other countries in managing their technological revolutions, though there are some comparative references and undoubtedly more lessons to be learned. We hope nevertheless that the essays presented here, primarily on domestic policies and institutions, will stimulate debate and discussion on the essential value questions.

We would like to thank the contributing authors for their generosity, cooperation, and patience in response to our many editorial requests. Special thanks are also due to Professors Ian Barbour, Patrick Hamlett, and Ned Woodhouse, who read and commented on parts of the manuscript. Among students who were forced to comment on earlier drafts or who provided research assistance, we give special thanks to Jolene Anderson, Chris Carlson, Peter Chiappinelli, Tamara Crockett, Bob Kaplan, Tom Lam, Ward Moberg, and John Palmer.

We also gratefully acknowledge financial and logistical support from the University of Wisconsin–Green Bay Research Council, the Herbert Fisk Johnson Professorship in Environmental Studies, the Carleton College Science, Technology and Public Policy Program, and a grant for the Carleton New Liberal Arts program from the Alfred P. Sloan Foundation. Finally, we thank Richard Rowson of Duke University Press for his understanding and encouragement in making this project a reality.

UNDERSTANDING TECHNOLOGY

PHILOSOPHY AND POLITICS

INTRODUCTION

Technology is increasingly seen as the metaphenomenon or defining characteristic of contemporary life. Looking backward, we can see that the use of tools and construction of artifacts has always distinguished man from other species and led from one stage of cultural evolution to another. But until quite recently the process of change was gradual and piecemeal, marked more by continuities than disruptions. As has been pointed out by the historian Lynn White and others, what we commonly think of as the industrial revolution of the eighteenth and nineteenth centuries can be traced back to innovations and ideas of progress in the Middle Ages.[1] But with gathering force in the past two centuries, the application of scientific knowledge and experimental technique has transformed the material and intellectual conditions of life in totally unprecedented ways.

We now depend on sophisticated technological systems to meet virtually every human need: food, housing, clothing, security, communication, transportation, health, entertainment, and learning. The practice of politics, and for millions even religion, is conducted through electronic media. The most intimate decisions about sexual reproduction, medical treatment, and prolongation of life are increasingly contingent upon technologies. We have machines to control machines: the computer is now the indispensable "command and control" device, the ultimate system manager, and the source of data and intelligence for human decision making.[2] Artificial intelligence systems are contemplated on a massive scale for ballistic missile defense in space and automated production on earth. At the same time, microbiologists are decoding the genetic markers that determine the cell structures and ontological properties of all living things. We are learning to create life itself, thus transcending the evolutionary processes and spiritual bounds that have defined our human nature until now.

It is not surprising that contradictory attitudes have developed toward the meaning and consequences of technology. As social change has accelerated, people have begun to question the moral, psychological, and cultural effects of technology.[3] The fear of many is that technological change is out of control and now threatens to overwhelm traditional human relationships and values. The twin dangers of nuclear holocaust and ecological destruction raise doubts about man's long-term survival. But even in the short run the distractions of modern technologies from VCRs to the latest composition of tennis racquets seem to reduce much of life to trivial pursuit (itself the name of one of the most popular family games of the 1980s). On the other hand, it is obvious that in many respects the quality of life has improved dramatically as a result of technical innovation. Most people enjoy technological conveniences and find them liberating. They cannot conceive of reverting to earlier life-styles or halting technological progress. Thus they are torn between two visions of technology, one negative and frightening, the other positive and exhilarating.

Such feelings underlie much of the political debate over technology, which often seems polarized between dire pessimists and optimists. But a deeper philosophical examination of technology is also underway. The discourse in this field is important in helping to clarify the nature of technological knowledge and its relationship to human ends. The question of whether man controls technology for his purposes or becomes a captive of the technological rules and systems he creates has been at the heart of this discussion. Philosophical inquiry of this kind in turn raises critical questions for political theory, especially concerning the practice of democracy in advanced technological societies.

The first chapter in this section, by Norman Vig, provides a general introduction to the book as a whole as well as an overview of the philosophical debate and its relationship to politics and government. Vig begins with a discussion of several levels of analysis in the new philosophy of technology. He points out that the term "technology" has different meanings to people: as a body of knowledge or way of "knowing," as a professional activity or way of "doing," as physical instruments and artifacts, as large-scale organized and integrated systems, and as the general environment or condition of contemporary life. It is important to understand which usage an author is employing in writings on technology. Vig then introduces three fundamental perspectives on the nature of technology: what he calls the instrumentalist, the social determinist or contextual, and the autonomous technology or technological determinist positions. He goes on to relate these perspectives to the theory and practice of democratic politics, stressing especially the debate over technocracy and the impact of communications technologies on the electoral process. The essay ends with an overview of the role of government in promoting, regulating, and managing technology in an increasingly competitive international environment. Vig concludes that while none of the theories of technology is conceptually adequate, each is useful in understanding part of the current political dilemma over the support and control of technological change. Together they bring out a critical need for much more political debate over the goals and consequences of technology and for much better foresight capabilities to prepare for the future.

The second chapter, "Do Artifacts Have Politics?" by the political theorist Langdon Winner, argues the controversial hypothesis that technical objects themselves can have political properties. While rejecting "naive" deterministic theories, he makes the case that certain technologies have important political qualities either (a) because they were explicitly designed to resolve political conflicts by supporting the power and authority of one group over another or (b) because they are only compatible with a particular type of governance structure. Several examples of each kind are given. The first type of technological politics is important because it refutes the notion that technologies are morally "neutral" unless they are utilized improperly. Rather, in designing a technology, we often restructure our social and political order as well. The second type is even more significant because it involves "inherently political" technologies; that is, technologies which cannot be designed in any way other than to require, or at least be conducive to, a particular authority structure. Either way, Winner suggests that "technological innovations are similar to legislative acts or political foundings that establish a framework for public order that will endure over many generations. For that reason the same careful attention one would give to the rules, roles, and relationships of politics must also be given to such things as the building of highways, the creation of television networks, and the tailoring of seemingly insignificant features on new machines."

The last chapter in this section, by philosopher Albert Borgmann, focuses on the theory of liberal democracy and the effect of contemporary technology on its practice. He suggests that the reason there is both a "crisis of democracy and a crisis of technology" is that democratic theorists have come to reject any substantive ideal of the "good life" and, consequently, the content of democratic politics has come to be specified by technology. Questions of equality and social justice have lost out to the pursuit of the material goods provided by technology, even though technological conditions have much to do with the unequal opportunities people have for self-development. This is in part because technological society has created a sharp division between the "foreground" of technological commodities that we celebrate and consume in our leisure and the almost forgotten "background" of labor required to produce these goods. Borgmann suggests that the decline of meaningful debate over political ends has increased citizen apathy and disengagement, while the role of the state is reduced to managing crises in the technological system. Borgmann thus concludes that technological progress can no longer be an excuse for avoiding the fundamental moral issues of democracy.

The ethical warnings of the philosophers do not mean that they are against all technology. Most critics would agree that technological innovation is essential for economic growth and to mitigate the social and ecological impacts of past technological excesses. Technological ingenuity will indeed be needed to sustain life on the planet as populations grow and resources dwindle.[4] However, the philosophers argue that it is essential that future technological development be appropriate to this end, and to maintenance of primary human values such as freedom, security, justice, equality, and community.

Two other points should be made to put this discussion in perspective. One is that technology does not simply advance by itself. Humans make decisions at every stage of the innovation process and always choose some designs and types of development over others. Indeed, far more inventions "fail," in the sense that they are never pursued or are tried and rejected, than "succeed" in getting developed.[5] In a variety of ways, including the expression of consumer preferences in the economic marketplace, some innovations are selected over others because they are believed to serve human needs. Technology is never completely "autonomous" or self-generating.

Finally, technology need not be "dehumanizing." Personal computers, for example, are entirely at the service of users and have arguably enhanced people's creativity and ability to communicate. In fact, the guiding principle behind much of the advanced research on information and communications technology today is that machines can be made to simulate the cognitive and thought processes of humans and to interact with them on an increasingly personal level.[6] Such interactive systems may be less inhibiting to individual thought and freedom than existing "mass media" technologies such as broadcast television.[7] Similarly, it may be that the new biotechnologies, which make use of the chemical and biological properties of living organisms, will prove far more benign to the natural environment than the older mechanical and chemical industrial technologies that have polluted it so badly.

However, much empirical research is needed on the precise social, psychological, and ecological effects of these and other technologies before we rush headlong into the next generation of machines. There is some troubling evidence, for example, that use of computer toys and games by children affects their cognitive mental development and, consequently, their self-conception and moral reasoning.[8] A variety of studies also indicate that computerization of offices and factories can have serious adverse effects on work relationships, morale, and job satisfaction.[9] While we need to be careful not to blame technology for all of the social ills and pathologies that afflict modern man,[10] we need to give far more thought to ways of evaluating and making collective decisions about new technologies than in the past. Subsequent sections of the book discuss institutional and analytical mechanisms for making such choices.

TECHNOLOGY, PHILOSOPHY, AND THE STATE:

AN OVERVIEW

NORMAN J. VIG

Any discussion of technology and politics must begin with a consideration of technology itself. Until quite recently, technology was conventionally understood to be the means by which man created tools and other artifacts for the improvement of material standards of living. Through the application of ever more sophisticated scientific principles, *homo faber* (man as toolmaker) could harness the forces and materials of nature to human ends, liberating himself forever from physical drudgery and poverty. Such human progress could not but further the advancement of democracy as well, many argued, for technology creates new opportunities for personal and political choice.[1] It was not by accident that the most technically advanced nations were also the most democratic.

This benign view of technology and its sociopolitical consequences has been shaken over the past quarter century. Although the prophets of technological optimism were never without their critics, not until the 1960s did wholesale questioning of the social and political benefits of technology begin. It was then perceived that affluent societies built on technological progress were beset with a host of new problems: decaying cities, rising crime and social violence, disintegrating families, polluted air and water, declining energy resources, mindless commercialism, and above all the capability to wage war beyond any sensible objective. It is not surprising that a new group of radical critics attacked "technological society" as a monstrous construction that had grown beyond man's control, a perversion of human intelligence that threatened to destroy both the natural ecology and the truly human values that had shaped our culture. Technology was increasingly seen as an agent of domination and oppression rather than liberation, as the source of the problem rather than the solution.[2] Democracy, in turn, required the abandonment of large-scale, centralized authority structures associated with big technology in favor of smaller communal units in which direct participation was possible. "Small is beautiful" referred to small-scale technology *and* democracy.[3]

While such extreme views have given way to more balanced assessments in the 1980s, they reflect a deep and growing concern over the nature of technological change and its political, economic, social, environmental, and ethical consequences. Economic problems are increasingly linked to international technological competition. At the same time, issues such as toxic and radioactive waste disposal, atmospheric and climatic modification, the militarization of space, the computerization of production, the dissemination of new reproductive and life-extending medical technologies, and the application of genetic engineering to a wide range of organisms and products outside the laboratory all raise fundamental moral and political controversies that are certain to intensify as we move into the twenty-first century. It is thus important to consider the broader philosophical implications of technological change as well as the more specific technical and political problems associated with individual technologies.

The two sections that follow examine the philosophical debate over technology in more detail, looking at the new focus on technology in philosophical discourse and differing basic conceptions of the nature of technology. We then turn to a discussion of the relationship between technology and democratic politics, with particular emphasis on the organization of power and the conduct of electoral competition. Finally, the role of the state in promoting and controlling technology is considered in light of both ethical concerns and current global economic and political pressures.

PHILOSOPHY AND TECHNOLOGY

A new subdiscipline focusing on the philosophy of technology has been emerging in the past few decades.[4] Its basic premise is that technology has become so central to our existence and way of life that it must be studied as a fundamental *human* characteristic. While the state of technology has always, in some sense, determined the possi-

bilities of social life, until recently technological conditions were relatively stable for long periods and did not radically alter the individual's role or sense of being over the course of a lifetime. From the end of
the eighteenth century, however, technological change greatly accelerated as it came to reflect the rapid advancement of scientific knowledge in Western societies. The new "scientific" technology of the industrial revolution enormously extended the power of humans to exploit
nature, fabricate products, and dominate each other. Each successive
wave of technical innovation has both enhanced living standards and
multiplied the potentials for mass destruction, inevitably impinging
more deeply on the consciousness of people subject to this Faustian
dilemma. But technology has also subtly changed the everyday pattern
of work, leisure, family life, learning, communicating, and thinking. It
is this deeper penetration of technology to the very definition and
expression of human character that concerns many philosophers.

   On an *epistemological* level, the pervasiveness of technology has
led to a broadening of its definition and conceptualization. Technology is no longer regarded simply as the cumulative stock of tools,
machines, and other artifacts (the "technics" of modern civilization),
but as a distinctive way of knowing and doing. As such, technology is
more than either applied science or engineering in the traditional
academic sense. Rather it is seen to embody a universalistic approach
to problem solving ("technique") and, according to some theorists, a
corresponding imperative for the rational organization of social
behavior.[5]

   When thinking about technology, it is important to be aware of
these different usages. "Technology" can refer to any of several things:
(a) a body of technical knowledge, rules, and concepts; (b) the practice
of engineering and other technological professions, including certain
professional attitudes, norms, and assumptions about the application
of technical knowledge; (c) the physical tools, instruments, or artifacts
resulting from this practice; (d) the organization and integration of
technical personnel and processes into large-scale systems and institutions (industrial, military, medical, communications, transportation,
and so on); and (e) the "technological condition," or character and
quality of social life resulting from the cumulation of technological
activity.

   Discussions of technology are often confused because the participants fail to clarify their usage of the term or alternate between one

usage and another. For example, many critics of technology are far more concerned about certain attitudes of professional technologists (b) or about the institutions which apply technology (d) than they actually are about technological knowledge (a) or artifacts per se (c), yet they are indiscriminately condemned as "antitechnological." Similarly, many proponents of "engineering" solutions to problems (a–c) may be critical of current technological systems (d) and share many concerns about the resulting quality of life; for example, pollution and congestion (e). Genuine philosophical dialogue requires mutual understanding of these semantic differences and of the underlying value premises.

But the problem of technology is not simply epistemological and linguistic. There is also a sense in which technology (in its many senses) is changing human nature itself. Philosophers have consequently devoted a good deal of attention to the *ontological* dimension of technology; that is, how technology reflects or relates to the essential nature of man.

The traditional view of technology derives from the classical Greek idea of *technē*, or the practical arts and crafts which humans developed to serve higher purposes. Thus in Aristotelian thought technology refers to a device or method created by man (and thus external to him) as a secondary means of achieving his primary ends (i.e., having only instrumental value). It is this root concept that has recently been challenged by a variety of thinkers who deny either that man is *homo faber* by nature or that technology involves only instrumental engagement with material reality.[6] The German philosopher Martin Heidegger held that technology is a profound way of "setting upon" and "unconcealing" truths about nature. But he warned that the cognitive framework underlying aggressive modern technology (what he called *Gestell*, or "enframing") also conceals and negates other ways of understanding human experience or "Being."[7] Many others argue that human character is altered through interaction with technology. Hans Jonas states that "the triumph of *homo faber* over his external object means also his triumph in the internal constitution of *homo sapiens*, of which he used to be a subsidiary part"; thus "man himself has been added to the objects of technology."[8] In the words of Langdon Winner, "As they become woven into the texture of everyday existence, the devices, techniques, and systems we adopt shed their tool-like qualities to become part of our very humanity."[9]

Indeed, according to some theorists, technological norms and modes of thought threaten to displace traditional "humanistic" values in virtually all areas of life. Combining ontological and epistemological critiques, this argument holds that "technical rationality," or what Manfred Stanley calls "technicism," has produced a radical reorientation of reason toward the means rather than the ends or purposes of life. This is manifested by intrusion of the language and metaphor of systems, control, planning, and problem solving into domains previously considered moral or ethical. At the extreme, technology itself becomes the imperative or end of life.[10]

These considerations, together with the enormous enhancement of physical powers conferred by modern technology, have led some philosophers to call for a new *social ethics* focused on the responsible use of technology. Hans Jonas, in particular, argues that traditional ethical systems are obsolete because they fail to appreciate the need for human restraint based on predictive knowledge; that is, knowledge of possible consequences of current actions for the remote future. Unless ethical responsibility and foresight are commensurate with empirical knowledge and power, he maintains, mankind will destroy its own future in an essentially utopian quest for technical progress.[11]

THREE VIEWS OF TECHNOLOGY

The nature of the ethical questions posed by technology depends on one's conception of how technology relates to human purpose. Much of the debate has revolved around three concepts of technology that I will identify as the *instrumentalist*, the *social determinist* or *contextual*, and the *autonomous technology* or *technological determinist* perspectives. This section discusses each of these concepts and points out some of their more important implications and weaknesses.

1. *Instrumentalism* holds that technology is simply a means to an end. Each technological innovation is designed to solve a particular problem or serve a specific human purpose. The only questions therefore are (a) whether the original purpose is socially acceptable; (b) whether the design is technically feasible; that is, whether the device "works"; and (c) whether it is used for its intended purpose. Of course, it is always possible that use of the technology can interfere with the exercise of someone else's rights—for example, if a machine creates so much smoke and noise that it lowers the value of a neighbor's property

—but these have long been matters for equity balancing in the courts rather than issues pertaining to the utility of the technology itself. It is the human beings who create and use technology that make it a force for good or evil: *technology itself is considered morally neutral.*

Emmanuel Mesthene, former director of the Harvard University Program on Technology and Society, stated a variation of this thesis when he wrote: "Technology . . . creates new possibilities for human choice and action, but leaves their disposition uncertain. What its effects will be and what ends it will serve are not inherent in the technology but depend on what man will do with the technology."[12] In Mesthene's view, the consequences of technology may be more unpredictable and open-ended than the simple instrumentalist hypothesis would suggest, but he is nevertheless confident of our ability to manage technology for social benefit. Technology is thus more or less synonymous with progress.

This kind of optimism has predominated in American (and European) attitudes toward technology since the industrial revolution. Many of the largest corporations were built on technological innovation or monopoly, making the utilitarian concept of technology especially important to the business community. Even today, corporate leaders have a strong vested interest in the instrumentalist doctrine since it justifies constant product innovation and minimizes public concern over the social effects of their activities. Indeed, this approach divorces technology from its social consequences.[13]

Instrumentalism has also infused liberal theories of democracy. The idea that individuals are free to pursue their own interests, without interference from the state, implies that the social impacts of technology are minimal. Indeed, insofar as there are social problems, technology rather than coercion or fundamental socioeconomic reform can often provide a solution (i.e., "technical fix").

From this perspective, no special ethical problems are presented by technology, since technology only provides the means for implementing values that are grounded elsewhere. To be sure, insofar as modern technology creates unprecedented powers for waging war or creating other potentially catastrophic situations, due caution must be exercised by those who control the technology to ensure that it is used appropriately. But this moral burden is not qualitatively different from that required in the past since it is the motives (or interests) of people, rather than the technology itself, that determine how the new powers will be used.

However, the rapid advancement and dissemination of technology have made this position increasingly difficult to defend. In the first place, it assumes that the designers and users of technology fully understand its purposes, while in reality they cannot foresee more than a narrow range of consequences. One discovery or innovation typically leads to another, and the cumulative process of invention may have little to do with original intent. One of the characteristics of technology is that it continually generates new applications and uses simply because "the technology is there." In fact, many of the most enthusiastic proponents of technology argue that its future impacts cannot be predicted.[14]

It is increasingly apparent that the second and third order consequences of technology include severe damage to the natural environment as well as social and cultural disruption. Many of these effects are difficult to predict due to long latency periods (as in the case of many cancers) or gradual dissemination through biological, geological, or social systems. To be sure, scientific and technical advance itself now allows monitoring of some of these processes with far greater accuracy than in the past (for example, many chemical residues can now be detected at parts per billion or even parts per trillion). Even so, the biological and social consequences of a technology may not be known for many years or decades after deployment, making ongoing decisions about use and control highly uncertain.

It is also very difficult to halt development of a technology once major economic investments and institutional interests are committed to it. One need only think of the modern automobile, chemical, or computer industries. It is ingenuous to claim that technology is neutral if it vastly increases the power of those who control it, allows one group to dominate others, or consistently produces changes that are opposed by substantial segments of the population. But even if they are perceived as benign, technologies become an integral part of the social order once they are developed and institutionalized.

2. This has led many students of technology, especially historians and sociologists, to adopt what may be called a *social determinist* or *contextual* approach. This perspective holds that technology is not a neutral instrument for problem solving but an expression of social, political, and cultural values. That is, technology embodies not only technical judgment but the broader social values and interests of those who design and use it. As John M. Staudenmaier puts it,

contextualism is rooted in the proposition that technical designs cannot be meaningfully interpreted in abstraction from their human context. The human fabric is not simply an envelope around a culturally neutral artifact. The values and world views, the intelligence and stupidity, the biases and vested interests of those who design, accept, and maintain a technology are embedded in the technology itself.[15]

The origins of technological innovations must thus be understood in terms of their particular social context. For example, the development of mechanical clocks in medieval monasteries can be traced to the importance monks attached to regular prayer observance. Or, to cite modern examples, Henry Ford's decision to mass-produce a simple, inexpensive automobile and Apple's decision to market a personal home computer over half a century later both reflect and reinforce an American preference for individual freedom, privacy, and convenience. Conversely, neglect of the nation's railway system and failure to develop alternative energy technologies demonstrate a weaker commitment to provision of collective goods, as well as the power of vested interests in the motor vehicle and petroleum industries. Decisions about which technologies are developed and who benefits from them are shaped more by cultural preferences and the distribution of financial and political power than by specific problems or technical opportunities.[16]

Marxist theory embodies a variant of this interpretation. Although Marx saw technology as a revolutionary force in creating new "forces of production," he argued that the consequences of technology depend on the "social relations of production"; that is, the economic system determines which class interests are served by technology, and thus ultimately what kinds of technology are developed. In the Soviet Union, all leaders from Lenin onward have attempted to utilize technology to create a new social and economic order, stressing the construction of large, centrally controlled industrial and agricultural systems. Many of these technologies are now regarded as obsolete, and the leadership looks to a new "scientific-technological revolution" to carry the USSR forward to "full communism." In practice, the Soviets are taking an increasingly instrumental approach to technological modernization.[17]

The social contextual approach is perhaps most valuable in tracing the origins of particular inventions and in explaining why certain intercultural variations occur in patterns of technological innovation.

The problem is that it may not tell us much about technology as a distinctive modern phenomenon. Explanation is simply moved one step backward, to social structure or culture, and technology is reduced to one form of cultural expression among others (the same could be said of art, literature, and music). Moreover, the chain of causation between social context and technology is difficult to establish; it can as well be argued that technology shapes culture, or that there are always reciprocal influences. In any case, whatever ethical issues arise would relate primarily to underlying social structures and values rather than to the *technology* involved.

Another difficulty with this approach is the ease with which technology transfer now takes place between cultures. In areas such as electronics and automobiles, manufacture is now worldwide, and countries which initially license or borrow foreign technology may quickly develop the capacity to engineer their own products. Multinational corporations can produce many "high-tech" goods almost anywhere, and the diffusion of organization and management techniques that results may profoundly affect other cultures. However, the "globalization" of technology also poses serious economic and political problems for originating countries (such as the United States), which find it increasingly difficult to compete with new producers.[18] Thus it seems fruitless to explain the nature of contemporary technology in terms of any particular social or cultural context; rather, technology appears to be an increasingly independent and universalistic phenomenon. The third perspective takes up this idea.

3. *Technological determinism* or the *autonomous technology* perspective regards technology as its own governing force; that is, technology advances according to its own logic and now shapes human development more than it serves human ends. The most complete expression of this view is found in Jacques Ellul's widely read books, *The Technological Society* and *The Technological System*, in which technology (or what Ellul calls *la technique*) is pictured as an autonomous force that now permeates man's thinking and daily patterns of life to such an extent that he has lost control over his destiny. Other critics of modern technology such as Lewis Mumford, Herbert Marcuse, and E. F. Schumacher argue that the type of large-scale, production-oriented "monotechnics" that have come to dominate advanced industrial societies are dehumanizing and authoritarian, if not totalitarian.[19]

This radical critique of technology was espoused by many intellectuals associated with the New Left in the 1960s and 1970s, but with much broader resonance. The Vietnam War, with its massive bombing raids, chemical defoliation program, and "electronic battlefield," and the proposed antiballistic missile (ABM) and supersonic transport (SST) systems became symbols of technological hubris to many. The environmental movement put much of the blame for ecological destruction on new chemical and pesticide industries. It was argued that such technologies are not value-neutral because they assert certain values—notably the will to power, the quest for absolute efficiency, and the profit motive—over other human needs (including those of future generations) and against the integrity of nature. They also concentrate economic, social, and political power in the hands of a narrow elite: those relatively few who command sufficient wealth, technical skill, or managerial authority to manipulate what Mumford called the "megamachine." This leads to technocracy, or rule by an elite of unaccountable experts (discussed later in this essay).

On a more theoretical level, Ellul and others argued that the conventional "tool/use" dichotomy is a false one. "There is no difference at all between technique and its use. The individual is faced with an exclusive choice, either to use the technique as it should be used according to the technical rules, or not to use it at all."[20] That is, once technological systems are employed, they demand a high degree of conformity, regardless of the intention of the "user." They also govern the "user's" life in many respects, particularly if the "user" is an ordinary person who has no direct control over the system he or she is "using." In this sense the consequences of technology are inherent in the technology; they are "designed in," whether the designer was fully aware of them or not.

Technological determinism theories, like the others, are open to some fairly obvious criticisms. In Ellul's work, for example, "technique" becomes an obscure and almost mystical force that defies empirical understanding. The concept implies a total absence of human volition at the societal level, yet we cannot deny that choices are made by those who create and manipulate technology. Nuclear weapons have not, after all, been used since 1945. Furthermore, specific technologies vary greatly in their societal impact and modes of control; not all are centralized "megasystems" that control peoples' lives, nor do they embody a single set of values. Personal computers, such as the one this is being written on, can enhance freedom of expression as well as economic efficiency. Environmentalists support laws such as the Clean Air Act that rely heavily on "technology forcing" to solve pollution problems. At the same time that DDT was banned in this country because it imperiled several species of birds, in India it was credited with saving millions of lives that would otherwise have been lost to malaria. The moral consequences of a technology are clearly relative to its social context.[21]

Such considerations have led many theorists to adopt a modified approach often referred to as "soft determinism." In this version —which could also be considered a distinctive fourth perspective —technologies are seen as "conditioning" or "encouraging" (rather than fully determining) certain types of political and social structural change which may or may not be appropriate to a given society's value system. Langdon Winner, for example, has elaborated and refined Ellul's concept of autonomous technology to emphasize the implications of different technologies for political authority arrangements (see chapter 2). He compares technological systems to political constitutions or legislation in the sense that, once implemented, they establish many of the "rules" by which people live.[22] While there is nothing inevitable about the direction of change, he warns against a pattern of "technological drift"; that is, a largely random and thoughtless process of technical and social change to which people adapt like "somnambulists."[23]

Albert Borgmann similarly suggests that we unconsciously conform to "invisible" social paradigms that are increasingly defined by technology:

When a social paradigm is deeply entrenched, it not only informs most human practices but it also patterns the organizations, institutions, the daily implements, the structures of civilization, and even the ways in which nature and culture are arranged and accessible. All of reality is patterned after the paradigm, and in this sense we can say that the paradigm has acquired an ontological dimension. When applied to technology, this is not to explain the paradigm's origin but to highlight the extent and intensity of its rule. When the pattern is so firmly established, it also tends to become invisible. . . . The relation to technology is neither one of domination by technology nor one of conscious direction of technology. It is perhaps best called one of implication in technology.

Living in an advanced industrial country, one is always and already implicated in technology and so profoundly and extensively that one's involvement normally remains implicit. The rule of technology is not the reign of a substantive force people would bear with resentment and resistance. Rather technology is the rule today in constituting the inconspicuous pattern by which we normally orient ourselves.[24]

The ethical implications of technological determinism, whether in "hard" or "soft" versions, are far more complex than those of instrumentalism and social determinism. On one level, man becomes the victim of his own invention, as in the old tales of Frankenstein's monster and the sorcerer's apprentice. To prevent such tragedies it is necessary to exercise much greater foresight and control at the *design* stage as well as in the *implementation* of technology. This suggests the need for much greater foresight and political control over the introduction of new technologies; indeed, once a technology is fully deployed it may be too late to avoid unwanted consequences. On another level, man must consciously affirm his ontological nature or human values if technological drift is not to define his purposes for him. The tendency for technological opportunism, or artifice, to displace human ends requires far more attention to value definition.

These concerns, which accord with those of many contemporary philosophers of technology, in turn raise a host of fundamental questions about politics. Does the state have the political and institutional capacity to control technology? To what extent is such control possible in a democracy? How are citizens to participate in the choice of technological alternatives that affect their lives? And how has technology shaped the political process itself? We take these issues up in the remainder of the chapter.

TECHNOLOGY AND DEMOCRACY

What is the relationship of technology to democracy? Although relatively few political theorists have addressed the question directly, most would probably agree that, historically, the progress of science and technology has been an important force in liberating peoples from traditional submission and poverty, and thus in establishing the preconditions for democratic citizenship. Some would argue further that technology has had an increasingly egalitarian and democratic impact on society by making the good things in life available to everyone.[25] Others have even suggested that technology may finally allow us to transcend preoccupations with material consumption and concentrate on the fulfillment of other human capabilities.[26]

A great deal obviously depends on one's definition of democracy and how one interprets recent developments. Of course the meaning of democracy has been debated for centuries and continues to evolve. But perhaps we can agree on a working definition with three critical elements: freedom, equality, and participation. Freedom requires protection of one's personal and civil liberties against the state via the rule of law. Equality entails both equality before the law and equal opportunity to develop one's abilities in the marketplace, which in practice implies some minimal degree of fairness in the overall distribution of income. Participation involves the right of citizens to elect their leaders and to communicate their political preferences actively in other lawful ways.

Now if we look at each of these components in light of contemporary levels of technology, there are clearly some troublesome aspects. A number of studies have recently been conducted on the effects of technological development on constitutional rights, especially First Amendment guarantees of freedom of the press, the evolving right to privacy recognized by the Supreme Court, private property rights, and the rights of the accused in the criminal justice system.[27] Many of these issues involve very sensitive questions such as the rights of individuals to protect themselves against unauthorized use and dissemination of computerized information, including medical records, and public access to new sources of information that may fall under national security restrictions. They also raise many new questions about the rights of the unborn and the terminally ill, the right to patent genetically engineered organisms, and the rights of employees against company-imposed electronic surveillance and medical screening.[28]

The impact of technology on social and economic equality is also debatable. During many periods of history technological change has reduced the living standards of many while benefitting new social groups. And although in the long run technology has reduced overall levels of inequality by creating economic opportunities, it has also produced immense corporate organizations and other centers of concentrated wealth and power that are controlled by relatively few people. Currently the transition from manufacturing to service industries in technologically advanced societies is lowering real wages and incomes for a large part of the work force by rendering many jobs and skills obsolete. Whether the new jobs created by technology are enhancing equality of opportunity and the chances for self-development is an open question, but recent trends toward greater inequality in the United States do not suggest that this is the case.[29]

Finally, does advanced technology lead to greater political participation or improved communication between government and citizens? On the one hand, there can be little doubt that modern communications media, especially television, have greatly reduced the "distance" between leaders and the public and made a truly national politics possible. On the other hand, it is also obvious that mass political communication can be used by authoritarian and totalitarian elites to manipulate mass participation and totally subvert democracy.[30] What we are concerned about here is whether recent developments in broadcast and other communications technologies in democratic systems enhance the quality of citizen participation or not. For example, what has the effect of TV been on election campaigns? Has it improved public information and knowledge of issues or detracted from serious debate? Does the public become more or less engaged in politics through the electronic media?

We will return to this issue shortly, but first we need to consider some of the more traditional concerns about the impact of technology on the governmental process. Technocracy, or rule by an elite of scientific or technical experts, has long been a concern of democracy.[31] At least since the time of Francis Bacon's *New Atlantis* (1627), utopian schemes have been proffered for delegating governance to those with specialized scientific knowledge. In the twentieth century social theorists from Thorstein Veblen to John Kenneth Galbraith and Daniel Bell have traced the rise of a new technical-managerial class in advanced industrial societies. Galbraith described the emergence of a new "technostructure" linking managers and planners in government and the corporate sector against those to whom they are nominally accountable. Bell predicted that knowledge—especially scientific and technical knowledge necessary for "rationality, planning, and foresight" —would become an increasingly important source of power and authority in "post-industrial society."[32] Similarly, Harvey Brooks warned of an "increasing relegation of questions which used to be matters of political debate to professional cadres of technicians and experts which function almost independently of the democratic political process."[33] Others claimed that technology has contributed to the centralization and bureaucratization of government. It was argued that the sheer scale and complexity of modern technological systems has increased the need for public coordination, management, and planning. Mesthene, for example, pointed out that "the physical dispersion made possible by transportation and communication technologies tends to enlarge the urban complex that must be governed as a unit."[34] The same tendency operates in the private sector, leading to greater corporate centralization. Others have stressed the impact of modern data-processing and communications technology on the capacity of the state to monitor and control private economic and social activity.

However, the claim that private and public power is increasingly concentrated in a centralized technocratic or bureaucratic elite has not fared well. Victor Ferkiss and others have effectively made the case that technology can lead to decentralization as well as centralization, and that in technological society power has been dispersed among ever more functional organizations and specialized interest groups.[35] Both he and Don K. Price have portrayed the scientific-technical elite as only one of several "estates," and hardly the most powerful.[36] More recently, Patrick W. Hamlett has described technological development as the result of decision making within, and interaction among, seven different "policy arenas" in our system: corporate-managerial, executive, congressional, regulatory, academic-professional, consumerist-environmental, and organized labor.[37] Indeed, the political problem is increasingly seen as one of extreme pluralism and fragmentation of decision making.

This does not, however, mean that technical expertise and influence are irrelevant or evenly distributed in society. Organizations that control the most economic resources usually have the greatest access to scientific and technical talent as well. Large corporations often have a monopoly or near-monopoly of technical information on their operations, making it very difficult for government to regulate their activities. The mismatch is even greater when citizen groups attempt to challenge such organizations; only recently have public interest groups begun to acquire comparable expertise. There are also imbalances within the government structure. Some executive agencies and congressional committees have built up overwhelming expertise in specific policy areas, particularly when they have allied with related corporate interests outside government.

The classic example was the alliance of the Atomic Energy Commission, the armed services, the Joint Committee on Atomic Energy of the Congress, and the reactor construction and utility industries which dominated nuclear energy policy in the United States from 1946 until the breakup of the AEC in 1974, and which arguably pushed nuclear power far beyond its economic justification.[38] Hamlett speaks of a "dominant configuration" of interests that has supported military research and development since World War II.[39] The secrecy and complexity surrounding defense projects also makes democratic control and accountability especially difficult. In other fields as well, private interests with a major economic stake in technological developments have worked to restrict public access to scientific and technical knowledge.[40]

The impact of technology on mass politics has also received increasing attention, especially the effects of the communications media on electoral politics. Twenty years ago Nathan Rotenstreich predicted that the advent of TV would lead to the intrusion of nonpolitical factors into politics and lowering of the standards of political reporting to meet mass tastes. The impact of events and personalities that can be projected visually and dramatically would increase in importance.

> Political life must perforce be dramatic, otherwise it would not answer the professional demands of appearing on TV. This dramatic aspect cannot be due to a conflict between ideas; it must, therefore, be based on a conflict between persons. In the absence of this drama, the attention of the anonymous individual will not be attracted, and he will not turn his thoughts to the public domain. Technology determines the shape of politics, and it is the taste of the consumer that determines what technology will bring to his home.[41]

Thus, although in theory modern communications technology increases political awareness and creates the possibility of "direct democracy" on a vast scale, in practice, Rotenstreich suggested, it facilitates a different kind of participation: what he called "*observer-participation without decision, that is, a nonactive participation.*"[42] (Italics in original.)

In retrospect, Rotenstreich's warning appears to have been justified.

Many political scientists have since demonstrated that political cynicism and declining voter turnout have accompanied the rise of television in American politics. Most studies have posited a direct linkage between "televisual" politics and the deterioration of party politics.[43] They have documented a dramatic increase in expenditures for TV advertising and media consultants by individual candidates in electoral campaigns, which have taken on an increasingly negative and personal character.[44] The new campaign technologies put a premium on candidates who are well financed and have a favorable television image, regardless of their issue positions or party attachment. Televised candidate debates and staged "media events" have done little to enlighten the voters on the issues. Meanwhile, the rapid proliferation of political action committees (PACs) and direct-mail fund-raising made possible by computer technology has increased the influence of special interest groups.

What is perhaps most striking, however, is the constant use of public relations techniques by those in power to shape public perceptions of their actions. While this can backfire when things go wrong —witness the Iran-contra scandal in the Reagan administration—it is nevertheless the case that public reaction to major political events and issues is almost totally dependent on television coverage.[45]

On the other side, it can be argued that the same communication technologies have increased public awareness of many political issues, including controversies over technology. Although the press and broadcast media have been heavily criticized for inaccurate and sensational reporting (see chapter 7), they have also taught the public that technology involves serious risks to health and the environment and that scientific "experts" can disagree about the solutions. As has often been pointed out, opposition to the war in Vietnam, the environmental movement, and the antinuclear campaign, among others, owe much of their success to television. More broadly, citizen and public interest groups have adopted computerized mailing lists and similar techniques for mobilizing support and fund-raising. Finally, new technologies such as satellite broadcasting, interactive cable television, videotex, and computer networking also have the potential for increasing citizen communication and participation in decision making. Thus far, however, local "direct democracy" and citizen education projects utilizing such technologies have had only very limited success.[46]

What, then, can be said in summary about the condition of democratic politics in an age of high technology? It would appear that, despite the Baconian thesis that "knowledge is power," it is not a unified class of scientists and engineers who govern. Nor has technology created an all-powerful central state. But strong political coalitions defend particular technologies in Congress and elsewhere in government. Technology has also fostered new organizational methods and entrepreneurial techniques for mobilizing political power, conferring additional benefits to groups with access to such resources. It has thus enhanced some forms of political participation—notably by organized activist groups promoting particular interests or causes —while at the same time reducing the effectiveness of mass participation through traditional channels such as political parties. Whether this is functional to the overall health of democracy is doubtful since it undermines representative processes and contributes to political fragmentation and alienation. As indicated at the beginning of this section, technological change also raises new ethical and constitutional issues that may become increasingly difficult to resolve. With these broad concerns about democracy in mind, we can now turn to the role of government in promoting and regulating technology.

THE ROLE OF THE STATE

In the wake of the Soviet launching of Sputnik, Walter McDougall writes, "states took upon themselves the primary responsibility for generating new technology. This has meant that to the extent revolutionary technologies have profound second-order consequences in the domestic life of societies, by forcing new technologies, *all* governments have become revolutionary, whatever their reasons or ideological pretensions."[47] Whether as an instrument of national power or as a distinctive goal in itself, national technological prowess has clearly become an important concern of states everywhere. Governments in all of the industrialized nations now finance a major portion of national civilian as well as military research and development (R&D), and seek to promote new fields of "high technology" that promise to revolutionize the world economy.[48]

Government support of technology is not, of course, new. Greek and Roman states, as well as medieval city-states, commissioned military weaponry and fortifications, built elaborate public works, and supported new agricultural and commercial ventures. By the eighteenth century European governments supported specialized poly-technical schools, while in the United States free public education and the development of land-grant colleges after the Civil War rapidly spread technical training and research. Congress also promoted the development of railroads, canals, and the telegraph, protected the rights of inventors through the patent system, and fostered private technolog-ical innovation through tax incentives and in countless other ways. However, as McDougall and others point out, our government took a relatively laissez-faire attitude toward the planning and direction of technological development until World War II, when for the first time the state engaged massively in R&D projects: the development of radar, the atomic bomb, computing devices, jet engines, synthetic materials, and operations research generally. After the war, support of R&D be-came a permanent and institutionalized function of government.[49]

But the goals and functions of state intervention regarding tech-nology have become more complex over time. During the war, the objectives were relatively simple: to develop tactical and strategic weap-ons before the other side did. Since then, competition in advanced weapons systems has seemingly institutionalized the arms race, and military security has been the dominant priority in U.S. (and Soviet) technology policy. For much of the postwar period, military R&D has accounted for two-thirds or more of the federal research budget. But war has always been the principal motivation for state support of technology.

A second goal, international political power and prestige, is closely related, but can be differentiated in that it involves direct technologi-cal competition in nonmilitary projects such as the manned space programs of the 1960s. The symbolic importance of such programs was bluntly stated by Vice-President Lyndon Johnson in a report to President Kennedy in 1961: "To reach the moon is a risk, but it is a risk we must take. Failure to go into space is even riskier. . . . One can predict with confidence that failure to master space means being sec-ond best in every aspect. In the crucial areas of our Cold War world, in the eyes of the world, first in space is first, period. Second in space is second in everything."[50] Although civilian space projects lost much of their support in the 1970s, they are again becoming important sym-bols of international stature and prestige, much as national airlines and nuclear power plants are in many parts of the world.

A third goal, international economic competitiveness, has become far more important in the past decade as U.S. and European manufacturers have steadily lost markets to more efficient Asian producers. Governments have long attempted to support certain kinds of basic research that are considered important to national economic growth but that are not financed adequately by the private sector, and some countries are now turning toward national "industrial policies" that include large R&D components. Technology transfer is now so prevalent that it is debatable whether "national" technologies can be said to exist.[51] Nevertheless, governments rush to support critical fields of research such as biotechnology, semiconductors, and now superconductivity, and much of the debate over economics and technology in the United States and other countries centers on protecting national industries from international technological competition.

Two further goals also became immensely important in the 1970s: the *promotion of health and safety,* and *protection of the natural environment.* These goals obviously differ from the first three in that they involve the state more as *regulator* than *promoter* of technology. To be sure, governments have for some time supported medical research and education, and acted to control certain diseases and other health hazards. Since 1970 they have greatly extended central regulation to protect citizens against many technological hazards as well—through consumer protection laws, occupational health and safety laws, environmental protection laws, and tighter safety regulation of such dominant technologies as automobiles and nuclear power plants. Protection of the environment involves a host of new regulatory programs designed to mitigate the impacts of technology on natural ecosystems. As Barry Commoner pointed out at the height of the environmental movement, most of our worst pollution problems stemmed from technologies developed since the war.[52]

It is sometimes overlooked that governments are also major *consumers* of technology, and thus have a direct interest in supporting R&D. In some sectors, notably defense production, the state is the sole user and customer. But in a great many other fields government provides a large share of the market or incentive structure for technological innovation and application. For example, the U.S. government was the first large-scale user of electronic data-processing equipment and communications satellites, and consequently played a major part in the development of the computer and telecommunications industries.[53] Of course many other policies, such as tax and securities laws, have major indirect effects on industrial research and development.

The list could be extended, but it is clear that government is a major participant in the promotion, regulation, and use of technology. The problem is that despite the growing importance of state technological functions, there has been little success in achieving policy coordination and cohesion. Most of what passes for national science and technology policy in the United States in fact emerges from the activities of middle-level federal agencies and bureaus. Although they rely on scientific committees and expert consultants for advice, these agencies are primarily concerned with carrying out their own special missions. Hence they do not usually consider the broader implications of their decisions or seek to integrate them with others.[54] This is partly because there has been little strategic planning and leadership at the presidential level. The result is a fragmentation and dispersion of programs that reflects the centrifugal forces of politics (see chapters 4 and 6).

Presidents have often initiated major technological programs for political reasons without the support of expert technical advice. It is well known that President Kennedy decided to send a man to the moon against the counsel of his science adviser, Jerome Wiesner, and the scientific establishment. Lyndon Johnson's decision in 1967 to deploy a "thin" ABM system against China owed more to anticipated Republican allegations of a "missile gap" than to threats from nonexistent Chinese missiles. Richard Nixon's all-out support of the SST and ABM system was opposed by leading members of the president's science advisory committee, leading Nixon in 1973 to abolish the committee.[55] And although President Carter was more cautious, he endorsed an ill-advised $20 billion synthetic fuels program in the wake of the Iranian revolution and 1979–80 oil crisis.[56]

All of these decisions reflect the political appeals of crash technology programs and the ideological context of technological decision making rather than the logical or autonomous development of technology. Perhaps the best example of the instrumental uses of technology for political ends is President Reagan's announcement of the Strategic Defense Initiative (SDI) or "Star Wars" program on March 23, 1983. It has been widely reported that Reagan's speech was prepared without consulting the Pentagon or his science adviser, George Keyworth, until a few days before it was given.[57] The timing of the announcement suggests that it was at least in part intended to discredit the nuclear freeze resolution then being debated in Congress.[58] The feasibility of the SDI program remains one of the most controversial legacies of the Reagan administration and suggests the need for a more permanent and institutionalized source of science and technology advice in the White House.

Congress has also promoted many technologies without foresight or as "pork barrel" projects. As noted above, Congress is generally fragmented and disorganized, leaving the initiative for specific proposals to individual committees and their clienteles. It is only now beginning to formulate a comprehensive approach to technology policy.[59] However, it has been more sensitive to the social costs of technology and has made important efforts to control the deployment and use of technology. In 1969 it passed the National Environmental Policy Act (NEPA), which requires executive agencies (and through them, private contractors and developers) to conduct environmental impact assessments before proceeding with federal projects. This was followed by numerous regulatory statutes to control the specific ecological and health effects of technology. The Technology Assessment Act (TAA) of 1972 went a step further in establishing the congressional Office of Technology Assessment (OTA) to study the long-term impacts of technologies *before* they are developed.[60] Along with NEPA, TAA is the best example we have of policy based on the recognition that technologies can have irreversible adverse consequences for society unless their design and deployment are carefully monitored and controlled (see chapter 5).

Much of the new regulatory legislation of the 1970s attempted to place responsibility for what economists refer to as the "external costs" of technology on the businesses causing pollution or other threats to public health and the environment. In some cases, such as the Toxic Substances Control Act (1976), the burden of proof for establishing the safety of new products was clearly shifted to the producers. The Environmental Protection Agency, the Occupational Safety and Health Administration, the Food and Drug Administration, the Consumer Products Safety Commission, and other agencies that implement these policies now conduct extensive "risk assessment" in setting regulatory standards, but the methodologies utilized in analyzing risks and benefits remain highly controversial (see chapters 8–10). Citizens increasingly feel they should have a say in making risk judgments (see chapter 12). The courts have also become much more active in evaluating technology both as a result of a dramatic increase in private liability suits and in reviewing the decisions of regulatory agencies.[61] Indeed, the United States is unique in the extent to which disputes over technological risks are ultimately resolved through litigation, reflecting in part a continuing lack of consensus on who should bear responsibility for the social consequences of technology.

There has been a marked reemphasis on the promotion of technology in the Reagan administration. Much of the focus has been military: the percentage of the federal R&D budget allocated to military purposes increased from 50 percent in 1980 to over 70 percent in the mid–1980s. On the international level, major efforts have been made to deny the Soviet bloc access to strategic Western technologies and to enlist the support of allies in the SDI program.[62] Although certain other areas of science and technology have also received increased funding, the administration has cut support for many programs (such as energy conservation and alternative technologies) on the grounds that commercial development is best left to the economic marketplace (an argument not applied to certain other technologies such as nuclear power). In his first term Reagan also attempted to cut back many of the environmental, health, and safety regulations enacted in the 1970s.[63]

Meanwhile, the diffusion of technology is rapidly undermining the hegemony of the superpowers and restructuring the world economy. Japan, Taiwan, South Korea, Hong Kong, and Singapore, as well as Brazil, Mexico, India, China, and a host of other countries, are undergoing their own technological revolutions at often breathtaking speed. Reactions to economic competition from these and other countries are likely to govern national technology policies in the coming decade. In countries such as the United States that are experiencing relative economic decline, there will be increasing pressure for state intervention to protect uncompetitive industries and to slow technology transfer by restricting technology exports and limiting foreign ownership of high technology firms in critical sectors (as in the recent case of the U.S. semiconductor industry). This might be accompanied by a more active government role in industrial planning and closer partnership between the state and private enterprise generally.

Protectionism could lead to trade wars and a breakdown of international commerce as in the 1930s. However, the alternative of free market competition for control of essentially global technologies also carries serious risks of conflict, and could lead to the abandonment of domestic policies to direct and control technological development. Technology would then indeed determine human purposes as the philosophers fear. McDougall may be right in suggesting that international technological competition is the revolutionary force of the late twentieth century.[64]

CONCLUSION

Political debate over the nature and consequences of technology is deeply rooted in ethical questions about man's ability to understand and control his own creations. Since technology vastly extends human powers, it may be a force for enormous good or evil, but it is not clear that the choice rests entirely in the hands of the users. Technological development now has a competitive momentum of its own, undermining the autonomy of the state as well as the stability of life.

Unfortunately none of the existing theories of technology is completely adequate. Instrumentalism assumes that decisions on the introduction and use of technology are made by rational individuals and institutions pursuing traditional human ends, but ignores the cumulative social and ethical constraints imposed by technological systems. Social determinism illuminates the cultural, political, and economic forces that shape technology, but tells us less about the distinctive character and increasingly universalistic impacts of technology itself. Technological determinism holds that technology itself embodies values and organizational imperatives to which man must increasingly conform, but minimizes the potential capacity of humans to make ethical choices in the design and implementation of technologies.

What is perhaps needed is not the abandonment of these concepts so much as a more complex understanding of both the character of present technologies and their ethical consequences. Such an understanding must include recognition of the dangers of "technological drift," with its continual transformation of social organization and living patterns; of the political seductions of technology and its corrosive effects on the democratic process; and of the destabilizing and potentially catastrophic impacts of international technological competition.

Although substantial efforts were made for the first time in the 1970s to anticipate and mitigate the adverse consequences of technology, it cannot be said that a coherent national policy has emerged in the United States, nor that an appropriate and lasting balance has yet been achieved between technological development and regulation anywhere. Uncoordinated government policies and private economic markets continue to encourage technological innovation and change. Even regulatory policies are premised for the most part on the technocratic-instrumental assumption that risky technologies can be managed responsibly. Only the National Environmental Policy Act and Technology Assessment Act recognize that certain technologies may simply be incompatible with nature and human life. Unfortunately these laws are only advisory, containing no requirements for action other than the preparation of impact statements and reports.

But if the philosophers are correct in warning that human understanding of technology has fallen considerably behind our technical capacity for action, we need to invest far more, rather than less, in research and education on technological change itself. Current methods of technology assessment, risk assessment, and environmental impact assessment must be further institutionalized and strengthened through major efforts to improve long-term foresight capabilities.[65] Limits must also be placed on television advertising and other campaign technologies that trivialize political issues and discourse. The public must be encouraged to participate in debate and decision making about the ends of technology. Finally, political leaders, including the president and other heads of state, require much better information and advice on technological developments and trends, and such information must be shared by the international community. The integration of global markets and diffusion of military weaponry will make the world infinitely more vulnerable without such foresight and cooperation.

DO ARTIFACTS HAVE POLITICS?

LANGDON WINNER

No idea is more provocative in controversies about technology and society than the notion that technical things have political qualities. At issue is the claim that the machines, structures, and systems of modern material culture can be accurately judged not only for their contributions to efficiency and productivity and their positive and negative environmental side effects, but also for the ways in which they can embody specific forms of power and authority. Since ideas of this kind are a persistent and troubling presence in discussions about the meaning of technology, they deserve explicit attention.

Writing in the early 1960s, Lewis Mumford gave classic statement to one version of the theme, arguing that "from late neolithic times in the Near East, right down to our own day, two technologies have recurrently existed side by side: one authoritarian, the other democratic, the first system-centered, immensely powerful, but inherently unstable, the other man-centered, relatively weak, but resourceful and durable."[1] This thesis stands at the heart of Mumford's studies of the city, architecture, and history of technics, and mirrors concerns voiced earlier in the works of Peter Kropotkin, William Morris, and other nineteenth-century critics of industrialism. During the 1970s antinuclear and prosolar energy movements in Europe and the United States adopted a similar notion as the centerpiece of their arguments. According to environmentalist Denis Hayes, "the increased deployment of nuclear power facilities must lead society toward authoritarianism. Indeed, safe reliance upon nuclear power as the principal source of energy may be possible only in a totalitarian state." Echoing the views of many proponents of appropriate technology and the soft energy path, Hayes contends that "dispersed solar sources are more compatible than centralized technologies with social equity, freedom and cultural pluralism."[2]

An eagerness to interpret technical artifacts in political language is by no means the exclusive property of critics of large-scale, high-technology systems. A long lineage of boosters has insisted that the biggest and best that science and industry made available were the best guarantees of democracy, freedom, and social justice. The factory system, automobile, telephone, radio, television, space program, and of course nuclear power have all at one time or another been described as democratizing, liberating forces. David Lillienthal's *T.V.A.: Democracy on the March*, for example, found this promise in the phosphate fertilizers and electricity that technical progress was bringing to rural Americans during the 1940s.[3] Three decades later Daniel Boorstin's *The Republic of Technology* extolled television for "its power to disband armies, to cashier presidents, to create a whole new democratic world—democratic in ways never before imagined, even in America."[4] Scarcely a new invention comes along that someone doesn't proclaim it as the salvation of a free society.

It is no surprise to learn that technical systems of various kinds are deeply interwoven in the conditions of modern politics. The physical arrangements of industrial production, warfare, communications, and the like have fundamentally changed the exercise of power and the experience of citizenship. But to go beyond this obvious fact and to argue that certain technologies *in themselves* have political properties seems, at first glance, completely mistaken. We all know that people have politics; things do not. To discover either virtues or evils in aggregates of steel, plastic, transistors, integrated circuits, chemicals, and the like seems just plain wrong, a way of mystifying human artifice and of avoiding the true sources, the human sources of freedom and oppression, justice and injustice. Blaming the hardware appears even more foolish than blaming the victims when it comes to judging conditions of public life.

Hence, the stern advice commonly given those who flirt with the notion that technical artifacts have political qualities: What matters is not technology itself, but the social or economic system in which it is embedded. This maxim, which in a number of variations is the central premise of a theory that can be called the social determination of technology, has an obvious wisdom. It serves as a needed corrective to those who focus uncritically upon such things as "the computer and its social impacts" but who fail to look behind technical devices to see the social circumstances of their development, deployment, and use. This view provides an antidote to naive technological determinism —the idea that technology develops as the sole result of an internal dynamic and then, unmediated by any other influence, molds society to fit its patterns. Those who have not recognized the ways in which technologies are shaped by social and economic forces have not gotten very far.

But the corrective has its own shortcomings; taken literally, it suggests that technical *things* do not matter at all. Once one has done the detective work necessary to reveal the social origins—power holders behind a particular instance of technological change—one will have explained everything of importance. This conclusion offers comfort to social scientists. It validates what they had always suspected, namely, that there is nothing distinctive about the study of technology in the first place. Hence, they can return to their standard models of social power—those of interest-group politics, bureaucratic politics, Marxist models of class struggle, and the like—and have everything they need. The social determination of technology is, in this view, essentially no different from the social determination of, say, welfare policy or taxation.

There are, however, good reasons to believe that technology is politically significant in its own right, good reasons why the standard models of social science go only so far in accounting for what is most interesting and troublesome about the subject. Much of modern social and political thought contains recurring statements of what can be called a theory of technological politics, an odd mongrel of notions often crossbred with orthodox liberal, conservative, and socialist philosophies.[5] The theory of technological politics draws attention to the momentum of large-scale sociotechnical systems, to the response of modern societies to certain technological imperatives, and to the ways human ends are powerfully transformed as they are adapted to technical means. This perspective offers a novel framework of interpretation and explanation for some of the more puzzling patterns that have taken shape in and around the growth of modern material culture. Its starting point is a decision to take technical artifacts seriously. Rather than insist that we immediately reduce everything to the interplay of social forces, the theory of technological politics suggests that we pay attention to the characteristics of technical objects and the meaning of those characteristics. A necessary complement to, rather than a replacement for, theories of the social determination of technology, this approach identifies certain technologies as political phenomena in their own right. It points us back, to borrow Edmund Husserl's philosophical injunction, to the things themselves.

In what follows I will outline and illustrate two ways in which artifacts can contain political properties. First are instances in which the invention, design, or arrangement of a specific technical device or system becomes a way of settling an issue in the affairs of a particular community. Seen in the proper light, examples of this kind are fairly straightforward and easily understood. Second are cases of what can be called "inherently political technologies," man-made systems that appear to require or to be strongly compatible with particular kinds of political relationships. Arguments about cases of this kind are much more troublesome and closer to the heart of the matter. By the term "politics" I mean arrangements of power and authority in human associations as well as the activities that take place within those arrangements. For my purposes here, the term "technology" is understood to mean all of modern practical artifice, but to avoid confusion I prefer to speak of "technologies" plural, smaller or larger pieces or systems of hardware of a specific kind.[6] My intention is not to settle any of the issues here once and for all, but to indicate their general dimensions and significance.

TECHNICAL ARRANGEMENTS AND SOCIAL ORDER

Anyone who has traveled the highways of America and has gotten used to the normal height of overpasses may well find something a little odd about some of the bridges over the parkways on Long Island, New York. Many of the overpasses are extraordinarily low, having as little as nine feet of clearance at the curb. Even those who happened to notice this structural peculiarity would not be inclined to attach any special meaning to it. In our accustomed way of looking at things such as roads and bridges, we see the details of form as innocuous and seldom give them a second thought.

It turns out, however, that some two hundred or so low-hanging overpasses on Long Island are there for a reason. They were deliberately designed and built that way by someone who wanted to achieve a particular social effect. Robert Moses, the master builder of roads, parks, bridges, and other public works of the 1920s to the 1970s in New York, built his overpasses according to specifications that would discourage the presence of buses on his parkways. According to evidence provided by Moses's biographer, Robert A. Caro, the reasons reflect Moses's social class bias and racial prejudice. Automobile-owning whites of "upper" and "comfortable middle" classes, as he called them, would be free to use the parkways for recreation and commuting. Poor people and blacks, who normally used public transit, were kept off the roads because the twelve-foot tall buses could not handle the overpasses. One consequence was to limit access of racial minorities and low-income groups to Jones Beach, Moses's widely acclaimed public park. Moses made doubly sure of this result by vetoing a proposed extension of the Long Island Railroad to Jones Beach.

Robert Moses's life is a fascinating story in recent U.S. political history. His dealings with mayors, governors, and presidents; his careful manipulation of legislatures, banks, labor unions, the press, and public opinion could be studied by political scientists for years. But the most important and enduring results of his work are his technologies, the vast engineering projects that give New York much of its present form. For generations after Moses's death, when the alliances he forged have fallen apart, his public works, especially the highways and bridges he built to favor the use of the automobile over the development of mass transit, will continue to shape that city. Many of his monumental structures of concrete and steel embody a systematic social inequality, a way of engineering relationships among people that, after a time, became just another part of the landscape. As New York planner Lee Koppleman told Caro about the low bridges on Wantagh Parkway, "The old son of a gun had made sure that buses would never be able to use his goddamned parkways."[7]

Histories of architecture, city planning, and public works contain many examples of physical arrangements with explicit or implicit political purposes. One can point to Baron Haussmann's broad Parisian thoroughfares, engineered at Louis Napoleon's direction to prevent any recurrence of street fighting of the kind that took place during the revolution of 1848. Or one can visit any number of grotesque concrete buildings and huge plazas constructed on university campuses in the United States during the late 1960s and early 1970s to defuse student demonstrations. Studies of industrial machines and instruments also turn up interesting political stories, including some that violate our normal expectations about why technological innovations are made in the first place. If we suppose that new technologies are introduced to achieve increased efficiency, the history of technology shows that we will sometimes be disappointed. Technological change expresses a panoply of human motives, not the least of which is the desire of some to have dominion over others even though it may require an occasional sacrifice of cost savings and some violation of the normal standard of trying to get more from less.

One poignant illustration can be found in the history of nineteenth-century industrial mechanization. At Cyrus McCormick's reaper man-ufacturing plant in Chicago in the middle 1880s, pneumatic molding machines, a new and largely untested innovation, were added to the foundry at an estimated cost of $500,000. The standard economic interpretation would lead us to expect that this step was taken to modernize the plant and achieve the kind of efficiencies that mechani-zation brings. But historian Robert Ozanne has put the development in a broader context. At the time, Cyrus McCormick II was engaged in a battle with the National Union of Iron Molders. He saw the addition of the new machines as a way to "weed out the bad element among the men," namely, the skilled workers who had organized the union local in Chicago.[8] The new machines, manned by unskilled laborers, actu-ally produced inferior castings at a higher cost than the earlier pro-cess. After three years of use the machines were, in fact, abandoned, but by that time they had served their purpose—the destruction of the union. Thus the story of these technical developments at the McCor-mick factory cannot be adequately understood outside the record of workers' attempts to organize, police repression of the labor movement in Chicago during that period, and the events surrounding the bomb-ing at Haymarket Square. Technological history and U.S. political his-tory were at that moment deeply intertwined.

In the examples of Moses's low bridges and McCormick's molding machines, one sees the importance of technical arrangements that precede the use of the things in question. It is obvious that technologies can be used in ways that enhance the power, authority, and privilege of some over others; for example, the use of television to sell a candidate. In our accustomed way of thinking technologies are seen as neutral tools that can be used well or poorly, for good, evil, or something in between. But we usually do not stop to inquire whether a given device might have been designed and built in such a way that it produces a set of consequences logically and temporally *prior to any of its professed uses.* Robert Moses's bridges, after all, were used to carry automobiles from one point to another; McCormick's machines were used to make metal castings; both technologies, however, encompassed purposes far beyond their immediate use. If our moral and political language for evaluating technology includes only categories having to do with tools and uses, if it does not include attention to the meaning of the designs and arrangements of our artifacts, then we will be blinded to much that is intellectually and practically crucial.

Because the point is most easily understood in the light of particular intentions embodied in physical form, I have so far offered illustrations that seem almost conspiratorial. But to recognize the political dimensions in the shapes of technology does not require that we look for conscious conspiracies or malicious intentions. The organized movement of handicapped people in the United States during the 1970s pointed out the countless ways in which machines, instruments, and structures of common use—buses, buildings, sidewalks, plumbing fixtures, and so forth—made it impossible for many handicapped persons to move freely about, a condition that systematically excluded them from public life. It is safe to say that designs unsuited for the handicapped arose more from long-standing neglect than from anyone's active intention. But once the issue was brought to public attention, it became evident that justice required a remedy. A whole range of artifacts have been redesigned and rebuilt to accommodate this minority.

Indeed, many of the most important examples of technologies that have political consequences are those that transcend the simple categories "intended" and "unintended" altogether. These are instances in which the very process of technical development is so thoroughly biased in a particular direction that it regularly produces results heralded as wonderful breakthroughs by some social interests and crushing setbacks by others. In such cases it is neither correct nor insightful to say, "Someone intended to do somebody else harm." Rather one must say that the technological deck has been stacked in advance to favor certain social interests and that some people were bound to receive a better hand than others.

The mechanical tomato harvester, a remarkable device perfected by researchers at the University of California from the late 1940s to the present, offers an illustrative tale. The machine is able to harvest tomatoes in a single pass through a row, cutting the plants from the ground, shaking the fruit loose, and (in the newest models) sorting the tomatoes electronically into large plastic gondolas that hold up to twenty-five tons of produce headed for canning factories. To accommodate the rough motion of these harvesters in the field, agricultural researchers have bred new varieties of tomatoes that are hardier, sturdier, and less tasty than those previously grown. The harvesters replace the system of handpicking in which crews of farm workers would pass through the fields three or four times, putting ripe tomatoes in lug boxes and saving immature fruit for later harvest.[9] Studies in California indicate that the use of the machine reduces costs by approximately five to seven dollars per ton as compared to hand harvesting.[10] But the benefits are by no means equally divided in the agricultural economy. In fact, the machine in the garden has in this instance been the occasion for a thorough reshaping of social relationships involved in tomato production in rural California.

By virtue of their very size and cost of more than $50,000 each, the machines are compatible only with a highly concentrated form of tomato growing. With the introduction of this new method of harvesting, the number of tomato growers declined from approximately 4,000 in the early 1960s to about 600 in 1973, and yet there was a substantial increase in tons of tomatoes produced. By the late 1970s an estimated 32,000 jobs in the tomato industry had been eliminated as a direct consequence of mechanization.[11] Thus, a jump in productivity to the benefit of very large growers has occurred at the sacrifice of other rural agricultural communities.

The University of California's research on and development of agricultural machines such as the tomato harvester eventually became the subject of a lawsuit filed by attorneys for California Rural Legal Assistance, an organization representing a group of farm workers and other interested parties. The suit charged that university officials are spending tax monies on projects that benefit a handful of private interests to the detriment of farm workers, small farmers, consumers, and rural California generally and asked for a court injunction to stop the practice. The university denied these charges, arguing that to accept them "would require elimination of all research with any potential practical application."[12]

As far as I know, no one argued that the development of the tomato harvester was the result of a plot. Two students of the controversy, William Friedland and Amy Barton, specifically exonerate the original developers of the machine and the hard tomato from any desire to facilitate economic concentration in that industry.[13] What we see here instead is an ongoing social process in which scientific knowledge, technological invention, and corporate profit reinforce each other in deeply entrenched patterns, patterns that bear the unmistakable stamp of political and economic power. Over many decades agricultural research and development in U.S. land-grant colleges and universities has tended to favor the interests of large agribusiness concerns.[14] It is in the face of such subtly ingrained patterns that opponents of innovations such as the tomato harvester are made to seem "antitechnology" or "antiprogress." For the harvester is not merely the symbol of a social order that rewards some while punishing others; it is in a true sense an embodiment of that order.

Within a given category of technological change there are, roughly speaking, two kinds of choices that can affect the relative distribution of power, authority, and privilege in a community. Often the crucial decision is a simple "yes or no" choice—are we going to develop and adopt the thing or not? In recent years many local, national, and international disputes about technology have centered on "yes or no" judgments about such things as food additives, pesticides, the building of highways, nuclear reactors, dam projects, and proposed high-tech weapons. The fundamental choice about an antiballistic missile or supersonic transport is whether or not the thing is going to join society as a piece of its operating equipment. Reasons given for and against are frequently as important as those concerning the adoption of an important new law.

A second range of choices, equally critical in many instances, has to do with specific features in the design or arrangement of a technical system after the decision to go ahead with it has already been made. Even after a utility company wins permission to build a large electric power line, important controversies can remain with respect to the placement of its route and the design of its towers; even after an organization has decided to institute a system of computers, controversies can still arise with regard to the kinds of components, programs, modes of access, and other specific features the system will include. Once the mechanical tomato harvester had been developed in its basic form, a design alteration of critical social significance—the addition of electronic sorters, for example—changed the character of the machine's effects upon the balance of wealth and power in California agriculture. Some of the most interesting research on technology and politics at present focuses upon the attempt to demonstrate in a detailed, concrete fashion how seemingly innocuous design features in mass transit systems, water projects, industrial machinery, and other technologies actually mask social choices of profound significance. Historian David Noble has studied two kinds of automated machine tool systems that have different implications for the relative power of management and labor in the industries that might employ them. He has shown that although the basic electronic and mechanical components of the record/playback and numerical control systems are similar, the choice of one design over another has crucial consequences for social struggles on the shop floor. To see the matter solely in terms of cost cutting, efficiency, or the modernization of equipment is to miss a decisive element in the story.[15]

From such examples I would offer some general conclusions. These correspond to the interpretation of technologies as "forms of life" presented in an earlier book of mine, filling in the explicitly political dimensions of that point of view.

The things we call "technologies" are ways of building order in our world. Many technical devices and systems important in everyday life contain possibilities for many different ways of ordering human activity. Consciously or unconsciously, deliberately or inadvertently, societies choose structures for technologies that influence how people are going to work, communicate, travel, consume, and so forth over a very long time. In the processes by which structuring decisions are made, different people are situated differently and possess unequal degrees of power as well as unequal levels of awareness. By far the greatest latitude of choice exists the very first time a particular instrument, system, or technique is introduced. Because choices tend to become strongly fixed in material equipment, economic investment, and social habit, the original flexibility vanishes for all practical purposes once the initial commitments are made. In that sense technological innovations are similar to legislative acts or political foundings that establish a framework for public order that will endure over many generations. For that reason the same careful attention one would give to the rules, roles, and relationships of politics must also be given to such things as the building of highways, the creation of television networks, and the tailoring of seemingly insignificant features on new machines. The issues that divide or unite people in society are settled not only in the institutions and practices of politics proper, but also, and less obviously, in tangible arrangements of steel and concrete, wires and semiconductors, nuts and bolts.

INHERENTLY POLITICAL TECHNOLOGIES

None of the arguments and examples considered thus far addresses a stronger, more troubling claim often made in writings about technology and society—the belief that some technologies are by their very nature political in a specific way. According to this view, the adoption of a given technical system unavoidably brings with it conditions for human relationships that have a distinctive political cast—for example, centralized or decentralized, egalitarian or inegalitarian, repressive or liberating. This is ultimately what is at stake in assertions such as those of Lewis Mumford that two traditions of technology, one authoritarian, the other democratic, exist side by side in Western history. In all the cases cited above the technologies are relatively flexible in design and arrangement and variable in their effects. Although one can recognize a particular result produced in a particular setting, one can also easily imagine how a roughly similar device or system might have been built or situated with very much different political consequences. The idea we must now examine and evaluate is that certain kinds of technology do not allow such flexibility, and that to choose them is to choose unalterably a particular form of political life.

A remarkably forceful statement of one version of this argument appears in Friedrich Engels's little essay "On Authority," written in 1872. Answering anarchists who believed that authority is an evil that ought to be abolished altogether, Engels launches into a panegyric for authoritarianism, maintaining, among other things, that strong authority is a necessary condition in modern industry. To advance his case in the strongest possible way, he asks his readers to imagine that the revolution has already occurred. "Supposing a social revolution dethroned the capitalists, who now exercise their authority over the production and circulation of wealth. Supposing, to adopt entirely the point of view of the anti-authoritarians, that the land and the instruments of labor had become the collective property of the workers who use them. Will authority have disappeared or will it have only changed its form?"[16]

His answer draws upon lessons from three sociotechnical systems of his day, cotton-spinning mills, railways, and ships at sea. He observes that on its way to becoming finished thread, cotton moves through a number of different operations at different locations in the factory. The workers perform a wide variety of tasks, from running the steam engine to carrying the products from one room to another. Because these tasks must be coordinated and because the timing of the work is "fixed by the authority of the steam," laborers must learn to accept a rigid discipline. They must, according to Engels, work at regular hours and agree to subordinate their individual wills to the persons in charge of factory operations. If they fail to do so, they risk the horrifying possibility that production will come to a grinding halt. Engels pulls no punches. "The automatic machinery of a big factory," he writes, "is much more despotic than the small capitalists who employ workers ever have been."[17]

Similar lessons are adduced in Engels's analysis of the necessary operating conditions for railways and ships at sea. Both require the subordination of workers to an "imperious authority" that sees to it that things run according to plan. Engels finds that far from being an idiosyncrasy of capitalist social organization, relationships of authority and subordination arise "independently of all social organization, [and] are imposed upon us together with the material conditions under which we produce and make products circulate." Again, he intends this to be stern advice to the anarchists who, according to Engels, thought it possible simply to eradicate subordination and superordination at a single stroke. All such schemes are nonsense. The roots of unavoidable authoritarianism are, he argues, deeply implanted in the human involvement with science and technology. "If man, by dint of his knowledge and inventive genius, has subdued the forces of nature, the latter avenge themselves upon him by subjecting him, insofar as he employs them, to a veritable despotism independent of all social organization."[18]

Attempts to justify strong authority on the basis of supposedly necessary conditions of technical practice have an ancient history. A pivotal theme in the *Republic* is Plato's quest to borrow the authority of *technē* and employ it by analogy to buttress his argument in favor of authority in the state. Among the illustrations he chooses, like Engels, that of a ship on the high seas. Because large sailing vessels by their very nature need to be steered with a firm hand, sailors must yield to their captain's commands; no reasonable person believes that ships can be run democratically. Plato goes on to suggest that governing a state is rather like being captain of a ship or like practicing medicine as a physician. Much the same conditions that require central rule and decisive action in organized technical activity also create this need in government.

In Engels's argument, and arguments like it, the justification for authority is no longer made by Plato's classic analogy, but rather directly with reference to technology itself. If the basic case is as compelling as Engels believed it to be, one would expect that as a society adopted increasingly complicated technical systems as its material basis, the prospects for authoritarian ways of life would be greatly enhanced. Central control by knowledgeable people acting at the top of a rigid social hierarchy would seem increasingly prudent. In this respect his stand in "On Authority" appears to be at variance with Karl Marx's position in Volume I of *Capital*. Marx tries to show that increasing mechanization will render obsolete the hierarchical division of labor and the relationships of subordination that, in his view, were necessary during the early stages of modern manufacturing. "Modern Industry," he writes, "sweeps away by technical means the manufacturing division of labor, under which each man is bound hand and foot for life to a single detail operation. At the same time, the capitalistic form of that industry reproduces this same division of labour in a still more monstrous shape; in the factory proper, by converting the workman into a living appendage of the machine."[19] In Marx's view the conditions that will eventually dissolve the capitalist division of labor and facilitate proletarian revolution are conditions latent in industrial technology itself. The differences between Marx's position in *Capital* and Engels's in his essay raise an important question for socialism: What, after all, does modern technology make possible or necessary in political life? The theoretical tension we see here mirrors many troubles in the practice of freedom and authority that had muddied the tracks of socialist revolution.

Arguments to the effect that technologies are in some sense inherently political have been advanced in a wide variety of contexts, far too many to summarize here. My reading of such notions, however, reveals that there are two basic ways of stating the case. One version claims that the adoption of a given technical system actually requires the creation and maintenance of a particular set of social conditions as the operating environment of that system. Engels's position is of this kind. A similar view is offered by a contemporary writer who holds that "if you accept nuclear power plants, you also accept a techno-scientific-industrial-military elite. Without these people in charge, you could not have nuclear power."[20] In this conception some kinds of technology require their social environments to be structured in a particular way in much the same sense that an automobile requires wheels in order to move. The thing could not exist as an effective operating entity unless certain social as well as material conditions were met. The meaning of "required" here is that of practical (rather than logical) necessity. Thus, Plato thought it a practical necessity that a ship at sea have one captain and an unquestionably obedient crew.

A second, somewhat weaker, version of the argument holds that a given kind of technology is strongly compatible with, but does not strictly require, social and political relationships of a particular stripe. Many advocates of solar energy have argued that technologies of that variety are more compatible with a democratic, egalitarian society than energy systems based on coal, oil, and nuclear power; at the same time they do not maintain that anything about solar energy requires democracy. Their case is, briefly, that solar energy is decentralizing in both a technical and political sense: technically speaking, it is vastly more reasonable to build solar systems in a disaggregated, widely distributed manner than in large-scale centralized plants; politically speaking, solar energy accommodates the attempts of individuals and local communities to manage their affairs effectively because they are dealing with systems that are more accessible, comprehensible, and controllable than huge centralized sources. In this view solar energy is desirable not only for its economic and environmental benefits, but also for the salutary institutions it is likely to permit in other areas of public life.[21]

Within both versions of the argument there is a further distinction to be made between conditions that are internal to the workings of a given technical system and those that are external to it. Engels's thesis concerns internal social relations said to be required within cotton factories and railways, for example; what such relationships mean for the condition of society at large is, for him, a separate question. In contrast, the solar advocate's belief that solar technologies are compatible with democracy pertains to the way they complement aspects of society removed from the organization of those technologies as such.

There are, then, several different directions that arguments of this kind can follow. Are the social conditions predicated said to be required by, or strongly compatible with, the workings of a given technical system? Are those conditions internal to that system or external to it (or both)? Although writings that address such questions are often unclear about what is being asserted, arguments in this general category are an important part of modern political discourse. They enter into many attempts to explain how changes in social life take place in the wake of technological innovation. More important, they are often used to buttress attempts to justify or criticize proposed courses of action involving new technology. By offering distinctly political reasons for or against the adoption of a particular technology, arguments of this kind stand apart from more commonly employed, more easily quantifiable claims about economic costs and benefits, environmental impacts, and possible risks to public health and safety that technical systems may involve. The issue here does not concern how many jobs will be created, how much income generated, how many pollutants added, or how many cancers produced. Rather, the issue has to do with ways in which choices about technology have important consequences for the form and quality of human associations.

If we examine social patterns that characterize the environments of technical systems, we find certain devices and systems almost invariably linked to specific ways of organizing power and authority. The important question is: Does this state of affairs derive from an unavoidable social response to intractable properties in the things themselves, or is it instead a pattern imposed independently by a governing body, ruling class, or some other social or cultural institution to further its own purposes?

Taking the most obvious example, the atom bomb is an inherently political artifact. As long as it exists at all, its lethal properties demand that it be controlled by a centralized, rigidly hierarchical chain of command closed to all influences that might make its workings unpredictable. The internal social system of the bomb must be authoritarian; there is no other way. The state of affairs stands as a practical necessity independent of any larger political system in which the bomb is embedded, independent of the type of regime or character of its rulers. Indeed, democratic states must try to find ways to ensure that the social structures and mentality that characterize the management of nuclear weapons do not "spin off" or "spill over" into the polity as a whole.

The bomb is, of course, a special case. The reasons very rigid relationships of authority are necessary in its immediate presence should be clear to anyone. If, however, we look for other instances in which particular varieties of technology are widely perceived to need the maintenance of a special pattern of power and authority, modern technical history contains a wealth of examples.

Alfred D. Chandler in *The Visible Hand*, a monumental study of modern business enterprise, presents impressive documentation to defend the hypothesis that the construction and day-to-day operation of many systems of production, transportation, and communication in the nineteenth and twentieth centuries require the development of particular social form—a large-scale, centralized, hierarchical organization administered by highly skilled managers. Typical of Chandler's reasoning is his analysis of the growth of the railroads.[22]

> Technology made possible fast, all-weather transportation; but safe, regular, reliable movement of goods and passengers, as well as the continuing maintenance and repair of locomotives, rolling stock, and track, roadbed, stations, roundhouses, and other equipment, required the creation of a sizable administrative organization. It meant the employment of a set of managers to supervise these functional activities over an extensive geographical area; and the appointment of an administrative command of middle and top executives to monitor, evaluate, and coordinate the work of managers responsible for the day-to-day operations.

Throughout his book Chandler points to ways in which technologies used in the production and distribution of electricity, chemicals, and a wide range of industrial goods "demanded" or "required" this form of human association. "Hence, the operational requirements of railroads demanded the creation of the first administrative hierarchies in American business."[23]

Were there other conceivable ways of organizing these aggregates of people and apparatus? Chandler shows that a previously dominant social form, the small traditional family firm, simply could not handle the task in most cases. Although he does not speculate further, it is clear that he believes there is, to be realistic, very little latitude in the forms of power and authority appropriate within modern sociotechnical systems. The properties of many modern technologies—oil pipelines and refineries, for example—are such that overwhelmingly impressive economies of scale and speed are possible. If such systems are to work effectively, efficiently, quickly, and safely, certain requirements of internal social organization have to be fulfilled; the material possibilities that modern technologies make available could not be exploited otherwise. Chandler acknowledges that as one compares sociotechnical institutions of different nations, one sees "ways in which cultural attitudes, values, ideologies, political systems, and social structure affect these imperatives."[24] But the weight of argument and empirical evidence in *The Visible Hand* suggests that any significant departure from the basic pattern would be, at best, highly unlikely.

It may be that other conceivable arrangements of power and authority, for example, those of decentralized, democratic worker self-management, could prove capable of administering factories, refineries, communications systems, and railroads as well as or better than the organizations Chandler describes. Evidence from automobile assembly teams in Sweden and worker-managed plants in Yugoslavia and other countries is often presented to salvage these possibilities. Unable to settle controversies over this matter here, I merely point to what I consider to be their bone of contention. The available evidence tends to show that many large, sophisticated technological systems are in fact highly compatible with centralized, hierarchical managerial control. The interesting question, however, has to do with whether or not this pattern is in any sense a requirement of such systems, a question that is not solely empirical. The matter ultimately rests on our judgments about what steps, if any, are practically necessary in the workings of particular kinds of technology and what, if anything, such measures require of the structure of human associations. Was Plato right in saying that a ship at sea needs steering by a decisive hand and that this could only be accomplished by a single captain and an obedient crew? Is Chandler correct in saying that the properties of large-scale systems require centralized, hierarchical managerial control?

To answer such questions, we would have to examine in some

detail the moral claims of practical necessity (including those advocated in the doctrines of economics) and weigh them against moral claims of other sorts, for example, the notion that it is good for sailors to participate in the command of a ship or that workers have a right to be involved in making and administering decisions in a factory. It is characteristic of societies based on large, complex, technological systems, however, that moral reasons other than those of practical necessity appear increasingly obsolete, "idealistic," and irrelevant. Whatever claims one may wish to make on behalf of liberty, justice, or equality can be immediately neutralized when confronted with arguments to the effect, "Fine, but that's no way to run a railroad" (or steel mill, or airline, or communication system, and so on). Here we encounter an important quality in modern political discourse and in the way people commonly think about what measures are justified in response to the possibilities technologies make available. In many instances, to say that some technologies are inherently political is to say that certain widely accepted reasons of practical necessity—especially the need to maintain crucial technological systems as smoothly working entities—have tended to eclipse other sorts of moral and political reasoning.

One attempt to salvage the autonomy of politics from the bind of practical necessity involves the notion that conditions of human association found in the internal workings of technological systems can easily be kept separate from the polity as a whole. Americans have long rested content in the belief that arrangements of power and authority inside industrial corporations, public utilities, and the like have little bearing on public institutions, practices, and ideas at large. That "democracy stops at the factory gates" was taken as a fact of life that had nothing to do with the practice of political freedom. But can the internal politics of technology and the politics of the whole community be so easily separated? A recent study of business leaders in the United States, contemporary exemplars of Chandler's "visible hand of management," found them remarkably impatient with such democratic scruples as "one man, one vote." If democracy doesn't work for the firm, the most critical institution in all of society, American executives ask, how well can it be expected to work for the government of a nation—particularly when that government attempts to interfere with the achievements of the firm? The authors of the report observe that patterns of authority that work effectively in the corporation become for businessmen "the desirable model against which to compare political and economic relationships in the rest of society."[25] While such findings are far from conclusive, they do reflect a sentiment increasingly common in the land: what dilemmas such as the energy crisis require is not a redistribution of wealth or broader public participation but, rather, stronger, centralized public and private management.

An especially vivid case in which the operational requirements of a technical system might influence the quality of public life is the debates about the risks of nuclear power. As the supply of uranium for nuclear reactors runs out, a proposed alternative fuel is the plutonium generated as a by-product in reactor cores. Well-known objections to plutonium recycling focus on its unacceptable economic costs, its risks of environmental contamination, and its dangers in regard to the international proliferation of nuclear weapons. Beyond these concerns, however, stands another less widely appreciated set of hazards—those that involve the sacrifice of civil liberties. The widespread use of plutonium as a fuel increases the chance that this toxic substance might be stolen by terrorists, organized crime, or other persons. This raises the prospect, and not a trivial one, that extraordinary measures would have to be taken to safeguard plutonium from theft and to recover it should the substance be stolen. Workers in the nuclear industry as well as ordinary citizens outside could well become subject to background security checks, covert surveillance, wiretapping, informers, and even emergency measures under martial law—all justified by the need to safeguard plutonium.

Russell W. Ayres's study of the legal ramifications of plutonium recycling concludes: "With the passage of time and the increase in the quantity of plutonium in existence will come pressure to eliminate the traditional checks the courts and legislatures place on the activities of the executive and to develop a powerful central authority better able to enforce strict safeguards." He avers that "once a quantity of plutonium had been stolen, the case for literally turning the country upside down to get it back would be overwhelming." Ayres anticipates and worries about the kinds of thinking that, I have argued, characterize inherently political technologies. It is still true that in a world in which human beings make and maintain artificial systems nothing is "required" in an absolute sense. Nevertheless, once a course of action is under way, once artifacts such as nuclear power plants have been built and put in operation, the kinds of reasoning that justify the adaptation of social life to technical requirements pop up as spontaneously as flowers in the spring. In Ayres's words, "Once recycling begins and the risks of plutonium theft become real rather than hypothetical, the case for governmental infringement of protected rights will seem compelling."[26] After a certain point, those who cannot accept the hard requirements and imperatives will be dismissed as dreamers and fools.

The two varieties of interpretation I have outlined indicate how artifacts can have political qualities. In the first instance we noticed ways in which specific features in the design or arrangement of a device or system could provide a convenient means of establishing patterns of power and authority in a given setting. Technologies of this kind have a range of flexibility in the dimensions of their material form. It is precisely because they are flexible that their consequences for society must be understood with reference to the social actors able to influence which designs and arrangements are chosen. In the second instance we examined ways in which the intractable properties of certain kinds of technology are strongly, perhaps unavoidably, linked to particular institutionalized patterns of power and authority. Here the initial choice about whether or not to adopt something is decisive in regard to its consequences. There are no alternative physical designs or arrangements that would make a significant difference; there are, furthermore, no genuine possibilities for creative intervention by different social systems—capitalist or socialist—that could change the intractability of the entity or significantly alter the quality of its political effects.

To know which variety of interpretation is applicable in a given case is often what is at stake in disputes, some of them passionate ones, about the meaning of technology for how we live. I have argued a "both/ and" position here, for it seems to me that both kinds of understanding are applicable in different circumstances. Indeed, it can happen that within a particular complex of technology—a system of communication or transportation, for example—some aspects may be flexible in their possibilities for society, while other aspects may be (for better or worse) completely intractable. The two varieties of interpretation I have examined here can overlap and intersect at many points.

These are, of course, issues on which people can disagree. Thus some proponents of energy from renewable resources now believe they have at last discovered a set of intrinsically democratic, egalitarian, communitarian technologies. In my best estimation, however, the social consequences of building renewable energy systems will surely depend on the specific configurations of both hardware and the social institutions created to bring that energy to us. It may be that we will find ways to turn this silk purse into a sow's ear. By comparison, advocates of the further development of nuclear power seem to believe that they are working on a rather flexible technology whose adverse social effects can be fixed by changing the design parameters of reactors and nuclear waste disposal systems. For reasons indicated above, I believe them to be dead wrong in that faith. Yes, we may be able to manage some of the "risks" to public health and safety that nuclear power brings. But as society adapts to the more dangerous and apparently indelible features of nuclear power, what will be the long-range toll in human freedom?

My belief that we ought to attend more closely to technical objects themselves is not to say that we can ignore the contexts in which those objects are situated. A ship at sea may well require, as Plato and Engels insisted, a single captain and obedient crew. But a ship out of service, parked at the dock, needs only a caretaker. To understand which technologies and which contexts are important to us, and why, is an enterprise that must involve both the study of specific technical systems and their history as well as a thorough grasp of the concepts and controversies of political theory. In our times people are often willing to make drastic changes in the way they live to accommodate technological innovation while at the same time resisting similar kinds of changes justified on political grounds. If for no other reason than that, it is important for us to achieve a clearer view of these matters than has been our habit so far.

TECHNOLOGY AND DEMOCRACY

ALBERT BORGMANN

We are experiencing a crisis of democracy and a crisis of technology. The crisis of democracy manifests itself in the growing apathy of the citizens, in the loss of common purpose, the weakening of governmental authority, and in the fragmented and nasty character of civic life.[1] The crisis of technology comes to the fore in the question of whether our planet can continue as a resource and dumping ground for a high and, so it is hoped, rising standard of living. The two crises are linked and reinforce each other. It is often thought that if the crisis of technology leads to a substantial decline in the standard of living, the crisis of democracy will become mortal.[2] Conversely, the disarray of democracy makes us unable to deal effectively with the twin crises of technology: energy and pollution.

These are serious matters, and we are indebted to the people who are laboring to solve them. The task of philosophy, however, does not consist in accepting and commenting on what is commonly thought to be urgent or important, but in taking the measure of the visible concerns to see if they truly and fruitfully reflect our best insights and our deepest aspirations. I believe the common view of the crises of democracy and technology fails to do this. There is something persistently superficial in the normal understanding of the crisis in which we seem to find ourselves. The crucial task today is not that of solving the crises as they are commonly understood, but one of recovering the

Reprinted with permission from *Philosophy and Technology*, vol. 7, pp. 211–28. Copyright 1984 by JAI Press Inc.

capacity for a fundamental and fruitful crisis. It is only from such a capacity that a worthwhile reform of technology and revival of democracy can arise. More specifically I want to argue that the character of this country has been shaped by two promises, the promise of democracy and the promise of technology. In saying this, however, I do not mean that every one of the remarkable features of the United States is traceable to these promises alone. The grandeur of this continent, along with the cultures of the native and immigrant Americans, have conspired to give us the present variety and colors of life. But what is characteristic of our time comes from the forces of modern democracy and technology, and also from the sciences, which are not our concern here. Yet democracy and technology have put a decisive imprint on all natural and traditional elements.

Nevertheless, both promises have been beset with ambiguities. Those of democracy persist to this day whereas those of technology have been resolved into a definite style of life. In the joint development of modern democracy and technology, the continuing vagueness of democracy was largely specified by the definiteness of the technological style of life. This has led to a severe impoverishment of public and private life. The recovery of genuine wealth in our lives can be accomplished only if the reform of technology and the revival of democracy are undertaken at the same time. Let me now develop these theses.

THE LIBERAL THEORY OF DEMOCRACY

I turn first to the promise of modern democracy. Of the intricate development and network of democratic theory, the strand that is most pertinent to our present concern is one that is part of the liberal tradition. Like others, I use liberalism here in a broad sense.[3] Its distinctive tenet has been accepted by all people in the mainstream of democracy. It is a specification of the notions of liberty and equality, and it has been made prominent by John Stuart Mill who in turn found its best articulation in Wilhelm von Humboldt's writings. It serves as a motto for Mill's On Liberty and says: "The grand, leading principle, towards which every argument unfolded in these pages directly converges, is the absolute and essential importance of human development in its richest diversity."[4] This principle, as Mill recognized, came out of German Idealism and was inspired by classical notions of human culture.[5] Though the cultural conditions of human development have changed radically in the nearly two hundred years since Humboldt developed his liberal democratic theory, his principle is still thought to be crucial to liberal democracy presently and for the future. According to C. B. Macpherson, a liberal democracy is "a society striving to ensure that all its members are equally free to realize their capabilities."[6] This formulation contains the promise of liberal democracy, the promise to provide everyone with the means for self-development.

We must now consider the uncertain force and fate of this promise. Macpherson opens the way with his claim that the principle or promise of liberal democracy competes with a commitment of liberal democracies to "a capitalist market society."[7] He suggests "that the continuance of anything that can be properly called liberal democracy depends on a downgrading of the market assumptions and an upgrading of the equal right to self-development."[8] In Macpherson's view, the unsolved problem of liberal democracy is its relationship to the class division that is entailed by capitalism. Liberal democratic theorists began, so he argues, by sanctioning the established classes at the expense of equality. Then they thought the class division to be a merely accidental obstacle to liberal democracy. In the early twentieth century, they believed that classes had given way to a pluralism of interests. Finally, around the middle of this century, they recognized the rule of an elite which was periodically elected and approved by the people at large. Ronald Dworkin, to the contrary, has argued that a free market system least prejudges the opportunities that are offered to people in pursuit of their self-development and that it allocates opportunities most efficiently. Admittedly, the market leads to inequalities, but these can be curbed through taxation and transfer payments.[9] Macpherson and Dworkin agree however that a moral principle is central to a truly liberal democracy. "Mill's model of democracy is a moral model," Macpherson says. Its moral significance lies in its concern to foster equal "chances of the improvement of mankind."[10]

There were exemplars of a fully developed human being when Humboldt first formulated the principle, and so there was an understanding of the direction in which one had to move if mankind was to be improved. But little argument is needed to maintain that Goethe, for instance, or Humboldt himself no longer constitute widely agreed-upon models for the improvement of mankind. Does it make sense to urge a social and political commitment to the ideal of people "acting as exerters and enjoyers of the exertion and development of their own capacities" as Macpherson has it, when it is quite unclear what the direction of such development should be?[11] Dworkin gives an emphatically affirmative answer and argues that it is in fact distinctive of liberalism that it subscribes to a theory of equality which "supposes that political decisions must be, so far as possible, independent of any particular conception of the good life, or of what gives value to life. Since the citizens of a society differ in their conceptions, the government does not treat them as equals if it prefers one conception to another, either because the officials believe that one is intrinsically superior, or one is held by the more numerous or more powerful group."[12] For Dworkin, this position does not betray a retreat from moral issues but is itself the "constitutive political morality" of liberalism.[13] "Its constitutive morality," he says further, "provides that human beings must be treated as equals by their government, not because there is no right and wrong in political morality, but because that is what is right."[14] To arrogate to oneself the determination of the good life for others is to practice paternalism.[15] I think Dworkin accurately captures the function of the state that is accepted by nearly all. The universe of political discourse in this country is delimited by Dworkin's principle of liberalism. This is well illustrated by the national debates that are engendered every four years by the presidential elections. Those debates are entirely devoted to the question of how the means toward the good life can be secured and improved. They deal with the problems of how our lives can be made more secure, internally and internationally, how economic growth can be promoted, how access to opportunities can be broadened. The question of what the good life itself is never comes to the surface.

Different kinds of societies agree, of course, in offering their members different conceptions of the good life. We normally think it distinctive of a modern liberal democratic society that it offers its members more equal opportunities and a greater range of them. But this is partly false and partly misleading. In the work world of this country, for instance, opportunities are sharply predetermined by one's sex, race, and above all by the social stratum into which one has been born.[16] The popular imagination is fond of illustrations which seem to show that this is the land of opportunity and upward mobility. And tales of the self-made man are no doubt used as instruments of social stability. They are thought to explain and justify the social order. This phenomenon belongs to the question of social justice and will concern us later. At any rate, the common misunderstanding in regard to the opportunities which a liberal democracy provides in the work world does not concern the ideal of equal opportunity itself but rather the gap between the ideal and reality. It is therefore an error which is remedied when we are ready to face the facts of inequality. This is increasingly the case. To act on the recognition of inequality turns out to be extremely difficult for the body politic, and this problem too leads to the question of social justice.

If in our society a principle of selection and limitation governs the distribution of work opportunities, then the principle indirectly determines social and material opportunities as well. The resulting inequalities are an embarrassment to liberal democracies. But that also means that in principle at least the conceptual resources of liberal democratic theory are adequate for the analysis of these problems. It is far different when we try to grasp the *nature* of the opportunities that have in fact been provided by the liberal democracies. It is undeniable that in respect to health, comfort, mobility, and access to culture the gap between the most and the least privileged is narrower in liberal democracies than in many other societies. And technology is surely the decisive factor in the narrowing of this gap. This achievement has been celebrated many times.[17] It is precisely in the area where the promise of liberal democracy has been fulfilled and there seem to be no further problems that the distinctive character of the opportunities provided is most often misunderstood. For it is not so much the degree of equality and the range which distinguish those opportunities; it is the nature of the opportunities which sets them apart.

Opportunities in a pretechnological society were to be grasped and acted out as a destiny. More precisely, one opportunity among others, however few, was to be taken up and lived out in a lifelong commitment; and all other opportunities ceased to be open and to exist. In a liberal democracy, on the other hand, any one opportunity is realized in a context of opportunities that have remained open. Ronald Dworkin's principle of restraint is taken to the extreme point where in political decisions even the expectation of a commitment to a destiny would be arrogant. Ironically, Gerald Dworkin allows interference by authorities, that is, paternalism, in the choice of persons only when that interference is needed to "preserve the liberty of the person to make future choices. This gives us a principle—a very narrow one—by which to justify some paternalistic interferences. Paternalism is justified only to preserve a wider range of freedom for the individual in question."[18] Dworkin has in mind interference with "decisions which are far-reaching, potentially dangerous and irreversible" or "which are made under extreme psychological and sociological pressures" or those that entail "dangers which are either not sufficiently understood or appreciated correctly by the persons involved."[19] But Gerald Dworkin's principle is really a guide for the shaping of society, and it is so in the broad sense in which the principle is formulated at the end of the quotation above. But how, concretely, do we act on this principle? It is clear that things that are to be taken up and relinquished easily must be free of contextual ties. If taking something up is to enter into strong and manifold bonds, then to abandon that thing is to suffer the trauma of the disruption of those ties and of injury to one's faculties.

How is a social structure of endlessly open opportunities possible? And what, more precisely, is the character of such opportunities and their effect on the worth of our lives? To answer these questions we must take account of the promise of technology and its convergence with the promise of liberal democracy.

THE CHARACTER OF TECHNOLOGY

Technology is here formally defined as the characteristic way in which we today take up with reality. The definition of technology is of course an intricate and controversial matter.[20] The formal and then increasingly substantive definition that I propose should be judged, I believe, by the extent to which it explicates our pretheoretical intuitions and by its heuristic fruitfulness.

The promise of technology was first formulated in the early decades of the seventeenth century by men such as Bacon and Descartes. It can be understood as the practical version of the Enlightenment; it saw the past as a time of toil, confinement, and suffering. Against those conditions it promised liberation and enrichment on the basis of the conquest of nature which was to be accomplished through the new natural sciences.[21] After an incubation period of a century and a half, the promise attained visible reality in the industrial revolution which, to be sure, at first considerably lowered the welfare of the people.[22] But in the nineteenth century the fruits of technology began to be reaped by the larger population.[23] In the United States particularly, the promise of technology accompanied industrialization as a commentary and exhortation in numerous variations, and it was often intertwined with the promise of democracy.[24]

The promise of technology is being reiterated even for today and tomorrow. It dominates implicitly the one truly national debate that we have every four years during the presidential campaigns. Occasionally the promise is made explicit, and one *locus classicus* of such explicitness is found in the April 13, 1976, issue of the *Wall Street Journal* where United States Steel in a full page advertisement asked "a prominent American to speak out." The invitation was issued to Jerome B. Wiesner, then president of the Massachusetts Institute of Technology. His statement begins with this paragraph: "More than any nation in the world, the United States has the opportunity to lead mankind toward a life of greater fulfillment. This opportunity is based on benefits from our continuing advances in science and technology. It is significant that people everywhere look to the United States to provide the science and technology which they need as they, too, seek to improve their condition."[25]

These remarks are typical not only in asserting a tight connection between a life of fulfillment and technology but also in its implication that the mature technology in an advanced industrial country is identical or continuous with the liberating technology which is needed to improve one's condition, presumably one of illiteracy, starvation, and disease. But while Wiesner's high seriousness is appropriate to the liberation from such misery, it becomes questionable, if not macabre, when we consider the language of liberation and enrichment that daily addresses us in advertisements such as these:

> Learning languages is not easy. It takes books, classes, cassettes, and hard work. Now, however, you have a choice. You can communicate in a foreign country without speaking the language, or you can learn the language more easily thanks to a new electronic miracle.[26]

> Now you can have some of the world's best dishes. Without leaving home. Without waiting. Without cooking. . . . Six new single-serving entrees come in speedy cooking pouches, so they're ready after just 15 minutes in boiling water.[27]

> There is now a new, fun way to jog. The new IS&A Computer is a solid-state system that lets you jog in place in the comfort of your

own home. . . . In just one week you'll notice the difference, feel great, have greater endurance, and you won't tire as easily.[28]

The promises here made with regard to liberation from toil and the advancement of literacy, eating, and health seem to be the direct descendants of the promises that one would want to make to the starving people in Third World countries. But beneath that appearance is a radical shift in the character of the promise of technology. That shift must lead one to doubt the soundness of the promise.

Wiesner acknowledges such difficulties. His statement continues: "Yet the survival of our own abundant society is being doubted by many thoughtful people who share a powerful concern, a reasonable apprehension about the impact of technology."[29] But such doubt can spring from very different concerns. One may be concerned whether technology can hope to be successful on its own terms, whether liberation in one place will not impose new burdens in another. This is Wiesner's concern when he says: "In this enormously complex world, each large-scale technological advance has costs, side effects often unanticipated."[30] One may further doubt whether technology can make good its promise in a socially just way, nationally and internationally, and Wiesner alludes to this problem when he speaks of "the more equitable and humane society which we all seek."[31] But there can also be a much more radical doubt about the promise of technology. One may ask not just whether the promise can be kept, but whether it is worth keeping, whether the promise is not altogether misconceived, too vaguely given at first, and harmfully disoriented where technology is most advanced.

A clue to the answer for this question can be taken from the advertisements cited before. Like most advertisements they depict the foreground of advanced technology, the world of commodities that are freely available for consumption. Here the promise of liberation and enrichment seems to have come to complete fulfillment. The greatest variety of food is at our fingertips without the burdens of harvesting, cleaning, preparing, and cooking. But the promise of technology has here suffered an ironical turn of which we are often uneasily aware.

Cartoons sometimes clarify sharply and suddenly a difficulty that has troubled us in a vague and nagging manner. There is a cartoon where a middle-aged woman stands in front of a chest of frozen dinners in a supermarket, holding up two packages, looking a little puzzled; and she says to her husband: "For the big day, Harv, which do you want? The traditional American Christmas turkey dinner with mashed potatoes, giblet gravy, oyster dressing, cranberry sauce and tiny green peas or the old English Christmas goose dinner with chestnut stuffing, boiled potatoes, brussels sprouts and plum pudding."[32] Harvey looks skeptical and a bit morose. The world of bountiful harvests, careful preparations, and festive meals has become a faint and ironical echo. Mabel is asking Harvey whether on December 25 he would rather consume this aggregate of commodities or that. To consume is to use up an isolated entity without preparation, resonance, and consequence. What half dawns on Mabel and Harvey is the equivocation in calling the content of an aluminum package a "traditional American Christmas turkey dinner." The content, even when warmed and served, is a sharply reduced aspect of the once full-bodied affair.

The availability of a technological commodity disburdens us from the work of preparing a meal; but for that reason, it also disengages us from the culture of the table. When a meal has become a commodity, it can no longer engage us; it can only be consumed. There are of course occasions where disburdenment from "slaving over the stove" is very much called for. At the moment I am not concerned to pass judgment on the ironical turn that the promise of technology has taken. Far less would I advocate the return to a culture of the table whose cost would be borne by women alone. I am rather concerned to point up a tendency which is prominently exemplified in our habits of eating. Let me elaborate that tendency further. To the foreground of easily and instantly available commodities which we take up in leisure and consumption there must of course correspond a background of machinery to which the inevitable burdens of procurement have been assigned. To the background of technology we attend in labor. A distinction between working and celebrating can be found in many pretechnological cultures. But the sharp division between labor and leisure is a characteristic which is crucial and unique to technological civilization.[33] It corresponds to the split between background and foreground and to the division in technological devices between their machinery and the commodity they procure. All three dichotomies constitute a peculiar version of the means-end distinction. Technology is devoted to the procurement of ends which can be enjoyed without the encumbrance of means. This ideal is foreshadowed in magic tales where there is effortless transportation on flying carpets and where you can have meals without growing, cooking, and serving on the table that sets itself. In technology the mere ends are commodities which rest on a machinery which is concealed and unobtrusive. We obtain light, warmth, music, and moving pictures by the flick of a switch; and the commodities emerge as from nowhere. We have a vague and cerebral grasp at best of their sources and channels and of the ultimate principles and the actual working of the supporting machinery. It is an instructive exercise to consider one's daily surroundings and to realize how they are composed of glittering and opaque commodities. It is enlightening also to consider the progress of technology and to see how the burdensome engagement with things is step by step replaced by easily available, but also impenetrable commodities.

The tendency of technology that I am considering moves through two phases. The first is the constructive phase where truly oppressive burdens were lifted from our shoulders, where the confinement of illiteracy and ignorance was broken through the availability of learning and letters. In the second and decadent phase, however, we have been freeing ourselves from ties that are necessary to give our lives vigor, depth, and orientation.[34] Pretechnological life was undoubtedly hard. This hardness has properly been seen as duress, and it has been successfully overcome. But the hardness of pretechnological life also constituted a firmness which we have lost along with duress. The loss of firmness in our lives is painfully apparent where duress has been most successfully eradicated, in the middle class of the advanced industrial countries, and in particular in the upbringing of its adolescents. It has been repeatedly remarked that we are at a loss as to the standards to which young people should be held.[35] Happily, brute economic necessity no longer requires them to be industrious, parsimonious, and continent. But no new discipline has taken the place of the old.

Necessity still reigns, of course, in the background of technology which we serve in labor. But there the mindlessness which in leisure has a pleasantly distracting air appears in the draining and demanding form of divided labor. We have been successful in shortening such work and in making it relatively safe and pleasant. But we have been unwilling or unable to guard the intrinsic dignity of work. Since divided labor like the machinery of devices and the background of technology has become a mere means, it is judged only by its productivity. This has led to the widespread degradation of most work through the loss of skill and initiative. Human labor has been adjusted to the requirements of a highly productive technological machinery. Such labor has, in spite of all regimentation, remained an imperfect component of production. Perfect production has no place for it. Eventually, then, the degradation of most work will yield to the elimination of much work, and this comes about through automation.

THE DEVICE PARADIGM

Let me now begin to establish the connections between technology and democracy. The first is naturally made by reflecting on the negative view that I have given of the normal quality of our leisure lives. What reaction comes most easily to such criticism? Normally people will not defend typical technological leisure, but rise to a point of order to exclude the matter from the agenda. This motion has a variety of forms. It is framed as the charge of elitism, as a reminder of the subjectivity of tastes, as a boasting of rich cultural pluralism, or a retreat to agnosticism. What undergirds these moves is the conception of liberal democracy where the state is not to prejudge the choice of a citizen's ends in any way, but should be restricted to providing the basis for individual choice. The state does this in cooperation with industry and the educational establishment. The procurement of means becomes the truly legitimate and eventually exclusive public concern. Thus the liberal democratic state shelters the technological way of life from examination and criticism. Technology in turn allows liberal democracy to execute at least a semblance of its program which, when one thinks about it, is hard or impossible to implement. As long as we live in a society and act in concert, we must after all do this and refrain from doing that. If the crucial measures by which one wants to shape one's life are really left open, nothing gets done, and we sink into chaotic and radical individualism. But if we agree on a sharp separation of means and ends and on the construction of a realm of means that allows for a seemingly endless variety of ends, we appear to have the best of two worlds: social discipline and cooperation in the means, and unencumbered individual choice in the selection of ends. What is overlooked, of course, is that the technological separation of ends and means does not leave the question of the good life open, but furnishes a radically new and consequential answer to it.

In addition to the consonance between technology and liberal democracy, there is a still deeper connection which runs mainly from technology to democracy. To see this tie we must first acknowledge the basic and implicit understanding that people have of technology. That is, they understand that their world is sharply divided between the means of labor and ends of leisure, that leisure is devoted to the consumption of commodities and that one pays one's dues in labor, that labor is a mere means and a necessary evil, that the progress of technology will procure more commodities and more refined ones, and that the machinery of technology exists, to be sure, but is normally beyond our understanding and intervention. The promise of liberal democracy is now understood technologically. Self-realization is more fully realized the more we are freed from burdens and furnished with the good things of life. Liberation and enrichment in turn are taken to be the disburdenment through technological devices and the consumption of commodities.

Through the device paradigm, technology provides a principle of organization, and through its promise of liberation and enrichment it provides an animating force.[36] Technology thus undergirds our political and social system. The system therefore comfortably survives crises that should be grave threats to it were it capitalist or democratic in the pure senses of these terms. This country has had riots in the big cities, lost a war, had a president resign in disgrace, had inflation and interest rates approach 20 percent, and seen its energy basis erode. But the common pace of life has hardly been affected. Political action, when it faces a crisis, finds its orientation in the device paradigm. Politics has become the metadevice of the technological society. Whenever subsystems of technology clash or founder, there is a call for political action to procure ease and safety for the system as a whole. Jürgen Habermas is correct in seeing that government has become strangely meliorative and remedial.[37] It is the agency of last resort and yet barren of positive guidance. But this becomes intelligible when we recognize the government as the ultimate servant to technology.

As the machinery of government becomes more sophisticated and powerful, disturbances change from unforeseeable crises to deviations from a standard state which are anticipated in their range if not their details and met through homeostatic adjustments. Society then becomes a nearly closed system. Aldous Huxley's *Brave New World* is the exemplar of such a society, and Manfred Stanley has provided a theoretical outline of it under the heading of "the libertarian technicist society."[38] It appears clearly from Stanley's sketch that when government becomes a perfect technological device, political disengagement becomes complete as well. Though there is a discernible tendency in that direction, government, at least now, is still an open system.

It is open in two very different senses. From the technological point of view it is negatively open, open in the sense of being incomplete. From the standpoint of a critique of technology, it is positively open, that is, it affords an institutional forum of discourse and action where the citizens could preserve and make room for engagement. A member of the technological society is largely impotent vis-à-vis corporations and government agencies when he is called upon to act as a consumer and taxpayer. But as a citizen his scope of action is undeniably wide and genuine. It is to take a condescending view of people's energy and judgment to blame the politicians, the lobbies, and the media for civic apathy. Complacency bespeaks a general acceptance of the technological society. Acceptance, of course, ranges from quiet resentment to chauvinist affirmation.[39] The positive opening within technology, at any rate, lies fallow for the most part. This is clearest in regard to the electoral process, where the openness of the social order is most evidently institutionalized. There is some indication that voters in recent years have become more consistent in their decisions.[40] But the general political awareness is still deplorably low, and participation in voting has generally been declining since the second World War. In 1976, only 54 percent of those eligible to vote cast a ballot in the presidential election.[41] This is often seen as a failure of technology since it is, supposedly, the poor and uneducated who typically do not vote; and it is seen as a failure of democracy because, so it is said, many are alienated from the political process due to its overpowering size, remoteness, and corruption. But Arthur Hadley has found that the largest single group of the nonvoters consists of people who are apathetic out of contentment.[42] And while the people who vote represent little more than half of those who are eligible to vote, the people who participate in the shaping of the political issues and in the selection and promotion of the candidates to be voted on constitute only a quarter to a third of the eligible voters.[43] Finally, when we look at the character of the political activity that does take place in the electoral realm, we must recognize, as was remarked before, that it engenders no searching debates about the good life or the common good and hence no radical decisions and actions. Beyond the common implication in the technological order there is little sense of civic responsibility. Voters and interest groups typically look at a candidate as a potential supplier of a commodity that is only obtainable politically. And a candidate sees himself or herself in large measure as a broker of various and often conflicting interests whose strength is measured by the size of the voting constituency.

CONSEQUENCES FOR DEMOCRATIC LIFE

The technological specification of democracy has two perilous consequences. The first is that it may permanently suppress the avowed liberal democratic goal of equality. The second is that it may resolve the liberal democratic vagueness as to the public significance of the good life in a way which is definite and consequential, but which is neither clearly and explicitly recognized by the people nor answers our deepest and best aspirations.

As regards the first danger, the social inequalities in this country are obvious. Precisely when we accept the technological concept of well-being, viz., the availability of commodities, we see that availability is not equal for all; some peoples' lives are clearly more commodious than others. This requires explanation since the democratic call of equality for all still has force and is to this day the battle cry of reforms.[44] But why have reforms not been more successful when the formal elements of liberal democracy are certainly at hand and when technology, quite apart from having specified the notions of equality and self-development, has provided powerful means of information and communication which should aid the cause of the less privileged?

As the distribution of wealth in technologically advanced socialist countries shows, technology is not by its nature socially unjust. It may in fact have a weak tendency toward equality. The inequalities in this country (and in all Western democracies) derive from historical circumstances. This illustrates once more *both* that technology is not the sole structuring force of contemporary reality *and* that it decisively transforms almost all traditional forces. To see this we must look more closely at the shape of inequality.

It is generally recognized that a satisfactory treatment of the question of equality requires an antecedent understanding of whether all humans are in fact equal and if so in what respect, given that there are obvious ineradicable differences. Assume that this question has been answered along Kantian lines. We are all equal because each of us belongs to the realm of morality as a member and as a sovereign. Each of us regards herself or himself and everybody else as an end in herself or himself.[45] The question then arises what we, acting socially, owe one another as equals. How, in the arrangement of our lives, is respect for equality to be made manifest? Different answers are conceivable. We might be concerned to secure equality of education, or of political power, of moral excellence, aesthetic sensibility, of skill and responsibility in the work world, or in other ways. But it is clear that in general we have no such concerns. Equality is measured solely by wealth and income. It is controversial whether wealth or income is a better measure of equality and inequality.[46] Wealth seems to bestow power. But wealth does not provide power that could be used against the paradigm of technology and the common allegiance that it commands. Within the paradigm, there is a range of options, but it is narrowly circumscribed. Personal income yields no directive power at all against technology. There is controversy also as to the way in which income should be measured.[47] But whether it is measured this way or that, the unchallenged significance of income is that it in turn is the measure of what is technologically available to a person. It determines how many commodities are at one's disposal. Income is a measure of equality that is consonant with technology, and so it has become the standard of living in a technological society.[48] It is again an indication of how deeply entrenched technology is that there is controversy whether, by the standard of income (or wealth), justice or prudence requires equality.[49] But there is no challenge to the standard itself.

What is the shape of inequality in this country, measured by income? There are two crucial features. First, there is a sharp difference between the incomes of the richest and poorest families. In 1970, the lowest fifth earned 5.5 percent of total family income, the highest fifth made 41.6 percent.[50] In 1978 the bottom 8.2 percent of all families made under $5,000 annually whereas the top 3.6 percent made $50,000 and over. Second, between these extremes, there is a fairly linear slope of inequality. As one goes up in $5,000 increments of annual family incomes for 1978, one picks out roughly 16 percent of the families with each step, except for the increment from $25,000 to $50,000 which corresponds to the largest group of families with 24.3 percent.[51]

The origin of inequality lies in the ranks of late medieval Europe, which developed into the class divisions of the early modern period, which in turn were smoothed into the present wage differences and contours.[52] The latter have considerable stability, but they no longer divide families into clearly delimited classes. The blurring of income differences is strengthened through the increasing number of families where two moderate incomes, one from the husband and one from the wife, may lift the family into the top quarter of family incomes.[53]

But given that liberal democracy has provided a notion of equality and has advocated it and given that the machinery of government to implement that notion is available, why is inequality so generally accepted?[54] It is clear that it is resented by the poorest families. They are excluded from the blessings of technology, and for them the promise of liberation and enrichment has retained some of its early and genuine appeal. But there is a broad middle class which is clearly poorer than the really rich and which could muster the political power to enforce greater equality, but fails to do so. It fails to act, I believe, because inequality is a motor and stabilizer of technological progress, and since the middle class is committed to the latter, it tolerates the former. Inequality promotes technology because the relative deprivation of the poorer people provides an unfailing rationale for an increase of the gross national product. Inequality helps to stabilize technology because in times of economic crises it provides a principle of selecting those who are to carry the burden of the downturn. The poor are made to suffer while the loyalty of the wealthier and active middle class remains secure.

The peculiar conjunction of technology and inequality that we find in industrially advanced Western democracy results in an equilibrium which can be maintained only as long as technology advances. The less affluent must be able to catch up with the more affluent at least diachronically; they must be able to attain tomorrow what their wealthier neighbors have today. If the general standard of living comes to be arrested for the indefinite future, inequality will become stationary and more manifest and will require a new solution.[55] At the moment, it is clear, the tendency is to maintain the dynamic balance of technology and inequality by maintaining technological progress through a rearrangement of energy resources.

As long as the tendency remains largely unquestioned, politics will remain without substance.[56] It will not be the realm where the crucial dimensions of our common life will be guarded or altered.

These are always and already determined by technology. Politics is merely the metadevice of the technological order. This is not all there is to politics. Traditional notions of service, leadership, and civic responsibility still move some people to political action which goes beyond technology. But the technological cast of politics constitutes its presently central features. Politics in this sense is well understood by people and used when they face an otherwise unsolvable problem. But a device, once designed and in use, does not engage or even permit engagement. The calls for participatory democracy which are oblivious to the substance of politics and merely recommend new forms of transaction are pointless and will remain inconsequential. One may as well call for participation in pocket calculators. A calculator not only disburdens one of the intricacies of computation. It resists efforts at engagement. It is beyond our care, maintenance, and radical intervention. One can of course study its history and construction. And one may find new and more frequent uses for it. But the first course of action is entirely cerebral and inconsequential, and the second is entirely playful if it goes beyond the genuine requirements of technological life. And so it is with politics within a technological society.

The substance of politics, I think, should be the direct concern for the good life. Such a concern must and can be bracketed or suspended in the public realm according to liberal democracy, and technology provides the semblance of such a suspension. In fact, however, modern technological democracy, primarily through its economic politics, has created circumstances which have given our lives a deeply uniform character which is thinly veiled by superficial variations. Our intuitions and personal experiences which tell us that most people divide their lives between unloved labor and distracting leisure are borne out by the surveys of social scientists.[57] And there are numerous examinations of the quality of technological culture with indicative titles such as *The Decline of Pleasure, The Harried Leisure Class,* or *The Joyless Economy.*[58] The technological specification of democracy makes it difficult for us to recognize this deep-seated malaise. Our recent economic policies and the great hopes that have been tied to the microelectronic revolution show that the force of the promise of technology is not yet spent. But the first thing and the least that we should recognize is that we have not left open the question of the good life; we have answered it in a definite and disquieting way. Once this is recognized, the question of the reform of technology and of the revival of democracy arises; and in reply and conclusion I can do no more than give a sketch of first steps.[59]

TOWARD DEMOCRATIC ENGAGEMENT

When I speak of the need for a revival of democracy, I mean a public return to the substance of our lives. The formal elements of democracy such as the universal franchise, free elections, and constitutional government are mostly in place and well preserved, and the formal well-being of democracy in this country surely constitutes reason for gratitude and pride. But without attention to substance, the forms of democracy become hollow and in the long run are in danger of collapse. The substance of the good life has already been delineated from without by the critique of the technological style of life. The good life then must be one of engagement, of vigor, of discipline, and of joy. Putting it this way, I am still speaking approximately, for the good life depends in the end on the forces that engage us, that inspire vigor, that rightfully call for discipline, and finally fill us with joy. Such forces cannot be invented, but they can be found, and in fact they are all about us in simple splendor. We find them in the wildness of nature, in the making of music, in the exercise of sports, in the celebration of meals, and most importantly and ambiguously perhaps in religious worship. We know from history that many of these forces used to grace people in eminently common and public ways, as in the enactment of the Greek tragedies or in the religious celebrations of the Middle Ages. Today none of the engaging forces is celebrated as an affair of the state. Engagement is an essentially private matter even where numerous private parties join together.

This must be accepted and will remain so for the foreseeable future. What can and must be done publicly, however, is to make our world more hospitable again to the forces of engagement. This is to be done in two ways. First we must reawaken a public conversation about the good life. We must recognize that we as a society are impressing even more strongly a definite, narrow, and dubious mold on the manner in which we take up with reality. We must take the measure of this approach to the world and speak up on behalf of the forces that are hollowed out by the technological approach. In instigating such a conversation we must remember some of the legitimate reasons why people have become wary of it, that is, the fear of dogmatism, bigotry, and presumption. Therefore a public examination of the good life can only be undertaken in a spirit of enthusiasm, sympathy, and tolerance. Enthusiasm is the knowledge that one has been graced by something other than oneself. Sympathy is the concern for the integrity and final well-being of one's fellow human beings and their enthusiasms. Tolerance is the realization first that I may be mistaken about the greatness of what I am enthused by, second that any fellow human being can be a witness to something greater than myself, and third that the greatness to which I want to testify is compromised if my testimony is accompanied or replaced by force.

Public, and that is political, action to make the technological world more hospitable to the forces of engagement can take guidance from the distinction between the standard of living and the quality of life. The standard of living is measured by the number of commodities that are available, that is, by the number of goods and services that are producible, marketable, and privately consumable. The quality of life is composed of the social goods and background features of our lives that, in general, we own in common or not at all.[60] These goods and features include clean air and water, open spaces, public safety, schools, museums, and orchestras. To raise the quality of life is both to restrict the cancerous growth of technological consumption and to promote the calm and the openness in which engagement and celebration can flourish. It is also to undertake public policy which has a more knowing and affirmative relation to the good life.

II

GOVERNING TECHNOLOGY

INSTITUTIONS AND PROCESSES

INTRODUCTION

The idea of "governing" science and technology is relatively new. Since progress in science requires unfettered intellectual inquiry, attempts to interfere with such freedom, from the trial of Galileo to Joseph Stalin's patronage of Trofim Lysenko, have been universally condemned. In regard to basic research there is an inherent tension between the needs of scientists to steer their own course and the rights of the many to participate in a democracy.[1] But this is much less so in the case of technology. Governments now support applied research and development on a vast scale and have numerous policies for promoting and regulating technologies with direct economic and social impact. Thus decisions must be made on funding priorities, on the design and implementation of programs, on the roles of the private and public sectors, and on the social benefits and risks of technology. The issue is not whether technology is governed, but how.

The American constitutional system is unique in the extent to which it divides and fragments authority among the various branches and levels of government. Thus the executive, legislative, and judicial branches at federal and state levels contend for power over many issues. But even within the major divisions of government there is a high degree of pluralism: Congress does its business through dozens of committees and subcommittees, and the executive branch is equally fragmented into departments, agencies, and offices. Thus governance in any field is immensely more complicated than in more unified constitutional systems.

Every study of policymaking for science and technology has

emphasized this problem. Indeed, from the Allison Commission, which investigated national scientific organization in the 1880s, to the President's Commission on Industrial Competitiveness in 1985, there have been repeated calls for more coherent federal policy or establishment of a national Department of Science and/or Technology. These reform efforts have had little impact, and policymaking for technology remains dispersed throughout government. Policy coordination and leadership is intermittent at best.[2]

The history of presidential science advising illustrates the difficulty of achieving policy coordination. During World War II, Dr. Vannevar Bush served as head of the Office for Scientific Research and Development and became a very influential adviser to President Roosevelt. But after the war this arrangement lapsed, and it was not until after the Soviet launch of Sputnik in 1957 that President Eisenhower appointed a personal science adviser. He also created the President's Science Advisory Committee (PSAC), a body of prestigious scientists and engineers who consulted in Washington several days a month (an executive Office of Science and Technology was added in the Kennedy administration). PSAC had considerable influence on weapons development, arms control, the establishment of NASA, and other areas of technology policy in its early years. However, its access waned under President Johnson as new social issues arose, and eventually it was abolished by President Nixon in 1973 after some of its members publicly opposed the Vietnam War and major technology projects such as the antiballistic missile (ABM) and supersonic transport (SST).[3] A somewhat weaker Office of Science and Technology Policy (OSTP) was restored under Presidents Ford and Carter for coordinating agency initiatives and commissioning review panels to study scientific and technical issues.[4] In the Reagan administration OSTP has been relegated to the outer reaches of the White House, and the science adviser has largely functioned as an advocate of the president's policies, including the Strategic Defense Initiative (SDI).[5]

The history of PSAC and OSTP suggests that expert bodies of this kind are only useful if they also serve the president's political interests. In fact, presidents give only intermittent attention to science and technology policy when major projects are at stake. The first chapter in this section, by W. Henry Lambright and Dianne Rahm, sets out a model of the policymaking process and analyzes the role of recent presidents in shaping technology policy at various stages of the process. The variability in presidential leadership is illustrated by four case studies: the Apollo program, the Space Shuttle, the Breeder Reactor, and SDI. Lambright and Rahm conclude that "strategic" policy for technology does not exist and will only be possible if some way is found to sustain presidential leadership over several terms.

Congress has developed somewhat greater institutional capacity for long-range policy analysis through the Office of Technology Assessment (OTA), the Congressional Research Service, the General Accounting Office, and the Congressional Budget Office. The OTA, established by the Technology Assessment Act of 1972, is particularly important as it is the only government agency designed specifically to conduct objective, nonpartisan studies of the long-term impacts of new technologies. In chapter 5 John Gibbons, the director of OTA, and Holly Gwin explain the origin, rationale, and functions of this remarkable body. They point out that the range of subjects covered by OTA has expanded greatly over the years as congressional interest and confidence in the office has grown, and that many other countries have shown interest in establishing similar institutions for technology assessment.

The last two chapters in the section are more critical. In chapter 6 economists Roger Noll and Linda Cohen argue that the politics of the institutional environment often interfere with efficient selection and management of public research programs. After explaining the economic rationale for government R&D, they suggest that political conditions may nevertheless preclude its success in certain areas of technology. In particular, short-term electoral and distributional incentives lead politicians to support "safe" but visible projects that will pay off quickly and benefit them politically. In the management of large projects this also leads to a tendency to foreshorten the relatively inexpensive but critically necessary basic research stages to capture the political benefits that flow from later stages of technological development— often jeopardizing the long-term success of the project. How to make needed long-range research politically viable is thus a major institutional problem in our system.

In chapter 7 sociologist Allan Mazur addresses another difficult issue: whether the mass media do an effective job of educating the public on controversies involving technologies. Since the public is relatively uninformed on scientific and technical matters, the press plays a crucially important role in interpreting and reporting events such as major technological accidents. The initial coverage also influences the agenda-setting process in government (i.e., the process of identifying problems and bringing them to the attention of policy-makers). Mazur's detailed analysis of reporting on the Love Canal chemical waste dump, the Three Mile Island nuclear power plant accident, and other mishaps and catastrophes suggests that media coverage bears little relationship to the inherent importance of such events. He argues that this failure is due less to the political bias of reporters than to the incentive structure of the major communications media, which often leads to overdramatization of events and reporting of unsubstantiated evidence of risks. Mazur concludes with a plea for journalistic restraint in these matters. Others would argue for complete freedom of the press or the public's right to know about potential hazards and disagreements among experts when the probability and magnitude of risks are uncertain.[6]

Several further points should be noted about the chapters in this section in light of the discussion in part I. First, with the exception of the chapter on OTA, the definition of "technology" is fairly restrictive; that is, the other chapters focus on big technology projects and accidents such as the Space Shuttle, Strategic Defense Initiative, and Three Mile Island. This is understandable since such technologies are the direct responsibility of government and receive the widest public and political attention. However, much of the decision making on or governance of "ordinary" technologies that most affect daily life occurs in private institutions or is dispersed throughout the economic, social, and political system. As is clear from the list of studies recently completed by OTA, "technological" issues now encompass virtually all areas of life and extend far beyond the traditional functions of government.

Secondly, this extension of technological problems shows no respect for established governmental jurisdictions. Many problems, such as atmospheric and ocean pollution, the uses of space, and the regulation of nuclear facilities, are now truly global in scope and require international governance. Yet many of the institutions involved, such as national public utilities, military and intelligence services, and large multinational corporations, are immensely powerful and difficult to control through international agreements. At the same time, subnational state and local authorities have focused increasing attention on developing regional technological facilities, especially high tech industries that can stimulate economic growth. The competition among states and regions for technological resources and projects has created new political strains in our federal system as well as among different nations.[7]

Another issue raised in part I and implicit in these chapters is the extent to which technology should be regarded as an inherently "political" phenomenon. The discussion of the role of the president by Lambright and Rahm suggests that technological programs are inevitably politicized at the highest levels of government. While they would obviously like to see more professional and consistent management of such programs, they do not view technology policymaking as fundamentally different from that in other areas. On the other hand, Noll and Cohen, and to some extent Mazur, decry the political biases that affect the funding and management of technologies and suggest that a more "rational" and "scientific" approach to technology is necessary. The implication is that technological decision making should be left to the experts. Interestingly enough, though, the Office of Technology Assessment, while charged with the conduct of nonpartisan technical analyses, makes no such sharp distinctions between political values and technical expertise. Indeed, OTA has shown considerable sensitivity to the political needs of congressmen as well as the concerns of the public in developing policy options.

Finally, it is important to put the American system in comparative perspective. While the United States has been the leader in developing technology assessment and regulation, other nations appear to have evolved more coherent processes and strategies for guiding national scientific and technological development.[8] The Japanese, in particular, have been successful in anticipating and planning for change in strategic areas of technology. In Europe, too, there has been considerably more cooperation and planning within and between governments, and between public and private sectors, than in the more laissez-faire United States.[9] The fragmented, politicized, and inefficient style of governance described in this section raises fundamental doubts about our institutional capacity to compete in the world arena.[10] But we need much more research on how governmental structures affect the course of technological innovation.

In sum, the chapters in this section raise questions about how technology issues are put on the public agenda, how institutional structures and processes influence their consideration, and what criteria should be applied to governing technology in a democracy. How can the short time horizons and lack of technical expertise on the part of elected officials, the media networks, and the public be offset by other mechanisms for expert assessment and planning? Can institutions such as OTA foresee the technical viability and social consequences of new technologies? Should economic efficiency be the principal criterion for public support of research? And how important is it to warn the public of potential health and environmental risks when the evidence is highly uncertain?

These issues are taken up in more detail in the next two sections of the book. Part III focuses more sharply on problems of regulating technology, including the growth of regulation and the development and use of different methods for technology assessment. Part IV considers several policy areas in which alternative approaches for resolving technical disputes and making ethical choices are considered necessary or are being tried. The question of the appropriate scope for expert decision making and for public participation is raised throughout these sections.

PRESIDENTIAL MANAGEMENT OF TECHNOLOGY

W. HENRY LAMBRIGHT AND DIANNE RAHM

Just as presidents deal with foreign and economic policy, so they are enmeshed in science and technology policy. They make decisions, in particular, that affect the course of large-scale technology programs —billion-dollar development efforts that often span a decade or more. These programs—the Strategic Defense Initiative (SDI) is a recent example—are initiated by one president but left for later presidents to speed, slow, or terminate. Like it or not, presidents are directly or indirectly engaged in the management of big technology. They can do it well or poorly, but they cannot escape the responsibility.

Presidents, to be sure, do not act alone. Programs deeply involve Congress and agencies as well. Often programs must be adjusted as the pressures of adjudication, special interests, and public opinion are felt. These conflicting pressures are a significant factor affecting the fate of controversial technologies. The success or failure of national technological programs is determined in large part by the pull and haul of these various actors. But presidents play a special role, for presidents enunciate national policy and priorities.

Much of the literature on science and technology policy has concentrated on advisory bodies such as the now-defunct President's Science Advisory Committee (PSAC). This orientation reflects an emphasis on scientists and government rather than government and scientists. A presidential perspective would show scientists as one group among the many that seek to influence presidential decisions. Presidents have to deal with a host of federal agencies as well as Congress in policymaking. This makes presidential decision making in science and technology subject to most of the same kinds of political pressures as other programs. Scientists might wish presidential science and technology policy were "different" (i.e., less political in the general sense), but it is not.

In dealing with science and technology, as in other areas of national policy, presidents must choose. They have limited time, resources, and political capital and therefore must concentrate on a few priorities. The political incentive structure, as pointed out by Noll and Cohen in chapter 6, leads presidents to concentrate on a few large programs with political payoffs, such as the programs to be discussed in this chapter. Cronin has shown that presidents spend most of their time on programs with a high national security or economic policy content.[1] In doing so they inevitably become involved with science and technology policy. But their involvement is not the result of any coherent or strategic approach to policy in this area.

Presidents are often pulled into science and technology policy in reaction to the pressures of agencies and other vested interests.[2] Their decision making is fragmented, ad hoc, and often quite short term. When they deal with science and technology they ordinarily focus on specific decisions concerning large-scale technology programs in the absence of any strategic context. This makes for uncoordinated programs, in which the president's role is sporadic and variable as the programs move through the cycle from initiation to implementation.

In this chapter we examine the presidential role in four major technologies that have experienced different outcomes. Did the presidential decisions help or hinder these programs? If either, how and why? After our look at these four technologies, we discuss presidential decisions on programs in terms of the larger issue of presidential-level, strategic national technology policy.

PRESIDENTS AND THE POLICY PROCESS

In examining the president's role it is useful to consider the president's involvement in a policy cycle or process affecting technology programs. A considerable literature on policy cycles exists. This literature customarily takes an evolutionary or process approach and focuses on stages in that process and key actors in those stages.[3] The number and specificity of those stages can vary. In a recent book, which serves to some extent as a foundation for this chapter, W. Henry Lambright used a four-stage model.[4] Elsewhere, he has used a six-stage model.[5] What matters is not the number of stages, but the questions being asked and the appropriateness of the model to those questions. One writer has organized a well-known book around one stage.[6] For present purposes we would like to focus on three stages in the policy process. These three stages will illuminate the presidential role (or roles). The stages are: (1) initiation, (2) early implementation, and (3) later implementation.

By initiation we refer to that stage during which a president makes a formal decision to commence a program. Early implementation is the period immediately following presidential commitment, when the implementing agency defines more precisely the program and the organizational design to carry it through, and then starts sponsoring and managing the requisite R&D. Later implementation, a less clearly defined stage, occurs after the program has been under way for a while and "results" are coming in (or not coming in). It is possible to speak of additional stages or decision points along a policy cycle (for example, termination).[7] But these three general stages are sufficient to highlight what is at issue here, namely the role of the president in the science and technology program process.

Programs can be initiated in different ways, with goals that are more or less clear, and statements of presidential intent more or less emphatic. The strength of initiation has much to do with the success or failure of a program. Programs in which the president has an active personal interest seem to fare better than programs espoused by the president for other reasons. The president must also be cognizant of the technological and political environment that will greet the new program. The presidential role here is that of initiator.

Similarly, there can be major presidential decisions in early implementation. Programs are most vulnerable at the outset, and their course is determined by a variety of choices made usually by the same president who makes the initiation decision. The president can strengthen the program by rhetoric aimed at the country as a whole, by giving attention to the organizational capacity of the agency charged with the program, by assuring an adequate budget, and by actively lobbying Congress so as to gain coalition support for the fledgling program. The initiating president thus has to be cognizant of his role as implementor.

Finally, in the later implementation phase, when the program has been in action for a while but is still not yet completed, the president

can be a key actor again. In this stage the program is subject to evaluation which can be triggered by either political or technological considerations. Due to the fact that most programs have longer cycles than
presidents have terms in office, this later implementation phase often
occurs under a president other than the one who initiated it. The force
of the decision either to recommit to or turn away from a program
hinges, in part, on the ability and willingness of the president to use
rhetoric, the budget, organization, and lobbying to secure the stated
goal, just as success of early implementation rests on these factors. But
later implementation is complicated by program entrenchment. The
longer a program remains on the national agenda and the more time its
advocates have to build grass-roots support for the program (usually in
terms of jobs), the more difficult it is to derail. Simply put, the presidential use of rhetoric, budget, organization, and lobbying is more
effective in the stage of early implementation than in later implementation. Presidential roles associated with this phase can be maintainer,
reorienter, rescuer, or terminator.

PROGRAMS AND OUTCOMES

To address these issues associated with national technology policy, we
examine four programs—all of which can be said to be presidential
technologies in the sense that they are affected by the presidential
interest. All of them have been influenced by the nature of presidential decisions and the roles played by presidents over time. They represent a range of technologies and are sufficiently well known that
they have been the object of considerable scrutiny by researchers.

APOLLO

Apollo was a program initiated by Kennedy, maintained by Johnson,
and completed by Nixon. Apollo is generally regarded as the most
successful technology program in history and as such serves as a model
for the ability of the nation to set a goal and see it through. The only
possible rival is the Manhattan Project, but that was a secret project
conducted under World War II conditions and is therefore not a very
useful model for comparison. To the degree that Apollo achieved its
goals, it provides insights into facilitative presidential decision making.

THE SPACE SHUTTLE

The Space Shuttle is an ongoing program. Initiated in 1972 by Richard Nixon, it was regarded in 1987, one year after the *Challenger* disaster, as a failure in terms of its initial presidential goals. Shuttle goals were more incremental than strategic; indeed, NASA saw it merely as the means to the desired end of a space station. The Shuttle was maintained by Ford and Carter. Reagan was cast in the role of reorienter. The "evaluation" that forced this role on Reagan was that of the Rogers Commission, established because of the *Challenger* disaster.

THE BREEDER REACTOR

The Breeder stands as a monument to inconsistent presidential decision making, and it also reveals the difficulty of having a strategic long-term science and technology policy within the U.S. system. The Breeder was initiated by Nixon in 1971 and maintained by Ford. Carter attempted to terminate the program but failed. Reagan inherited a troubled program and tried to rescue it, but failed. When the program ended in 1983, it had cost the taxpayers well over a billion dollars and had not progressed beyond the design stage of development.

THE STRATEGIC DEFENSE INITIATIVE, OR STAR WARS

The Star Wars program was initiated by Reagan in 1983, with the look of a national technology policy. It is still under way at the time of writing (November 1987). Hence, the "final" outcome depends on future presidents. However, the prognosis is reorientation from original presidential goals. Indeed, Star Wars is uncommon in that this reorientation is coming so quickly—under the same president who initiated the program. This does not bode well for the future of Star Wars.

A comparative analysis of these four programs lends insight into questions concerning the feasibility of American national technology policy. The nature of presidential decisions cannot be separated from the fate of these technologies. They are not the ordinary technological programs buried in agencies and invisible to all but specialists. They are highly public because presidents have made them so. Their fate tells us a great deal about the strengths and weaknesses in presidential leadership in this area of national policy, as well as the prospects for long-term or strategic technology policy.

INITIATION

To evaluate the presidential decision to initiate a program, we need to ask about both the ripeness of the environment for the decision and the quality of the decision itself. We will deal with ripeness first. By ripeness of environment we mean technical and political readiness. Was the presidential decision based on a consensus among scientists that a program was technically feasible? Political ripeness refers to congressional and public environments. Were those who would have to provide resources (Congress) ready for a presidential decision in terms of support? Was this a decision of more general public salience?

In the case of Apollo there had been considerable previous technical planning by the time Kennedy was ready to make his decision. NASA had had Apollo on its agenda for two years and had attempted unsuccessfully to get the Eisenhower administration to consider it.[8] Under Kennedy, and his appointee as NASA administrator James Webb, NASA refined its planning and even tried to work, incrementally, toward the goal of a lunar landing. Hence, on a technical level, there was sufficient planning prior to the decision—the technology was ready. On a political level there was also plenty of input. The Cold War and the perceived "crisis" of the Soviet threat made Congress anxious to have a dramatic presidential initiative in space. Additionally, Vice-President Lyndon Johnson was an effective broker for Kennedy and Congress in assuring support, should Kennedy articulate a program. Hence, technically and politically, there was a positive environment for the decision.

In no other case was the environment as ripe for decision. In the case of the Shuttle there was plenty of technical agency planning.[9] However, political support was lacking. There was no great crisis to unify support behind the venture save the "crisis" that NASA had no mission beyond Apollo and, without a decision, NASA's capacity would atrophy.[10] With the Breeder Reactor the story was basically the same. A senior member of the Joint Committee on Atomic Energy (JCAE) had advocated the development of the technology, but this advocacy was more a final effort to do something really "big" before his retirement than a response to a real energy need at the time. The agency push for Breeder technology began in 1967, long before the energy crisis of 1973–74.[11]

Star Wars represents a case of minimal advanced technological and political planning. The lack of political ripeness is clearly seen by the surprise that greeted the president's announcement from White House aides, the Pentagon, and official Washington alike.[12] Shortly after the president's speech of March 23, 1983, there was a gust of congressional hearings, diplomatic cables, official and unofficial studies, and speeches.[13] Star Wars' future was turned over to two major study groups initiated by National Security Study Directive (NSSD) 6-83. The most important study resulting from this directive—the Fletcher Report—spanned some seven volumes. All this planning and study came *after* the decision.[14] The technological ripeness of the defense shield was an issue from the very start. Within two days of the March 23 initiation speech, major scientists were debating the feasibility of President Reagan's proposal in the press.[15] (See chapter 13 by Masters and Kantrowitz.) Within four days seventeen scientists (many of them Nobel Prize winners) and arms experts had signed a petition urging Reagan to adopt policies banning weapons from space.[16] Although there was a certain ripeness owing to Reagan's defense modernization strategy, this did not fully reach to Star Wars because the Soviet threat in this particular area seemed uncertain.

In terms of environmental ripeness, then, Apollo had the best initiation of the four technologies at issue here. But successful initiation must also be judged based upon the quality of the decision. Was the decision clear and unambiguous? Did the president personally show interest in the technological program or was the presidential decision merely used to make political gains in other areas? How committed was the president?

The presidential decisions varied in a number of respects. Apollo, for example, was absolutely clear and unambiguous. A decision was reached to set a foreign policy goal—to beat the Russians to a goal sufficiently challenging and distant that the United States, then behind, could win. There was a personal presidential commitment behind the decision, as Kennedy himself asked his advisers for a goal he could set in competition with the Soviets.[17] While others, particularly James Webb, administrator of NASA, influenced the rhetoric, unquestionably Kennedy wanted a national goal for personal reasons—namely, the need to reinstill pride and command in a presidency wounded by the debacles of the Bay of Pigs and the Gagarin first-man-in-space flight. Viewed within the context of science and technology policy, Apollo was a strategic decision. Its aim was to move the country forward toward a broader goal of preeminence in space vis-à-vis the Russians. It was a presidential leadership decision, rather than a decision in which the president acquiesced to a coalition of forces seeking more incremental national policy. While a decision NASA wanted, it was truly one Kennedy made his own.

In contrast, the Shuttle was an acquiescence decision. The president made the decision following a difficult coalition-building process led by NASA, which bargained and negotiated with the Office of Management and Budget and the Defense Department to get to the president. The president essentially accepted what had been worked out—a much compromised technology—at lower levels. He did so for reasons that were his, rather than NASA's or OMB's. But his reasons hardly involved presidential leadership.

The Breeder decision was cut from the same mold as the Shuttle decision. Nixon's call for the Breeder came not so much from a dedication to a new form of energy as it did from the need for a political compromise with the then-powerful chair of the House Government Operations Committee, Chet Holifield, who also sat as a charter member of the JCAE. As member of the JCAE, Holifield championed the development of the Breeder reactor. But Holifield's position on the House committee placed him in a central position to determine the success or failure of Nixon's proposed government reorganization plan.[18] The decision was a politically motivated incremental addition to already established nuclear energy policy.[19] Although lacking the personal dedication of the president, the decision was quite clear. In his 1971 energy address to Congress Nixon called for the development of the Breeder by 1980, calling it "our best hope today for meeting the nation's growing demand for economical clean energy."[20] Despite the clarity of the decision, the program suffered. The president had little interest in maintaining his decision.

Star Wars, in certain respects, is more like Apollo than either the Breeder or the Shuttle. Reagan set forth a vision beyond incrementalism. This was the notion that a space-based defense would render nuclear weapons "impotent and obsolete."[21] This was strategic, like Apollo—a broad decision setting a course of policy, within which technologies would be advanced, rather than a technology in search of a policy like the Breeder and the Shuttle. The president firmly believed in Star Wars. He had a long personal history of not liking the policy of Mutual Assured Destruction.[22] Like Apollo, Star Wars was a Cold War foreign policy decision. But unlike Apollo, Star Wars also had an overriding domestic political context. The growing influence of the Nuclear Freeze movement threatened the president's commitment to an arms buildup.[23] The Freeze movement offered the solution of disarmament. This solution, no doubt unpalatable to Reagan, needed to be undercut. Star Wars gave him the opportunity to call for a "moral" defense and undermine the influence of the Freeze movement.

Unlike Apollo, however, SDI had no clear goal, and shortly after the speech much attention was focused on answering the question of just what SDI would be. And, unlike Apollo, Star Wars had no completion date set by the president, who said only that the effort "may not be accomplished before the end of this century."[24] There was much ambiguity and room for changing the goal. Hence, the analogy with the Apollo decision is more an appearance than a reality, particularly as is seen in the next phase of presidential decision making.

EARLY IMPLEMENTATION

The early years of a big technology program tell a great deal about presidential commitment. These are critical years, when a program is most vulnerable. This is the time when it must be organized and provided with staffing and resources for the long haul. Presidents can help new programs in various ways: securing necessary funds, giving public support through rhetoric, lobbying Congress, and backing the implementing organization in the bureaucratic politics of the executive branch.

In Apollo, Kennedy helped NASA by making it clear to the Bureau of the Budget (BOB) and Congress that he wanted the funds NASA thought necessary to carry out the decision. When NASA and his science adviser got into a major dispute over the way to go to the moon (earth vs. lunar rendezvous), the president backed NASA. When the head of NASA and his principal subordinate for Apollo engaged in a power struggle over priorities and congressional strategy, the president cut short an end-run and supported the administrator. In these and other ways the president strengthened the hand of the agency responsible for Apollo. By the time Kennedy was assassinated, NASA had

Apollo off to a strong start, and there was great momentum going into the next administration.[25]

In the Shuttle program Nixon quickly withdrew from the scene after the initiating decision, leaving NASA unsupported in the task of fighting with OMB and Congress for dollars year to year.[26] Nixon gave little rhetorical support in public when he had power, and none once he became engulfed in the Watergate scandal. NASA was on its own. An agreement for a long-term stable budget, presumably established between NASA and OMB at the time of the president's initiating decision, quickly unraveled as OMB saw the president distracted by other priorities.[27]

The scenario of the Breeder was much like that of the Shuttle. Nixon had supported the program with some degree of rhetoric, but budgetary support was not forthcoming.[28] The Nixon administration had determined that the cost of development of the Breeder was to be shared with the private utilities, which would financially benefit from the operation of Breeder plants. The utility companies were hesitant to assume the open-ended costs of development associated with the Breeder, having had substantial losses on early light-water reactor designs.[29]

Despite this problem, the Nixon administration stayed firm on the budgetary necessity of private industry assuming its part of the cost. Nixon's support for the agency charged with the implementation of the Breeder program was also in question. Instead of supporting the AEC, Nixon recommended its reorganization.[30] If lack of budgetary and organizational support from the president were not enough, the program also came under court supervision. An environmentalist activist group called the Scientists Institute for Public Information won a court battle against the AEC which required the agency to submit a long-term environmental impact statement on Breeder technology.[31] The Breeder, increasingly enmeshed in technological controversy, was delayed. Opponents aimed at preventing the building of a demonstration plant on the Clinch River in Oak Ridge, Tennessee. When the impact statement was finally issued, the Environmental Protection Agency (EPA) joined the fray by rejecting AEC's statement and supporting the environmentalists.[32] The early implementation stages of the Breeder were thus lacking critical elements of presidential support —budgetary and organizational support—while at the same time the program was being delayed in the courts and vilified by critics in the press. The Breeder was wounded at the outset.

Star Wars, being the personal property of Reagan, did not have the problems with OMB or other bodies within the executive branch that afflicted the Breeder. The program was given influence by being established directly under the secretary of defense in a new organization, the Strategic Defense Initiative Organization (SDIO), established by DOD directive on April 24, 1984, specifically to nurture and develop the effort. Lt. General James Abrahamson, former director of the Space Shuttle program, was appointed director of SDIO and was given a vastly increased budget from past SDI-related programs—$1.4 billion for FY1985, with $26 billion sought through FY1989.[33] The strength of the president's commitment was proved again and again by his rhetoric to the American people, lobbying with Congress, and particularly his refusal to compromise Star Wars in negotiations with the Russians at Reykjavik.[34]

In early implementation, however, certain problems became apparent owing to difficulties at the point of the initiating decision. First, the decision was neither politically nor technically ripe. It was immediately criticized by both the Pentagon and Congress, revealing the political problems of the notion.[35] Debate centered on the undermining of the ABM treaty and the possibility of arms escalations in defensive as well as offensive munitions.[36] Within one year of the initial presidential announcement, the Office of Technology Assessment had concluded that the prospects for success of Star Wars were "so remote that it should not serve as the basis for public expectation or national policy."[37] At the 150th annual meeting of the prestigious American Association for the Advancement of Science, certain members called for a limit on the development of technologies for Star Wars.[38] Even the Defensive Technologies Study Team, chaired by James Fletcher, despite its optimistic attitude toward newly emerging technologies was not able to indicate when such a system would work, how well it might work, or what it would cost.[39]

Second, the ambiguity of the president's decision (based on his words and those of executive officials interpreting him) created problems in implementation. Was this a decision to have a leak-proof, space-based defense for people or was it a decision to have an ABM-style missile defense system using space technology? As early as May 1984 evidence indicated that Abrahamson was reorienting the focus of the program. Before the House Appropriations Committee's military subcommittee he testified that plans for Star Wars included the fielding

of weapons in space to protect strategic missiles instead of populations.[40] By the end of 1984 scientists in charge of research for SDI were
saying that plans had been substantially scaled back, from trying to
create an impenetrable defense of the nation to protecting the nation's
land-based nuclear arsenal.[41] Still, the president and many of his high
ranking officials, like DOD Secretary Caspar Weinberger, insisted that
the goal of Star Wars was a population shield.[42] SDIO had the problem
of implementing a program whose goal was not clear—maybe not
feasible—and whose budget, while large, was under pressure from the
beginning.[43] Scientific and political debate over the ripeness of the
project continued unabated and even escalated.[44] There was no
"honeymoon" for Star Wars as there was for Apollo. There was slip-
page in schedule, dampening of objectives, and congressional cut-
backs in funds, all under Reagan.

Indeed, concern for what might happen to the program may have
forced the early reorientation away from the exotic R&D required for
the population shield to more obtainable weapons which would defend
only land-based missiles. The aim became to deploy sooner, thus providing a demonstration fait accompli and a harder program to cut or
terminate by the successor.[45] Another part of the strategy was to have
SDI firmly entrenched in the grass-roots economy of the nation by
attracting universities through grants and private enterprise through
contracts. "Sharing the wealth" might serve SDI in the same way it
served the Breeder—by creating resistance in Congress to cut budgets
which monetarily benefited local constituencies.[46] That became the
Reagan strategy for making his successor a maintainer rather than
terminator.

LATER IMPLEMENTATION

Initiating presidents can do only so much to secure "their" programs.
What happens to Star Wars depends on who follows Reagan as president and the circumstances of that administration. It is rare indeed
that a successor president has the same sense of ownership of a program as the initiator. So much can happen in the environment of a
program that is unforeseeable and that can make it easier for a president beset by other problems to let a program slide. Even Apollo was
under enormous difficulty in the late 1960s, when Johnson focused
his attention and budgets on Vietnam and the Great Society. But John-

son had been advising Kennedy to make the Apollo decision, and he regarded Apollo as his program as well as Kennedy's. Hence he resisted pressures from Congress, mayors, and especially his budget director to let the Apollo goal slip. Also, at Apollo's darkest moment, the fire in 1967 which killed three astronauts, Johnson made a critical decision to charge NASA with conducting the investigation of what went wrong. While NASA was forthright in its technical examination, the fact that it was in command gave the agency more opportunity to contain damage and control the recovery process. Johnson also provided rhetorical and congressional support for Apollo, as needed, throughout his administration. He did cut NASA's budget, but he took the cuts from the non-Apollo programs.[47]

The nature of the initiating decision was critical to what Johnson and Congress did to maintain Apollo in the late 1960s. The goal was so clear and unambiguous that NASA was in a position to point the finger at those "responsible" for preventing the agency from succeeding. Most legislators did not want to be so labeled, and neither did Johnson. For him, Apollo was a personal commitment. After Nixon assumed power, his major decision was the nondecision of letting the Apollo landing take place as scheduled. He took whatever credit he could from being in office at the appointed hour.

Ford, by contrast, had relatively little impact on either the Shuttle or the Breeder. Succumbing to continued agency battles between EPA and the newly created Energy Research and Development Administration (ERDA) over environmental issues, Ford tried to slow the development of the reactor but was not successful.[48] By this time the project had secured grass-roots support, and Congress resisted attempts to cut the budget.[49] Bowing to congressional pressure, in the 1976 energy address to Congress Ford committed himself to the Breeder program.[50] But shortly thereafter he reversed himself by announcing a program curbing weapons spread, which was to include a reevaluation of the domestic use of plutonium and thus the Breeder (which bred plutonium).[51]

Ford's wavering position on the Breeder made him ineffective. He paid lip service to the program in the early part of his administration, then reversed himself. He never actively campaigned against the technology, but neither did he foster it. He was an ambivalent maintainer.

One of Carter's first acts, however, was to cut the budget of the project. The budget revision for fiscal 1977 and 1978 cut millions from the Breeder program. Carter added rhetoric to his budgetary actions by announcing that the United States would adopt a policy not to use plutonium fuel for nuclear power and by remarking that "there will be no need for a Breeder reactor plant such as Clinch River."[52] Carter allowed the demonstration plant design to be completed but fought all construction efforts. He brought the power of the presidency to bear on his decision, and in April 1977 ERDA announced that it was canceling all contracts for the Breeder.[53] Carter's opposition to the Breeder had two bases. First, when the energy crisis came, it brought with it a host of competing technologies, some of which, like solar and conservation, were embraced by environmentalists opposed to nuclear power. At the same time Carter made halting nuclear weapons proliferation a foreign policy priority. Carter saw the Breeder as more a foreign policy problem (nuclear proliferation) than an energy solution.

Carter's attempts to terminate the program were unsuccessful, despite a long battle with the legislature involving vetoes and supplemental appropriation bills.[54] The Breeder program survived all Carter's bold attempts to terminate it, but with the coming of the Reagan administration the program faced another round of reevaluation.

Energy was not a major focus of the Reagan administration, and the mood and membership of the legislature had changed. Reagan made a halfhearted attempt to save the Breeder by proposing $200 million for the completion of the Clinch River demonstration plant.[55] But after the retirement of its main congressional supporter, Senate Majority leader Howard Baker of Tennessee, an unlikely coalition of fiscal conservatives and environmental liberals finally terminated the project.[56] By the end of 1983 the long-lived Breeder Reactor was a program of the past. It had lasted for over a decade and cost $1.5 billion.[57]

Carter tried to kill the Breeder for reasons of foreign policy, not energy or science and technology policy. Similarly, when he rescued the Shuttle from a severe budget problem in 1979, he acted not so much for reasons of space policy but for reasons of defense and foreign policy. What happened was that the nation was gradually coming to rely exclusively on the Shuttle for launching. This meant that the ability to verify past and future SALT agreements with the Soviets depended on launching huge spy satellites via the Shuttle rather than expendable rockets. When NASA revealed that the Shuttle was running late and costing far more than originally forecast—an original forecast based more on what it took politically to obtain an initiating decision than on economic reality—Carter found himself listening to DOD as well as NASA. The upshot was that Carter gave NASA what it needed to move the program forward. He restricted the program, however, by cutting the number of planned shuttles from five to four and giving DOD priority in future launches.[58]

When Reagan became president, the Shuttle program seemed to have recovered and reached its goals, albeit at a much higher cost than anticipated. That is, NASA proclaimed it was moving from an R&D program to a reliable operational system. Reagan accepted this and approved NASA's request to move to its next major R&D program, the Manned Space Station, in 1983. Reagan did not question NASA's claim that the Shuttle was so reliable that it could carry civilians in space. But then came the *Challenger* disaster in January 1986.

Unlike Johnson, Reagan made no effort to contain the damage afflicting NASA. He appointed a group beyond NASA's control (the Rogers Commission) to investigate what went wrong. They found much that was "flawed" in NASA decision making.[59] Safety had been compromised as management strove increasingly for greater cost-effectiveness. As a frantic shake-up occurred within NASA management, the Shuttle program was put on hold. While recovery will eventually take place, there is little question that Shuttle failed to reach its major goal. It is a long way from the cost-effective, operational system it was supposed to become by the early 1980s. Possibly those goals were unrealistic. Certainly they had little hope of realization given the absence of support to NASA in meeting them over most of the 1970s. NASA's decision making was not all that was flawed. There was also presidential decision making, beginning with Nixon and continuing through Reagan.

CONCLUSIONS

What does this discussion tell us about presidential management of science and technology? Are these major programs part of a strategy for science and technology policy, or are they a result of ad hoc pressures and historical accident? Is there hope for long-term R&D programs in an environment of short-term presidential calculations?

The answer is that there is some hope, but it is based on the consistent coupling of presidential decisions over a series of presidents rather than a clearly stated science and technology policy. Presidents are politicians and problem solvers; they develop policies as solutions to problems with political implications. Those problems may be Russian competition (Apollo), cooperating with the Joint Committee on Atomic Energy (Breeder), how to keep NASA and America's space capability alive (Shuttle), or how to neutralize a growing Nuclear Freeze movement while finding an alternative to Mutual Assured Destruction (Star Wars). In solving immediate problems, presidents can make leadership or acquiescence decisions. Acquiescence decisions are likely to be next steps in existing programs, pushed by agencies or congressional allies. Leadership decisions are larger decisions, based more on personal presidential priorities than on bureaucratic momentum. Leadership decisions are far more likely to have both presidential commitment and strategic dimensions, in the sense of having policy drive technology, rather than the reverse.

The most serious issue where these large-scale programs are concerned is not one president's strategic decision, but the slim chance that another president will share that decision. Strategic policy is long term, and of the four programs examined here only Apollo was implemented by a president with the same sense of priority as his predecessor. This was an unusual case. Sustaining presidential leadership is the key problem that prevents strategic decision making and successful long-term technology programs most of the time.

Of course, it can be argued that this is all to the good. It can be said that it is important for new presidents to take a critical look at old programs, evaluate them, and reorient or terminate them. True, not all programs are equally worthwhile. Moreover it fits the political incentives of presidents to make their mark by distinguishing their decisions from those of predecessors. But that does not obviate the need for some staying power on the part of presidents behind programs that are initiated and evaluated in accord with some strategy that supersedes any one president.

This need is most likely to be met if there is a high-quality initiating decision backed by widespread congressional support. This requires a broad consensus based on national need rather than bureaucratic momentum or coalition politics. In such cases presidential decisions are more likely to be truly national decisions. This was true of Apollo but was not of the Breeder or the Shuttle. The more technically and politically ripe the technology, the clearer and less ambiguous can be the decision and the better chance it will have of being sustained by future presidents. It also helps immensely if the initiating president, in the early implementation stage, is attentive to the need for a capable agency with strong leadership to be an advocate throughout the process. Frequently, there will be problems affecting a technology along the way, after the initiating president goes. When those problems come, it is up to the successor president to evaluate the program. The successor president will have more information based on experience about the continued technical and political ripeness of the program and desirability of maintaining it. The better the decisions prior to this stage, the more likely that maintenance will be the choice.

Beyond that it is hard to say what else can be done—or should be done—in the U.S. system to make presidential technology management more stable and effective. For better or for worse, the election of relatively short-term presidents as well as legislators promotes change. What technological programs need is political stability. It would be ideal if both change and continuity were guided by a better sense of strategy in science and technology policy. The cases studied here suggest how difficult it is to obtain such a strategic policy. Perhaps the closest the American system can come to this ideal is a tighter coupling of successive presidential leadership decisions.

TECHNOLOGY AND GOVERNANCE:

THE DEVELOPMENT OF THE OFFICE

OF TECHNOLOGY ASSESSMENT

JOHN H. GIBBONS AND HOLLY L. GWIN

Upon this gifted age, in its dark hour
Falls from the sky a meteoric shower
Of facts . . . they lie unquestioned,
    uncombined,
Wisdom enough to leech us of our ill
Is daily spun; but there exists no loom
To weave it into fabric.
—Edna St. Vincent Millay

The search for a means to weave scientific endeavor into the fabric of man's existence is very old. Applied science, technology, has long been viewed as both release from bondage and as a terror, a force that simultaneously presents the promises of heaven and the perils of hell. The ancient Chinese sought to expand agriculture and build cities, but perceived that the resulting deforestation could lead to dire consequences—harmful effects on stream flow and the quality of lowland soil, not to mention the loss of a natural barrier to horse-riding barbarians.[1] Sophocles lauded the inherent power of the plow,[2] but Plato described the negative side of that power, deforestation and soil erosion.[3]

Each century the power of technology has intensified; it continues to do so today. The twenty-five years preceding World War II have been characterized as a period of sweeping revolution in basic science, particularly in physics and chemistry, and in the years following the

An earlier version of this article appeared in *Technology in Society*, vol. 7, pp. 333–52.

war, technology rapidly transformed the nature of industrial and agricultural production.[4] The belief that technology delivered us from the carnage of prolonged war encouraged the expectation of technical solutions, those demanding little or no change in human values or ideas of morality,[5] for all problems, especially those that technology creates.

The natural companion to the desire to use new technologies is the yearning to know just where the applications will lead. Indeed, good governance requires an appreciation of the profound ability of science and technology to shape our lives, surroundings, and future. The environmental crises of the 1960s made Congress acutely aware of the importance of foresight. Only after DDT had been used extensively throughout the country did the public become aware of its consequences. Technologies developed and applied with only the best of intentions threatened clean air and clean water, resources long taken for granted. If the national legislature were to act as "all wise rulers must: cope not only with present troubles, but also with ones likely to arise in the future, and assiduously forestall them,"[6] it would need an institutional mechanism for foresight, one that would make analysis of the consequences of technology a methodical enterprise.

THE INSTITUTIONALIZATION OF FORESIGHT

Congress was called upon to debate several issues in the 1960s that had critical impact on the decision to institutionalize foresight. Budget limitations, as usual, were very influential. Spending for scientific research and development had increased from $3 billion in 1954 to $18 billion in 1972, yet Congress was being asked to allocate even more money to technology development without being able to clearly foresee the outcome—good or bad—of such investment.[7] But a new urgency regarding the public health and welfare dominated the debate. For example, in 1972 Senator Edward Kennedy, as chairman of the Senate Subcommittee on Health, conducted an investigation of the effects of lead poisoning. Learning that about 400,000 children suffered from lead poisoning, and that each year about 200 children were dying from ingestion of thirty-year-old, lead-base paint, he wondered whether Congress could have anticipated this problem and enacted legislation which would have spared thousands of children the effects of this poison.[8]

Maintaining the separation of powers of the legislative and executive branches of government was also an important objective. The debates over the supersonic transport (SST) and the antiballistic missile (ABM) treaty emphasized the paucity of information available to Congress and the public that supported anything other than the administration's views on the issues. Contention over testing of nuclear weapons in the atmosphere drove home the growing problem of relying on outside scientific experts for perfect foresight and unbiased advice. Although expert scientific advice had become increasingly important to good decision making, Congress properly reserved to itself the responsibility to make policy. Thus a better internal understanding of science and technology that would decrease the need to rely on the administration, and outside experts, all with causes to advocate, would be needed if Congress were to maintain equality with the executive branch.

Congress found exasperating the fact that scientists and other experts often disagree, frequently to the extent that their testimony, allegedly with respect to the facts, is flatly contradictory. It became clear that technical information can be diffuse, judgmental, uncertain, and thus confusing to policymakers as well as scientists.[9] Not only did the debate over the SST suffer from congressional overdependence on information from the executive branch and outside advocates, it deteriorated from disagreement among the experts.[10]

Experts testifying on atmospheric testing of nuclear devices presented another dilemma. Those in favor of nuclear testing reported health effects in terms of an individual's increased cancer risk as a result of exposure to fallout. So expressed, the risk seemed minimal. Critics of testing expressed the identical facts in terms of the extra deaths that would occur worldwide within a period of fifty years. This calculation, seemingly a high figure, aroused concern.[11]

Congress soon realized that scientists, too, can be politicized, and that the needed "facts" cannot be lifted directly from the scientific journals and plugged into the policy debate.[12] Rarely are clearly established facts central in a policy debate. It is almost always the unknowns and credibly disputed claims—such as in cases of acid rain or nuclear safety—that are at issue. Some leaders felt that the dilemma posed by scientist-advocates and selective presentation of information might be diminished or even avoided altogether if Congress could do a careful and independent job of anticipating the effects of technological advances and working to mitigate the undesired consequences.

Serious legislative consideration of a congressional foresight mechanism began in 1967, around the time the term "technology assessment" was coined. The stakes were rising in technological gambles —billions of public dollars were spent on the SST before Congress decided to abandon it; the nation's security was at risk in the consideration of the ABM treaty—and this promoted a great deal of congressional concern about the legislature's level of scientific sophistication. Congress wearied of governing technology by muddling through. Responsible government requires clear knowledge of the consequences of actions, knowledge that was all too often unavailable to elected representatives.[13]

There grew an ambition to create for Congress a nonpartisan, analytic staff that could: (1) provide expert analysis independent of the executive branch; and (2) convert complicated technical information accurately into a form easily used by Congress. Reports by the National Academy of Engineering (NAE)[14] and the National Academy of Sciences (NAS)[15] articulated the need for this type of impartial governmental analysis of new technologies, and indicated that Congress would be an appropriate body to house an agency to perform technology assessments. The deliberations culminated, in 1972, in an act "to establish an Office of Technology Assessment (OTA) for the Congress . . . to provide early indications of the probable beneficial and adverse impacts of applications of technology and to develop other coordinate information which may assist the Congress."[16]

HOW OTA EMERGED

A review of OTA's enabling legislation and legislative history reveals that Congress hoped to obtain a unique set of services from this new agency. Technology assessment was to be a new type of research not performed by any other congressional research group. In the collective congressional view, technology assessment meant that OTA would:[17]

- Provide information especially suited for the policy process. Not only was OTA to convert scientific information into laymen's terms, it was also to distill the vast body of information available to its essence for decision making. The goal was to help focus congressional debate and thereby to help resolve issues.

- Anticipate technological issues, and provide an "early warning" system for Congress. Congress wanted very much to avoid repeating fiascos like that of the SST.
- Identify and describe policy options and their likely consequences. This would include descriptions of the social, economic, and political effects of the policy options—for better as well as for worse.
- Assure objectivity. This was to be accomplished, at least in part, by involving people from outside government in analysis, advice, and review, yet OTA was to maintain institutional responsibility for the results. Appreciating the fact that scientists often serve as advocates, and may argue for policies that do not necessarily follow from "facts," Congress wanted the services of an agency whose loyalties were owed to the Congress as a whole, not to particular groups or causes.
- Provide the public with information about the likely consequences of possible governmental decisions. A government for the people and by the people requires that the public have access to the information used by Congress in policy formation.
- Not substitute for the policy decisions of elected legislators. Congress wanted to avoid leaving to technical experts decisions that were the proper domain of elected representatives. OTA was challenged to narrow, if possible, the uncertainties and conflicts of science and technology, and to provide a reasonable range of options or alternatives for public policy, but not to recommend particular legislative actions.
- Contribute to restoring and supporting public confidence in the wisdom of the congressional decision process.[18]

Interested Congress-watchers were definitely of two minds about this unique set of services. Early champions of OTA envisaged an agency that would be able to curb the influence of the technology optimists, who were frequently able to inspire congressional enthusiasm for technologies and activities with popular appeal but questionable technical merit. Early critics, on the other hand, felt that OTA might constrain the development of science and its transformation to technology.

Proponents viewed OTA as a place to conjoin a variety of technical experts to act as a shared resource for Congress, an agency where unbiased analyses of technical claims could be performed. Opponents feared that the agency, rather than acting as a nonpartisan, shared resource for all congressional committees, might too easily be used to build the empire of a particular committee, member, or group of members, and press particular points of view upon Congress.

Promoters of OTA anticipated an agency that—with extensive public participation—would comprehensively analyze the major sociotechnical issues of the day, and integrate the results into a package that would inject greater national wisdom into congressional debate. Detractors opposed the insertion of a new, untested, and unpredictable actor into the delicately balanced process of policymaking. And the complaint that "there is too much analysis already," indicative of the belief that studies had often been used to justify delays in decisions, was not uncommon.

Given these disparate views, it is not surprising that OTA would prove a disappointment to some, while pleasantly surprising others. OTA's founders, however, embedded in the authorizing legislation several features that helped the agency grow and develop even in the face of controversy. Chief among them are:

- An active, bipartisan, bicameral, congressional Technology Assessment Board (TAB), which meets on numerous occasions throughout the year to establish agency policy, review progress, and approve initiation of assessments;
- Specific designation as a shared congressional resource, to be responsive to requests from committees in both the House and Senate, and from either side of the aisle;
- Flexibility in employment and contracting authority vested in OTA's management; and
- A Technology Assessment Advisory Council (TAAC), comprising eminent intellectual leaders from across the nation, the comptroller general of the United States, and the director of the Congressional Research Service. TAAC provides oversight of OTA's work.[19]

The fact that OTA involves the interested public in its work by use of advisory panels and external reviewers, while retaining responsibility for the finished product, has also contributed to its level of acceptance and its standing in the technical community.

Learning by Doing

One must learn
By doing the thing, for though
you think you know it,

You have no certainty, until you try.

—Sophocles

OTA learned by doing. Starting a new organization is always difficult, especially when the designated role is new, imprecise, and threatening. Earlier attempts to perform technology assessments had been on a much smaller scale and well outside the legislative arena, so there was no operational paradigm. The first few years are particularly treacherous for an organization that seems to infringe on established territories. In an open letter to the Speaker of the House in June 1975, an early TAB member, the Honorable Charles A. Mosher, identified several organizational shortcomings that would need attention in the succeeding years:[20]

- OTA would need to establish appropriate linkages with the Congressional Research Service (CRS), the General Accounting Office (GAO), and the National Science Foundation (NSF), and also to work with the executive branch to assemble relevant and available facts;
- TAB and TAAC would need to establish a closer relationship, which would require a better understanding regarding procedures, assignments, and authorities;
- The House of Representatives would need to make better use of OTA's resources; and
- OTA would need to give attention to small as well as large requests (i.e., address mundane but important questions as well as the intellectually intriguing issues).

Today, formalized, proven procedures exist for coordinating OTA's activities with those of the Congressional Budget Office (CBO), CRS and GAO. Extensive use is made of information available from the academies of science and engineering, NSF, and the executive branch agencies, as well as from the private sector and international sources. The original tension between TAB and TAAC—largely the result of an early debate over what kind of body should govern OTA—has essentially disappeared, and their roles are now complementary.

Requests for OTA assistance, which originally came predominantly from the Senate, are now almost evenly divided between the Senate and the House. Finally, OTA examines a broad range of issues, assessing, for example, air traffic control as well as outer space, and strip-mine control technologies as well as high-technology polymers and

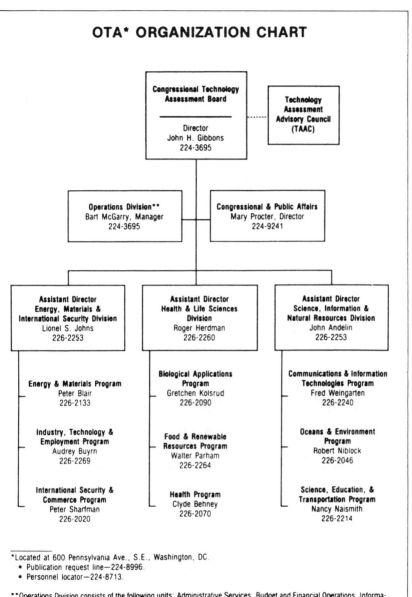

OTA* ORGANIZATION CHART

Congressional Technology
Assessment Board
───────────
Director
John H. Gibbons
224-3695

Technology
Assessment
Advisory Council
(TAAC)

Operations Division**
Bart McGarry, Manager
224-3695

Congressional & Public Affairs
Mary Procter, Director
224-9241

Assistant Director
Energy, Materials &
International Security Division
Lionel S. Johns
226-2253

Assistant Director
Health & Life Sciences
Division
Roger Herdman
226-2260

Assistant Director
Science, Information &
Natural Resources Division
John Andelin
226-2253

Energy & Materials Program
Peter Blair
226-2133

Biological Applications
Program
Gretchen Kolsrud
226-2090

Communications & Information
Technologies Program
Fred Weingarten
226-2240

Industry, Technology &
Employment Program
Audrey Buyrn
226-2269

Food & Renewable
Resources Program
Walter Parham
226-2264

Oceans & Environment
Program
Robert Niblock
226-2046

International Security &
Commerce Program
Peter Sharfman
226-2020

Health Program
Clyde Behney
226-2070

Science, Education, &
Transportation Program
Nancy Naismith
226-2214

*Located at 600 Pennsylvania Ave., S.E., Washington, DC.
 • Publication request line—224-8996.
 • Personnel locator—224-8713.

**Operations Division consists of the following units: Administrative Services, Budget and Financial Operations, Information Center, Personnel Office, Publishing Office, and Telecommunications and Information Services.

Figure 5-1

Office of Technology Assessment

Congressional Board of the 100th Congress

MORRIS K. UDALL, *Arizona, Chairman*

TED STEVENS, *Alaska, Vice Chairman*

Senate	**House**
ORRIN G. HATCH *Utah*	GEORGE E. BROWN, JR. *California*
CHARLES E. GRASSLEY *Iowa*	JOHN D. DINGELL *Michigan*
EDWARD M. KENNEDY *Massachusetts*	CLARENCE E. MILLER *Ohio*
ERNEST F. HOLLINGS *South Carolina*	DON SUNDQUIST *Tennessee*
CLAIBORNE PELL *Rhode Island*	AMO HOUGHTON *New York*

JOHN H. GIBBONS
(Nonvoting)

Advisory Council

WILLIAM J. PERRY, *Chairman* *H&Q Technology Partners*	CLAIRE T. DEDRICK *California Land Commission*	RACHEL McCULLOCH *University of Wisconsin*
DAVID S. POTTER, *Vice Chairman* *General Motors Corp. (Ret.)*	S. DAVID FREEMAN *Lower Colorado River Authority*	CHASE N. PETERSON *University of Utah*
EARL BEISTLINE *Consultant*	MICHEL T. HALBOUTY *Michel T. Halbouty Energy Co.*	JOSEPH E. ROSS *Congressional Research Service*
CHARLES A. BOWSHER *General Accounting Office*	CARL N. HODGES *University of Arizona*	LEWIS THOMAS *Memorial Sloan-Kettering* *Cancer Center*

Director

JOHN H. GIBBONS

Figure 5-2

composites. The scope of OTA assessments varies as well. Some studies are very broad, for example, *Effects of Technology on the American Economic Transition*, while others are relatively focused, like *Managing High-Level Commercial Radioactive Waste*. Completion of analyses takes anywhere from a few days for a very brief staff memorandum to a few years for the most lengthy assessments.

Requests for assessments, testimony, and briefings have increased to a level that now clearly exceeds resources. The acquisition of internal expertise and institutional memory was essential to the organizational maturity such a level of activity implies. Though OTA relies heavily on outside contracts for analytical work, a core professional staff whose tenure goes beyond the term of an assessment is essential, since much of the value of OTA's work is received through follow-on communications with Congress after publication. Also, many of OTA's assessments are interrelated, and staff continuity is very productive.

OTA has moved toward a larger, fulltime, professional staff, devoting about 60 percent of resources to internal support and 40 percent to contracting. This has worked to OTA's advantage, particularly as it aids the performance of broad and diverse assessments. Nevertheless, flexibility in making contracts and employing temporary staff is an essential attribute of OTA's ability to adapt to changing needs of Congress and to quickly access new sources of expertise.

THE ASSESSMENT PROCESS

Evolution of OTA's assessment process is an example of learning by doing. The steps each assessment takes are critical to the objectivity and value of the resulting analysis, yet there was no certainty of how to proceed when OTA's operations first got under way.

Today, the genesis of assessments is complex. Formal requests for assessments must come from the chairman or ranking minority member of one or more committees, or from TAB itself. OTA may not undertake assessments at the request of individual members, but does try to accommodate their requests for information, if the material can be drawn from past or currently authorized work.

A well-coordinated cross-referral service between the congressional agencies and other sources of information, such as the National Research Council (NRC), is used to satisfy many of the requests OTA receives from committees and members. The formal written request

for a major assessment is generally the culmination of extensive dialogue between the interested committee(s) and OTA. These preliminar-
ies sometimes last many months, and clarify what is needed, including the scope of the analysis and timing of delivery, and what resources
are potentially available at OTA.

Proposals are prepared with the object of synthesizing a research
plan that best accommodates the various interests of the different
committees of jurisdiction. Before a project is presented to TAB, satisfactory answers are required to inquiries such as the following:

- Is this now or likely to become a major congressional issue?
- Can OTA make a unique contribution, or could the requested activity be done effectively by the requesting committee or another agency
  of Congress?
- How significant are the costs and benefits to society of the various
  policy options involved, and how will they be distributed among
  various affected groups?
- Is the technological impact major and enduring?
- How imminent is the impact?
- Is there sufficient available knowledge to assess the technology and
  its consequences?
- Is the assessment of manageable scope—can it be bounded within
  reasonable limits?
- Is the cost of the assessment appropriate?
- Is there enough time to do the assessment properly?
- What is the likelihood of congressional action in response to this
  assessment?
- Would this assessment complement other OTA projects?[21]

After TAB approval, management of a project is centered in one of
OTA's nine programs (see figure 5–1). The program areas reflect major,
enduring, sociotechnical areas, a structure that allows a sequence of
distinct but related assessment projects to be carried out within a
larger, coherent framework. Program focus can and does change over
the years, reflecting the changing urgency of various issues. The OTA
analytical staff is about evenly divided between natural scientists and
engineers on the one hand, and social scientists, doctors, and lawyers
on the other. Each program is designed to reflect a broad issue area,
and typically works on three major assessments at a time, in addition
to special projects. OTA management encourages interprogram coordi-

nation to ensure that full advantage is taken of all ongoing and completed work and agency expertise, as well as to ensure agency-wide
consistency and quality.

One of the first tasks the project team—which is composed of a
project director and two to four analysts—undertakes is to select, with
the review and approval of the director, an ad hoc advisory panel to
guide and critique the work. The panel, typically twelve to eighteen
people, includes representation of all parties-at-interest to the issue.
Through meetings, three or more over the course of the project, and
comments on draft work products, the panel provides OTA with assurance that the work is comprehensive, accurate, fair, and as free as
possible from bias and advocacy. The panel neither writes nor approves
the final document, but the project staff attempts to understand and
reflect all legitimate concerns of the panel in the final draft. Fair representation of panelist views is a primary goal of the assessment process, and OTA advisory panels often reach consensus over the course of
the assessment about the range of specific options for Congress to
consider.

The OTA staff coordinates its assessment activities with the work
in other federal agencies and in the private sector. The literature and
experts, as well as the stakeholders, on the controversial issues studied must be well known. Every effort is made to pace OTA's assessment
projects to complement and benefit from others' work.

When an assessment nears publication, the advisory panel's expertise is supplemented by other individuals chosen to provide critical
review and comment on the final draft. Extensive peer review of OTA
documents is part of a series of checks on the work's accuracy and
objectivity. The Technology Assessment Board reviews final drafts and
gives authorization for release, but does not take a position of approval
or disapproval of the results. Actual delivery and public release of OTA
documents are coordinated with requesting committees, but, again,
they do not approve or disapprove the results.

An OTA report provides several discrete types of information. Enu-
meration of the relevant facts and their corollaries is an early priority
in the assessment process. This step leads to another critical function
of the office—identifying where consensus exists on an issue and
where there is disagreement, and explaining the basis for disagreement. This one step can be invaluable to Congress, whose members
are daily confronted with conflicting information that cannot possibly

be analyzed in the individual offices or in each committee with jurisdiction.

The final step consists of pulling all the pieces together to identify plausible options for federal action. When OTA has examined the full extent of a technology's implications—the economic, social, and legal (in addition to the technical aspects)—that information is synthesized for decision makers. The options presented are explanations of the choices reasonable people of various persuasions might make, given scientific and political realities, and the ramifications of such choices.

SUBSTANTIVE CHALLENGES ENGAGING OTA

OTA works on some of the most critical and controversial problems facing the nation. The current agenda is full. In the spring of 1987 OTA was conducting assessments of:

Technology and the American economic transition
High technology ceramics and polymer composites
Star power: the U.S. and international quest for fusion energy
Competitiveness of domestic copper
Technological risks and opportunities for future U.S. energy supply and demand
Increased competition in the electric power industry
International competitiveness in the service industries
Technology, innovation, and U.S. trade
Technology transfer to China
New technology for NATO: implementing follow-on forces attack
Seismic verification of nuclear test ban treaties
Advanced space transportation technologies
Strategic Defense Initiative: survivability and software
Low resource agriculture in Africa
Technology and public policy to enhance grain quality in international trade
Monitoring of mandated Vietnam veteran studies
Technology and child health
Nontraditional methods of cancer treatment: science and policy issues
The quality of medical care: information for consumers

Diagnostic medical tests: impact on public and private policies toward health care

Drug labeling in developing countries

Life-sustaining technologies and the elderly

New developments in biotechnology

Infertility prevention and treatment

Mapping the human genome

New communications technology: implications for privacy and security

Technology, public policy, and the changing nature of federal information dissemination

Communications systems for an information age

Science, technology, and the Constitution in the information age

Seabed minerals: exploring the nation's ocean frontier

New Clean Air Act issues

Sustaining the national technological base: education and employment of scientists and engineers

Educational technology: an assessment of practice and potential

Safety in the commercial aviation and motor carrier industries

Also ongoing were special responses drawn from past experience on such diverse topics as infrastructure materials and construction technologies, mammography screening for the Medicare population, machine translation of scientific and technical information, the technology/ecology fit in aid to developing countries, and a progress report on waste reduction.

Concern about increased governmental spending—both on R&D and in general on matters of technological import—was a major impetus to OTA's creation. In this time of huge budget deficits, OTA is called upon more and more often to look at areas of both increased and decreased spending. Many of OTA's assessments reflect the wish of Congress to constrain the public as well as external (e.g., environmental) costs of technology, while still encouraging its development and use.

For example, the Strategic Defense Initiative will cost billions of dollars to research, and many billions more if implemented. OTA was asked to study this issue, and produced documents on ballistic missile defense (BMD) and antisatellite (ASAT) technologies. To help Congress with the complex decisions it will have to make regarding these technologies, the study developed criteria for assessing potential BMD systems and their components. It identified a range of possible objectives for a deployed system, and translated these into technical performance requirements. Assessment criteria were also developed for evaluating the effects of potential BMD systems on crisis and arms race stability, arms control, alliance relations, and foreign relations generally. The objective of this assessment was to identify performance levels that can reasonably be expected in specific time frames, and to assess proposed technologies and systems on the basis of feasible rather than ideal levels of performance. The assessment also examined technical risks and benefits to national security.

Similarly, Congress is also looking at ways to reduce federal expenditures on nondefense issues. For instance, OTA was mandated to undertake a study involving Medicare costs as a result of the Deficit Reduction Act of 1984. In the resulting study of physicians and medical technology OTA examined current patterns of physician expenditures and use, identifying areas of inefficient or inequitable technology use for Medicare beneficiaries, and developing options for physician payment under Medicare to address the problems identified. Congress is interested in providing fees on a prospective diagnosis basis, taking into account different technologies and different physician specialties; incentives for the use of primary care and other technologies; moderation of increases in Medicare expenditures; participation of physicians in Medicare; access to care by Medicare beneficiaries; and quality of care provided.

The complicated and swiftly changing agenda of Congress makes it difficult to predict specifically OTA's future studies, but the general issue areas are fairly clearly defined. For example, the handling and managing of externalities, particularly waste by-products of industry and energy conversion, will be of continuing concern. Those problems, especially energy and environmental concerns, instigated much of the public outcry that resulted in governmental environmental impact and technology assessment. Many OTA reports address these issues. OTA recently completed an intensive study of nuclear waste issues, *Managing Commercial High-Level Radioactive Waste*. Work on this project was unusual in that OTA actually undertook to advise Congress on the specific requirements of legislation to control nuclear wastes. OTA also is actively involved in assisting Congress with the oversight of implementation of that legislation by the executive branch.

OTA's study of acid rain, *Acid Rain and Transported Air Pollutants: Implications for Public Policy*, provided briefings, special analyses, and testimony for committees of jurisdiction, in addition to the comprehensive report. In support of the analysis OTA developed atmospheric models that continue to be used, in part because they were carefully designed to be "policy driven," or helpful in evaluating the specific implications of alternative policy choices.

Superfund Strategy identified just how large the costs of cleaning up hazardous wastes were going to be, and examined alternative technologies and strategies for effective, long-term resolution of the problem. OTA's current study of disposal of waste in the ocean examines the different technologies used or proposed for disposal of different types of waste in the ocean. The study addresses policy issues related to the role of oceans within an overall waste management context, alternative strategies for managing these wastes in coastal areas, the pretreatment of wastes prior to disposal, and research and development priorities. The environmental, economic, international, and institutional implications of different policy options are being evaluated.

Other issues, such as the impact of technology on jobs, privacy, freedom, and national security, also are subjects of OTA assessments. How to handle the transfer of technology to developing and competing industrialized countries is of major concern to the United States. OTA currently is investigating opportunities and potential problems presented by technology transfer to the People's Republic of China. Technology transfer could enhance economic growth for both countries. On the other hand, technologies such as computers, telecommunications equipment, and nuclear reactors, even if sold for commercial use, could be directed toward military purposes.

Of even more immediate concern to many people, OTA's study, *Technology and Structural Unemployment: Reemploying Displaced Adult Workers*, examines the role of technology in changing the skills that workers will need for success in the U.S. workplace. OTA is evaluating an array of reemployment and retraining programs and alternatives to displacement, such as continuing education, plant conversion, and worker buyouts, with respect to their ability to avoid or minimize displacement problems. Patterns in international trade and changing technology are also being examined in OTA's efforts to assist Congress in addressing the problem of structural unemployment.

OTA is frequently asked to examine questions about sustainability of resources. Several recently published and ongoing assessments reflect congressional interest in this area—*Energy from Biological Processes, Sustaining Tropical Forest Resources, Technologies to Maintain Biological Diversity*. OTA has just begun a related assessment, *Low-Resource Agriculture for Developing Countries*. Most people in developing countries are subsistence farmers who cannot obtain or afford the fertilizers and pesticides upon which high-yield (Green Revolution) technologies are based. Thus, as populations grow, and fuel and other input prices rise, low-resource agriculture technologies are receiving increased attention from donors and researchers. For this study OTA is building upon the results of a previous technical memorandum, *Africa Tomorrow: Issues in Technology, Agriculture, and U.S. Foreign Aid*. By examining low-resource agricultural technologies worldwide OTA will help Congress evaluate programs and identify policies related to both U.S. agriculture and foreign policy. In order to do this, OTA will: (1) Determine which of these technologies might increase African food production in socioeconomically and environmentally sustainable ways; (2) Identify alternative U.S. roles in technology development and transfer; (3) Assess actual and potential benefits to the United States from participation in international agricultural research on low-resource methods; and (4) Evaluate certain aspects of the Sahel Development Program as a case study in U.S. public and private assistance to Africa.

Another area of continuing inquiry is least-cost paths for the provision of goods and services. It is known that, in industry, technological process changes often lead to economic and materials savings, as well as less severe environmental impacts. For example, as OTA found in *Technology and Steel Industry Competitiveness*, steel mini-mills are both energy- and materials-efficient, because they use a great quantity of scrap steel, and can produce certain kinds of steel more cheaply than can conventional plants. A follow-up study to work on hazardous wastes and Superfund is investigating industrial technologies that could economically prevent the production of toxic by-products.

Finally, investigation of the accommodation of society to changes in technology will continue. For example, OTA is currently involved in assessing the effects of computers on people's lives—in terms of office automation, civil liberties, and intellectual property. Another very broad undertaking nearing completion is a study called *The Effects of Technology on the American Economic Transition* (ET). There is a growing feeling in the United States that new technologies, growing international competition in manufacturing and service markets once dominated by U.S. suppliers, and dramatic changes in the cost and availability of oil and other critical resources may lead to a fundamental change in the structure of the U.S. economy. These changes could also affect the utility of major classes of public policy. The ET assessment was undertaken to describe ways in which the national economy may change during the next two decades; explore the ways these changes may alter prospects for employment and profitable investment in different major classes of economic activity; describe how the changes may alter critical aspects of the quality of life in America; and examine the implications of these changes for national policy. The results of this project, as well as others OTA has undertaken, could help Congress understand better not only how society can accommodate new technologies, but how technology could be molded to enhance those aspects of society that are valued.

ORGANIZATIONAL AND PROCEDURAL CHALLENGES

Overcoming the inherent problems in using technical information in public policymaking is a major challenge for OTA. The assessment process is specifically designed to deal with the problem of defining areas of certainty and uncertainty, and to help disentangle technical concerns from values. Still, reports are no good unless they are used, and there is constant effort to find the most effective routes to Congress, to determine the real needs of the customers for OTA's work in its various levels of detail.

It has been noted that "perhaps the cardinal attribute of the successful report is felicitous timing,"[22] but matching the output of OTA's work to the congressional schedule is difficult. After nearly a year and a half of study, *Technology and Soviet Energy Availability* was delivered to the Congress during the same week Chairman Brezhnev arrived in Germany to sign the contract for long-term delivery of Soviet natural gas. Because of its timeliness, the report had greater impact on Congress (and other decision makers) than earlier or later delivery might have produced. But in the typical situation, OTA's work is tapped by Congress from the outset and used throughout the course of a project, which is timed to closely parallel the decision-making process.

During times of intense debate, highly specific analyses in response to committee requests for quick assistance take precedence over writing the formal report. Consequently formal completion (printing) of an assessment can be delayed. Congress profits from OTA's accommodations in project scheduling, for they enable OTA to direct its special resources into timely and focused work. But it can also lead to criticism of the "excessive" amount of time that OTA takes to complete a report. Still, the notion of OTA as a "shared resource" for Congress depends upon the flexibility in timing and priorities required to meet the needs of its numerous clients.

Delivery of OTA's analyses is a process, rather than a single event. The analysis and information developed in an assessment exist in varying degrees of certitude throughout the course of a project. OTA must be prepared to deliver information—with appropriate caveats regarding its preliminary nature—when requested by Congress. Interim products, based on the assessment and in a variety of formats —testimony, technical addenda, background papers, case studies, and staff memoranda—are delivered as appropriate. In the end, the results are provided to a much broader audience, including the general public and policymakers at all levels of responsibility, nationally and internationally, through sales of the reports by the U.S. Government Printing Office. The domestic and foreign commercial press commonly republish OTA reports.

Postpublication, follow-up activities are an essential part of the delivery process. Requests to synthesize material gathered in past assessments for easier consumption by Congress are common. Over the past several years, for instance, OTA has published several industry-focused studies that deal, in varying degrees, with U.S. industrial competitiveness. OTA now receives requests to draw upon the findings of all of those assessments to help Congress address broader issues of international trade and industrial policy.

Establishing the appropriate mix of long- and short-term studies contributes to the problem of defining OTA's role. Much like the ongoing debate over whether to spend more R&D dollars on basic research or applied science, this question may never be resolved, but a balance must be struck. The balance between short- and long-term analyses may shift slightly as congressional needs change, but there will always be a mixture of projects. OTA was founded during a time of much greater interest in expansive government solutions to long-term, emerging issues. Today, the Congress is wrestling with budgetary problems of a magnitude not even envisioned five or ten years ago. Complying with the legislative mandate, while staying sensitive to the changing needs of Congress, is difficult, and requires constant attention.

A continuing question is how close OTA should get to the legislative decision process. OTA must be careful not to prescribe policy for the Congress, or it becomes part of the technology advocacy community and much less valuable to Congress. It can be frustrating for committee staff to work with a group of experts who refuse to take that final step of telling them what to do or what they would do, if they were members. But that orientation is an important though difficult part of OTA's job. It appears that nonpartisan technical analysis can be a helpful part of resolving tough issues within a frequently partisan and adversarial process, and there is increasing interest in stimulating its further adoption, both in the United States and abroad.

STATUS OF TECHNOLOGY ASSESSMENT

Technology assessment has gained fairly widespread acceptance in the United States. OTA's experience has assisted with the adoption of both the concept and the practice. In the United States, where the assumption generally exists that more thoughtful analysis can improve the chances for wise decisions, there are a variety of activities related to technological analysis.

— Industry analysts apply their tools to the tasks of anticipating and identifying potential markets for new products and learning how to increase their competitiveness. They must also spend time assessing any potential liabilities for environmental or safety hazards posed by a new product or its manufacture.
— Public interest groups use analytic tools to estimate the various costs and benefits of activities that interest them (e.g., public projects, environmental regulations).
— NSF supports research on *methods* of analysis of technology and its impacts, including attention to improved ability to project future developments that can arise from advances in science and engineering.
— The NRC, including its parent academies of science and engineering and the institutes of medicine, carries out a wide variety of studies, mostly for the federal executive branch agencies. These range in scope from highly focused studies of specific equipment to broad

overviews (e.g., science and research policy), and require six months to four years to complete. The academy reports represent the consensus—or lack of it—of an expert group. Typically, NRC reports contain both findings and recommendations for action.

– The Office of Science and Technology Policy (OSTP), located within the executive branch, also conducts studies related to technology. It draws mostly upon resources of other executive branch agencies. OSTP's work is generally not publicly available, but is carried out and delivered to the White House for consideration.[23]

The congressional Office of Technology Assessment is unique in many respects. It is the only such organization responding directly to the needs of congressional committees. It avoids the kind of advocacy required in corporate and other private interest group analysis of technical issues, and though OTA uses executive branch information, it makes a much broader investigation of issues and its reports are publicly available. OTA's advisory panels are also distinct from other advisory groups, in that OTA panels give well-heeded advice, but do not approve reports nor take direct responsibility for the final product.

In addition to other U.S. institutions performing technology assessments, it is encouraging to note the increasing global interest in the field. OTA is frequently visited by foreign officials who are interested in OTA's organizational structure, as well as its substantive work. There was frequent communication between OTA and the government of France during their successful attempt to establish a legislative body to do technology assessment. The new Parliamentary Office for Evaluation of Scientific and Technological Options is set up to inform the Parliament of the consequences of potential scientific and technological decisions. The office, which is similar to a joint committee of Congress, collects information, implements study programs, and makes evaluations. The office is constituted much like TAB in that it is composed of eight deputies and eight senators, with proportional representation of political groups within each assembly. A fifteen-member scientific council, similar to TAAC, advises the office, which can also seek outside advice from national organizations and parties at interest to legislation. Requests for assessments can come from: (1) a group chairman; (2) sixty deputies; (3) forty senators; or (4) special or permanent committees. One major difference between the French office and OTA is that the French office's work is confidential until the requester has had the opportunity to comment on the work, or, in the case of specially undertaken assignments, until the assembly making the request grants permission for its release.[24] It is still much too early to tell how successful the office will be; it will have to overcome many of the same hurdles OTA originally faced.

OTA has also provided advice and assistance to the Federal Republic of Germany and to Great Britain in their attempts to establish OTA equivalents, but resistance to the idea in those countries so far has prevented adoption of legislative technology assessment. At least part of the reason for this may be the fundamental differences between the U.S. system of government and the parliamentary system.[25] A primary reason for establishing OTA within the Congress was to assure independence from the executive branch. In a parliamentary system, the majority party in the legislature, or a coalition, makes up the executive branch ("the government"), thus there is no natural tension between the executive and legislative branches—no separation of powers to maintain. In the parliamentary system, then, an OTA that included equal representation of each party could give added political power to the opposition without any perceived offsetting benefits to the legislative body itself. There is a perception of no inherent need on the part of the legislature to assert its independence from the executive, while there is clearly reason to continue to withhold information from the opposition parties. This difference, combined with the fact that any new organization can be viewed as a threat to established centers of power, may pose a formidable barrier to legislative technology assessment in a parliamentary system.

Germany's attempts to establish legislative technology assessment are still in the experimental stages. OTA continues to assist the Ministry for Research and Technology as it attempts to establish technology assessment elsewhere in the government. As recently as the summer of 1985 OTA was visited by members of the Bundestag still searching for a way to set up a parliamentary office. Germany's most recent efforts are reflected in the creation of a committee comprising eight members of the Bundestag and seven members of the public who will take approximately eighteen months to study the possible applications of technology assessment techniques in the German legislature. As part of the study, two technology assessments—one on information technologies and one on an environmental problem, possibly groundwater—will be performed as a test of their usefulness to the legislative debate. It will be interesting to see the results of the experimental technology assessments, as well as the overall findings of the committee. In Great Britain the Steering Committee of the Parliamentary and Scientific Committee has set up a working group to advise Parliament on how it can best go about replicating OTA in Britain.[26]

The methods of technology assessment have been widely adopted throughout the Western world, though not necessarily within legislatures. Under the leadership of the Austrian Ministry of Science and Research, an Institute for Socio-Economic Development and Technology Assessment has recently been established in the Austrian Academy of Sciences. The Institute will respond to requests for analysis from both the Ministry and the Parliament.

A project under way in The Netherlands is notable because it involves both a national government and an international organization. The Project on Future Health Technology, sponsored by the Steering Committee on Future Health Scenarios, an advisory body to the government of The Netherlands, and the World Health Organization's European Region, has two main objectives. The first is the identification of future health technologies and the establishment of methods to monitor their development. The second phase will involve collection and analysis of information on the potential implications of high-priority technologies in advance of their diffusion into practice. The project is designed both to serve as an early warning system and to present information that can help guide actions that might hasten, alter, or avoid aspects of the future of health technology, or be used to take advantage of opportunities posed by coming events. The possible audience for the results, other than the sponsors, include ministries of health and other agencies (both government and private sector), particularly in the European Member states of WHO and the health-related professional community.

Developing countries are demonstrating a growing interest in incorporating technology assessment at an early stage in their industrialization. The People's Republic of China (PRC) is looking for help from OTA in establishing technology assessment within its government. It is very exciting to see this concept adopted so early in China's industrialization, since it could aid the development of new technologies as well as help avoid some pitfalls that have been encountered in the West.

Technology assessment is continuing to develop as a concept and a technique, and seems to be flourishing throughout the world. It is sometimes identified with other works—maximizing the appropriateness of technology development—in attempts to avoid the negative reactions that sometimes attend the term,[27] but the techniques themselves are still utilized and valued.

TECHNOLOGY AND GOVERNANCE

A popular government, without popular information, or the means of acquiring it, is but a prologue to a farce or a tragedy, or, perhaps, both. . . . A people who mean to be their own governors must arm themselves with the power which knowledge gives.—James Madison

U.S. democracy depends upon its leadership to define shared national goals and help all the fragments of this pluralistic society work together toward these purposes.[28] OTA's mission is to assist Congress in its pursuit of that high degree of leadership as it faces the bewildering array of issues in which technology is a facet. Wise application of scientific knowledge has long been a national shared purpose that complements basic research, and Congress works exceedingly hard to assure that available, beneficial technologies are widely applied, and that new technologies are researched and developed. Yet the availability, potential, and breadth of new technologies make it increasingly difficult for laymen to differentiate promising from questionable technological directions, to discern the differences between facts and values. It is essential that Congress remain in touch with the citizens who will be affected by the use of technologies, and that advocacy groups retain their access to their elected representatives, but it is crucial that Congress also have available to it information and analytical resources that are as free as possible from bias and advocacy. Congress looks to OTA for such information and assistance, for help in sustaining—in a complex and pluralistic arena—the intellectual clarity to find a workable consensus on scientific and technological issues. Over the past decade, OTA has tested ways to analyze highly complex and controversial issues surrounding technology and federal policy and ways to transfer the results to Congress, for sound decisions are based on sound information. Thus OTA is asked to identify costs, good and bad effects, dangers and, most importantly, uncertainties associated with emerging technologies.[29] There are fundamental differences between supplying information to decision makers and entering the decision process itself. OTA is competent in the former, but it leaves to the elected members of Congress the latter, much more exacting task.

ECONOMICS, POLITICS, AND GOVERNMENT

RESEARCH AND DEVELOPMENT

ROGER G. NOLL AND LINDA R. COHEN

Public officials and policy analysts long ago developed logically compelling rationales for active government promotion of research. The basic argument has two components. First, research and development (R&D) is desirable because it promotes economic growth, strengthens national defense, and contributes to national prestige, not to mention that it creates new knowledge that may be a valued end in its own right. Second, the private sector, if left to its own devices, undertakes insufficient R&D. The second component, although having numerous elements, for the most part boils down to an argument about the appropriability of new knowledge. People who invest their resources in R&D are unable to reap all the benefits to society that their discoveries create and hence have insufficient incentives to invest as much in R&D as is socially desirable. Moreover, even if a result of R&D is appropriable, those who possess it can have a monopoly in the new technology or product. This is inefficient to the extent that monopoly prices are charged for the output of the new technology.

The argument described above is used to justify the three major types of government-supported research and development. First, government supports R&D to improve the performance or to reduce the costs of the goods and services that it uses. For goods produced virtu-

This essay is a synopsis of the authors' joint research project and forthcoming book, *The Technology Pork Barrel*. The authors are grateful for research support from the Caltech Energy Policy Studies Program, the Brookings Institution, the Guggenheim Foundation, the Center for Advanced Study in the Behavioral Sciences, the National Science Foundation, and the Hoover Institution.

ally entirely for government, such as defense weapons systems, this makes sense, because government thereby can reduce its own costs and direct R&D in ways that serve its own needs. Second, government can contribute to the general technological base of the nation by supporting basic research in science and technology. Advances in basic knowledge can be applied widely in numerous industrial settings and so have great potential economic value. At the same time, new basic knowledge usually becomes public quite quickly, and so is difficult to convert to profit if done entirely by private enterprise. Consequently, there is reason to expect that too little basic research will be undertaken if government does not support it actively. Moreover, by supporting basic research, government can assure that the results are available freely and disseminated widely to produce maximal economic benefits. Third, governments may elect to undertake developmental work to produce new commercial technology for a specific sector of the economy if that sector is especially weak at innovating on its own. For example, the firms in the industry may be so small and specialized that they cannot undertake commercial development of new technology efficiently, as has been argued to be the case in agriculture since the establishment of the land-grant colleges and the Agricultural Extension Service in the nineteenth century.

For these rationales to be valid reasons for public action, two additional issues must be resolved satisfactorily. First, a plausible case must be made that the government is able to select the R&D activities that most clearly fit the rationales. Second, government agencies must be capable of adept management of R&D programs. Both of these issues refer to more than the cognitive capacities of government officials —henceforth we will assume that elected and bureaucratic public officials are capable of effective program selection and management. The primary concern in this chapter is with the institutional structure in which government officials operate, the incentives that affect decisions in the public sector, and the information flows on which decisions must be based. The principal message is that there are serious political barriers to the efficient implementation of some types of R&D policies. These political phenomena, when taken into account, can alter substantially a prospective analysis of the expected benefits and costs of a government R&D program.

POLITICAL INCENTIVES AND R&D POLICIES

The political institutions of the American system of government create certain broad incentives that affect policymaking. The focal point of the American political system is elections. Whereas public officials have complex motives and may even seek to serve such public-spirited objectives as improving the nation's defense, prestige, and economic performance, all face the stark reality of reelection. A public official cannot achieve either altruistic or selfishly personal goals in public service unless he or she takes account of the necessity for elected politicians to be successful in seeking reelection. This fact not only influences the strategies of elected officials and their political appointees, but also those of career civil servants who must establish enduring working relationships with political officials in both Congress and the executive branch.

Recent research on how the need for reelection affects policy choices has focused on three especially important aspects of the electoral process. The first is the inability of voters or politicians to make creditable or enforceable commitments for longer than one term of office.[1] Because one session of Congress cannot bind subsequent sessions except by constitutional amendment, public officials cannot enter into a long-term contract with the public to complete a program as established and promised initially. The second important feature of the electoral system is the relatively low information content of voting. Voters have only a simple, dichotomous signal to send to incumbent officials—simple approval or disapproval. Moreover, as far as national policymaking is concerned, voters often cannot assign credit or blame accurately for a change in policy. Power in the American governmental system is so diffused that rarely can it be said that any single public official, even the president, is clearly responsible for a policy decision. Hence, in making decisions about voting, it makes sense for voters to focus on a relatively small number of highly important issues —and issues for which individual roles in policy can be assessed.[2]

The third important property of the electoral system is that the net social consequences of a policy are only one element of its overall political importance. Individuals also care whether their communities and businesses receive a fair share of the government's expenditures for goods and services. In a few industries economic well-being is highly dependent on who gets government contracts. Hence voters will evaluate political leaders in part on the basis of the distribution of expenditures, as well as on the net social benefits of the program that the expenditures make possible.[3]

These basic features of the electoral process produce several incentives that are important from the point of view of government R&D policies.[4]

IMPATIENCE

The political process is biased against programs that take a long time to pay off. First, elected officials who undertake such programs face several intermediate reelection campaigns before a very long-term project will produce benefits for which credit can be claimed. All other things being equal, political actors prefer to allocate the budget to policies with more immediate payoffs that will help them through the next election. Voters, too, are wary of programs promising long-term payoffs, for they have to take into account the prospect that, an election or two down the road, politics will change, the program will be cancelled, and they will be left having floated some of the costs without receiving any of the benefits. Contracting firms and their employees also will be skeptical of the desirability of undertaking long-term commitments to participate in a program for the same reasons. This implies that firms will require extra financial inducements to commit their resources to a program that may be cancelled in midstream.

RISK AVERSION

Public officials are reluctant to undertake programs if they cannot identify potential beneficiaries, both the users of the program's ultimate outputs and the recipients of its contracts. Remote and uncertain benefits are unlikely to motivate voters. Uncertainties about the ultimate contractors undermine an official's ability to take political credit for the program with the people whose incomes will benefit, and in any case the contracting benefits may well go to constituencies that do not serve the reelection interests of the politicians. Public officials would prefer to appropriate funds to projects whose beneficiaries are known at the beginning, so political credit can be claimed effectively for the next election.

Risk aversion is induced further by the fact that elected officials usually face a very high probability of reelection. Incumbents are far more likely to win than to lose. Hence, undertaking risky programs —programs that have a high expected political value but also a substantial probability of failure—presents a relatively unattractive gamble. If the program fails, it can undermine a high reelection probability. If the program succeeds, it cannot add very much to a reelection probability that, in the absence of the risky program, is still very high.

DO NO POSITIVE HARM

All else being equal, political leaders favor programs that are relatively uncontroversial, where the results are perceived widely to be benefits (and not really costs), and the act of contracting does not inflict significant damage on competitors of the contractor. The latter is accomplished by having most competitors share in the program, either through extensive subcontracting (as with defense) or by dividing the program into many separate, small components (as with basic research grants to universities).

The way these three factors relate to R&D is as follows. A defining characteristic of R&D is that its results are uncertain and normally take considerable time to bear fruit. Research is a search for unknown, new pieces of knowledge. Until the research is done, one does not know what new knowledge will emerge, or what use is likely to be made of it. Moreover, the act of pursuing an R&D program to its ultimate end can take a very long time, especially for the radical changes in technology that are most likely to produce a fundamental change in industrial practice. Finally, fundamental changes can do positive harm. For example, the firm undertaking government-sponsored research may gain a substantial advantage over its competitors, even if the results are made public. Indeed, whole industries may be made obsolete when the new technology is adopted.

IMPLICATIONS FOR THE SELECTION OF R&D PROGRAMS

The principal implication to be drawn from the preceding summary of the political aspects of R&D decisions is that very long-term, fundamental work to transform technology is unlikely to appear attractive politically. For an R&D program to be maximally attractive to political officials, it must have the following characteristics:

1. It can be connected readily to one of the very few salient political issues on which elections normally turn. One example is the state of national defense, and another was energy policy after the rapid increase in the price of oil in the 1970s.
2. It can be spread easily to all the important components of the contracting industry. This is easiest to accomplish when the industry is concentrated (so that a few contracts and subcontracts do the job) or, in an unconcentrated industry, when the program can be subdivided into numerous small projects without a substantial loss of efficiency.
3. It promises relatively short-term payoffs in politically visible social benefits and expenditures to politically important constituencies.
4. It is unlikely to produce an embarrassing failure that will lead to investigations and scandal. This is most easily assured when the government itself controls the decision to adopt the new technology and thereby to declare it a success.

The type of R&D that is most attractive politically is short term in nature; is directed at the production of government goods (defense or space exploration, for example) so that it can lead to utilization regardless of the shortfall in performance or overrun in costs; is addressed to a widely accepted, generally uncontroversial national objective; and is undertaken without altering substantially the distribution of market advantages in the private economy. Least attractive are programs that address unsensational goals (such as economic growth), require very large contracts for a relatively small fraction of an industry, not only have uncertain results but can end in obvious failure, and are unlikely to produce tangible evidence of success for a long period.

For each of the three categories of research mentioned at the outset, the implications are quite different. For research aimed at the production of government goods and services, prospects are best, but a few problems do emerge. Because all research is necessarily uncertain, some projects are bound to fail, yet political incentives militate against allowing failure. Hence the government will be prone to continue projects that have gone sour rather than admit bad fortune, even though the continuation can create difficulties in the efficient provision of government goods. This tendency is enhanced further by the political unattractiveness of canceling economically significant contracts enjoyed by major groups of constituents. This type of R&D also faces the problem of making the best trade-off between short-term projects promising relatively quick but small technical advances versus riskier, longer-term projects that may produce revolutionary changes in technology. However, because the government is the consumer of the product and because political officials will be held accountable for the state of technology in important government areas (such as defense) over a sustained period, impatience and risk aversion are likely to be least important in this particular category of projects.

The principal difficulty with the second category of R&D activities, the promotion of basic research in science and technology, is that rarely is basic research a response to a salient political issue. A notable exception is the connection between biomedical research and medical care policy—especially the war on cancer. But usually basic scientific research is difficult to connect to a symbolic national issue and so conveys less promise as a device for claiming political credit. Of course, basic scientific research usually is long term in character. However, the government has succeeded in making it appear more immediate by relying on short-term grants to researchers. This creates frequent opportunities for announcing major grants and for taking credit for each step along the path toward the creation of important new scientific knowledge.

Most problematic is the third R&D category, the development of new technology for a specific industry or sector. Here the best indicator of success is whether the industry adopts the new technology freely, which happens only if it is a technical and economic success. The government therefore has relatively little leverage on whether the image of the program is successful. As a result, such activity carries greater political risks. In addition, if the program cannot support R&D in all firms efficiently, some firms will not be able to participate in the program. Such firms are likely to oppose the program, and so too will their elected political leaders. Hence the prospects for the program to survive multiple appropriations through several future elections are dim.

As with programs for the production of government goods, commercially oriented R&D projects tend to favor relatively short-term, low-risk activities. But here there is no countervailing tendency working against the pursuit of incremental advances because of the absence of a salient national political issue and because of the inability of the government to use procurement expenditures to cover at least some of the failures. The problem is especially acute for commercial R&D because, typically, the kinds of technology development projects that are easiest to rationalize as requiring government assistance are ones that are risky, long-term, and large compared to the capabilities of firms in the industry.

IMPLICATIONS FOR PROJECT MANAGEMENT

In addition to the forces influencing the selection of government R&D projects, two political factors affect the choice of management strategies.

In the first and third categories of government research programs, the objective is to develop a useful new technology, either for the government or for the private sector. Usually such projects involve a sequence of activities, beginning with parallel research to test alternative design concepts before a commitment is made to develop prototypes and working models of the chosen method. The purpose of the early research is to undertake relatively low-cost activities that increase the probability that a right choice will be made when the time comes to commit major resources to the program. However, since the latter step is so highly valued by political decision makers as the first visible sign of progress, political incentives push program management to foreshorten the research phase of a developmental research program and commit too early to a design. The consequence is that programs on the average cost more and perform less well than they would if they were managed with maximal efficiency (that is, to maximize the present value of benefits net of costs). Thus the factors that make such programs generally unattractive for the private sector—the need for protracted research and the uncertainties surrounding the pursuit of the unknown—also work to undermine optimal project management by government officials. Foreshortening research cuts the duration of the project and resolves the uncertainties regarding identification of some of the beneficiaries (including the contractors).

A second management choice is the extent to which the work in the program is done in-house by government agencies. Specifically, if the program is designed to advance technology in an industry in which there are more firms than can be supported efficiently, the political incentives are to build the research capability in-house to avoid, if possible, favoring one competitor over another. Generally it is more efficient to have the users of the technology develop the capacity for research. Undertaking research in one organization to advance technology that will be embodied in the product of another creates important informational problems. The users are likely to be more knowledgeable about their own needs than they are able or willing to communicate across organizational lines, especially for public consumption. Of course, if the users have substantial research capabilities already, and the industry is highly concentrated, the government research efforts can take the form of contracts with industry research labs. Then organizations need not share information to assist in selecting research topics; however, this will lessen the extent to which new technical discoveries from government contracts are diffused through the entire industry.

The third management issue is the periodic evaluation of the progress of a program and the decisions that must be made about continuing, altering, or canceling it. The key point to recognize is the asymmetry of political incentives between the prospective decision to undertake a major expenditure and the later decision to cut it back. Because constituents and hence political leaders heavily discount promises about future programs and evaluate programs primarily on the basis of current activity, the political benefits of promising a future program are less than the political costs of canceling an ongoing one of equal size. This leads to the creation of a threshold in the life of a major developmental research project. During the relatively low-cost exploratory research and concept development phase, programs can be evaluated relatively cleanly because the political costs of killing them are low. Only a decision to extend the research phase faces difficulty, because of the impatience and risk-aversion incentives acting upon political decision makers. But once the large expenditures associated with constructing prototypes and demonstration projects are undertaken, the distributive aspects of the program become much more significant. Important political benefits are to be reaped from granting the contracts—and important political costs can be suffered if they are canceled. Thus technology development programs are likely to be too sensitive to bad news in the research phase, but too prone to ignore bad news in the developmental/demonstration phase.

ILLUSTRATIONS FROM RECENT PROGRAMS

Far too many examples of government support in developing new technology are available to make a definitive, exhaustive treatment possible in a single paper. Yet empirical research on these types of programs has been quite vigorous since the mid–1970s. Although government support for R&D has been common for 200 years, the intensity of federal support for other than defense systems has increased dramatically since the early 1950s, when the federal government launched the program to commercialize nuclear power for electricity generation. The energy problems of the 1970s caused a dramatic, if temporary, increase in government support of nondefense R&D, directed primarily at the development of a wide variety of alternatives to oil and gas.

The following examples of government R&D activities illustrate some of the points made in the preceding sections.

THE CLINCH RIVER BREEDER REACTOR AND THE SPACE SHUTTLE[5]

Although ultimately facing different fiscal fates, the Clinch River Breeder Reactor and the Space Shuttle programs had quite similar lives. Both were conceived as part of important, but not the most crucial, national issues. The Space Shuttle was the follow-on to the highly successful and widely popular Apollo program that enabled Americans to explore the moon. Clinch River was a follow-on to the development of light-water nuclear reactors for generating electric power, a program that in the early 1970s also was widely regarded as a success. Both programs were justified to Congress as economically warranted. Clinch River was to be a means to guarantee relatively cheap fuel for nuclear reactors in anticipation of enormous growth in their use for generating electricity combined with pessimistic forecasts about the availability of uranium from reliable sources. The Space Shuttle was to be a means of lowering the cost of launching very large payloads and of retrieving payloads for repair and relaunch. Both programs eventually ran into significant problems—after the major parts of the expenditure programs were under way.

Clinch River faced massive delays and cost overruns, and eventually it became clear that it would not even be at the forefront of breeder technology. Moreover, the demise of the nuclear power industry in the late 1970s, owing to a slowdown in the growth of demand for electricity and unexpectedly high costs for nuclear plants, undercut the economic rationale for immediate commercialization of breeders. Nevertheless, the program continued for more than five years after it was clear that it should be either canceled outright or redirected more toward research and away from early commercialization.

The Space Shuttle faced cost overruns but, more importantly, also a critical performance underrun: the demise of the "Space Tug." In the initial benefit-cost studies to justify the program, approximately half of the benefits of the Space Shuttle were to be captured from its ability to retrieve and repair satellites. The Space Tug was to be carried aloft by the Shuttle and used to transport astronauts to geosynchronous orbit, where most of the investment in satellites resides. By the late 1970s the Space Tug idea had been scrubbed as technically infeasible. This eliminated most of the Shuttle's repair and retrieval benefits, which in turn made the net expected benefits of continuing the program turn negative. In addition, the costs and launch capability of the Space Shuttle turned out to be much worse than was predicted at the outset. The crisis period was from about 1978 until the first launch in 1981. During that period the optimal management decision probably was to stretch out the program, produce fewer orbiters, undertake more research, and terminate the plan for exclusive reliance on the Shuttle as America's launch vehicle for spacecraft. But with production expenditures in high gear, the program survived the crisis.

Both of these programs were tied to relatively important national issues that enter the normal political debate. Both were directed at relatively concentrated industries: aerospace and nuclear reactors. Both appeared economically attractive to political decision makers at the time they were proposed and for most of the early research phase. Both then suffered sufficiently serious setbacks so that they should have been rethought and reprogrammed. But the setbacks took place after the high-cost expenditure phase was under way, and so, like supertankers, they continued to lunge ahead pretty much according to the old plan—but with reduced capabilities and higher costs. Eventually one was killed, but long after many useless dollars had been spent and only after its performance became almost laughably short of initial expectations. The other continued, primarily because it did produce a significant visible product, the television pictures of astronauts in space. Because of the relatively low level of detailed knowledge that people have generally about program performance, the limited but highly visible success of the Space Shuttle was ample to keep it going despite its poor performance as a commercial technology.

COMMUNICATIONS SATELLITES[6]

In the wake of Sputnik the U.S. government launched a major effort to make use of earth-orbiting satellites. During the 1960s several generations of new technologies for satellites were developed with government support. Whereas the actual launches by the government were of mixed success, the program was widely regarded as successful. Many technical innovations developed under the auspices of the program were adopted by commercial satellite users and manufacturers. Then, in the early 1970s, the program was promptly killed, with Congress summarily removing from the budget the developmental funds for the next generation of experiments.

To find a technical or economic justification for the demise of the program is difficult, for the canceled projects do not appear to have any less promise than the ones that went before. Indeed, a major emphasis in the canceled programs was the development of new methods for using satellites for broadcasting—an innovation that the private sector and other nations began to explore on their own in the mid–1980s. Thus it appears that the government research program had detected a logical next step for an important commercial development.

What really happened to the satellite program was that the industry turned against it. When the program began, the satellite business was highly concentrated—indeed, initially only Hughes Aircraft Company was capable of putting satellites in geosynchronous orbit. But by the time the last project was being designed, the industry had become quite competitive. Several firms were capable of building the next experimental satellites. Moreover, the National Aeronautics and Space Administration (NASA), which administered the program, had attempted explicitly (to its credit) to encourage competition, to the point that Hughes was no longer even attempting to acquire the experimental contracts. When NASA did award the contracts for its last proposed experiment, the losers objected strongly. The NASA investigators found the decision to be a close call but certainly not tainted, and proposed to continue. But the issue had become a cause célèbre with members of Congress who represented districts in which the losing companies were located. Congressional investigations were launched and the contract award decision was reversed. Meanwhile, telecommunications utilities grew to fear that NASA was emerging as a competitor. Once the satellites were launched, they could be used for years—long past the period of R&D work. Hence the telecommunications industry conditioned its support for the program on the imposition of severe limits to the uses NASA could make of its satellites. Amid this growing opposition from both manufacturers and users of satellites, the program was killed.

The record of this controversy indicates that no technical or economic rationale for cancellation was developed. Some pointed with alarm to failures in past launches, but research projects are inherently risky, and these did not seem excessively unproductive—especially considering that the technologies which NASA developed were used subsequently in commercial satellites. The key argument appears to be that the new satellites would put the goverment in the business of competing with public utilities and determining which firms in a competitive manufacturing industry would have a lead in the next generation of satellites. Because the losers outnumbered the winners, and because the winners had no really substantial technical advantages over the losers, political actors decided that it was inequitable to have such a program, regardless of the technical benefits it might produce. Because the nature of the project precluded letting everyone in on the program, NASA had no effective response to this opposition. The scale of the project was simply too small to allow the use of subcontracting and project segmentation to overcome the disadvantage of harming key firms in the industry. The unfortunate consequence, however, was that American R&D fell precipitously after the program was canceled, allowing other nations to overcome their technical deficits by pursuing their own R&D programs.

SYNTHETIC FUELS

The energy shocks of the 1970s gave rise to a major effort by the federal government to promote development of technologies for creating liquid hydrocarbon fuels from coal, oil shale, and other exotic sources. Obviously, at inception these programs were part of the national response to a highly important political issue, the energy security of the nation. In the late 1970s funds were appropriated to begin major research programs, a few of which were for construction of prototypes and demonstrations, but most of which were to begin the more basic and conceptual work that would be a prelude to the expensive demonstration phase. Soon thereafter the Synthetic Fuels Corporation was created to finance the major projects.

Technically and economically, most synthetic fuels projects were not very exciting, and the early work offered no happy surprises. Moreover, not long after the 1979 oil shock occasioned by the Iran-Iraq war, energy supplies loosened substantially, real energy prices began to fall, and energy fell in priority as a national issue. All this took place before major commitments had been made to large construction projects (with a few notable exceptions). Consequently, the budgetary plans for subsidizing synthetic fuels plants could be scaled back relatively easily without doing harm to a large number of contractors and employees. Unlike the Clinch River Breeder Reactor and the Space Shuttle, changed circumstances and sober reflection about the program's merits could produce a reprogramming and scaling down because the most visible stage of the program had not yet been entered.

SEMICONDUCTORS AND COMPUTERS[7]

A major factor in the development of the modern computer and microelectronics industry was support from the Department of Defense (DoD) in the 1940s and 1950s. The Department of Defense sought high performance and was not terribly concerned with costs, because the new systems would be embedded in far more valuable weapons and communications systems. Hence DoD was a predictable, relatively sure market for any inventor or firm that could meet the performance requirements of the military.

These programs had two key features. First, as a consumer of the products to be produced, DoD had a clear idea of what it wanted and could work with industrial suppliers to push technology toward its well-articulated objectives. Second, DoD would decide on its own whether a new technology was worthwhile—it did not have to face an independent judgment from firms in the private sector, as was the case with the projects discussed above. Firms could be sure that if the technical objectives announced by the government were met, they would enjoy commercial success, since the agency specifying the objectives was also the potential customer. That these activities produced a commercially successful industry that was far larger than the market for defense electronics was something of a fortuitous stroke. Indeed, in the early 1950s conventional wisdom held that defense would dominate the market indefinitely.

An interesting aspect of the DoD projects is that however important they were in developing commercial production capabilities, DoD was not particularly successful in identifying the most promising basic research. Fortunately, the agency was flexible enough to begin supporting projects once it was apparent from their early successes that they were promising. But in computers and especially semiconductors, many of the major breakthroughs first were supported privately, by firms or universities, with DoD jumping in only after some progress had been made. This provides some evidence of the difficulties of communicating the relative merits of alternative lines of basic research and prospects for revolutionary advances across organizational boundaries.

CONCLUSION

The primary lessons to be learned from the marriage of the economic and technical analysis of R&D with the political factors affecting public decisions are as follows.

First, whereas government has a relatively low tolerance for risk and failure, research and development programs inherently are uncertain adventures. Indeed, a program that does not have some failures is probably not being sufficiently innovative. Public officials are likely to be leery of programs that might fail—and especially of programs in which the failure plausibly can be laid on their doorsteps. The lesson: Government is not likely to be a very effective source of support for developing radical new technological advances for the private sector. Probably the most palatable form of such policies is to distance government from the results of any single project, such as by providing support to general industrial R&D facilities. The Synthetic Fuels Corporation is an example of this kind of organization, although it was created to pursue technical ideas that were not very promising.

Second, whereas government is impatient, a well-managed R&D program requires some long-term research and the flexibility to speed up or slow down as the results from the research begin to roll in. The lesson: When government does become committed to develop a radical new technology, it is likely to foreshorten the research period and thereby produce a less-than-satisfactory result—including both performance underruns and cost overruns. The most likely successes will be in areas where the duration of each generation of technologies is relatively short (satellites, for example) or where there will be some valuable, visible success indicators along the way (such as pictures of astronauts in space).

Third, there is no automatic match between the conditions that give rise to inadequate private R&D and the political conditions that make a program possible and effective. If competitive industries with small firms are least likely to be innovative, they also may be least attractive as a target of a federal research effort because of the problem associated with creating winners and losers in the technology race. If radical new technologies present risks and gestation periods too great for private industry to accept, they may be equally unattractive to impatient, risk-averse public officials.

Fourth, the distributional aspects of a program affect its fate. Even long-term programs can survive if they provide short-term political benefits, through interim successes and contracts that are visible publicly and that allow public officials to claim credit. But this two-edged sword is dangerous. First, it can keep a bad program going, especially if the primary political benefit is large, ongoing government contracts rather than technical performance. Second, it can kill a good program that has the unfortunate side effect of harming part of the industry. The lesson: Do not overlook the distributional consequences of a program when it is being designed, and give special attention to the extent to which the work is done inside the government, diffused among a large number of small enterprises, or concentrated in a few large contracts.

Finally, by no means is continued support for basic research assured. It is most bountiful when it is tied to salient national political issues, as high-energy physics is tied to defense and biomedical research is tied to health. This suggests that continued support for basic research depends on the efforts of its supporters to publicize the results and their potential utility. It also is more viable politically if it is distributionally conscious; that is, if it is carried out by constituents of a large number of political leaders.

Heavy institutional, geographical, or even topical concentration of effort invites attack by those left out and can lead to reduced support for all. Unfortunately, this strategy is not likely to be the most efficient one for advancing the base of technical knowledge.

CONTROVERSIAL TECHNOLOGIES

IN THE MASS MEDIA

ALLAN MAZUR

The seventy-three-second flight of the Space Shuttle *Challenger* was shown so often on television that the pattern of plumes from its rent boosters has become an instantly recognizable logo for the disaster. Would public concern and the political impact of the accident have been so great if the vehicle and its crew had been lost outside the view of cameras?

Today few people would claim that the mass media can give extended coverage to an event or issue without shaping it in some degree. "Three Mile Island" and "Love Canal" have entered the language as synonyms for a disaster of modern technology, while other accidents that caused much greater morbidity are forgotten because they received less attention from journalists. During years when high coverage is given to nuclear power plants, energy shortages, toxic waste, or biomedical research, these issues hold the public's attention and take priority on the nation's political agenda, but when media coverage wanes, public and political interest falls too, even when the issue has not obviously lost its intrinsic importance.

Neither the public nor policymakers are very well informed about science and technology. Often there are great uncertainties or differences of opinion among experts about the significance of technological problems and events, and these ambiguities are easily politicized, with opposing sides making apparently contradictory technical claims. Usually both the public and policymakers learn about these controversial issues through the mass media, which have the difficult task of presenting relevant technical detail in an understandable manner. In doing so, the media determine which technological problems are salient to the public, and they influence the public's perceptions of technological events and risks.

The mass media are especially important in the "agenda-setting" stage of the policymaking process, in dramatizing events and identifying problems, in getting the attention of policymakers and mobilizing public concern, and in shaping initial perceptions of the problem and the kinds of policy responses that might be necessary. Once policies are formulated or actions taken, the press often loses interest unless there is a major mishap, and it rarely focuses on the later stages of policy implementation and evaluation which may be more important to the ultimate success of the policy. This is in part because the incentive structure of journalism is heavily weighted toward delivering readers or viewers to advertisers, and so journalists give most attention to the innovation and contentiousness of policy formulation, which are more interesting than the routine of implementation.

These effects of the media on policymaking are best described in the context of real examples of controversial technologies, and the cases of Love Canal and Three Mile Island will do nicely. But first it is necessary to give a brief description of the structure and operating procedures of the mass media in contemporary America.

Nearly every city has several radio and television stations and at least one newspaper. Despite this diversity, American news media speak with a fairly uniform voice when reporting events of national significance. Nearly all such stories are first reported by one or more of a small group of major news organizations that are collectively called "the national news media," including the New York Times and the Washington Post, the three television networks, Time and Newsweek magazines, and the two major wire services, Associated Press and United Press International. These organizations have the resources and connections to cover national and international events. They can afford specialized reporters who concentrate on science, energy, or environment, and who come to know one another from covering the same events and sometimes sharing accommodations and leisure hours. While there is competition among reporters to be first in publishing a story, there is also a good deal of cooperation and sharing of leads and background information.[1] Through repeated contacts, reporters develop personal relationships with important sources of news, including spokesmen for government, industry, and environmental groups. These relationships become channels for the flow of information, whether by formal news conferences, briefings "off the record," or leaks. Social relationships among sources and reporters thus support the reporting of routine events, and similar stories drawing on the same basic sources are produced by all the national news organs. Furthermore, each central organization watches the others for stories that have been missed, so these can be taken up if they seem worthwhile.

Every day the national news media collectively produce a menu of stories from which thousands of local organs select their news of the day, sometimes simply repeating stories as they come in, and sometimes embellishing them from local sources. Thus the public receives a fairly uniform body of news, whether directly from the national organs or indirectly through local outlets.

A "newsworthy item" that is not reported in the national news remains unknown to the public, as was the case with the fire in 1976 that destroyed both "redundant" control systems at the Browns Ferry nuclear power plant, leaving operators without control of the reactor. Recognized by experts as one of the most serious accidents to ever occur at a nuclear power plant, Browns Ferry was wholly ignored by the national media at that time. In contrast, events reported in the national media become news simply by virtue of appearing there. Pollution at Love Canal, recognized by local sources as a problem since 1976, was ignored by the national press until August 2, 1978, when literally overnight it became a news topic of major importance.

LOVE CANAL: AN EXAMPLE OF MEDIA EFFECTS

The Niagara Gazette first began reporting possible hazards at Love Canal in 1976, but the story was taken up more actively in February 1978 by Michael Brown, a young reporter for the Gazette who had written several articles on another waste dump in the area. As a result of Brown's articles, the U. S. Environmental Protection Agency (EPA) and the New York State Department of Health started health and environmental studies. By May they had concluded that there was a serious threat to the health of persons living near the edge of the old dump. Jon Swan later wrote in the Columbia Journalism Review that Brown had "delineated a story of national significance. But small newspapers do not determine such matters."[2] It required the arrival of the New York Times to bring the story to national attention.

The *Times* arrived in late July in the person of Donald McNeil, Jr., a twenty-four-year-old reporter, still in training, with an interest in environmental problems. Word of a story at Niagara Falls had reached Sidney Schanberg, then metropolitan editor of the *New York Times*, through connections with members of the New York State legislature, which was holding hearings on Love Canal. Schanberg had been especially interested in the toxic chemical issue at that time and, by his account, wanted someone young and energetic to cover the story. In McNeil's words, "Schanberg looked around for someone young and unmarried to send up to Buffalo, and it was me."[3]

McNeil had never heard of Michael Brown or his articles before meeting him the first day at Love Canal. He stayed at Brown's home that night, and the two men of similar age and interests became friends. Brown introduced McNeil to his sources among the homeowners, and they shared a common view of the events being reported.

By chance, McNeil had arrived shortly before the New York State health commissioner, Robert Whalen, announced his department's findings and recommendations to the governor. McNeil's first story, which appeared on the front page of the *New York Times* the morning of the press conference on August 2, told the history of Love Canal and cited anecdotal accounts of numerous maladies suffered by residents, implying that these were caused by the chemicals.[4] Though only a few reporters—including Brown, but not McNeil—attended Whalen's press conference in Albany, the commissioner's announcement, coming right after the morning article in the *Times*, of "a great and imminent peril" at Love Canal, and his recommendation that pregnant women and infants living at the edge of the dump move as soon as possible, was national news as soon as it was put on the wire. The evening network news programs on ABC and CBS reported it that night. McNeil, who had been ready to return to New York but for Schanberg's order to stay, produced stories every day, often for the front page, until August 10 when the *Times* stopped publication because of a strike. Love Canal had finally saturated the central news organs and flowed from there to local outlets across the country.

Love Canal's first appearance before a national audience lasted about a week, from McNeil's first story until the strike at the *Times*. By then Governor Hugh Carey of New York and President Jimmy Carter had made emergency funds available for the evacuation and purchase of the 239 homes closest to the canal. Although the purchase was announced as a direct response to the recently publicized "peril," it went substantially beyond the health commissioner's recommendations a few days earlier. The surge of publicity throughout the country almost certainly contributed to this solution, especially as Love Canal immediately became an issue in the gubernatorial campaign for the primary elections then in progress.[5] With the purchase of the houses accomplished and the New York Times on strike, attention to Love Canal rapidly receded.

The journalists had helped the homeowners win their first battle, but there would be two battles, and two fairly distinct stories. The first concerned the houses in the "inner ring," those closest to the canal where there was evidence of an excess of miscarriages, if not of other morbidity.[6] This was the story reported by Brown in the Niagara Gazette and by McNeil for the New York Times. It was essentially settled a week after Whalen's press conference by the arrangement to purchase the houses.

By this time residents of the "outer rings" further from the canal were concerned that they too might be at risk. Led by Mrs. Lois Gibbs, a minor character in the first battle, many of the remaining homeowners waged a new campaign, largely through the news media, for their houses to be purchased.[7]

Various measurements of both national and local media coverage show that attention dropped substantially after August 1978, when the problem of the inner ring was settled, but a lower level of attention remained fairly sustained during 1979, while remedial construction was under way at the canal to confine the wastes (figure 7–1). Gibbs was effective in holding the attention of the press during this period; she became the major source of news among the homeowners and appeared on the television networks, including the Phil Donahue Show, but she did not achieve the permanent relocation the homeowners sought.

The climax of the battle came on May 17, 1980, on the front page of the New York Times, where Irvin Molotsky reported that eleven of thirty-six recently tested residents of Love Canal "may have suffered chromosome damage from toxic chemicals buried there." The article further suggested that such damage is linked to cancer and genetic defects in offspring.[8] Molotsky had been told by unnamed sources of an exploratory study, conducted for the EPA, that soon became the focus of intense scientific criticism because of its lack of a proper control group, which left no way to determine whether the frequency of observed aberrations was abnormally high.[9]

A subsequent study with proper controls has since reported no excess of chromosome damage among Love Canal residents.[10] Molotsky had been given only fragments of the first study by his sources, and he has more recently told me that had he known there was no control group, he would have given less credence to the findings. Since the study had been leaked to the Buffalo press at about the same time, it would have appeared even if Molotsky had withheld his story, though

Figure 7-1. Number of Stories in Selected News Media on Love Canal (smoothed by running medians)

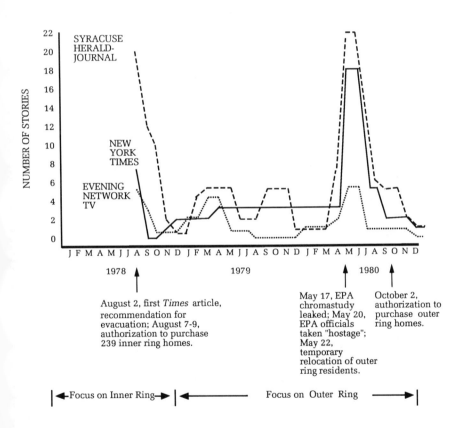

SYRACUSE HERALD-JOURNAL

NEW YORK TIMES

EVENING NETWORK TV

1978
1979
1980

August 2, first *Times* article, recommendation for evacuation; August 7-9, authorization to purchase 239 inner ring homes.

May 17, EPA chromastudy leaked; May 20, EPA officials taken "hostage"; May 22, temporary relocation of outer ring residents.

October 2, authorization to purchase outer ring homes.

◄Focus on Inner Ring► │ ◄ Focus on Outer Ring ►│

without the authority of the *New York Times* behind it. In any case, this dramatic story was widely disseminated and in my own city, Syracuse, N. Y., was published under a front-page banner headline.[11]

That afternoon the EPA held a press conference to discuss the study; this was unusual for a Saturday and almost certainly a reaction to Molotsky's story. It announced that the findings of chromosome damage might make it necessary to relocate the 710 families still living at Love Canal. A decision on the move was to be made in the next week, on the basis of a review of the chromosome study by geneticists.

The homeowners at Love Canal, who had gone through two years of worry about their health and that of their families, were highly disturbed by the chromosome story, particularly those who had been tested but not yet informed of the results. As hastily dispatched staff members from the EPA arrived to explain the tests, and journalists came to report the emerging story, frustration and anger grew in the community. That Monday, May 19, amid a crowd of homeowners and reporters, Gibbs took two officials of the EPA "hostage," a reference to the American hostages then being held at the embassy in Iran. She telephoned this information to the White House in what appears to have been a staged "media event" to influence the decision regarding relocation.[12]

The interest of press and public in toxic chemicals, which had been growing since 1976, stimulated attention to the Love Canal story and in turn was stimulated by it. With this heightened receptivity, the events of Saturday to Monday, May 17 to 19, received more journalistic attention than was given to Love Canal at any previous time (figure 7–1). By Wednesday, May 21, President Carter declared a state of emergency—although his advisers apparently regarded the chromosome study as invalid—permitting the federal government and the state of New York to relocate temporarily the families from the "outer ring." Once the residents had been moved from the area, the purchase of homes became inevitable and was approved that October. With the help of the journalists, the homeowners had won the second battle.

AGENDA-SETTING:
WHAT MAKES THE NATIONAL NEWS?

The disaster at the Chernobyl nuclear power reactor was newsworthy by any criterion and was eventually covered even by the Soviet press, which until that time rarely reported serious domestic accidents. The loss of *Challenger* and its crew, and the poison gas cloud that killed over 2,000 people at Bhopal, India, were obviously stories of inordinate importance. Nonetheless, factors extrinsic to the accidents appear to have influenced the kind and degree of attention that they received.

Challenger's loss was easy to cover, its destruction caught vividly on film that was shown over and over to television viewers. The subsequent federal investigation was largely open to reporters, including statements by engineers from Morton-Thiokol, manufacturer of the defective booster, that they had warned against a launch in cold weather but were overridden by their own management, apparently under pressure from NASA. This was grist for a long series of substantive news stories, including opportunities for first-rate investigative reporting.

In contrast, the Chernobyl explosion occurred out of reach of the Western press, which depended on rumor in its reporting, much of it inaccurate. Bhopal was also outside the usual range of Western reporters, who missed the accident in progress. Nonetheless, they were motivated to cover the story, not only for its death toll but because the plant was a subsidiary of an American corporation, Union Carbide. Furthermore, Bhopal followed by two weeks the explosion of a liquid gas tank in Mexico City which left nearly 500 known dead, not counting unregistered squatters whose bodies were incinerated to ash. The Mexico City explosion, which received less coverage than Bhopal and is barely remembered today, probably primed editors to devote more resources to Bhopal than they otherwise would have. Still, American coverage of the Indian tragedy was superficial, giving little information on the cause of the accident but focusing instead on the suffering of victims and later on American attorneys flocking "like vultures" to solicit liability clients.

These remarks emphasize the importance of the established channels between reporters and their primary news sources in government, industry, and environmental groups. Events occurring outside these routine channels, especially in the Third World or the Soviet Union, or even at Love Canal in upstate New York—the hinterland for East Coast journalists—are inaccessible and often reported superficially or missed altogether. When Love Canal did finally enter the agenda of the national press it became marked as an important event. Local attention increased immediately in nearby Buffalo and even in the *Niagara Gazette*, which had initiated the story and carried it for years, in recognition of Love Canal's new stature as national news.

Why did the accident at Three Mile Island, which killed no one, consume 40 percent of television network evening news during the first week, while the Browns Ferry fire three years earlier was ignored by the press? One answer is that Three Mile Island was uniquely severe. Yet there have been other accidents which may be regarded as equally severe, and which certainly caused more deaths, but which did not receive nearly as much attention. The worst airline accident in American history, the crash of a DC-10 killing 274 people as a result of a faulty engine-mount assembly, occurred two months after Three Mile Island but got far less attention. It is true that the *potential* effect of Three Mile Island was far greater, but the extreme seriousness and dramatic incidents there—the discovery of the hydrogen bubble, concerns about a meltdown and evacuation—only became apparent on the third day, after the site had been flooded with hundreds of reporters.[13]

The inconsistent relationship between severity of an accident and amount of media attention given to it is illustrated in figure 7-2, which lists the five accidents in nuclear power plants that experts consensually agree were the most serious and three that were relatively minor.[14] The amount of coverage in the *New York Times*, on television network news, and in the popular periodical literature is shown during the first two months after each accident (during the first two days for Three Mile Island). The fire at Browns Ferry in 1976, which was second only to Three Mile Island as a prelude to disaster, went unreported, as did the serious accident at Rancho Seco, California, in 1978. In contrast, after Three Mile Island, relatively minor accidents received as much or more attention than serious ones. Thus severity alone does not account for the amount of coverage.

The pattern of attention to these accidents is better explained by the increasing interest of editors and reporters in nuclear power during the 1970s. Like most people, journalists neither knew nor cared much about the technology at the beginning of the decade. But after the OPEC oil embargo in 1973, as the United States became concerned about energy and particularly the controversy about nuclear power, the attention given by journalists to atomic power plants gradually increased (figure 7-3). In the mid-1970s journalists were still insufficiently sensitive or informed to give their attention to the Browns Ferry fire, although the owner of the reactor, the Tennessee Valley Authority, held a formal press conference immediately after the accident.

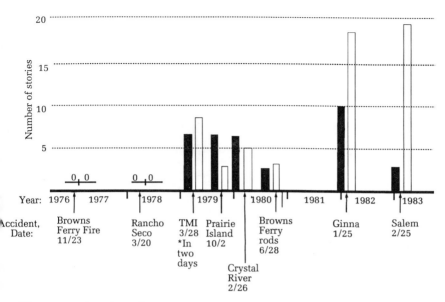

Figure 7-2. Number of Stories in Selected News Media within Two Months of Several Nuclear Power Plant Accidents. Notes: Television evening news stories are represented by solid bars. *New York Times* stories are represented by open bars. The five most serious accidents are shown with thick gray bars, the three less serious accidents with thin black bars. [a]Stories for Three Mile Island were reported in two days.

Perhaps if the accident at Three Mile Island had occurred in 1976, it too might have been ignored, at least initially. Coming in 1979, as President Carter was planning a major energy program and just as the antinuclear film *The China Syndrome* was showing across the country, Three Mile Island brought an immediate response from the media. Also, unlike Browns Ferry, Three Mile Island was in a populous area and easily accessible to journalists in nearby New York and Washington. The accident happened at the right time in the right place to become the center of attention. As events developed after the second day—the struggle with the bubble, the heroic actions of the nuclear engineers in averting disaster, the entry of the president, and the exodus of the frightened populace—it became a first-rank disaster story by any standard. With hundreds of journalists already on the scene, atten-

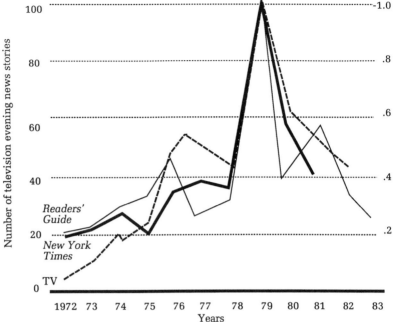

Figure 7-3. Mass Media Coverage of Nuclear Power Plants, 1972–83

tion in the press, radio, and television increased tremendously.

Once the awareness of the media and the public had been heightened by the accident at Three Mile Island and nuclear power was firmly in place on the journalistic agenda, subsequent nuclear accidents were invariably reported, whether or not they were serious. The attention given to the minor accident at Ginna, New York, in early 1982 was especially great, perhaps because a release of radioactivity into the atmosphere and the spillage of a large amount of radioactive water into the containment building were reminiscent of the Three Mile Island accident, though in this case the reactor was never out of control. On the other hand, the accident at Salem, New Jersey, which the chief of reactor regulation of the Nuclear Regulatory Commission (NRC), Harold Denton, called "the most significant . . . that we have had since Three Mile Island,"[15] received little television coverage, though it was well reported in the New York Times. In 1983, when the "energy crisis" seemed to have disappeared and attention to nuclear power plants was diminishing, television journalists were no longer interested.

Just as Three Mile Island became the paradigmatic nuclear accident, so Love Canal became the exemplar of the hazardous waste dump. Why Love Canal? It was not the obviously worst instance of chemical ground pollution known to the press at that time.[16] Perhaps the worst American example was the spread of the chemical PBB through Michigan in 1973, which resulted from its accidental mixing with livestock feed. By the time the accident was discovered in 1974, livestock were dying on a large scale, and many farm families displayed symptoms of PBB poisoning. The state of Michigan began a two-year program of slaughter, burying 35,000 cattle and at least a million pigs, sheep, and chickens, yet these events were little reported outside the area. Even with the animals gone, restocked farms remained contaminated, bringing new rounds of slaughters and burials in 1978, and eventually costing two million animal lives and probably substantial human morbidity.[17]

That the events connected with PBB in 1974 and 1975 should remain virtually unknown to the American public outside Michigan, while Love Canal was given great prominence in 1978, may be explained in the same way as the ignoring of the Browns Ferry fire in 1976 while Three Mile Island was intensively covered in 1979. Chemical pollution simply was not of major concern to journalists in 1974, so editors and reporters paid little attention to such an occurrence outside of their normal channels. The situation changed rapidly about 1976, with the confluence of major stories about PCB contamination in the Hudson River, the explosion of the chemical plant at Seveso in Italy—which spread dioxin over nearby residents—and the enactment by Congress of the Toxic Substance Control Act.

By mid–1978 chemicals were a topic of rapidly increasing attention in the American media (figure 7–4), and a story about chemical pollution was more likely than ever before to attract the interest of an editor. Love Canal, like Three Mile Island, appeared at the right time to receive enhanced coverage.

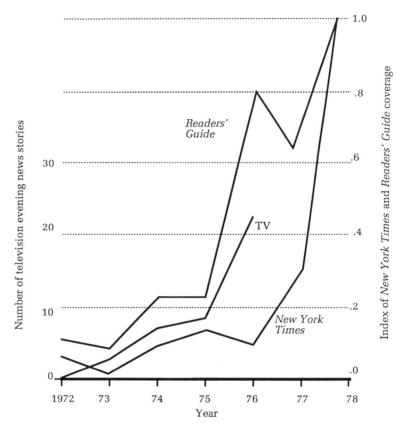

Figure 7-4. Mass Media Coverage of Chemical Waste–Related Issues, 1972–78. Note: The 1978 value for the *New York Times* is prorated from January-June data and therefore contains no stories on Love Canal.

INTERPRETING OR SHAPING EVENTS?

The media gave unusual emphasis to Three Mile Island, for example when Walter Cronkite told his national television audience on the third night that "the world has never known a day quite like today."[18] As a result, the commission created by President Carter to investigate the accident, under the chairmanship of John Kemeny, appointed a task force especially to examine the activities of the journalists. Inquiring if the hundreds of reporters who covered the story—usually with little technical understanding of the events before them—acted in a responsible manner, the task force concluded that they had done a creditable job under extremely difficult circumstances. Furthermore, it said that when the press produced erroneous reports, these errors were usually traceable to sources in government and industry rather than to journalists.[19]

Perhaps the most alarming but erroneous report during the accident was a story that a hydrogen bubble inside the reactor could explode, blow the head off the reactor, and release radioactive material into the atmosphere, possibly within two days.[20] The story appeared on Saturday, March 31, the fourth day after the accident began and one day after accurate reports that a hydrogen bubble in the reactor might interfere with the flow of coolant, causing a small but real possibility of fuel meltdown.

Joseph Hendrie, chairman of the NRC, had become concerned that oxygen gas, generated inside the reactor, could mix with the hydrogen, making it explosive. Hendrie mentioned at a press conference on Saturday afternoon that the bubble might become "flammable," but reporters there missed its significance, which may have been obscured by Hendrie's use of the word flammable, which did not sound as serious as explodable. In any case, the direct precipitant of the story was an employee of the NRC who telephoned the Washington bureau of the Associated Press (AP) on Saturday afternoon to say that the bubble might explode. Over the next few hours, AP reporters worked to fill out and confirm the story, which they were able to do largely through additional sources at the NRC. This is the most striking example of an error reported by newspeople but originated by the NRC, for it is now generally accepted that there was never any good reason to think that the bubble might explode.

The imminence of the potential explosion—within two days—was one of the most alarming features of the story. A closed meeting of NRC commissioners, lasting most of Saturday, repeatedly discussed how long it would take for the bubble to become explosive; "two or three days" was a rough, early estimate, although new calculations were providing evidence of longer periods. AP reporters, who were seeking out sources of information in government and industry, found it hard to make the timing precise because estimates were highly variable and uncertain. One source finally said "two days," and that estimate was incorporated into the story. The reporters who had heard the diverse estimates and finally chose the shorter one had as much hand as the NRC in constructing the false story.[21]

A survey of reporters and editors drawn largely from the national news media showed most to be political liberals and strong supporters of environmental protection but without bias against large corporations. On the specific issue of nuclear power plants, the journalists were skeptical, especially those in television.[22] Did this skepticism affect the reporting of Three Mile Island?

The Kemeny Commission was split on the matter but finally accepted its task force's conclusion that, with some glaring exceptions, journalists gave generally fair and accurate news reports about the accident. Whether or not that is a proper assessment of the reporting of the facts of the accident, there is much consensus that the "color" or "human interest" stories which supplemented the factual news were often biased. Three-fourths of the quotations of local residents were, according to the task force, presented in an alarming manner. Often journalists let the fears of laymen represent the actual situation. For example, an official statement that local milk was safe was reported in the words of a dairy farmer who was afraid to drink his own animals' milk. One team of television journalists asked bystanders to stay out of camera range, apparently to show abandoned streets near the reactor.[23]

The bias of "color" is well illustrated by the major news magazines, Time and Newsweek, which wrote factually accurate cover stories. Time facetiously compared the reassuring statements of the plant's spokesmen to the script of the film The China Syndrome, which depicts a nefarious executive of a nuclear power plant placing his own profit above his concern for public safety. Newsweek ran a picture of the film's control room set next to one of the real control room at Three Mile Island.

Newsweek was one of many organs to give attention to extreme claims of radiation hazard, in this case by Dr. Ernest Sternglass, who arrived on site during the second day of the accident. Over the years Sternglass has attributed extreme and varied effects to radiation, such as the national decline in scores on the Scholastic Aptitude Test, so that even opponents of nuclear power found fault with his claims. Nonetheless, Newsweek reported his prediction of a 5 to 20 percent increase in childhood leukemia in the area within a year—which did not occur—even while acknowledging that "Sternglass's warning was exaggerated"; it added, "But no one—not even radiation experts—can say for sure that he is totally wrong."[24]

Editorial cartoons are usually omitted from discussions of bias, yet their prominence on the page and easy absorption make them ideal vehicles to convey simple ideas. Unlike news stories, truth is purposely distorted in cartoons for satiric effect. These distortions were usually biased against nuclear power during the Three Mile Island episode, as when the spokesman for a utility was pictured near the radiating rubble of a nuclear plant, announcing: "There is no real cause for alarm."[25]

Although the media coverage of Love Canal has been studied less extensively than that of Three Mile Island, it is apparent that many journalists favored the position of the homeowners over that of industry or the relevant government agencies. According to the homeowners' account, residents suffered severe physical harm from chemical leakage; the fault lay with Hooker Chemical Company, which was remiss in both its initial methods of disposal and its subsequent refusal to accept responsibility; furthermore, state and federal governments were unsympathetic to the homeowners and reluctant to aid them in their plight. This is the basic account conveyed to the public by journalists. As at Three Mile Island, fears of local residents were represented as describing the real situation. The *New York Times* was technically accurate to report: "Residents say many in the neighborhood have died of rectal, breast and blood cancers,"[26] but the fact that residents said this does not mean that these people did indeed die of these cancers—and if they did, that the deaths were caused by the waste chemicals.

In fact, the degree of morbidity attributable to chemicals leaking from Love Canal remains uncertain and may be very low. Most claims of chemically induced illness were either anecdotal, such as those cited in the *New York Times*, were based on informal house-to-house surveys by the homeowners themselves, or were based on two small pilot studies. A committee of experts, appointed by Governor Carey to review most of those statements, concluded that they were of little scientific value and did not establish relationships between health and the hazardous wastes at Love Canal.[27] The firmest but still inconclusive additional evidence on morbidity comes from epidemiological data collected by the New York State Department of Health. It shows a relatively high rate of miscarriage among women living in "wet areas" of the neighborhood and among those living along one side of the dump, but not along the other side. Otherwise, chemicals have had little apparent effect on health in the community.[28] In contrast to this evidence, the mass media have conveyed the impression of a community suffering various severe health effects from leaking toxic waste.

While some degree of journalistic bias is undeniably present in reporting about controversial technologies, journalists are increasingly following a format that carefully balances conflicting claims.[29] Typically in this format, one paragraph quotes the position of an expert on one side of the controversy, and the following paragraph contains a rejoinder from an expert on the other side, and then the first expert rebuts the rejoinder, and so on. The reporter draws no substantive conclusion, leaving that to the reader who has been exposed to both positions in the debate. This format has the advantages of giving equal treatment to both sides, and of freeing the journalist from having to judge which expert to believe.

Unfortunately, this balanced format carries its own biases. First, it gives equal voice—and implicitly equal weight—to both sides, even when one position is representative of most reputable experts and the other is a fringe position. Second, a number of empirical studies show that consumers of such stories tend to shift their opinions about the technology toward opposition. At first glance this is a surprising outcome since a balanced treatment ought to promote balanced opinions, but apparently, in the case of a risky technology, the public takes a conservative position, as if thinking, "Why take a chance if there is any doubt?" Thus "balanced" stories seem to favor the opposition to a technology, and the greater the quantity of these stories, the more public opinion shifts against the technology.[30]

CONCLUSIONS

In many ways journalistic coverage of controversial technologies is like that of other controversial topics of national importance. As routine matters, they reach public attention through established channels between reporters from the major organs of the national media and their regular news sources. Unusual events are given more or less coverage—or ignored altogether—depending on their intrinsic newsworthiness, their accessibility to reporters, and whether or not the topic is on the national media's own agenda of current interests. The special interests of editors and reporters may change markedly from year to year; certainly they do in the reporting of technology and environmental matters.

At an earlier time, journalists often described themselves as mere reporters of events with little influence over the events themselves. Hardly anyone takes that position seriously anymore, especially as the mass media have become increasingly pervasive in American culture. However the belief persists that a truly unbiased media would have minimal effect on what is being reported. That view ignores the impact of a large quantity of coverage—even unbiased coverage—on public concern with a controversial topic.

The bias in journalistic presentation is insufficient to account for the dramatic effects that the news media have had in shaping public conceptions of major accidents and other controversial matters of technology. Without a large amount of attention, content alone—whatever its bias—would have little impact on the audience, as in the failure of reports favoring the homeowners to have much effect on Love Canal in the years before its emergence as an event of national importance. Surely the frequent repetition of unbiased television pictures showing the exploding Challenger intensified public grief beyond what it would have been if the level of coverage had been closer to that given the Apollo capsule fire in 1967 which killed three astronauts. The influence of media coverage is as much a function of salience as of content.

Once a controversial technology enters the journalists' agenda, reporters become the medium through which partisans compete for advantage. This would probably occur even if journalists were wholly unbiased. Corporations announce that their technologies cause minimal damage and deny fault. Those who challenge the corporations seek publicity for their claims of damage and for their charges of the culpability of industry, to prod government into action and to obtain compensation for their alleged injuries. Competition for favorable coverage may split the challengers themselves, as when the Lois Gibbs group dominated other factions of homeowners at Love Canal through her successful management of reporters.[31] Governmental agencies seek to discredit the challengers' extreme claims of damage while maintaining their own credibility as responsible sources of information. In the background are elected officials, sometimes with the ultimate power to resolve the controversies, but concerned about tight budgets, hasty judgments, and the image that the media conveys to their constituencies. Journalists themselves may become important participants, as in the accidents discussed here. That certain spokespeople and viewpoints receive inordinate amounts of attention may be attributable to the biases of the journalists—but even without such biases, the mere presence of reporters and cameras encourages words and actions that are aimed at the larger public audience rather than at individuals on the scene.

The intense public concern following Three Mile Island influenced proposals by both government and industry for solutions to the newly prominent problems of nuclear power, just as public concern with Love Canal encouraged legislation to create a "Superfund" to pay for cleaning up toxic waste dumps which rapidly became visible across the country. At the same time, residents living near these sites experienced high levels of anxiety over potential risks. These media effects may be applauded or attacked depending upon one's views regarding nuclear power, the chemical industry, and so on.

Journalistic ethics already condemn bias in reporting, but this stricture is applied less to "human interest" stories and "investigative reporting" than to factual news. Editors tend to assign technologically uneducated reporters to deal with events with large technical components, even when competent science writers are available for assignment. Science writers might avoid the common error of accepting anecdotes about morbidity as if they were the verified results of research, or of accepting fragments of scientific studies, leaked by biased parties, without inquiring into the research methods in sufficient detail to assess the credibility of such reports.

Journalists might consider a norm of moderation, attempting to avoid the extremes of overwhelming attention as at Three Mile Island, and virtual silence, as at Browns Ferry. A voluntary rule of moderation might discourage television news editors from supplementing one minute of factual reporting with nine minutes of "color" interviews. An emphasis on moderation would preclude sending tens or hundreds of inept, unqualified reporters to a scene of crisis, when a smaller group of technically competent journalists could provide reports without further complicating the understanding of an event that is already difficult enough.

III

REGULATING TECHNOLOGY

RISK ASSESSMENT AND

MANAGEMENT

INTRODUCTION

Technology has a pervasive influence, both positive and negative, on modern life. Its contributions to making life more pleasant and productive are justly praised. Its not-so-benign effects on society, for example, the "negative externalities" of production that we call pollution, are often cause for concern. Examples are easy to find. We love the personal freedom, mobility, and power that automobiles give us, but we also worry about the accidents and air pollution they cause. Similarly, we once celebrated rising levels of energy production as a sign of economic health; now we wonder about long-term threats of nuclear power plant waste and possible climatic changes attributable to burning fossil fuels.[1] When these kinds of fears are intense enough, the public demands that government intervene to regulate technology and its side effects.

Over the past several decades, the federal government in the United States, along with national governments in many other industrialized nations, has intervened on frequent occasions in an effort to respond to rising public concern about technology's effects on health, safety, and environmental quality.[2] As a result, not only have government regulatory programs grown in number, scope, and impact, but so has criticism of regulation as irrational, excessive, and costly.[3] The new and controversial status of regulation has led to reliance on a host of new methods and procedures used by government in its attempt to anticipate, prevent, and mitigate technology's negative impacts. In particular, during the last decade there has been a quantum leap in use of environmental impact analysis, technology assessment, and risk assessment. Not surprisingly, increased reliance on these methods has in turn spawned new interest in the effect of regulation on the economy and the potential contribution, as well as the limitations, of these methods.[4]

A range of important normative and empirical questions intrigue students of technology and its regulation. Among the major normative questions are such basic concerns as whether and to what extent we should attempt to regulate technology, whether the costs of doing so are acceptable given the benefits derived, what trade-offs might be necessary between economic growth and regulatory restrictions such as control of hazardous substances, and whether the technical experts, the general public, or its elected representatives should make such decisions.[5] There is also no shortage of important empirical questions such as what capacity government has to identify, measure, and prevent or reduce certain hazards or risks; how the public's preferences can be determined; how decisions on technology assessment and risk assessment are made in various bureaucratic settings; how trade-offs between competing values (e.g., the economic costs of regulation and the benefits of risk reduction) are handled; what conditions limit the use of these methods; and how the methods might be improved.[6]

The three chapters in this section selectively address these kinds of questions and provide an introduction to the leading disputes over contemporary governmental regulation of technology. Harvey Brooks is concerned primarily with some of the consequences of what he describes as a "sea change" in society's attitudes toward technology and its side effects. He argues that public skepticism toward technology has been affected less by an identifiable change in environmental conditions than public perception that risks are now worse. He also identifies a number of reasons for the greater responsiveness of government in the late 1960s and 1970s to new public demands for protection that grow out of such perceptions. Among the consequences of this "new policy towards the governance of technology" is a legal and regulatory structure that threatens to limit severely the development of new technologies. Brooks reminds us forcefully of the benefits that previous advancements in technology have provided, and wonders whether we will not pay a steep price for placing the restrictions we have on technological innovation. Will we, for example, delay viable solutions to urgent public problems while we wait for evidence of all possible negative effects of new technology? In light of those concerns,

he draws some comparisons to how other nations have governed technology, especially how they have used risk assessment and other
scientific information. Although the differences have been significant
in the past, he foresees a convergence between U.S. and European
styles of using science in policymaking and a regulatory science
that will become more and more subject to universalistic norms as
public problems and their solutions increasingly transcend national
boundaries.

Michael Kraft's chapter broadly surveys the recent growth in public concern about technological hazards, the rise of methods of risk
assessment, and their employment in federal regulatory agencies. Like
Brooks, he raises a number of questions about the legitimate role of
government in regulating technology, and in particular relying on risk
assessment for knowledge of the harm inflicted by modern technology.
He asks, for example, how we should make decisions about the levels
of risk that are acceptable, who should participate in such decisions to
insure that they are not dominated by technical experts in the bureaucracies, and what role values and ethics should play in shaping regulatory decisions of this kind. But his focus is more empirical than
normative. He offers a primer on methods of risk assessment and risk
evaluation to help the reader better appreciate the complexity of such
decisions and the inevitable disputes between proponents and critics
of these methods. He concludes that risk assessment is an important
and valuable tool for making decisions that seek to balance the benefits
of regulation against its costs despite some obvious methodological
limitations and considerable potential for misuse. He believes it would
be a better tool if there were improvements in data and methodologies,
new guidelines for communication of risk studies, and development
of various mechanisms to insure the accountability of agency decision
makers. These conclusions are consistent with much of the contemporary writing on the subject of risk assessment and its communication.[7]

Edward Woodhouse takes issue with some of the fundamental
assumptions behind modern risk assessment and thus does not agree
with Brooks and Kraft on the contribution that these analytic methods
might make to government regulation of technology. For example, he
questions whether we can know the risks we face and make both public and private decisions without significant errors. He argues that
uncertainty is so great in most cases of measuring technology's impact
that we delude ourselves if we believe we can forecast impacts or risks

with enough accuracy to rely upon these methods. Trial and error or incremental decision making might help, but Woodhouse alerts us to various barriers to error correction, including delayed symptoms, misperception of those symptoms, difficulties with feedback mechanisms, and irreversible or catastrophic effects. He suggests an alternative form of decision making which he terms sophisticated trial and error. Like ordinary trial and error, it allows us to learn from past mistakes and adjust our actions over time. But it improves upon that form of decision making by helping to guard against the worst consequences of error and to improve government's ability to learn from errors. These advantages can be gained through taking initial precautions against catastrophic loss, erring on the side of caution, testing risks through experimental procedures where possible, actively preparing to learn from experience, and setting priorities among risks to be regulated to make the task more manageable and rational.[8] Sophisticated trial and error in decision making cannot correct systemic flaws in the American political system, but it can help to ameliorate some of the worst characteristics of the regulatory process identified by all three authors in this section.

As much as we have improved our knowledge of these matters in recent years, there is much more to be learned about the regulation of technology. These chapters clarify both the potential and limitations of these analytic methods and the procedures we follow in making decisions about how technology is to be regulated. They also speak to the question of institutional capabilities and deficiencies with respect to such decision making and to the public's ambivalence about technology and governmental efforts to regulate it through bureaucratic procedures. But a number of important questions, both empirical and normative, remain insufficiently explored. For example, how are such studies actually used in making regulatory decisions, and how do decision makers deal with the methodological limitations that provoke so much concern? In regard to public preferences for how technology is to be regulated and the public's participation in such decisions, how do decision makers determine what the public wants, and to what extent is this a factor in deciding what to regulate and how? More normatively, how well do the various mechanisms of accountability—from White House oversight to media coverage and congressional investigations—insure responsiveness to the public as well as provide for effective decision making? Scholars have begun to examine all of these questions, and in the next several years we should be able to address more fully and precisely many of the relationships hinted at in the three chapters in this section.

CONTROLLING TECHNOLOGY: RISKS,

COSTS, AND BENEFITS

HARVEY BROOKS

EXPERIMENT AS A SOURCE OF ECONOMIC PROGRESS

In their provocative book, *How the West Grew Rich*, Rosenberg and Birdzell[1] summarize their answer to the question in the title in the following terms:

Our general conclusion is that the underlying source of the West's ability to attract the lightning of economic revolutions was a unique use of experiment in technology and organization to harness resources to the satisfaction of human wants. The key elements of the system were the wide diffusion of the authority and resources necessary to experiment; an absence of more than rudimentary political and religious restrictions on experiment; and incentives which combined ample rewards for success, defined as the wide-spread economic use of the results of experiment, with a risk of severe penalties for failing to experiment.

To these authors innovation and the social selection of successful experiments are the principal engines of Western economic growth, which distinguish it from the other great civilizations of the past and most of the non-Western societies of the present.

An important corollary of the proposition asserted above is: "In the West, the rewards [of innovation] are not subject to offset for the losses sustained by those injured by an innovation such as workers whose skills are made obsolescent or capitalists whose investment in superseded enterprises becomes worthless."[2] I might add that, until very recently in the West, this proposition has applied in effect to all, or almost all, negative externalities resulting from the introduction and diffusion of new technologies. Even where such externalities were to some extent offset, the costs tended to be redistributed across society as a whole rather than being borne by the deployer of the innovations. In this way the already substantial risks faced by the innovator were not augmented by the additional risk of having to bear the cost of unanticipated externalities, or publicly perceived externalities, and it was expected that there would therefore be more innovations whose aggregate incremental net benefit to society would exceed the aggregate cost to adversely affected groups, resulting in a higher standard of living for all than would otherwise have been the case.

EXEMPTION OF INNOVATORS FROM SOCIAL COSTS

Until very recently, the exemption of innovators from the risk of having to bear the social costs of their innovations was almost absolute—to a degree, in fact, that seems almost unimaginable today. But in the twentieth century this has begun to change, only slowly at first, but at an accelerating pace beginning in the mid-1960s in the United States and somewhat earlier in Europe. Part of my purpose in this chapter will be to analyze both the roots of these changes and their possible implications for the future evolution of Western-type societies and their place in the scheme of things. I will also be concerned with the somewhat different ways in which the changes have worked their way through different political cultures and with whether these differences are likely to intensify or attenuate in the future.

Initially, the changes in societal response to the negative externalities of innovation and growth involved mainly society as a whole assuming some measure of collective responsibility for income maintenance and for the economic welfare of those disadvantaged by the by-products of innovation and growth. These measures included social security, welfare, and some public subsidy for health care. Other measures, such as unemployment insurance and workmen's compensation, were insurance schemes with costs partly based on the experience of individual firms, and were thus rather modest measures for imposing externality costs on the firms responsible. None of these benefits were explicitly related to the by-products of innovation, however, nor were they considered as offsets to the benefits of innovation as such. Rather they represented the necessary social costs of economic activity in general.

The fact is that in the last hundred years the advance of technology has generated far more jobs than it has eliminated. Among the OECD countries, the employed work force has tripled in size while two-thirds of the jobs that existed in 1880 have disappeared.[3] Approximately one-third of the increased output per man-hour has been taken by society in the form of increased leisure and prolongation of education.[4] Nevertheless, social welfare programs have been important in mitigating the cost to temporarily displaced workers and their dependents, but these costs have not been imposed directly on the innovators (assuming it would have been possible to allocate responsibility for these costs, which is doubtful in most cases, since displacement most frequently occurs in firms different from those introducing the new technology. For example, skilled mechanical watchmakers are displaced by competition from electronic watches).

REALLOCATION OF SOCIAL COSTS

In the late 1960s and at an accelerating pace through the 1970s, especially in the United States (the trend had started earlier but proceeded more slowly in other countries), the cost burden of *other* negative externalities of innovations began to be shifted to the organizations responsible for deploying them. The primary mechanisms for this were legislatively mandated regulation and tort liability, both of which experienced explosive growth, driven by strong public support. Indeed the two mechanisms were closely interrelated, because the legislation that established regulatory standards and assigned regulatory authority to new agencies also greatly broadened the definition of *standing* in the courts to include large, diffusely affected groups who could now bring class action suits against polluters or even against regulators who were considered to be evading their legal mandates to enforce the standards against polluters. Most importantly, suits could in principle be brought against the originators of technologies deployed as much as thirty to forty years earlier whose adverse consequences had only just begun to be widely appreciated. The case of asbestos is, perhaps, the most dramatic example. Even in the case of employment displacement effects, suits were brought against the University of California for their support and conduct of research on mechanical vegetable pickers, which were alleged to have caused extensive displacement of agricultural workers.[5]

What were the changes in circumstances that led to this veritable "sea change" in society's approach to the negative externalities of technological innovation? I would assert that any real growth in the actual adverse effects of technological progress was far less important than the changes in public perceptions and sensitivities as well as changes in institutions and lifestyles which made it easier for citizens to register their concerns through the political and judicial processes. Public sensitivity and consequent reaction to the negative externalities of technology, especially environmental degradation, grew far more rapidly than the effects themselves. In some cases public concerns actually grew while the effects themselves were declining, for example, in the case of the more visible forms of air pollution such as smoke and soot. Indeed, average life expectancy has increased steadily during the period when many new threats were alleged to be entering the environment as a result of growing industrial activity.

I would summarize the factors leading to a new policy toward the governance of technology in the following terms:[6]

1. *The widening ramifications of technology and its "systemic" effects extending to consequences remote in space and time from its original place and time of introduction, many of these consequences having been unforeseen.*

One of the earliest examples was the global radioactive fallout from nuclear weapons testing in the atmosphere, which was a key factor in mobilizing public support for the partial test ban treaty of 1962. A more influential example was, perhaps, the publicizing by Rachel Carson in 1962 of the ecological side effects of the widespread use of DDT as an agricultural pesticide.[7] This may have had an especially big impact on opinion because the initial result of the introduction of DDT had been so dramatically beneficial. It was estimated to have saved some half billion human lives from insect-borne disease in the years since its first use during World War II, and it had been responsible for spectacular increases in crop yield in some areas.[8] The adverse effects were insidious, long in becoming apparent, and highly nonlinear with respect to scale of application, so that they came with considerable surprise and shock.[9] The public debate about the American program to build three prototypes of a proposed commercial supersonic transport (SST) was another triggering event in the public mind since, again, the preceding advances in commercial air transport had been so spectacular, and the side effects projected for a fleet of commercial SST's were so subtle and esoteric (and so surprising); in addition they were associated with the "dread disease" of cancer, to which the public had become especially sensitized.[10] These two well-publicized examples of the side effects of new technologies which had originally been thought of as highly beneficial dramatized for the public the two faces of technology and created a strong feeling that the proponents of new technologies did not always know what they were doing and might have built-in blinders when it came to foreseeing all the possible consequences of their brain children.

2. *Scientific progress that made possible earlier and better appreciation of the actual and potential risks of complex technologies.*

The ability to measure concentrations of contaminants in the parts-per-billion and even the parts-per-trillion range developed rapidly and led to discoveries such as the presence of DDT residues in Antarctic penguins and the presence of submicroscopic asbestos fibers in Lake Superior near the drinking water intake for the city of Duluth (an observation only possible with the use of the latest techniques of electron microscopy).[11] The ability to detect impurities in tiny quantities, combined with evidence of the long latency periods for the development of cancer as a result of exposure to small concentrations of carcinogens, caused scientists and politicians to suspect that the absence of short-term human epidemiological evidence of damage from environmental chemicals was no guarantee of their safety. In a similar vein, the modeling of improbable but potentially catastrophic accidents with computers—for example, with nuclear reactors or liquified natural gas (LNG) storage facilities[12]—made it possible to show that the absence of accidents within the short time that these technologies had been deployed could provide little assurance of the impossibility of such accidents in the future. Thus the greater the power of scientific measurement and analytical techniques became, the more insistent the public became that their full potential be brought to bear to assure the population against even the remotest risks from technology. Paradoxically, the growing power of one set of technologies—those for measuring and predicting risks—helped to point the finger of suspicion at the safety of other technologies.

3. *Political and social changes that encouraged and facilitated*

the registration of wider and more subtle social concerns in the political process than in the past.

These changes included: (a) growth of a professional and technical class with the leisure, education, and affluence to concern themselves with issues that affected more than their immediate livelihood and surroundings—a group more idealistic, politically active, and animated by values beyond their immediate economic self-interest than had been seen in the past; (b) growing economic security of a larger segment of the population, with a receding memory of the setbacks and hardships of the Great Depression and World War II, and a consequent sense that the economy was invulnerable and could be manipulated to produce greater social justice and better quality of life beyond the mere material; (c) growth in the staff resources of the Congress (including independent and nonpartisan congressional offices such as OTA, CRS, CBO, and GAO), driven by congressional desire for independent access to technical expertise to match the in-house expertise available to agencies in the executive branch; and (d) a subtle shift in the burden of proof required in political and judicial processes from the critics of new technology to its proponents, so that technology was increasingly viewed as guilty until proved innocent rather than, as in the past, innocent until proved guilty. An accompaniment of the shift in the burden of proof was that the public was less willing to accept assurances that a technological fix could and would be found for future adverse effects of a new technology. Therefore one could not afford to go full speed ahead with the deployment of a new technology without waiting until such fixes were specifically identified and proven in practice. The political struggles over high-level radioactive waste disposal in connection with commercial nuclear power is a prime example of this new policy climate. Had a similar policy been adopted for chemical wastes a generation earlier, many risks might have been avoided, but there might never have been a dynamic post–World War II chemical industry.

GROWING AMBIVALENCE TOWARD TECHNOLOGY

The dramatic change in the attitude toward science and technology that I have described contained a good deal of ambiguity and was by no means as skeptical of technology as might appear at first sight, or as some commentators have suggested. Despite public appreciation that "advances" in the application of technology could be a mixed blessing, the expectation persisted that sufficient political pressure could bring about technological solutions to many intractable environmental problems, ranging from automobile emissions to the cleanup of hazardous waste dumps. This indeed seemed to be the premise underlying much of the environmental, health, and safety legislation passed in the 1970s. "Technology forcing" through nondiscretionary legislated standards with tight deadlines became a major strategy for change. In fact its record in practice was mixed: technology forcing proved neither as impractical as its (mainly industrial) critics proclaimed in advance nor as successful as its (mainly public interest group) proponents hoped. Progress on auto emission controls and power plant stack gas scrubbers that were mandated as a result of the 1970 Clean Air Amendments exceeded the predictions of pessimists, but took longer to achieve with adequate reliability than environmental advocates insisted was possible. As a result legislated standards and deadlines were revised several times in subsequent sessions of Congress. In the end the timetable originally projected by the Nixon administration for the achievement of auto emission standards, and overridden by Congress in 1970, turned out to be the timetable which was actually followed as a result of the many changes in deadlines and standards allowed by the amendments.

Similarly, inflated expectations of immediate breakthroughs in the cost of solar energy installations were not met, but some solid technical progress was made, albeit accompanied by wasteful and ineffectual "demonstrations." Economic targets of cost-competitiveness or near cost-competitiveness of solar photovoltaics with more traditional energy sources proved wildly unrealistic.

These changes were also accompanied by loss of public confidence in the political neutrality of experts, and even of expertise in principle, as the final court of appeal in difficult public policy decisions involving science or technology. Too many of the experts appeared to be acting as "hired guns" for a variety of interest groups ranging from self-serving industrial interests to environmental activists. Subservient either to economic self-interest or to the (frequently) hidden political agendas of activists, these experts consciously or unconsciously exploited scientific uncertainties to use evidence or analysis selectively in support of their viewpoints; they often seemed to be mobilizing the whole panoply of science for the support of policy positions arrived at beforehand for essentially nontechnical reasons. Although these latter biases were not necessarily self-serving, this made little difference to public perceptions of expertise as unconcerned with the public interest. Polarization among the experts led to confusion among politicians and the public, who found it understandably difficult to sort out the reasons for often startlingly sharp differences about what appeared to the layman to be questions of fact or purely technical questions that ought to have a single right answer. At the same time many scientists, flattered by political or high-level policy attention to their views or to their fields of expertise, exaggerated the certainty of what was known and ignored uncertainties or contradictory evidence or argumentation.

THE INTERNALIZATION OF SOCIAL COSTS

But the most important outcome of the new political climate toward technology was to force more and more "internalization" of the costs and risks arising out of the negative externalities of innovation; that is, the innovating organization, as opposed to society at large or particular adversely affected groups, was compelled to bear these costs. This added a new class of risks or unpredictable costs to those already faced by the innovator. In addition to the risk that the innovation would run into unexpected technical snags in the course of its development, or that the resulting innovative product would not be accepted by the market or would be preempted by a competitor even if technically successful, there was the risk that the innovation would cause unforeseen damage to some individual or group—damage for which the innovator might have to pay either through compensation of victims or through expensive redesign of the product or manufacturing process long after the investment for producing and marketing the concrete embodiment of the innovation was already in place. In many cases, of course, these extra costs could be passed on to users through higher prices, and mechanisms of corporate restructuring were available to partially shield the parent corporation from the full potential liability. In particular, liberalization of bankruptcy laws has permitted corporations to avoid part of their potential liability, as in the case of Johns-Manville and the side effects of asbestos.[13] In other cases, as with electric utilities, regulatory policy has enabled the innovator to recover through higher rates the extra costs incurred as a result of

required retrofit of equipment deemed necessary for publicly acceptable safety. Nevertheless, additional risks are still present for the innovator even when they are partially shared with ultimate consumers. In
some cases where they have escalated, as for nuclear power plants,
state public utility commissions have shown increasing resistance to
allowing such costs in the rate base.

There is, of course, no paucity of arguments for why the innovator,
or his customers that are beneficiaries of the innovation, rather than
society as a whole, should bear the costs of the negative externalities
resulting from the economic use of his innovations. These include:

1. To encourage socially responsible innovations and discourage socially irresponsible ones.
2. To encourage a more thorough and comprehensive technology assessment prior to the decision to introduce an innovation to the
   market.
3. To reward socially responsible innovators by protecting them from
   being undersold by less responsible innovators with lower costs,
   and to drive the irresponsibles out of business.
4. By incorporating the cost of negative externalities in the price of
   new products, to reduce the consumption of these products and
   thereby to reduce the net cost to society of their introduction.

If a consequence of cost internalization was the loss of some socially beneficial innovations that would otherwise have been introduced,
this was increasingly regarded as a small price to pay for the avoidance
of future damage from innovations having high social costs. Behind
this view implicitly lay a changed assumption regarding the net balance between the goods and bads of the totality of innovations coming
into the market as compared with the past. There was greater public
and political sensitivity to the potential negatives relative to the posi-
tives of new technology.

There have been two principal mechanisms for the internalization
of the social costs of innovation, although both are aimed at economic
activity in general rather than specifically at innovation or new technology as such.

First is legislation authorizing regulation of industrial activities or
products by special agencies created for the purpose, for example, the
Environmental Protection Agency (EPA), or the Occupational Safety
and Health Administration (OSHA) of the Department of Labor. Here

there has been a trend over time to permit less and less discretion to regulators in the interpretation and implementation of the statutes, usually by incorporating quantitative standards and explicit time deadlines. This strategy has been based on the "capture" theory of the politics of regulation, which holds that over time regulators tend to become intellectually captive to the organizations they are regulating (through continual contacts and familiarity with their problems) and that therefore their discretionary authority to make policy judgments and interpretations of legislative intent have to be closely circumscribed.

Second is the extension of the concept of tort liability to include "strict liability" and "joint and several liability" and other concepts which do not necessitate a showing of intent or negligence (or sometimes even of direct causality) to make an organization liable for payment of compensation to individuals or groups believed to be damaged by the deployment of technology. Liability adjudicated in the courts goes beyond regulation in that an innovator is not exempt from the payment of damages (sometimes including punitive treble damages) even if he had strictly observed all the relevant statutes and administrative regulations existing at the time he introduced the innovation. The burden of proof is thus on the innovator to show that he essentially left no stone unturned, nor ignored any potentially relevant scientific evidence, in assessing the possible adverse effects of his technology before introducing it into the market.

IMPACTS ON THE RATE OF INNOVATION

The question that increasingly arises is what effect these new risks have on the rate of innovation and on economic application of new technology and, ultimately, on the overall rate of economic growth and improvement in the general welfare. In other words, what, if any, losses of welfare are being sustained by society as a result of the effort to deter socially irresponsible innovation by imposing its costs on innovators rather than society as a whole?

The first and most obvious thing that can be said in answer is that it depends more on the predictability of the costs to be borne by the innovator than on the exact magnitude of these costs. If the innovator knows the standards his product or process will have to meet, he should be able to incur most of the necessary costs of meeting them before he has to decide on the price that he will have to charge for his product. He can asses the potential market on the basis of that assumed price. Furthermore, he can be reasonably assured that at least his competitors in the *domestic* market will be held to the same standard. Only if he is forced to meet standards imposed retroactively, or is judged liable for damages because of side effects he failed to anticipate, will he face an unpredictable risk, and hence a cost not anticipated when he priced his product or service. In the case of regulation this has proved to be a problem only for a few technologies—most notably nuclear power—for which fairly extensive retrofitting has been required late in construction, or even after the plant has been in routine operation for some time. Even in this case it has been at least theoretically possible to recover such retrofitting costs through higher electricity rates over a period of time.

For foreign competitors in the domestic market, product standards are no different than for domestic manufacturers, so that it is only negative externalities or social costs incurred in the manufacturing process itself that can be a factor in competition. It does not appear to me that health, safety, and environmental factors have actually been a serious competitive factor compared to differential direct labor costs between foreign and domestic producers. Only in the case of a few extraction industries can one make much of a case for the effect of such regulation on competition, and here we are not dealing primarily with innovations but only with ongoing economic activity. When all competitors in a given market have to bear essentially the same costs of negative externalities, these costs can be passed on to consumers. Only if the relative costs of meeting regulatory standards differ significantly among individual producers will they affect competitive advantage. Also, if the demand for the product or service is highly price elastic, the rate of growth of the market may be significantly reduced by internalized costs, and this could be an important factor in the time required to recover initial development and introduction costs for a new technology. From a societal point of view, however, this restraint of demand for a product with serious externalities may be desirable.

There have been quite a few econometric studies of the direct economic impact of regulation, and the consensus conclusion which seems to emerge is that such impact has been quite modest, accounting for only a small reduction in the rate of economic growth or productivity growth. Even in the rather extreme case of nuclear power, unusually long planning horizons combined with much slower than expected demand growth (due more to slow overall GNP growth than to conservation of electricity), appear to have been more important than regulation per se as a cause of the reduced demand for new plants. Such economic impacts of regulation as there are seem to be due to the unpredictability of regulatory costs in individual instances rather than to the costs per se. Evidence for this is the wide variation in the construction costs of nuclear plants of very similar design in different utilities. While regulatory retrofit has doubtless been a factor here, it is not clear that it has been as important as just plain managerial competence.

However, the direct economic costs of regulation may be far from the whole story. The diversion of management attention from overall technological strategy in world markets to meeting regulatory requirements is hard to quantify in economic terms but may be much more important. It has put lawyers and accountants in the driver's seat and subtly changed the criteria of managerial performance from competitive success to satisfying the regulators and the vocal public interest groups. Managements have become defensive and public-relations conscious, paying more attention to the regulatory environment than to what their competitors are doing, especially their foreign competitors.

Judicial liability may be even more important in discouraging innovation just because it is more unpredictable and open-ended with respect to cost. A few extremely large and apparently capricious awards may change the psychological climate for innovation way out of proportion to the actual economic significance of average awards.

INTERNATIONAL COMPARISONS

In public discussion of the governance of technology in the United States, relatively little attention has been given to comparison with other industrialized countries. However, there have been a number of recent comparative studies on the use of scientific information by political authorities and regulators in different political systems. I recently chaired an international "forum" at the International Institute for Applied Systems Analysis (IIASA) on "science for public policy" which involved policy analysts from the United States, Western Europe, and several Eastern Bloc countries including the USSR.[14] Also,

Sheila Jasanoff of Cornell University has recently published a book on comparative risk assessment in Europe and the United States, based partly on her own research with Ronald Brickman and partly on an international conference on the subject held at the Rockefeller Foundation conference center in Bellagio.[15]

Howard Kunreuther of the Wharton School, University of Pennsylvania, recently edited a volume for IIASA on the comparative use of technical information and probabilistic risk analysis in decisions about the siting of storage facilities for liquified natural gas (LNG) in five countries.[16] Ronald Brickman and Dorothy Nelkin of Cornell have also published extensively on this subject.[17]

The results of this comparative work are in strong conflict with a widespread view that "good science" can be or ought to be the primary determinant of risk management policy. There are wide divergences in the way the same scientific information is used in different political systems and in the relative roles of scientists and politically accountable public officials in the establishment of policies and standards. Paradoxically, in the United States much more is expected from science and much more demanded of scientists in the regulatory process, but less weight is given to scientific judgments in actual decisions or in the establishment of broad policy. This is especially striking in the establishment of "cancer policy" in different countries, on which much of the research mentioned above has been focused. The fragmentation of political power in the United States both increases the demand for a clear and explicit scientific rationale for risk decisions and encourages sharp competition among different perceptions of risk by different pressure groups and different scientific elites. In the United States it is presumed that political policy judgments have to supplement (and sometimes precede) scientific evaluation of risks and that such policies can and should be formulated as explicitly written guidelines or "inference rules" available for public examination. In this way any weaknesses in scientific argument or inconsistencies with earlier policies or decisions are open to any interest group prepared to challenge a particular decision. Indeed, challenges in court or in administrative hearings to particular decisions are often used as a vehicle for raising the same generic issues repeatedly in different forums. An extensive, publicly available "paper trail," open to subsequent judicial review, accompanies every administrative decision.

In Europe, in contrast, risk decisions tend to be managed on a case-by-case basis by "neutral" civil servants with minimal externally imposed policy guidelines. These decisions are delegated to expert committees, whose deliberations are usually confidential, so that there is no clear record of the principles of scientific interpretation followed in individual cases or of changes in these principles over time as scientific understanding improves.

One consequence of these differences is that in the United States, advances in scientific knowledge pose a much more fundamental challenge to the continuity and internal consistency of the risk management process, since new knowledge almost invariably tends to throw doubt on established assumptions about risk and to reveal errors in past policy decisions. In the European process of delegation to expert committees, these inconsistencies can be papered over in the informal discretionary judgments of the experts. The public is generally inclined simply to accept these judgments without examining in detail the reasoning behind them. Thus, paradoxically, the European system seems to afford a better opportunity to adjust policy to changing science. Experts are under less political pressure to maintain consistency, in part because Europeans are much more accustomed to accepting qualitative judgments of professional civil servants who are above party and do not change with the political cast of the government in power. In fact, in the United States the greater proclivity for challenging expert judgments may be related in subtle ways to the decline of the party system.

The normal operation of science that does not have immediate policy implications allows a great deal more scope for informal, discretionary judgments and for intuition and subjectivity than the usual accounts of "scientific method" would have us believe. Indeed, without such informality, and the degree of mutual trust among scientists which it presupposes, science would advance much more slowly than it does. Yet in the American system of "science for policy," where everything has to be explicit and open to public challenge, the informality of normal science cannot be tolerated in regulatory science. Thus the rules of inference used in the interpretation of data have to be codified for the record and thereby become policy matters rather than purely scientific matters. For example, in "cancer policy" whether a substance is to be classified as a carcinogen on the basis of animal evidence alone is a policy matter, not just a matter of scientific judgment. In some cases, as in the famous Delaney Amendment, the rules of inference can become embedded in statute.[18]

In the United States, the necessities of policy science may actually feed back into the priorities for the conduct of normal science. This is because new scientific paradigms can quickly acquire broad social overtones (of which their originators may even be unaware) if they appear, or can be made to appear by others, to have policy implications that affect the prior public positions of influential players in the policy process. Because powerful interest groups are often working around the clock to seize on new paradigms to further their positions, the regulatory system's interest in closure and policy continuity can obstruct or distort the undertaking or utilization of research that tends to upset a bureaucratically acceptable approach to a problem such as risk management. The case of Bruce Ames's work on dietary carcinogens and mutagens of natural origin,[19] and the case of research on indoor radon concentrations resulting from energy conservation measures,[20] provide two striking examples of this. A plausible inference from the Ames work might be that much of the effort that has been devoted to regulation of industrially produced synthetic chemicals and wastes is misplaced from a public health standpoint, and that priorities should be shifted to the analysis and control of dietary carcinogens and anticarcinogens to which humans are exposed in larger numbers and in higher concentrations than industrial chemicals. A similar change in priorities away from the regulation of nuclear power toward attention to natural sources of radiation exposure might similarly be inferred from recent studies of the radon problem—if achievement of the greatest improvement in public health for a given expenditure of public resources is taken as the goal. I am not suggesting that these policy conclusions follow automatically or logically from the data, but interest groups have already seized on the research results to support the policies they have always advocated, while others have opposed such research as a smoke screen designed to undermine environmental laws.

LESSONS OF COMPARISON

What, then, can we learn from the comparative study of European and American approaches to the use of science for policy in the governance of technology and the management of risk? In the first place, it seems that actual outcomes of the regulatory process in other countries are, on average, little different from those in the United States, despite the much greater political turbulence and energy in the U.S. system. In particular, the United States appears to be ahead in the protection of public health from the effects of automobile emissions, while Europe appears to be ahead in the management of hazardous chemical wastes. Delegation of more discretionary authority to committees of experts, and the use of consensual modes of decision making involving industry, do not appear to have appreciably degraded standards, and in many cases have resulted in more expeditious establishment of *some* standard. Jasanoff states: "In their four-country survey of chemical control policies, Brickman et al. found that significant regulatory end points, such as the number of carcinogens subjected to public control, seem roughly comparable in all four countries over time. Badaracco's case study of vinyl chloride regulation reaches a similar conclusion."[21] The American system places much greater emphasis on process relative to outcomes than other national systems, and some evidence indicates that this tends to increase the perceived legitimacy of outcomes in the United States, though frequently at the expense of paralysis in decision making and long delays that are costly to producers and innovators and, at the same time, costly in delaying the implementation of needed environmental protection measures while the search for elusive scientific precision proceeds.

On the question of who should bear the cost of externalities, I believe that too doctrinaire insistence on the "polluter pays" principle, or its equivalent for other kinds of externalities, often holds up viable solutions to urgent problems. The demonstration effect of initial public investments in hazardous substance or effluent management may in many cases expedite the identification and validation of satisfactory (though perhaps less than ideal) solutions to externality problems, thereby accelerating their adoption and widespread deployment in practice. Demonstration through public investment of the feasibility and economics of waste management technologies on a realistic scale can be important in solidifying the political case for regulation. This appears to have been true for the management of hazardous solid wastes in Europe, for example. A balance has to be struck between the deterrence of irresponsible or premature deployment of new technologies and the deterrence of all innovation until all its potential external costs have been assessed and dealt with.

Yet it is also true that technology-forcing legislation has had desirable effects in stimulating innovation and even in rejuvenating the propensity for innovation in an entire industry because of synergy between the innovations required for health, safety, or environmental protection and other innovations for advances in productivity, efficiencies in resource consumption, or product performance. There is some indication that this is what happened in the United States auto industry as a result of the legislation forcing emission controls. A number of innovative companies such as Minnesota Mining and Manufacturing (3M) have found that the search for ways of reducing or eliminating unwanted effluents has led to the development of new and cheaper production processes. In addition, regulation has created brand new markets for analytical and effluent monitoring instrumentation and for safety devices. Indeed, one recent study of the effects of government intervention in markets on innovation suggested that competition in the development of technologies to meet government regulations was the single most important government-derived stimulus to technological innovation.[22]

As for the future, I think we may expect to see increasing convergence between U.S. and European styles in using science for regulation and policymaking. One reason for this belief is the observation that twenty years ago the U.S. approach to the role of science in regulation was very similar to what the European approach is now, as noted, for example, by Philip Harter, who has pointed out that in the original philosophy of regulation established during the days of the New Deal, public servants were regarded as viable custodians for "the public interest" which they could be trusted to determine in an impartial and objective manner with the aid of science.[23] In other countries, we will see a trend toward opening up the decision process to public participation much as has happened in the United States in the past twenty years. However, we will also see a trend toward the use of informal consensus-building among diverse stakeholders prior to formal regulatory processes in the United States.

Majone has pointed out that the universalistic norms of science vary a great deal from field to field.[24] Generally they are greatest in the most abstract fields, such as physics and mathematics, and are least in the fields of science that are generally most relevant to regulation and policymaking. But as international institutions become more important in the establishment of the scientific basis for regulation (e.g., because more and more environmental problems transcend national boundaries and because more and more goods affected by safety and health standards will move in international trade), it seems likely that regulatory science will become increasingly subject to universalistic norms, and this will probably spill over from the purely scientific into the procedural aspects of the interactions between science and policy.

CONCLUSIONS

In the history of Western economic development, experimentation and social selection of successful experiments has been a powerful engine of economic progress. To some extent the encouragement of experimentation has been believed to entail the exemption of innovators from having to pay for the "external" costs resulting from the economic utilization of their innovations, allowing such costs to be shifted onto society as a whole. In the last fifty to one hundred years—but at an accelerated pace in the last two decades—there have been growing political pressures to "internalize" these social costs, and thus make them an additional risk attached to the process of innovation and hence on the incentives to the innovator. The balance of benefits and costs to society of this internalization process is now a matter of intense public debate, which involves not only whether costs should be internalized but *how* they should be internalized. The "how" question also raises the issue of the appropriate role of experts in relation to the general public in the legislative, administrative, and judicial processes by which this internalization takes place. A growing divergence of practices between the United States and other countries does not appear to have produced any striking difference in *outcomes* either with respect to the protection of public health and the environment or with respect to the rate of innovation and its benefits to the public, but the jury is still out on this question. At the same time convergence seems to be taking place among differing national norms, so that the universality of science is likely to extend gradually to the *use* of science, both social and natural, in the process of controlling technology.

ANALYZING TECHNOLOGICAL RISKS IN

FEDERAL REGULATORY AGENCIES

MICHAEL E. KRAFT

Few question the manifold contributions of technology to modern life, from improved medical services to rising levels of material comfort. But as economists are fond of saying, there is no such thing as a free lunch. There is also no such thing as risk-free technology, as is evident in contemporary efforts to deal with carcinogens in drinking water, toxic pollutants in the air, and radioactive wastes from nuclear power plants, among other hazards. In return for the considerable benefits of modern technology and the economic growth it has made possible, we pay a price, not always knowingly or voluntarily, in exposure to a wide variety of what are usually termed technological risks. Sometimes these are referred to as hazards or threats, which suggests an absolute danger. More commonly today they are called risks, which implies uncertainty or variable probability of danger. Whichever term is used, increasingly they have received attention in the mass media and have become a major object of public concern.

Governments in the United States and other Western democracies have responded to this concern over the past two decades as one might expect when such issues become salient: there has been a vast out-pouring of legislation intended to eliminate the hazards, or more accurately, to reduce the risks. In particular, dozens of public policies focusing on health, safety, and environmental quality have been adopted and implemented by the U.S. government despite often intense and persistent opposition by the regulated parties, usually industry.[1] In order to meet their new, extensive, and complex responsibilities for managing technological hazards or risks, regulatory agencies such as the Environmental Protection Agency (EPA), the Occupational Safety and Health Administration (OSHA), and the Nuclear Regulatory Commission (NRC) have turned increasingly to formal methods of risk assessment. These methods have been seen as major tools for aiding decision makers in setting priorities among competing programs and risks, and in determining "reasonable" safety standards in light of the inevitable costs imposed by regulation.

But how should we determine the appropriate level of safety? What methods and procedures should be used to identify, measure, and compare risks? How accurate and reliable are those methods? Can they be used confidently when there is so much uncertainty over how risky certain technologies and activities are? Given the intensity of political conflict over regulation and its costs, a lively debate has arisen over just how much protection from various risks is necessary. There are sharp disagreements over who should make such decisions and how they should make them; these disputes extend to the question of the extent to which regulatory policy decisions should be based on risk assessment and related methods like cost-benefit analysis.[2]

In this chapter I examine public concern over risks and the consequent growth in demand for risk assessment, provide a brief overview of the leading methods and procedures, and try to sort out conflicting perspectives on the promise, pitfalls, and use of risk assessment. Much of the debate over these methods is innocent of empirical data; arguments are often based upon ideology, speculation, and faith in—or distrust of—science or analysis. But if recommendations are to be proffered for changing the way we use risk assessment in governing technology, we need to know more about the actual employment of the methods in regulatory agencies. For that reason, I also pay some attention to evidence of how agency staff and policy officials have used risk analysis in recent years, and the problems they most frequently encounter.

There is a thesis in what follows. It is that risk assessment is an important and valuable technique despite some obvious methodological limitations and the potential for misuse. It is not a panacea for dealing with the multiple risks of a technological society. It is not intended to replace political interaction, concern for important public values, and careful judgment by scientists, regulators, and the public about proper levels of safety, trade-offs between risks and benefits, or priorities for our regulatory efforts. But if employed judiciously, and especially with sufficient regard for the uncertainty of scientific knowledge, risk assessment can tell us more accurately than otherwise possible what risks we face and what choices we have for dealing with them. Thus like other methods of policy analysis, by providing crucial information risk assessment can help in making sensible and responsible decisions. We are better off having such information than not having it, but its effect depends on our collective intelligence and care in using it.

CONTEMPORARY RISKS AND PUBLIC CONCERN

There is an understandable tendency to view health, safety, and environmental risks as a uniquely twentieth-century phenomenon and risk assessment as a strictly modern technique. We forget that man has coped for thousands of years with natural disasters, epidemic diseases, pollution of land and water, contamination of foods, transportation accidents, and occupational injuries, which have taken an enormous cumulative toll in human lives. In large part because the greatest risks to life were eliminated or reduced through improvements in nutrition, medical services, sanitation, working conditions, and the standard of living, average life expectancy has increased strikingly in the past five hundred years; in particular infant and child mortality rates have dropped sharply from their previously high levels.[3]

But as some authors argue, if we are living longer and better, why is it that we are feeling worse about life's risks?[4] Poll data indicate that we *are* more concerned; recent surveys show that 80 percent of the American public believes that we are subject to more risks today than twenty years ago.[5] That concern has much to do with the nature of contemporary risks. As Covello and Mumpower argue, many are fundamentally different in character and magnitude from those which were encountered in the past.

These include nuclear war, nuclear power plant accidents, radioactive waste, exposure to synthetic pesticides and chemicals, supertanker oil spills, chemical plant and storage accidents, recombinant DNA laboratory accidents, ozone depletion due to emission of fluorocarbons, and acid rain. The magnitude of many of these risks cannot easily be estimated because historical or actuarial data do not exist or are extremely difficult to collect. Moreover, cause-effect relationships are often highly problematic for these risks. Of perhaps greatest importance, many of these new risks are latent, long-term, involuntary, and irreversible. At least some are conceivably globally catastrophic, and most are derived from science and technology (in contrast to risks from "acts of nature or God").[6]

Studies by Paul Slovic and others indicate that lay people's risk perceptions and attitudes are closely related to two factors in particular: dread risk and unknown risk. The former refers to perceived lack of control, catastrophic potential, fatal consequences, and the inequitable distribution of risks and benefits; nuclear weapons, nuclear power, and radioactive waste score highest on this factor. The latter refers to hazards judged to be "unobservable, unknown, new, and delayed in their manifestation of harm."[7] Chemical technologies (e.g., toxic and hazardous materials) score highest on this factor. In short, where scientists and regulators focus on actual risk as measured by the probability of death, illness, or accidents, the general public is more concerned with the uncertainties of life's perils and the seriousness of their potential effects. Risk perceptions of this kind are affected by the way hazards are reported in the media and by cultural norms (such as sensitivity to environmental degradation) that have changed in recent years.[8] Both help to explain how concern over risks can rise even while living standards and life expectancy increase.

Some other technical, social, and political developments have contributed to heightened awareness of the newer risks. Scientists are now better able to identify and measure risks through a variety of new techniques that allow, for example, measurement of parts per billion. Also there are more scientists and analysts studying and writing about risk; public interest advocacy groups (especially environmental organizations) whose activities help to publicize risks are now more numerous and better organized; and there is more intensified coverage of risk problems in the media.[9] In addition, for a variety of reasons having to do with changes in the American political system in the 1970s, public concern over technological risks and demands for greater protection from them are given more weight than previously, especially in Congress and state legislatures.

Governments at all levels face important choices about how to respond to public concern and how to deal with such risks. Yet conventional approaches to decision making in both legislatures and bureaucracies are often inadequate. They may result in one of two undesirable conditions. First, risks may be exaggerated, leading to imposition of unnecessary or excessive regulations because it is politically popular to regulate when public concern is high and media coverage is extensive. Here we pay a price in added costs of compliance with the regulation and possibly wasteful diversion of economic resources. Second, risks may be ignored or underestimated because policy officials lack mechanisms of foresight to alert them to the risk early enough, or they are reluctant to act for political reasons before a hazard is apparent and public demand for action exists. In this instance we may fail to protect human health and environmental quality sufficiently, and severe or irreversible damage may occur. Risk assessment is one of a number of tools used to supplement normal processes of decision making that, at least in theory, can help in both of these situations.

ASSESSING AND EVALUATING RISKS

Some definitions are necessary before proceeding further. *Risk* itself is usually defined as the magnitude of adverse consequences of an event or exposure, and implies uncertainty about precisely what the event, exposure, or consequences are. *Risk assessment* refers to a number of methods used to both identify risks and estimate the probability and severity of harm associated with them; the harm is normally stated in terms of injury, disease, premature death to persons (i.e., dying at an earlier age than expected), damage to environmental quality, or loss of property. That is, assessment is in part a matter of estimating the probability that certain events will occur (e.g., a nuclear power plant accident) and in part an estimate of how serious the consequences might be if it does occur. One of the reasons why risk assessment is difficult to grasp is that it is concerned with estimating probability, a concept unfamiliar to much of the public and many elected officials. In fact, risk can be expressed as probability multiplied by consequences. Thus some threats (e.g., natural hazards) are described as low probability–high consequence risks; they are not very likely to happen, but if they do, there may be severe results.

Deciding what to do about technological risks—"managing" them —involves more than simply estimating probabilities and consequences. At some point there must be judgments made about what level of risk is tolerable or acceptable to society, and what constitutes safety. Indeed, such decisions are made at many points in the governmental process and are subject to revision as new information or changing perspectives warrant. William Lowrance expresses the need for this kind of judgment in his statement of what safety means in this context: "a thing is safe if its risks are judged to be acceptable."[10] Safety does not mean zero risk, but rather a level of risk that society believes is sufficiently low.

Who participates in this judgment process (e.g., technical experts, regulatory officials, or the general public) and whose views are ultimately decisive is important. Government may not need to regulate a risk at all if it is thought to be lower than the accepted level. Extensive regulation. may be called for if risks are believed to be too high. But determining the acceptability of risk, which some call *risk evaluation*, is a political rather than technical task. It involves personal and social value judgments about life, health, safety, or environmental quality for which there can be no substitute by professional risk assessors. They may be able, however, to assist the public, elected representatives, and agency policymakers in those difficult choices by providing pertinent information.

THE EVOLUTION OF RISK ASSESSMENT AND RISK EVALUATION

Methods of risk assessment gained prominence in the late 1960s with efforts to measure the risks associated with nuclear power plants, in particular the risk of catastrophic accidents. A 1969 article by Chauncey Starr was particularly influential; Starr developed a method for comparing technological risks and benefits through the use of "revealed preference" to answer the question, "How safe is safe enough?" After examining patterns of "acceptable" risk-benefit trade-offs for several industries and activities, he defended nuclear power by emphasizing the small risk of accidents and hence the safety of the plants compared to other activities.[11] Other risk assessments of nuclear power followed, the most famous of which was the Rasmussen report of 1975, which also showed that nuclear power plants had less risk than what society accepted from other sources.[12] As the deficiencies in these approaches and calculations became prominent, there was growing skepticism toward risk assessment itself. Some concluded that the methodologies were inherently flawed and would result in antiregulation or protechnology decisions whenever used.

Four other developments were to propel *risk analysis* (a term many use to refer to the combination of risk assessment and risk evaluation, and others use interchangeably with risk assessment) to the center of debates over regulation in the late 1970s and 1980s. First, as a result of the National Environmental Policy Act (NEPA) and other new acts of Congress, by the late 1970s technology assessments and environmental impact statements had become familiar components in environmental and related policymaking. After a shaky beginning they were increasingly seen not only as competent analyses that could be produced by professionals in and out of government, but as helpful in making important policy choices. Their familiarity and perceived value helped to make other forms of policy analysis, such as risk assessment and cost-benefit analysis, more acceptable.[13]

Second, implementation of the several dozen new environmental and consumer protection policies between the mid-1960s and the mid-1970s created a demand for such analysis. Most of these policies require some form of balancing of risks, benefits, and costs for the agencies to set "reasonable" standards. Table 9–1 indicates the pattern with five examples from the 1970s. A related cause of concern was the use of different guidelines and procedures for risk assessment and risk evaluation in various policy areas. Congress prefers to express regulatory goals and standards in general terms as table 9–1 shows. But that delegates the important decisions to the agencies and forces them to design their own procedures and to set regulatory standards in ways that can create added controversy. Critics of the agencies often focus on these bureaucratic procedures.[14]

Third, the economic and political climate had changed considerably by the late 1970s. Far more concern was exhibited for limiting government regulation; thus there was increased interest in how methods like risk assessment and cost-benefit analysis could be used to provide relief from what critics saw as irrational, inefficient, and costly regulatory policies. As early as 1973, congressional committees criticized EPA for inadequate scientific and technical information to support its regulatory efforts; four years later the National Research Council substantiated these charges.[15] But the criticism of EPA and other regulatory agencies intensified during the Carter administration, and it became even more pronounced under President Reagan. Conservative public policy journals such as *The Public Interest* and *Regulation* frequently added fuel to the fire by publishing polemical critiques of overzealous regulation of what were described as trivial risks.[16] Court decisions in the early 1980s on OSHA's benzene and cotton dust regulations were also important in furthering the use of these methods.[17]

Finally, risk analysis has emerged in the last decade as an identifiable discipline and profession. It has its own professional societies, meetings, journals, and practitioners who are part of a risk community, chiefly in and around Washington, D.C. In line with those developments, the scientific literature on risk analysis has grown at a rapid pace, with considerable assistance from the National Science Foundation and other funding agencies.[18]

Against this backdrop, it is easy to understand both the widespread appeal of risk analysis in the 1980s and the continuing doubts by some about the wisdom of using these methods in regulatory agencies. After a review of the methods employed, I shall turn to some empirical data that help to assess the conflicting arguments of advocates and critics of risk analysis. That exercise also suggests some ways to meet the objections raised by the critics and yet improve the capacity of government to use these methods responsibly.

ANALYTIC METHODS AND THEIR LIMITATIONS

Most of the controversy surrounding risk analysis concerns the methods of risk assessment (that is, how we estimate the severity of risk), but there are additional concerns about risk evaluation methods and decisions about actual safety levels to be set. It is worthwhile to examine both.

Proponents of risk assessment often assert, as did former EPA administrator William Ruckelshaus in a frequently cited article in *Science*, that "there is an objective way to assess risk," even if there is "no purely objective way to manage it."[19] In distinguishing the two separate processes of estimation and management, Ruckelshaus was echoing the conventional wisdom dating back to William Lowrance's 1976 work and a later review by the National Research Council.[20] However, even Ruckelshaus noted that quantitative risk assessment is a product of "a shotgun wedding between science and the law."[21] The

Table 9-1. Examples of Health, Safety, and Environmental
Protection Policies That Require or Permit Balancing
of Risks, Costs, and Benefits

Policy	General Statement of Purpose	Basis for Agency Action or Degree of Protection	Basis of the Legislation
Safe Drinking Water Act (EPA) 1974	"To assure that the public is provided with safe drinking water"	Protect health to the extent feasible, taking costs into consideration.	Balancing
Consumer Product Safety Act (CPSC) 1972	"To protect the public against unreasonable risks of injury associated with consumer products"	"Standard shall be reasonably necessary to prevent or reduce an unreasonable risk of injury."	Balancing: "unreasonable risk"
Toxic Substances Control Act (EPA) 1976	"To assure that innovation and commerce in chemical substances do not present an unreasonable risk of injury to health or the environment."	Actions are based on "unreasonable risk" to health or the environment, or imminent and unreasonable risk to serious or widespread injury.	Balancing: "unreasonable risk"
Hazardous Materials Transportation Act (DOT) 1975	"To protect the nation adequately against the risks to life and property which are inherent in the transportation of hazardous materials in commerce."	Regulation of any hazardous material if there is an "unreasonable risk" to health and safety, and standards are "necessary or appropriate."	Balancing "unreasonable risk"; "necessary or appropriate"
Federal Insecticide, Fungicide,	"To protect against unreasonable risks to man or the envi-	Registration decisions are based on "unreasonable	Balancing: "unreasonable adverse effects"—

Table 9-1. (continued)

Policy	General Statement of Purpose	Basis for Agency Action or Degree of Protection	Basis of the Legislation
and Rodenti- cide Act (EPA) 1972	ronment, or survi- val of a species, from pesticides."	adverse effects on the environment or will involve unrea- sonable hazard to the survival of a species declared endangered."	"unreasonable risk to man or the envi- ronment taking into account the economic, social, and environmental costs and benefits."

latter comment may more accurately characterize the current state of the art in risk assessment. It *can* be objective, but there are major methodological problems in applying this approach to many contemporary risks, and no shortage of scientific disputes over theories, measurements, and assumptions even in areas where there has been extensive experience with these techniques, such as testing potential carcinogens.[22]

Some risks are easy to calculate and there is little reason to doubt the objectivity of the assessment. For example, reasonably good historical data tell us how many Americans are killed or injured each year in accidents (92,500 were killed in 1985, about 5 percent of all deaths, and another nine million suffered disabling injuries). Likewise, we know the frequency of natural hazards such as earthquakes, floods, and hurricanes. Thus an estimate of current or future risk can be made through statistical inference.[23] But in other policy areas the assessment is not so simple because there has been no experience with the risk. In many cases the only data available may come from experiments, which require extrapolation from an animal population to humans. The challenge of risk assessment in this situation should be described to better explain the skepticism often expressed about these methods.

For most regulatory decisions made by the EPA, OSHA, the Consumer Product Safety Commission (CPSC), and the Food and Drug Administration (FDA) which concern human health, and especially protection from potential carcinogens, there is a series of similar steps in performing a risk assessment: (1) a *hazard identification* (e.g., whether a specific chemical is or is not linked causally to particular health effects), (2) a *dose-response assessment* (determining the relationship between the magnitude of exposure and the probability of occurrence of a health effect), (3) an *exposure assessment* (determining the extent of human exposure before and after the application of regulatory controls), and (4) a *risk characterization* (a description of the nature and usually the magnitude of risk to humans, with its attendant uncertainty).[24] These components of risk assessment are portrayed in figure 9–1, which also shows the relationship between technical assessments and the larger process of risk management.

None of these activities is easy, and a good deal of uncertainty necessarily characterizes the whole process. Moreover, at each step a number of both scientific and policy judgments are required to determine which methods to use and how to infer human risk from limited data or data drawn from animal exposure. The data gathering itself is involved, time-consuming, and expensive. While there has been considerable agreement among the agencies mentioned on guidelines for making these kinds of decisions, efforts by the Reagan administration to alter them (to substitute less conservative or more risk-tolerant standards) indicate that they remain controversial.[25]

The scientific work is only the beginning of the risk management process, which includes risk evaluation, as figure 9–1 illustrates. Once the assessment itself is done, typically it is sent to an office of regulatory analysis, where some form of economic and policy evaluation is completed. A number of policy options may be considered at this stage. In some cases these are iterative processes, with repeated discussions among regulatory officials and scientific staff, involving multiple studies and draft reports. The National Research Council succinctly described the process: "After the various uncertainties are assessed, the policy choices may still be far from obvious. The policymaker has to consider, formally or informally, the alternative actions he or she might pursue, the intellectual and political constraints, value and ideological judgments, and so on. This is risk evaluation."[26]

Value judgments are an inherent part of risk evaluation and they are reflected in many decisions already made, for example in the laws, policies, moral principles, and other constraints on the process of evaluation, and in the choice of risk assessment methods themselves.

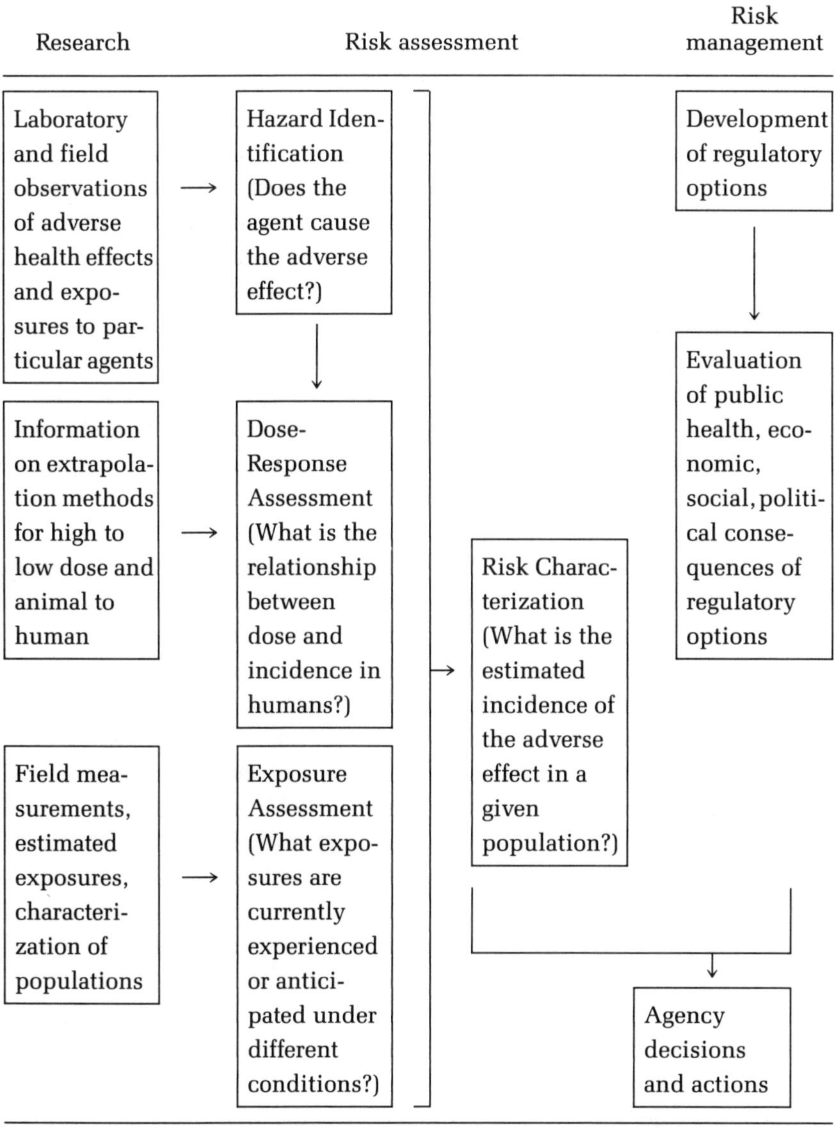

Research	Risk assessment	Risk management

Laboratory and field observations of adverse health effects and exposures to particular agents →

Hazard Identification (Does the agent cause the adverse effect?)

Development of regulatory options

Information on extrapolation methods for high to low dose and animal to human →

Dose-Response Assessment (What is the relationship between dose and incidence in humans?)

Risk Characterization (What is the estimated incidence of the adverse effect in a given population?)

Evaluation of public health, economic, social, political consequences of regulatory options

Field measurements, estimated exposures, characterization of populations →

Exposure Assessment (What exposures are currently experienced or anticipated under different conditions?)

Agency decisions and actions

Figure 9-1. Elements of Risk Assessment and Risk Management. Source: National Research Council, Committee on the Institutional Means for Assessment of Risks to Public Health, *Risk Assessment in the Federal Government: Managing the Process* (Washington, D.C.: National Academy Press, 1983), p. 21.

Because these values are a central part of determining safety levels, even if typically implicit rather than explicit, some writers such as Lowrance offer guidelines for making choices about risk acceptability. He includes such considerations as whether a risk is accepted voluntarily or is borne involuntarily, whether the effects are immediate or delayed, whether there are alternatives available, whether the risk is known with certainty or unknown, whether exposure is essential or a luxury, and whether the consequences are reversible or irreversible.[27]

Beyond such guidelines, there is wide acknowledgment that such value judgments must be made, that they are essentially political or policy decisions, and that, where permitted by law, they are likely to reflect the priorities and preferences of a given presidential administration. Thus it comes as no surprise that the Carter administration favored stronger environmental protection actions than the Reagan administration. However, risk analysts employ a number of methods to help inform the choices made by policy officials regardless of their initial preconceptions. These methods include four that merit special note: revealed preferences, expressed preferences, natural standards, and risk-cost-benefit analysis.[28]

The method of *revealed preferences* uses past risk-acceptance decisions as a basis for comparing the acceptability of new risks. The results are often stated in terms of the comparative probability of a fatality or a reduction in life expectancy as a consequence of engaging in different activities or exposure at a certain level. If the new risks provide similar benefits but do not exceed the level of risk that has been historically tolerated, they might be judged acceptable. As noted above, Starr used this approach in evaluating the risk of a severe accident in nuclear power plants. Many others have compiled risk compendiums in which a series of hazardous activities are compared in terms of their impact on life or longevity. Typically these include a number of ordinary activities, such as driving automobiles or riding a bicycle, from which one might infer people's "preferences" for safety; that is, one's tolerance of risk is supposedly revealed by such common (and thus accepted) behavior. Based on that assumption, one might say that people are probably willing to accept new or unusual risks of a comparable magnitude. In one such compendium, for example, Wilson found that the following activities are equally risky and likely to increase the chances of death by one in one million: smoking 1.4 cigarettes, living two days in New York or Boston (air pollution), traveling 150 miles by car (accidents), eating forty tablespoons of peanut butter (aflatoxin), or living 150 years within twenty miles of a nuclear power plant (radiation).[29]

These kinds of comparisons are often cited by critics of regulation, who especially note the wide variance in cost per life saved of government regulation of such diverse risks. For example, an Office of Management and Budget (OMB) economist reported that the cost ranged from $100,000 per life saved for steering column protection and ventilation requirements for space heaters to hundreds of millions of dollars for some rejected EPA regulations on radionuclides, benzene, and arsenic. Six final EPA rules examined were estimated to save a *total* of five lives per year, which is why the cost per life saved is so high in these cases. Such studies also show that safety regulation is far more cost-effective than health regulation.[30]

Instead of trying to infer risk preferences from behavior, the method of *expressed preferences* is more direct; public and expert opinion is measured through survey research that attempts to identify and explain the risks that are explicitly considered to be acceptable. Such research has indicated that public perception of risk is often quite different from actual risk, and that public ranking of risks differs markedly from expert judgment of the same risks. For example, the public fears nuclear power plants far more than experts think is reasonable and it underestimates the risk from other electric-generating plants and from X-rays. But the public and experts agree on the high risk of smoking and use of motor vehicles.[31] The public's perception is significantly influenced by the way the media report risks; hence research on expressed preferences may be helpful in improving communication among lay persons, technical experts, and decision makers. But there are some difficulties in using these studies, including biases in individual perceptions of risks and benefits which can vary both from individual to individual and over time for a given individual. Moreover, riskiness means more to people than, for example, the expected number of fatalities or cancers that may result from an increased exposure. For that reason among others, Paul Slovic, a major researcher in the field, urges that "attempts to characterize, compare, and regulate risks must be sensitive to this broader conception of risk."[32]

Use of the *natural standards* approach avoids the possible bias of both revealed preferences and expressed preferences by appealing to geologic and biological risk factors that are naturally occurring, and in particular are assumed to have been present during human evolution. If we have long tolerated such conditions, the level of risk represented may be taken as a kind of baseline against which technological (man-made) risks can be compared. Risks that are lower than natural standards (e.g., background radiation) might be considered to be acceptable and those which exceed those standards might be viewed as unacceptable.

Finally, *risk-cost-benefit analysis* is used to make explicit comparisons between the benefits derived from a hazardous activity and the risks, or costs, that are involved. If all major benefits and costs (direct and indirect, short term and long term) are considered, alternative courses of action might be compared to see which yields the greater balance of benefits over risks or costs. Of course, costs and benefits are not easily quantifiable, and some may not be considered at all. But where estimates can be made and a common denominator used (typically monetary), there can be a comparable basis for evaluating risks and determining which are acceptable. Given the prevailing concern over the economic impact of regulation, and the requirement of most statutes that "reasonable" standards be adopted, this method has an obvious appeal.[33] Under Executive Order 12291, issued by President Reagan in February 1981, cost-benefit analysis is required for major regulations. The order states that "regulatory action shall not be undertaken unless the potential benefits to society from the regulation outweigh the potential costs to society."[34]

Difficulties in using risk-cost-benefit analysis include the sensitive issue of how to value the benefits of reduced risk; this cannot be avoided in regulatory decision making although it is not always explicitly stated.[35] For example, as part of the effort to comply with the Reagan executive order, federal agencies have used dollar estimates for a human life that range from about $400,000 to $7 million, with an average of about $2 million.[36] Among other significant defects, the usual representation of risks, costs, and benefits is in terms of mortality averted (i.e., dollars per life saved). But a focus on lives alone ignores chronic or acute disease and discomfort, injury and incapacity, and loss of environmental amenities; hence only one important benefit (lives saved) may be counted. In addition, there is often little attention paid to whether the risks are imposed involuntarily on a population or are assumed voluntarily, which makes a great difference in how people judge their acceptability.

One could make a good case for improving the nation's capacity to anticipate, prevent, or reduce technological risks through use of these various methods of risk analysis. Several authors have tried to do so.[37] However, many students of regulatory policy—and technology and politics more generally—remain skeptical, and considerable controversy surrounds the conduct and use of these methods in regulating technology. The reasons are clear enough. Risk management policies are enormously important for public values such as health, occupational safety, and environmental quality. But many see the methods as insufficiently developed and subject to politicization within the agencies. These conditions help to explain the range of views on what some believe is a largely scientific enterprise and others consider to be little more than sorcery with numbers attached.

As discussed above, proponents of risk analysis argue that such an approach is necessitated by the wide range of technological risks of varying magnitude to which society is exposed and the numerous risk-reduction policies now in place. They believe that these methodologies are sound enough to contribute to what they regard as improvement in the rationality of regulatory decision making; they assume that reliable scientific data on the extent of risk can be compiled and that the costs of risk reduction can be calculated, thereby allowing for comparative risk analysis and priority setting.[38]

In contrast, critics of these methodologies, including spokespersons for many environmental and consumer protection groups, legislative staff members, and a number of academics, argue that risk analysis is an inexact science at best; they believe it is burdened by too many methodological limitations to be of much value in these kinds of decisions. They are skeptical that risks can be estimated accurately, that the benefits of risk reduction can be identified and measured as thoroughly as the costs, and that the risks, benefits, and costs can be fairly evaluated by all agencies.[39]

Some writers, for example Langdon Winner, suspect that the entire enterprise of risk assessment will have the effect of delaying or curtailing efforts to eliminate important societal hazards by portraying them as merely "risks" and thus possibly worth taking. Winner notes that the early stages of development of new technologies like passenger trains and jet aircraft have often involved a "period of trial and error in which people were killed or injured." But a "commonly accepted norm is that obvious sources of harm must be eliminated through either private or public action; otherwise the very usefulness of the device will be called into question."[40] What price do we pay, then, when society is deprived of that source of error detection and stimulus for reform (or elimination) of dangerous technologies?

In a similar vein, some critics have focused on the ethical implications of using such underdeveloped and, in their judgment, overly quantitative methods that seriously misrepresent hazards imposed on a population or ignore important value questions in dealing with them.[41] Many others have pointed to the politicization of risk decisions in the Reagan administration as evidence that their concern for misuse of these methods is warranted.[42]

RISK ANALYSIS IN PRACTICE: EXPERIENCE IN THE AGENCIES

Given all the uncertainty involved in risk analysis and the passion with which liberals and conservatives argue about the merits of governmental regulation, it is easy to understand that the methods themselves often become the focus of debate. The proponents of risk analysis assume that if the right methods are used, the outcome will naturally yield rational (superior) decisions; many critics believe that the methods are so flawed that no use at all is warranted, and that somehow we should be able to make better decisions without them. Both may be faulted on the grounds of unwarranted technological determinism; that is, they believe the methods themselves determine the outcome one way or the other. But this is rarely the case. *How* the methods are used makes a difference. A more logical argument is to acknowledge that the methods have serious limitations, some of which are inherent, that they may be misused by those unfamiliar with or insensitive to those limitations, and thus that some procedural safeguards are needed to insure that they are used properly. Those procedures might include peer review of scientific assumptions, data, and findings; guidelines for communication of risk studies (e.g., how to report uncertainty); and various mechanisms to insure the accountability of agency decision makers.

To find out how methodological inadequacies and biased judgments in use of risk analysis actually affect government regulation, we need to examine the record of agency actions. Empirical studies of agency decision making are scarce, and rely primarily on public hearings, court decisions, and agency files. To add perspective to the written evidence, in 1981 I interviewed technical staff and policy officials using risk analysis at EPA, OSHA, NRC, CPSC, FDA, and the Materials Transportation Bureau of the Department of Transportation, which regulates the shipment of hazardous materials. The research is reported elsewhere, and I will refer here only selectively to the findings.[43]

To begin, it was apparent even in 1981 that the use of risk analysis within the agencies was increasing compared with five to ten years earlier. Most of those interviewed supported continued use of these techniques, especially when accompanied by methodological refinements and greater sensitivity to their limitations as tools of policy analysis. But attitudes of staff and policy officials ranged from highly positive to strongly negative, and I found significant variation among agencies in their use of risk analysis. In some it was merely reviewed and discussed by technical staff, whereas in other agencies the analyses were a major influence in policy decisions. However, there were only rare instances where the analysis itself was the determinative factor in a policy decision.

There are many reasons for the distinctions among agencies. They deal with different kinds of policy problems, operate under different statutory mandates, are affected by their varied institutional settings, and recruit different kinds of staff and policy officials. The agencies also have quite different levels of resources and capabilities for performing or using risk analyses, which can be expensive. Of course, some of these patterns may have changed since 1981, particularly given the imposition of Executive Order 12291 early in the Reagan administration; as noted above, that order required cost-benefit analysis for all major proposed regulations, and thus both increased the need to conduct risk assessments and the probability that they would be influential. There has been a good deal of popular commentary on some of these changes and their effects, but no systematic study of comparative agency behavior.[44]

Along with the increased use of risk analysis, the interviews indicated that there was a consensus emerging in the early 1980s on the best methodologies to use; this was especially true for assessment of suspected carcinogens. Thus one OSHA staff member acknowledged, "We use EPA methodology in a lot of our work. The work has undergone critical reviews and represents a reasonable state-of-the-art approach, we feel, to some of these problems." There was no consensus, however, on the best procedures to follow in the agencies for integrating risk analyses with the other tasks involved in setting and enforcing regulations.

The interviews also elicited widespread acknowledgment that despite such consensus on methods, risk analysis presented a host of technical and evaluation problems. Those most often mentioned included an inadequate data base (e.g., insufficient data on the incidence and causes of illness and death), the difficulty of estimating the impact of low probability–high consequence hazards, the challenge of analyzing phenomena at the limits of scientific understanding (e.g., acid rain or global climatic changes from carbon dioxide buildup), uncertainty over how to measure the benefits of risk reduction, and lack of agreement on how to express (and consider) uncertainties when establishing acceptable levels of risk. In short, these problems were recognized and taken into account by the technical staff and by most other decision makers within the agencies. As one biostatistician put it, "I would say people are realistic here. You do the best you can. We're dealing with the best available evidence." Even more revealing is an observation made by a top regulatory official at the NRC on how information is evaluated given all these uncertainties:

Most regulators make decisions in a fashion that's quite similar. Information is put on the table, technical information, and the regulator looks at it, circles the table three times, and casts a judgment column on the table. And that's a regulatory decision. And then the regulator tries to defend that decision through a hearing process or a public comment process or whatever the regulator has to do. The real issue is what's the information you put on the table and how do you sort it out? Because in the last analysis it does boil down to judgment. In any complex regulatory field no simple formula will suffice.

Policy officials in many of the agencies believe they have adapted well to these limitations, in part through reliance on informal procedures for bringing together the scientists and the regulatory office staff to review differences of outlook and opinion. That is not to say the agencies function satisfactorily when confronting these issues. But this perspective does suggest how institutional adjustments can help prevent misuse of risk analysis. In the FDA, for example, there was said to be a "collaborative effort between the scientists, on the one hand,

and the consumer safety officers on the other. They work it out in a collaborative, cooperative way." The dialogue continued up through the hierarchy of the commissioner's office. One official defended the process in this way: "The reason you need all of this interaction between science and policy . . . to come to a regulatory decision is that because of the softness, because of the uncertainty, we cannot, should not, be capricious. And if you just left the technical people to their own devices, they can, unwittingly, be quite capricious. Because they are not the guardians of the overall process, that assures some degree of consistency."

These types of procedural adaptations seem particularly important given the methodological weaknesses that preoccupy the critics of risk analysis. The collaborative dialogue and interaction help to minimize the use of poor analysis or poor data by subjecting the risk estimation and economic analyses to review by a diverse set of participants. Maintenance of such a pluralistic decision-making process is an important characteristic of agencies which seem to have adjusted well to the need to perform such analysis.

At the same time the individuals interviewed expressed concern that there was considerable potential for misuse of risk analysis precisely because these methodological problems exist. Special note was made of the way executive office officials and members of Congress respond to risk analysis studies, with criticism voiced about their tendency toward "technique fascination" and "terminal bottom line illness," an inability or reluctance to probe beyond the numbers at the conclusion of a report. Given the increased oversight of the agencies by the OMB since 1981, one would expect to find a good deal more concern about the misuse of risk analysis today, particularly because many believe that the OMB has used these techniques as part of a more general effort to overreach its authority. According to an account in the *Washington Post* in 1986, OMB was considering "developing more specific guidance for performing risk assessments" in the agencies; in response, one critic of the new OMB role in regulation, MIT Professor Nicholas Ashford, described the OMB regulatory review staff as operating with "arrogance, ignorance, and nonaccountability."[45]

What might be done differently in the agencies to help insure that risk analyses are performed competently and not abused either within the agency or at a higher level? The interviews yielded some suggestions and others can be pulled from more recent writing on the subject. There is nothing surprising about the recommendations which are usually made, and perhaps little that is particularly helpful. Simply put, they involve improvements in the methods of risk assessment and evaluation, greater consistency in the use of methods from one policy and agency to another, improved data bases (e.g., records on illness, death, and occupational safety), and better ways to deal with uncertainty and to present it more clearly in risk reports.

Also widely recognized was the fact that agency resources are often too limited to expand the use of risk assessment significantly. The fiscal situation worsened in the 1980s. At the same time that critics of regulation have demanded better scientific knowledge to justify government actions, the EPA and other agencies have sustained severe cuts in research and development budgets.[46] Thus one cannot expect too rapid an improvement in research in the short term.

Other aspects of institutional capacity are also important. For example, there would be improved accountability for risk-oriented decision making if the Congress were to engage in closer supervision of the agencies through use of its oversight and budgetary authority. It does have considerable institutional resources at its disposal, including the Office of Technology Assessment, the Congressional Research Service, the General Accounting Office, and the Congressional Budget Office. But with a few exceptions, members of Congress have been reluctant overseers, in part because careful oversight is time consuming and rarely is politically rewarding.[47] In addition, calls for regulatory reform, which include building greater consistency into regulatory law and providing more explicit guidelines for agency decisions on risk, have not yet succeeded in producing many changes. Those patterns are likely to continue without greater demand from the American public for increased oversight and other changes. In recent years there have been some exceptions, which indicate how public attitudes influence regulatory policy; for example, public criticism of the Reagan administration's regulatory relief efforts led Congress to revise a number of statutes to set explicit (and higher) standards of protection and tighter deadlines for agency decisions precisely because Congress no longer trusted the agencies to enforce the law as it intended. A case in point is the Resource Conservation and Recovery Act (RCRA), the major federal policy governing regulation of hazardous waste. When Congress strengthened that act in 1984 it was clearly responding to public concern over earlier abuse of authority in the EPA under Anne Burford, Reagan's first administrator.[48]

Those concerned especially about the role of values in risk analysis have raised questions that need to be addressed, such as problems related to treatment of individual rights in comparing risks and benefits, the moral implications of imposing risks on a population, and equity in the distribution of risks, benefits, and costs, including intergenerational equity in cases involving long-term risks. Numerous suggestions have been offered for how such values might be more explicitly considered in agency decisions.[49] One way is for agencies to hire more social scientists and humanists (including professional philosophers) who can bring new perspectives to decisions about risk. For example, many philosophers would take issue with the way human lives are valued in benefit-cost analyses, and they might suggest a different approach that more nearly reflects acceptable ethical reasoning. In fact both the EPA and the OTA have employed political scientists and philosophers in recent years, and the practice could be expanded and extended to other agencies.

Finally, many suggestions represent attempts to respond to the heightened controversy over risk and regulation by proposing new mechanisms for risk communication and the building of greater public confidence in the bureaucratic processes that determine safety levels. Public knowledge, participation, and political legitimacy cannot be entirely separated. In recent years, several organizations (including the EPA, the Conservation Foundation, the National Science Foundation, and Tufts University's Center for Environmental Management) have sponsored conferences on how to improve risk communication in an effort to facilitate more informed reporting of risk events, studies, and policies. The conferences have also attempted to improve public knowledge and participation in the framing and review of community and societal risk-management decisions.[50] As is true of many actions involving science and technology, there is no simple way to educate and involve the public in decision making about risk; moreover, hearings and conferences are often used to co-opt citizens and persuade them to accept ongoing practice rather than to seek their views out of a more genuine concern for improving policymaking.[51] We need to search for more promising ways of involving the public in decisions about risk if the legitimacy as well as the quality of those decisions is to be improved.

206 Michael E. Kraft

CONCLUSION

There is no question that risk analysis methods are problematic. Many of the criticisms reviewed above are entirely appropriate, and skepticism over the way such methods have been used in regulatory decision making on health, safety, and environmental quality is certainly warranted. The question is not, as some put it, whether we should make *any* use of these methods. There is very little choice about that given the present statutes and recent court decisions.[52] But aside from those practical constraints, it would be foolish to reject these methods on a wholesale basis since they do promise to provide information that is useful in reaching answers to questions that need to be asked, such as: What are the risks that we face, both in the short term and the long term? How much planning or protection is necessary? How should our limited dollars be spent to have the maximum beneficial impact on human health, safety, and environmental quality?[53] A study by EPA staff in early 1987 demonstrated the value of such work. It found that the problems posing the greatest risk to human health and environmental quality in the United States "do not correspond well with EPA's current program priorities." EPA's priorities, it turned out, were more closely aligned with public opinion than with actual risks.[54]

As I have argued throughout this essay, the mere conduct of risk analyses or the consideration of them in a regulatory agency does not oblige public officials to base their decisions on the results. The analyses are intended to inform policy choices, not to make them. The methods themselves are not perfect, but neither are they as dangerous as some make them out to be. If our aim is to make better policy choices, we need to insure that the methods of risk analysis and the institutional capacity to use them wisely and effectively are improved.

To do this requires that journalists and the attentive public (including leaders and activists in relevant interest groups) as well as elected officials take more responsibility for informing themselves about the technical and policy problems faced and participate more fully in those decisions. This is especially needed with respect to the political task of evaluating risks and determining policy directions. Information about risks needs to be distributed more widely and discussed more thoroughly and critically. In particular, we must insure that the policy choices and the decisions made receive the coverage in the media and attention by the public that they so obviously merit. Over time the media and various policy actors may become more familiar with risks and their assessment and more adept at playing the important roles that democratic governance of technology requires.

Governing technology is a complicated task that typically dictates the use of considerable scientific expertise, and for that reason the process often is thought to be at odds with democratic principles. Regulating technological risks is no exception to the rule. If we are to avoid becoming too dependent on technical experts in remote or suspect bureaucracies, increased public involvement is essential. Many people understandably approach the challenge of active participation on such issues with trepidation. But there are abundant signs in the late 1980s that more people (and organized groups) than ever are concerned enough about these critical choices and they are willing to make the effort. As a result, our capacity to understand and respond to societal risks with the care and intelligence they demand should improve in the future.

SOPHISTICATED TRIAL AND ERROR IN

DECISION MAKING ABOUT RISK

EDWARD J. WOODHOUSE

If decision making about technological risks had to be characterized in one word, it would be "disagreement." Spokespersons for industry and environmental groups barely seem to be talking about the same universe when debating health risks from chemicals or safety risks from nuclear power. Media commentators criticize anything that goes wrong. Scientists who assess risks routinely disagree with each other — much to the frustration of Congress and the public. And the general public is about equal parts frightened, fatalistic, apathetic, confused, and angry. But these disparate observers do act as if they agree on two points: we can know the risks we face, and we can make public and private decisions that are free from significant errors. Unfortunately, neither belief is realistic.

This chapter begins with an explanation of why considerable uncertainty about ultimate consequences is inevitable at the outset of a new technological endeavor. High uncertainty implies that major errors are quite likely, so some form of trial, error, and error correction has to be a normal part of political decision making. The predicament, however, is that risky technologies have potentially catastrophic consequences and other characteristics that make error correction even more problematic than it is for most social problems. The second section of this chapter examines the implicit and explicit strategies

This chapter draws in part on the research and analysis in Joseph G. Morone and Edward J. Woodhouse, *Averting Catastrophe: Strategies for Regulating Risky Technologies* (Berkeley: University of California Press, 1986). I am indebted to Morone for portions of the analytic framework and case materials.

society has evolved for coping with this situation. Five of the strategies, if used jointly as an integrated approach to risk regulation, constitute a system of "sophisticated trial and error," which guards against the worst potential consequences of error while actively preparing to learn from whatever errors do occur. Later sections of the chapter briefly discuss the fit between sophisticated trial and error and other approaches to risk regulation such as technology assessment and benefit-cost analysis, and speculate on what decision making about risk has to teach us about prevention and mitigation of other problematic aspects of technology.

UNCERTAINTY AND TECHNOLOGY POLICY

Decisions about technological risks like ozone depletion and hazardous waste are hindered by most of the difficulties facing other complex social problems as well as some additional characteristics that make problem solving difficult. Any successful approach to decision making about technology must take these characteristics into account.

The starting point for technological decision making is to face up to the inevitability of uncertainty. Many people believe that disagreement is a pathology of politics, which could somehow be dissolved by sufficient talk or analysis or logic. If only we had the right elected officials, or bureaucrats, or scientists, with sufficient competence and motivation, we could arrive at an agreed, correct answer. As a former senator from Rhode Island put it, "We have had a lot of gobbledegook from both sides of this question, a lot of verbiage that sometimes is hard for the average citizen (or senator?) to understand. I wish at some time somebody would come before this committee and tell the committee categorically a nuclear reactor is safe or isn't safe, so that the public will know exactly where it stands."[1]

But disagreement seldom can be avoided in any realm of political life, because there are good reasons for it. In decision making about technology (and elsewhere in politics), one of the main sources of disagreement is that risks typically cannot be calculated very exactly. Consider the case of lead. We might hope simply to measure damage caused by lead to humans, animals, and the environment and then to set standards that offer adequate protection. Among many obstacles, however, are the following:

1. There is no way to measure the amount of lead to which a person has been exposed over the course of a lifetime: blood lead levels measure only the amount absorbed in recent weeks, so a person with high exposure in the past might test the same as a person with consistent, moderate exposure.
2. "Cross-laboratory calibration of measuring instruments is both difficult and time-consuming and is often a source of major error," so results of one study are not necessarily comparable with results from other laboratories.[2]
3. Because only a few children and adults accidentally take in large quantities of lead, there is not much of a population to test.
4. Laboratory animals may or may not respond to lead the same way humans do, and in any event, not much testing with animals had been done by the time policymakers needed answers in the 1970s.
5. Without knowing how much lead a person ingested through food, drink, dust, or lead paint, it is impossible to calculate the percentage actually being absorbed; if it is 3 percent, the implications for lead precautions are very different than if 33 percent is absorbed.

As a result of such obstacles to definitive lead studies, EPA over a period of years offered more than a dozen technical claims regarding the need to take lead out of gasoline; every one of the claims was plausibly rebutted by the Ethyl Corporation, the major manufacturer of lead additives for gasoline. For example, EPA claimed that "since lead has not been shown to have any biologically useful function in the body, any increase in body burden of lead is accompanied by an increased risk of human health impairment." Ethyl Corporation countered: "Experiments on animals seem to show that lead is, after all, an essential element. . . . [Moreover] years of experience with occupationally exposed groups show blood lead levels well in excess of those found in the normally exposed population to be perfectly safe."[3]

The result, according to technology policy analyst David Collingridge, was that:

Both sides set out to build up the best technical case they could. . . . Scientific evidence which fits the case is cited without criticism, while that which undermines the case is subject to the most intense scrutiny. . . . There is a huge technical literature available to those opposing the case . . . which can be dipped into as needed.

There is therefore ample room for each side to build up a case, changing it as time goes on, as new reports supplement the stock of literature and in response to one's opponent's criticisms. With such opportunities, there is no possibility of one side losing to the other, having to accept on scientific grounds the technical case made out by its rival.[4]

Much the same can be said of nuclear power plant safety and many other health, safety, and environmental issues. The range of legitimate disagreement can be narrowed, but often not far enough to be of much use to policymakers. There is near consensus among atmospheric scientists, for example, that there will be climate warming from combustion of fossil fuels. But they disagree markedly regarding how much warming, how soon, and what should be done about the greenhouse effect.[5] Even for debates we think of as settled, such as smoking and lung cancer, inspection of the scientific literature often reveals a lively minority viewpoint.[6]

In addition to factual uncertainties, interpretations of risks require controversial value judgments, on which disagreement is certain. Should a new hazardous waste disposal facility be sited far away from cities, for example, to minimize the number of people potentially exposed if problems occur? Or should it be located near cities, so those who benefit from activities generating waste also bear a fair share of the risks? Should risk regulations aim to fully protect the most vulnerable members of the public, or should they aim to protect the average person? How much weight should be given to professional expertise compared with citizen perceptions? Several thoughtful, logical opinions can be given to each of these questions, none of which is obviously conclusive.[7]

Another aspect of uncertainty about risks concerns the uses to which a technology will be put, and the magnitude and frequency of its use. Even a dangerous activity on a small scale may not create much of a problem; but what if it escalates? Peter Drucker argues that "the future impact of new technology is almost always beyond anybody's imagination."[8] Thus

- The original DDT researchers did not think of using the chemical as a pesticide for controlling insects on crops.
- Inventor Philo T. Farnsworth did not foresee anything like the massive social changes produced by his television tube, and early devel-

opers did not even conceive of remote electric vision systems as instruments for picking up over-the-air broadcasts.

– As recently as 1958, three experts on technical innovation concluded that "the Electronic Digital Computer seemed to have so uncertain a commercial future that we decided to exclude it from our case histories" of important twentieth-century inventions.[9]

– In 1972 the Atomic Energy Commission predicted that the United States would have 1200 nuclear power plants by the year 2000 (we will actually have about 110).

Does this mean that studies by the Office of Technology Assessment and others are useless? Surely not. It is merely a reminder that new scientific and engineering developments, business entrepreneurship, and consumer responses will dynamically evolve unexpected combinations and extensions of whatever exists at the time a forecast is attempted.[10] So egregious errors are inevitable.

ERROR CORRECTION AND BARRIERS TO IT

If unforeseen problems inevitably occur in complex policymaking, then there is no complete substitute for trial and error.[11] (Partial substitutes are discussed later in this chapter.) So decision makers must adjust their policies on the basis of feedback, as experience is gained and the various ramifications of a technology and its regulation become known. What conditions would need to prevail for error correction to proceed relatively satisfactorily?

1. Errors must generate noticeable symptoms.
2. Someone must perceive these symptoms.
3. This feedback must be communicated to those with competence to interpret it.
4. Such interpretations must then be communicated to those with authority to take action.
5. The error must be correctable and/or compensable.

After that come all the normal steps in political decision making, many of which can interfere with error correction (such as disagreement between president and Congress). But if technological risk problems are to stand roughly as good a chance of error correction as other social problems (which may not be very good), they must satisfy these five conditions at least as well as other social problems do.

First, will errors generate symptoms that can be perceived? A *long delay before information emerges* about an error may interfere with the perception that a problem even exists. Thus the harmful effects of DDT were not persuasively documented for a quarter century after the pesticide's initial use. Other chemical releases, begun in the 1940s and 1950s, have contaminated some underground drinking water sources; but not until the 1980s did compelling evidence of the phenomenon begin to emerge. Such delayed feedback allows undesired consequences to accumulate and persist; it may also allow the error to become embedded in the economy. As a congressional committee noted in frustration when the dangers of vinyl chloride were becoming apparent, it is prior to the first manufacture that "human suffering, jobs lost, wasted capital expenditures, and other costs are lowest. Frequently, it is far more painful to take regulatory action after all of these costs have been incurred."[12] It also is more difficult to overcome the opposition of business.[13]

Even if errors begin to generate symptoms relatively quickly, the negative feedback may not be perceived due to the *esoteric nature* of some problems caused by use of technology. Unless a pollutant creates visible symptoms or has a distinctive smell or taste, normal human senses may be inadequate to detect an error. In the case of ozone depletion, most U.S. environmental groups relaxed their vigilance after fluorocarbon aerosol sprays were banned in 1978. And for a while most atmospheric scientists believed that the ozone threat was diminishing. By the late 1980s, however, it became apparent that several dozen human-made chemicals deplete ozone through much more complex (and delayed) processes than previously recognized. So almost a decade was lost before renewed concern emerged.[14]

In cases where these first two problems do not apply, the sheer *number* of important problems may prevent early recognition of errors. More than 60,000 different chemicals are produced and used in the United States, and several hundred new ones are marketed each year. Even keeping up with just the six hundred or so chemicals used in pesticides is a formidable task: in 1972 Congress ordered EPA to review all the pesticides registered before 1970, and by 1987 the agency was only about halfway through the assignment! If we added together all the new scientific-technological activities undertaken each year, the nontrivial ones that deserve monitoring surely would exceed a thousand. A sensible response seemingly would be "to deal with problems in order of importance. Unfortunately, the information needed to establish priorities is not available; the collection of such data might itself swamp the system."[15]

Fourth, when errors are discovered, they may be partially or wholly *irreversible*. Improper disposal of toxic wastes could affect humans and other species for many generations, because it is so difficult to completely clean up contaminated soils, and because contaminated drinking water aquifers can require centuries to regenerate. Even less reversible is the extinction of thousands of potentially valuable species of plants and animals as tropical rain forests are destroyed. And errors that are reversible in principle may prove inflexible in practice. This was an important part of what went wrong with the nuclear power industry: by the time mistakes were widely recognized, too much had been invested to start over. In hopes of achieving low cost through economies of scale, utilities purchased huge nuclear reactors that ended up costing as much as $5 billion each. A decade or more was required to plan, construct, license, and begin to use such machinery; so by the time it became clear that nuclear power was unacceptable to much of the public, too expensive, and perhaps unnecessary due to changes in energy supply and demand, the utilities were largely stuck with their original decisions. As Collingridge argues, these inflexibilities made nuclear power "a technology which is not open to the normal process of political control."[16]

Finally, mistaken judgments can bring *potentially catastrophic consequences*. The "trials" in technological endeavors sometimes affect large areas of the globe almost simultaneously, with billions of people potentially at risk. The magnitudes of risks to health, safety, and environment have escalated as technologies have become increasingly potent. Even the purely social effects of new technologies can quickly and radically modify long-established cultural patterns in ways that some observers consider culturally catastrophic. For example, the seemingly innocent use of snowmobiles for herding reindeer had tragic effects on the Skolt Lapp society in Finland.[17] Overall, then, merely waiting for errors to show up does not look like a very promising approach to decision making, because the costs of error can be so severe.

In addition to these special barriers to error correction that apply disproportionately to technological issues, there obviously are more general tendencies in politics to create and continue errors. These include aspects of the present electoral system that lead elected officials to worry more about reelection than about social problem solving.[18] Red tape and a multitude of communication problems interfere with effective performance by bureaucratic organizations.[19] Flaws in human information-processing abilities lead to rampant misperception and to mislearning the lessons of history.[20] Inequalities in access and resources routinely shut some interests out of the political process while inviting others in.[21] Finally, the fundamental structure of U.S. government established by the Constitution may be "too congenitally divided, too prone to stalemate, too conflict-ridden to meet its immense responsibilities" in a technological era.[22]

As a combined result of the above, errors are not always perceived, and those who recognize a problem may not be able to get the attention of others. There is no common yardstick such as businesses have when sales slump; once alerted, political actors are likely to disagree diametrically over whether an "error" is occurring.[23] Even if they agree on wanting to correct a problem, resources typically are inadequate, knowledge of how to improve may be shaky, and implementation is virtually certain to be difficult.

The dilemma, then, is that many decision problems pertaining to technology have characteristics which render them unsuited for the normal process of trial, error, and error correction. Yet major errors and disagreements are inevitable, and some errors carry potentially catastrophic consequences. Thus society is relatively vulnerable to error from the normal operation of the decision-making system for new technology: the bright ideas of scientists and engineers, the normal behavior of business, and affluent consumers' willingness to purchase innovative products—all encouraged by government.[24]

STRATEGIES

In principle, what are the options for reducing the extent of society's vulnerability? If, as argued above, trial and error is inevitable, can we somehow make a more sophisticated effort to head off the worst problems and do better at correcting others? It turns out that decision makers have half-wittingly evolved at least five strategies for adapting policymaking to delayed feedback and the other barriers to error correction.

First, even in highly uncertain endeavors, it is possible at the outset partly to foresee and protect against some of the worst risks. Homeowners, for example, do not have to calculate the likelihood of their house burning down; merely knowing that it is an unacceptable possibility is enough to warrant obtaining insurance as an *initial precaution* against catastrophic loss. Likewise, rather than relying entirely on preventing all accidents, U.S. nuclear decision makers required containment buildings around civilian reactors; most of the radioactivity released during the Three Mile Island accident was thereby prevented from entering the environment. If the Soviets had taken this precaution instead of assuming impeccable performance by their nuclear plants, the 1986 accident at Chernobyl probably would have had less serious consequences. Other tactics are appropriate for other types of problems, but the basic idea is to take some kind of initial precautions rather than merely hoping for the best. The precautions will not prevent errors, but will make them less costly.

If uncertainty is high and consequences are potentially severe, a second strategy is to *err on the side of caution*. Thus in 1976–78 the United States had to decide whether to take action on potential depletion of stratospheric ozone by fluorocarbons. There was no solid, direct evidence that such depletion was occurring, and the American Chemical Society complained that proposed legislation would constitute "the first regulation to be based entirely on an unverified scientific prediction." A DuPont spokesperson likewise argued, "We're going a very long way into the regulatory process before the scientists know what's really going on."[25] Nevertheless, Congress and EPA acted to ban most aerosol fluorocarbon sprays, even though few other nations did so. Another aspect of proceeding cautiously is to put the burden of proof on advocates of risky activities; whereas government once had to go to court to prove a pesticide unsafe, manufacturers now are required to demonstrate that their products are not unduly dangerous. This tactic is imperfectly applied in current pesticide regulation, but the burden of proof has shifted significantly toward proponents of risky chemicals.

A third strategy calls for speeding up negative feedback instead of just waiting for it to arise naturally; this is accomplished by *testing the risks*. After numerous bad experiences from chemicals such as PCBs, vinyl chloride, and the chlorinated hydrocarbons, Congress in 1976 decreed that all new commercial chemicals would have to be approved by EPA prior to marketing; toxicology testing is a component of this premanufacture notification program. And instead of waiting for possible global ozone depletion from chlorofluorocarbons and other chemicals, atmospheric researchers are conducting research in hopes of finding out whether the ozone hole over Antarctica is an early warning sign. More generally, most scientific research pertaining to technological risks can be considered a way of speeding up negative feedback which otherwise might be long delayed.

Deliberately *preparing to learn from experience* is a fourth strategy. Well-designed trial and error is not purely reactive but expects error, carefully monitors initial trials, and prepares for error correction. Even though each nuclear power plant is customized to suit its particular location, for instance, a lot can be learned from experiences elsewhere. When the Davis-Besse reactor suffered a potentially serious problem due to a stuck valve, a report on the incident was sent to the Nuclear Regulatory Commission. If prompt learning had occurred, it would have been possible to prevent the subsequent accident at Three Mile Island, caused in part by a similar valve problem. As investigations after the accident revealed, however, the Nuclear Regulatory Commission lacked a satisfactory method for identifying the important information in the thousands of reports submitted to it each year.[26] Few programs anywhere in society yet do very well at such deliberate preparation for learning from error.

A fifth strategy, *priority setting*, works interactively with advance testing and deliberate learning from experience. Where the number of trials is large, and the potential problems legion, there are only two choices: be confused and haphazard, or set priorities. Because all 60,000 chemicals in commerce cannot be tested in any given year (or decade), the Toxic Substances Control Act of 1976 established a mechanism for setting priorities. An Interagency Testing Committee, composed of representatives from most of the federal agencies with relevant responsibilities, selects a dozen or so chemicals each year that it recommends to the Environmental Protection Agency for priority testing. The chemicals selected generally are those which are in relatively widespread use, are close analogues of chemicals known to be carcinogens, or otherwise are identified by regulatory personnel and toxicological experts as suspicious and underemphasized.[27] As sensible as such priority setting seems, it is by no means widely applied. Thus, in the case of the greenhouse threat, the National Research Council and the relevant research communities appear to be trying to study everything at once.

In sum, whereas ordinary trial and error merely hopes for the best and corrects when failures become apparent, sophisticated trial and error restructures decision making to make it more appropriate for dealing with high uncertainty and potentially catastrophic consequences. Decision makers protect against catastrophe by taking more stringent initial precautions than are really expected to be necessary. They then actively set out to reduce uncertainty about the magnitude and probability of the hypothesized risks, through prioritized testing and careful monitoring of early trials. If uncertainty can be substantially narrowed, the initial precautions then are revised. Precautions can be relaxed when threats prove less serious than feared, enhanced when threats prove more dangerous than initially suspected, and otherwise refined to make them more effective and perhaps less costly.

Is this a utopian hope? Clearly not, for every element of sophisticated trial and error already is being applied in the regulation of some risky technology. Perhaps the most thorough application to date was in early research on recombinant DNA, the scientific procedures which led to the emerging biotechnology industry. Scientists organized a voluntary moratorium on the potentially risky research in the early 1970s and worked out a regulatory strategy through the National Institutes of Health. Six classes of especially risky experiments were prohibited altogether, and precautions were adopted for the others, varying in stringency according to the degree of risk each type of experiment was believed to pose. The aim was essentially to make the research forgiving of error: special laboratory facilities were used to prevent bacteria from escaping from the research building; and intentionally enfeebled strains of an especially well known bacterium were used for most of the research, so that even if bacteria escaped they would have great difficulty surviving outside the favorable conditions of the lab.

Once precautions had been taken to protect against error—precautions more stringent than many scientists believed necessary—rDNA researchers attempted to reduce uncertainty. Priority was given to worst-case experiments, which aimed at finding out whether researchers might accidentally create virulent new organisms; another priority was improved understanding of the behavior of E.coli K-12, the most common host bacterium. There was some disagreement about the interpretation of some tests, but the great majority of observers found reassurance from the priority testing and from the absence of negative feedback from hundreds of ordinary rDNA experiments around the nation. As uncertainty was reduced, more experiments were allowed at lower levels of containment; by the early 1980s most of the containment requirements were dropped, and no type of experiments remained altogether prohibited.[28]

Both in principle and in practice, then, sophisticated trial and error appears a workable strategy for many types of technological risks. It is not, however, an automatic process that specifies exactly what should be done in any given situation. All the ordinary work of policy analysis and political negotiation still must go on.

THE FIT WITH OTHER DECISION TECHNIQUES

How does sophisticated trial and error fit with other decision techniques, such as technology assessment, risk-benefit analysis, and benefit-cost analysis? Are they alternatives to one another or supplements? (For further detail on some of these techniques, see chapters 8 and 9.)

When problems with technology were garnering widespread concern in the late 1960s and early 1970s, advocates of "technology assessment" called for comprehensive, advance analyses of technological actions that might have significant social or environmental impacts.[29] The intention was to identify impacts early, frame policy options for "obtaining maximum public advantage," and then hope that normal political processes would act to head off the problem, or at least mitigate it.[30]

In pursuit of these goals, Congress required environmental impact assessments as part of the National Environmental Policy Act of 1969; early assessments helped cast doubt on esoteric proposals for seeding hurricanes, increasing snowfall in the Rockies, and building a fleet of SSTs. The Office of Technology Assessment, established in 1972, started off timidly but now turns out a steady stream of sensible analyses.[31] Starting in 1973, the National Science Foundation awarded grants to academics to conduct technology assessments on everything from the checkless-cashless society to solar energy, biological pesticides, and integrated hog farming. Whole new intellectual fields sprang up, embodied in professional associations such as the International Association for Impact Assessment.

The Office of Technology Assessment and the impact assessment enterprise more generally have had some success in sensitizing policymakers to the negative side effects of technical innovation. The information base for governmental decision making clearly has improved, and siting of noxious new facilities like hazardous waste treatment plants now routinely incorporates assessment activity, public participation, and sometimes financial and other forms of impact mitigation. Technology assessments are very useful for condensing a lot of information on a topic into a format accessible to policymakers, and for providing a systematic checklist of important considerations that might otherwise be missed. But this decision technique runs the danger of degenerating into the platitude "Consider Everything," which can never be done for complex problems, especially at the outset of a new technological endeavor. And technology assessment per se does not decide what is to be done, so it must be used in conjunction with other decision techniques and strategies.

Risk-benefit analysis is one such technique, based on the idea of balancing the overall benefits of a proposed regulation against its overall risks. While the general idea makes sense and is applied in a rough-and-ready fashion in many sorts of decision making, full implementation of it is bound to require controversial judgments. As economist Lester Lave asks, for example, "Are only health risks to be considered, or are risks to the present and future environment (air, water, louseworts, snail darters, and tundra) relevant? . . . How can the risks to louseworts be added to those of the health of our great grandchildren and of current workers? Similarly, there is no guidance about how to quantify benefits: what is the value of an increase in the supply of food or electricity?"[32] Risk-benefit analysis is not a way out of uncertainties and disagreements, though the technique can help to systematize and perhaps narrow them.

Benefit-cost analysis is a more quantitative and formal version of risk-benefit. It requires translating all values and judgments into dollars, in order to calculate the net value of many hypothetical policy options. The goal is to select policies with high net benefits. One obstacle to achieving this for risk problems is that most people find it unpalatable to put an explicit dollar value on the benefits of prolonging a life. In addition, there is no agreement about how to compute interest on future effects or costs, and the notion of what constitutes a benefit is in the eye of the beholder, varying with cultural background, time horizon, and personal goals. In practice, moreover, this technique sometimes is used "as a tool for defending the status quo. It is rarely used to consider *who* benefits or pays, and it focuses on the present, giving short shrift to even the near-term future. . . . [Moreover,] the more important non-economic concerns are, . . . the less helpful this framework will be."[33] Still, sensibly employed benefit-cost analysis can be a powerful framework for helping to "establish regulatory priorities, weed out the least desirable alternatives, and increase the efficiency with which government" acts.[34]

Whatever their shortcomings, technology assessment, risk-benefit analysis, and benefit-cost analysis all provide information in a form that is potentially quite helpful to decision makers and their staffs. Sophisticated trial and error provides no such information, only a strategic framework. On the other hand, the various analytic techniques do not provide a means for overcoming the barriers to learning from error. So technology assessment and the other decision techniques cannot be a substitute for a decision *strategy*, nor do they eliminate the need for sensible political judgments. But they can be very helpful when used in support of sophisticated trial and error, in helping formulate sensible initial precautions, setting priorities, and otherwise preparing to learn from error at an acceptable cost.

CONCLUSION

In sum, there are inherent difficulties in patching up and reversing errors in risky technologies when feedback is delayed, problems require esoteric knowledge, the number of trials is huge, and the consequences of error are potentially catastrophic and irreversible. Sophisticated trial and error can do nothing about the ordinary institutional problems and power imbalances that characterize political life. But where political majorities are willing, the characteristics that make technological problems especially difficult can be ameliorated by enacting stringent initial precautions in the face of high uncertainty and potentially severe consequences. Following prioritized testing of the risks and active learning from experience, the precautions can be relaxed or strengthened.

There are very significant areas of risk not yet brought under the umbrella of this system, of course. It required accidents at Bhopal, India, and Institute, West Virginia, to bring chemical plant safety forcefully onto government's agenda. Programs to combat indoor air pollution—especially radon—are just getting underway in the late 1980s. Even where sophisticated trial and error has been applied, moreover, its implementation tends to be underfunded and rife with other shortcomings. Still, decision making about health-safety-environment risks has typically used far more sensible strategies than has decision making pertaining to purely social impacts such as technological unemployment, community abandonment, and the stress of rapid social change.

The term "risk" has become almost synonymous with "health-safety-environment" in both public discussion and professional literature about technological policymaking. On reflection, however, we all recognize many other aspects of technology that pose threats to values we care about. Over the past century or so, changes in technology have transformed the nature of housework and the family, our occupational opportunities, what we eat, how we spend our leisure time, friendship patterns and sexual relationships, and even religious beliefs. Technological innovation thus has a tremendous cumulative impact on social institutions and on what kind of people we are. Indeed, health/safety risks were secondary compared with the more purely social, psychological, political, and economic consequences of automobiles, telephones, radio and television, computing, factory automation, commercial airliners, and other twentieth-century innovations. So even if we could be guaranteed zero health-safety-environment risks from new technology, a majority of the disconcerting effects might still be with us.[35]

What are the implications for our understanding of decision making about technology? Affluent societies have established elaborate procedures for making governmental decisions of all kinds, with especially elaborate procedures including expert peer review and public participation for many health-safety-environment threats. But society's other main decision-making system is not subject to the same degree of public scrutiny and potential control. The decision system comprised of scientists, engineers, business executives, and consumers is delegated the responsibility of developing and diffusing most innovations, yet none of the participants has much incentive or capacity to ward off long-term threats to society.

Because technological arrangements often become relatively resistant to change once established, it seems important to have more systematic procedures for taking initial precautions to protect society from market transactions that "govern" the introduction of new technologies. Also needed are mechanisms to learn from early errors, instead of waiting until a technical arrangement is embedded in the economy and in social habit. Effective learning, of course, requires authority to act on the perceived error. This almost certainly would mean substantial encroachment on what is now perceived as the prerogative of the technical and business communities to act as they see fit in most aspects of technical innovation that do not directly threaten health, safety, or environment. This will be a difficult task, in part because of the powerful interests which support relatively unbridled technological change. Perhaps equally responsible for the present situation, however, is the fact that few of us have yet recognized that all major technological decisions — not just safety risks — have public consequences that need to be regulated by a sensible society. Sophisticated trial and error provides one way of conceptualizing the task, if and when the political will is forthcoming.

IV

EVALUATING TECHNOLOGY

CASES AND CONTROVERSIES

INTRODUCTION

In part I we dealt with basic philosophical issues raised by technology and its influence on politics. Parts II and III focused on institutions and their capacity to govern technology and diverse perspectives on how we attempt to regulate technology. In this last section we turn to different ways in which technology might be evaluated. In many respects this returns us to the concerns that drive the essays in part I on philosophical and normative issues.

The problem of evaluation is central to any serious consideration of technology and politics. It includes a concern for whether a given technology will perform as expected and with what possibly unanticipated side effects, the role of technical experts in judging the merits of technology and the compatibility of such expertise with democratic principles, how important issues of values and ethics are addressed both within and outside of governing circles, how private individuals and groups can participate in the framing and assessment of technical questions that are at the heart of most important public policy disputes involving technology, and how the federal government can or should share responsibility with state and local governments in making decisions about technology.[1]

Increasingly, as the essays in this book make clear, there is intense conflict over the impact of a wide range of technologies on our public and private lives. Controversies over decisions concerning energy production, environmental protection, space exploration, biotechnology, medical technology, and national defense, among others, are more complex, visible, and protracted than ever before; they also involve a wider range of participants and have a broader and more extensive impact on society and the economy than in the past.[2] Yet public knowledge of the issues and governmental capacity to resolve bitter disputes over technology and its uses are often inadequate. Given those conditions, what is the most appropriate way to evaluate technology? What mechanisms or approaches are suitable for assessing issues of both fact and value? What is most promising about them, and what limitations are of greatest concern? How might they be changed to improve our overall capacity to understand and deal intelligently and humanely with technology and its impact?

We try to address such questions here by using case studies of three quite different problem areas to illustrate the range of technology's influence on public affairs and individual well-being. The cases include the ethical and political dilemmas faced in deciding how to develop and employ the vast range of new biomedical technologies, the challenge of disposing of high-level nuclear waste from power plants given public fears about contamination, and disputes over the Strategic Defense Initiative (SDI) proposal—in particular the use of Scientific Adversary Procedures to help assess the factual components in that debate.

Case studies are both limited and enlightening ways to view such problems. They are limited because they focus on a single case or area of technology and public affairs and hence do not easily lend themselves to generalizations about the larger universe of cases of which they may not be representative.[3] On the other hand, case studies afford a much more detailed and richer examination of the complexity of issues and decision making than is otherwise possible. Where we are often prone to oversimplify issues of technology and politics, case studies bring us back to the messy reality of individuals struggling to resolve major conflicts in imperfect institutions operating under uncertainty. The three cases we have chosen here cannot represent all major controversies over technology. But they cover enough of them to offer some insight into the politics of technology in several different and informative ways.

The technologies considered by the authors of these three chapters are a varied lot: new ideas and techniques in medicine and genetic engineering and their use, the hardware and software to be used in SDI and the impact of those developments on U.S.-Soviet relations and world peace, and the techniques and management approaches to be

used in disposal of nuclear waste and the implications for public
health and environmental quality. As Norman Vig points out in chapter 1, "technology" can refer to many things, ranging from what is "in
the heads" of specialists and professionals, to the tools, products, and
by-products of industry, to large-scale institutions and systems which
shape the quality of modern life. All of these usages are evident in the
three chapters in this section.

In chapter 11, Robert Blank provides an overview of major policy
issues raised by the rapid development of a broad array of biomedical
technologies such as genetic screening, prenatal diagnosis, psychosurgery, and organ transplants. He focuses on the ethical and conceptual
issues that arise in applying such technologies, particularly those dealing with human genetic and reproductive technologies, and raises a
large number of questions which policy officials and others concerned
with such technologies need to address. As with other technologies,
innovations in biomedicine are neither risk free nor easily understood. Blank argues that we need to confront the issues posed by
further development and use of these technologies head on. For example, critical choices must be made about allocating scarce economic
resources and rationing certain kinds of treatment. Which programs
deserve funding and which do not? And who decides which patients
receive certain kinds of care, such as organ transplants? Once largely
private concerns, the provision of medical care and the regulation of
these new technologies are now important issues on the public agenda.
Consequently, policymakers must pay more attention to the value issues
and ethical dilemmas tied inextricably to these changes and they must
cope somehow with the difficult policy choices that need to be made.
If they don't do so intelligently, he warns, biomedical policies are
likely to fail.

In chapter 12, Michael Kraft explores the problem of nuclear
waste disposal, which requires unprecedented technical and managerial achievements to isolate these highly toxic wastes from the biosphere for thousands of years. The requirements for securing public
and state approval for a waste repository are equally formidable. After
decades of complacency, in the 1980s the federal government finally
tried to select possible sites for the disposal of these wastes, only to
discover that public fear and opposition were far too intense to allow
the program to move ahead. Kraft explores the difficult question of
how democratic governments can deal with the conflict between the

imperative of waste disposal and protection of public health and environmental quality, and in particular the conflict between technocratic and democratic approaches to problem solving. He focuses on how public participation can help to evaluate technology and its attendant risks and thereby can assist in making the necessary public policy choices. He does that by reviewing critical issues in the evaluation of technological risks like nuclear wastes, major approaches to public education and participation that might be used in evaluating such risks, and how those approaches might have made a difference in the outcomes to date in governmental efforts to design and implement a disposal policy. He concludes that without greater participation in the important decisions over nuclear waste disposal, the U.S. government is unlikely to gain public acceptance for its siting program. Much the same could be said of other Western democracies facing the same problem of public concern and the familiar NIMBY (Not-In-My-Back-Yard) syndrome.[4] Kraft also extends the analysis to other issues involving risky technologies, particular where public involvement is critical to resolving disputes over their use.

In chapter 13 Roger Masters and Arthur Kantrowitz focus on one particular institutional mechanism for evaluating technology, Scientific Adversary Procedures, and apply it to the case of the SDI. Originally called the "Science Court" when proposed in the 1970s, Scientific Adversary Procedures are a new and more effective alternative for isolating and verifying scientific facts that are an inevitable part of every conflict over technology. The purpose of these procedures is not to make a decision on policy proposals but to facilitate scientific agreement by providing a forum in which public cross-examination by differing scientific or technical experts occurs in an academic context. The hope is that such a setting and procedure will make possible a more responsible dialogue among experts, the public, and policymakers by separating personal opinion and political passion from the scientific facts. The chapter reports on the application of these procedures to the hotly disputed case of the SDI, which was examined in several experiments at the University of California, Berkeley, and at Dartmouth. The authors conclude that there is much promise to the Scientific Adversary Procedures for this and other controversial debates over technology.

Where others despair of the possibility of the lay person playing much of a role in decisions involving technology, Masters and Kantrowitz suggest that we need to reconceptualize the public's contribution. Nonexperts can indeed assist in evaluating technology, but it is increasingly difficult for them to challenge the scientific facts themselves. In such cases we need to create public forums in which equally qualified experts may contest the facts and thereby assist the nonexperts, both the public and policymakers alike, in making difficult choices about technology. Mechanisms like the Scientific Adversary Procedures offer the hope that responsible decisions in evaluating technology can be made without abandoning the legitimate and important contributions we expect from the public and its elected representatives. The timing, focus, and structure of such procedures must, however, be carefully planned if they are to serve democratic purposes.[5]

The research presented in these chapters contributes to our understanding of how conflicts over technology might be resolved, and each chapter offers some prescriptions for evaluating technology in the future. Additional studies might examine parallel cases, for example, the use of Scientific Adversary Procedures for issues other than SDI or the appropriateness and effects of various kinds of public participation in policy disputes other than those over nuclear waste disposal. Such studies might be conducted at the state level as well as the national level in the United States and in other nations; the latter would allow cross-national comparisons of conditions facilitating promising processes for dispute resolution such as negotiation or compensation. Other studies might look at how well policymakers deal with the kinds of ethical questions posed in Blank's chapter. To what extent are the ethical dilemmas recognized and how well do policymakers respond to them? How might our capacity to make ethically justifiable decisions be improved?[6] Increasingly scholars are examining such questions, and thus we can look forward to improved understanding of how well the various approaches to evaluating technology discussed here are likely to work during the next decade.

ETHICS AND POLICY:

ISSUES IN BIOMEDICAL TECHNOLOGY

ROBERT H. BLANK

Although the biomedical technologies now available pale in comparison to what is promised for the future, they represent an impressive array of methods for human intervention. The possibility of indefinite artificial maintenance of life, new methods of creating as well as aborting life, organ transplantation, and new applications of psychosurgery are but a few of the rapidly advancing techniques that will help reshape our destiny. While offering new hope for many persons, however, these innovations are creating ethical and political dilemmas unparalleled in the past. Changes in technology have always demanded redefinition of issues and policies, but the new discoveries and applications in genetics and medicine represent perhaps the greatest challenge our species has yet faced—the alteration of our most basic definitions of humanhood. Although each innovation raises a unique set of opportunities and problems, they share broader social and political ramifications which must be evaluated in a systematic and timely fashion.

This chapter provides an overview of the policy issues created by the rapid emergence of a broad assortment of biomedical technologies, which according to Amitai Etzioni represent a "new revolution."[1] It is clear that the intensity and scope of the issues in human genetic intervention (e.g., eugenics, sex selection, genetic counseling, and genetic screening), reproductive technology (e.g., abortion, sterilization, prenatal diagnosis, artificial insemination, in vitro fertilization, and fetal research), and biomedical intervention in the human life process (e.g., psychosurgery, electrical brain stimulation, drug therapy, organ transplants, and euthanasia) challenge traditional values and social structures at an accelerating rate. Together these issues present a formidable set of policy concerns which vividly demonstrate the critical ethical aspects that underlie all technological applications. To illustrate these policy implications in a focused manner, this chapter emphasizes human genetic and reproductive technologies.

BIOMEDICAL ETHICS AND POLICY

Major alterations in the U.S. health care system will be necessary in the coming decades if we are to avert a crisis of immense proportions. Many seemingly unrelated demographic, social, and technological trends promise to accentuate traditional dilemmas in medical policy-making. The aging population, the proliferation of high-cost biomedical technologies designed primarily to extend life, conventional retroactive reimbursement schemes by third-party payers, and the realization that health care costs are outstripping society's perceived ability to pay all lead to pressures for expanded public action. At the same time public institutions appear incapable and unwilling to make the difficult decisions in an area traditionally viewed as outside the political arena.

The constraints on economic resources now apparent in the United States are certain to be compounded by the confluence of the trends noted above. Even with all the current measures to contain costs, health care expenditures will increase from $387 billion in 1984 to $690 billion in 1990 and $1.9 trillion by 2000, representing almost 15 percent of the GNP.[2] Increased competition for scarce resources within the health care sector will necessitate resource allocation as well as rationing decisions.[3] In turn, these actions are certain to exacerbate the social, ethical, and legal issues and intensify political action by affected individuals and groups. Although public officials might continue to avoid making critical decisions and attempt to resolve long-term problems with piecemeal solutions, they can no longer avoid becoming major participants in the health care debate.

Medical decision making, until very recently, has been a matter of private, not public, policy. Even the emerging emphasis on "bioethics" in the last several decades and the inclusion of the ethical dimension into medical decision making did not necessarily place such decisions in the public sector. The introduction of ethical considerations and their perceived escalation in importance did, however, contribute to the expanded role of public officials in medical policymaking by requiring some form of institutional protection for the interest of the weaker parties. If the ethical dimension was critical, some agent was needed to ensure that these concerns were properly considered before action was taken. Increasingly, public officials found themselves drawn into medical decision making to guarantee that these ethical concerns were honored and the consumers of medicine protected. Tradition to the contrary, medicine was quickly drawn into the realm of public policy.

Although there is a historical tie between the emergence of interest in biomedical ethics and in biomedical policy and the two approaches overlap, the emphasis in policy analysis is critically different from that of bioethics. Three policy levels are crucial in health care issues. First, decisions must be made concerning the research and development of the technologies. Because substantial medical research is funded either directly or indirectly with public funds, it is logical that public input be required at this stage. The growing, although still limited, interest in forecasting and assessing the social as well as technical consequences of health care technologies early in research and development represents one attempt to facilitate a broader public input.

The second policy level relates to the individual use of technologies once they are available. Although direct government intrusion into individual decision making in health care ought to be limited, the government does have at its disposal an array of more or less implicit devices to encourage or discourage individual use. These include tax incentives, provision of services, and education programs. Whether or not explicit rationing of health care resources will be a feasible future policy option remains to be seen. However, some observers feel that as the social costs of certain forms of treatment become high, we must reassess our notion that physicians ought to act primarily as agents of the patients and give consideration to a role as trustee of scarce medical resources.[4]

The third, and perhaps most critical, level of health care policy centers on the aggregate societal consequences of widespread application of a technology. For instance, what impact would wide diffusion of artificial heart transplants have on the provision of health care? Adequate policymaking here requires a clear conception of national goals, extensive data to predict the consequences of each possible course of action, an accurate means of monitoring these consequences, and mechanisms to cope with the consequences if they are deemed undesirable. As technologies become available which allow for sex preselection, surrogate motherhood, reversible sterilization, and gene surgery, social patterns will be affected. Policy planners must account for these potential pressures on the basic structures and patterns of society and decide whether provision of such choices is desirable.

Before policy decisions are made on particular innovations, there is a need for delineation of broad societal goals toward biomedicine and public health in general. Only by explication of such goals can the direction of medical research and development and the priority attached to each potential application be ascertained. In addition to setting national goals, a future-oriented public agenda for achieving these objectives must be established. Nowhere is the need for cautious evaluation of options prior to the development and widespread use of the innovation more vital than in biomedical technology. Early technology assessment must include a considerable focus on the first- and second-order political, ethical, and social consequences of each option.

The need for integrated and clearly articulated policy objectives to deal with the expanding arsenal of high-cost technologies is clear. However, it must be acknowledged that their attainment is difficult given the inextricably complex cultural, social, and political context of medical decision making. In a pluralist society, there are many conceivably legitimate but contradictory goals, especially on issues as fundamental as those that relate to human life and death. Moreover, because these issues are not amenable to bargaining and compromise techniques, it is a formidable task to attain a rational balance among the competing goals.

At its foundation, much of the controversy surrounding the development and application of biomedical technologies centers on conflicting goal criteria. Some of the competing goal orientations which frame public policy to varying degrees are the maximization of: (1) individual freedom and choice, (2) social or public good, (3) scientific and technological progress, (4) quality of life, (5) human dignity, (6) efficiency, (7) social stability, and (8) alternative concepts of justice themselves based on goals of equity, merit, or need. Reactions to specific innovations, as well as to science and technology in general, will vary depending on the predominant social values.

Although the threat of technological innovations to traditional values and institutions is not a new phenomenon, as medical technology expands into previously uncharted directions it becomes crucial to assess the social benefits and costs of each potential application. The diminishing lead time between initial research on a technique and its widespread dissemination, along with the potential irreversibility of many applications, demand that analysis of technology be instituted early in the research and development process. David Freeman argues that technologies must be assessed before "unwanted, unanticipated and damaging" consequences inflict "intolerable amounts" of harm to mankind.[5] He is concerned that by the time negative consequences are learned, technologies are often "frozen" into technical and institutional patterns. In such cases, planned change to correct and control the adverse consequences is extremely costly and difficult.

One barrier to the creation of effective biomedical policy centers on expectations of unlimited availability of medical technology both among consumers and providers. These expectations fuel unrealistic public demands which, in turn, are encouraged by many providers of health services. There is little doubt that the suppliers of high-technology goods and services have a large stake in the continued growth of the health care industry. Furthermore, the infusion of corporate medicine and for-profit hospitals into the health care community heightens the stakes.

All political decisions involve trade-offs as goods and services are distributed across a population. No matter what allocation scheme is applied, some elements of society will benefit and others will be deprived. The philosophical debate has long centered on what criteria ought to be used to determine whether a particular policy is just or fair. Do we select those policies that maximize the good for the greatest number, help those who are least well off, or concentrate goods in a small elite on the assumption that somehow benefits might "trickle down" to those on the bottom? Since Plato first argued that health resources should not be wasted on the sickly and unproductive, the distribution of these limited resources (money, technologies, skilled personnel, and time) has been part of a public policy debate. Although the dominant policy in the United States has been to minimize direct governmental intervention in the allocation of health care resources, for reasons discussed above this policy perspective must undergo revision.

Until now there has been a clear tendency in the United States to avoid making the difficult decisions regarding the distribution of scarce medical resources. Most often the "solutions" merely shift costs from the individual to the government or from one agency to another. Aaron and Schwartz, for instance, see a pattern toward reliance of policymakers on prospective reimbursement schemes to solve health cost problems.[6] Although this approach gives the appearance of resolving the problem, these shifts only delay the need to make the hard choices at a later date. As William Brandon notes, we are running out of easy options and purported panaceas.[7] Despite these interim shifts in the burden of payment, the prevailing approach fails to address the critical issues relating to the need to establish policy priorities and set limits on the use of certain high-cost medical technologies. Neither policymakers nor the public are willing to face the futility of simply shifting costs and make the difficult choices which increasingly are becoming necessary.

Biomedical issues are particularly problematic and sensitive within the U.S. cultural and institutional context. Central to our value system is a tendency to look for the easiest solutions. The dependence on increasingly higher levels of technologies to avoid more difficult changes in lifestyle is obvious. Ought society continue to encourage this perspective and develop technologies to provide a "fix" for these problems or should it make efforts to alter life-styles such as obesity, smoking, and sedentary life found in an affluent society? Few technologies more vividly illustrate the dilemmas concerning individual rights, social needs, and responsibilities than biomedical technologies, because they deal with human life and death directly. While the scope of "fundamental" rights has expanded, conflict is intensified by introducing technologies that confer different rights and responsibilities across a variety of divisions in society. Basic questions focus on the scope of individual rights, the extent to which society ought to intervene in these freedoms, and how such constraints, if any, might be justified. If a person abuses himself or herself, what responsibility does society have to that individual? Ought the concept of community be expanded to take into account the rights of and responsibility toward the unborn, toward future generations, and toward other species?

Table 11-1.   Selected Human Genetic and Reproductive Technologies

Characteristic Screening Techniques	Carrier Screening
	Neonatal Screening
	Sex Preselection
	DNA Analysis
Prenatal Intervention Techniques	Amniocentesis
	Chorionic Villus Biopsy
	Ultrasound
	Fetoscopy
	DNA Probes
	Fetal Surgery
	Gene Therapy
Reproduction-Aiding Techniques	Artificial Insemination
	In vitro Fertilization
	Embryo Lavage
	Embryo Transfer (Surrogate)
	Cryopreservation
	Egg Fusion

ETHICAL ISSUES IN HUMAN GENETIC AND REPRODUCTIVE TECHNOLOGY

Among the myriad ethical/policy dilemmas arising from biomedical technology, none are more troublesome and challenging than those of human genetics and reproduction. Because they give us the capacity to intervene in the most fundamental of life processes, more than any other biomedical developments they generate intense reactions both for and against their use. The scope of human genetic/reproductive technologies is illustrated in table 11−1. Although there is overlap among the categories, attention here is directed toward the third category, reproduction-aiding technologies.

Infertility is a growing problem for many American men and women. In 1982 an estimated one in six couples was infertile. Although the causes of infertility are complex and poorly understood, they include environmental, heritable, pathological, and sociobehavioral factors. Although drug therapy and microsurgical intervention are effective in treating infertility in some instances, increasingly couples are turning to reproductive technologies. According to the Office of Technology Assessment, the demand for these services is attributable in part to several factors:

1. Couples are delaying childbearing, thereby exposing themselves to the higher infertility rates associated with advancing age.

2. An increased proportion of infertile couples is seeking treatment due to an increased awareness of the availability and successes of modern infertility services coupled with a decreased supply of infants available for adoption. In 1983 about 50,000 adoptions took place in the United States, but an estimated two million couples wanted to adopt.

3. A greater number of physicians offer infertility services than in previous years. An estimated 45,600 physicians provide infertility services, a statistic that exceeds by 25 percent the number of physicians providing obstetric care.[8]

TECHNOLOGIES OF HUMAN REPRODUCTION

The most widely used form of reproduction-aiding technology today is artificial insemination (AI). Approximately 30,000 to 60,000 AIs are performed annually, resulting in 6,000 to 10,000 live births.[9] Semen is deposited by a syringe in or near the cervix of a woman's uterus in an effort to achieve conception. AI is a relatively simple medical procedure; in fact, one researcher suggests that a "home insemination kit" might not be far off. Biologically, it is irrelevant whether the sperm used is the husband's or a donor's, but the ethical, psychological, and social problems surrounding third-party insemination are more complex. Artificial insemination by donor (AID) is usually used when the husband is wholly infertile or is known to suffer from a serious hereditary disorder such as Huntington's disease. AID is also used for single women wishing to bear a child outside of a sexual relationship.

Although the first reported child was conceived through AID a century ago, use of this method has expanded in the last few decades through the introduction of cryopreservation techniques, which freeze and preserve sperm indefinitely by immersion in liquid nitrogen. Cryopreservation has led to the establishment of commercial sperm banks, some of which now advertise their products to the public. Sperm banks also make it possible for a man to store his semen prior to undergoing a vasectomy, as a form of "fertility insurance." More importantly, they also facilitate eugenic programs, such as the Repository for Germinal Choice which will inseminate women of "high intelligence" with sperm of "superior men."

In vitro fertilization (IVF) is the procedure by which eggs are removed from a woman's ovaries, fertilized outside her body, and reimplanted in her uterus. This procedure is called for when the oviducts are blocked, preventing the egg from passing through the fallopian tubes to be fertilized. The National Academy of Sciences estimates that up to 1 percent of all American women who are otherwise unable to bear children might be able to do so through IVF.[10]

The first stage of IVF is to obtain an egg from the woman's ovary. A small incision is made in the woman's abdomen and a fine hollow needle is inserted, aspirating the mature egg contained in follicular fluid. Often "superovulation" through hormonal treatment is used to provide multiple eggs during a single ovulation. The fluid is then deposited in a medium that allows the ova to mature completely prior to fertilization. Concurrently, semen (either fresh or frozen, husband or donor) is placed in a carrier solution that capacitates it so that it is able to fertilize the egg. The two mediums containing the egg and the sperm are then diluted to simulate conditions found in the fallopian tubes. A few hours after the fertilization occurs, the zygote is transferred to a solution that supports cell division and embryo maturation. When the embryo reaches the 8- to 16-cell stage after several days, it is transferred to the uterus of the egg donor, or to another woman. With the ability to freeze the human embryo has come the capacity to preserve the several-cell embryo for transfer at a later time. This has already resulted in the births of twins sixteen months apart. Hypothetically, in combination with embryo splitting or "twinning" techniques, this would offer future persons the possibility of having their twin embryo as a child. In any event, there is a clear trend toward the use of frozen embryos in conjunction with IVF.

In vitro fertilization expands considerably the possible combinations of germ material and further complicates the concept of parenthood. This technique also illustrates the speed at which these technologies become diffused. In 1978 the first in vitro baby, Louise Brown, was born in England. In January 1980, after considerable political debate, Norfolk General Hospital obtained governmental approval to make the technique available. In its first year of operation the Norfolk In Vitro Fertilization Clinic treated forty-one patients and had a pregnancy rate of about 15 percent. On December 28, 1981, Elizabeth Carr became the first in vitro baby born in the United States. Within five years the number of clinics offering IVF has expanded to 130 and the number of children born through this method totals well over 1,000. Moreover, most clinics continue to have long waiting lists of women who are willing to pay $4,000 to $5,000 for a chance of becoming pregnant. In most cases, the final cost of pregnancy is in excess of $20,000 because more than one attempt is necessary. Despite this investment, up to 80 percent of the women who undergo in vitro fertilization do not become pregnant.

This heavy demand for reproductive-aiding technologies led in 1983 to the first birth through the embryo lavage technique. In this particular case, twelve potential donor women were artificially inseminated with the sperm of a married man. After a sophisticated procedure where the menstrual cycles of the donor women and the man's wife were synchronized, the embryos were flushed from the donors at about five days and microscopically screened. The "best" embryo was selected and transferred to the wife who carried it to term. Although the procedure was performed at Long Beach Memorial Hospital, both the procedure and the computer software were patented by a Chicago firm, Fertility and Genetics Research, Inc.

One especially controversial social innovation culminating from these technological breakthroughs is surrogate motherhood. Here an infertile woman and her husband contract with another woman (the surrogate) to be artificially inseminated with the sperm of the husband. After fertilization, she carries the fetus to term; once the baby is born she relinquishes her rights to it and gives it to the couple. Surrogate motherhood raises new legal and moral problems because the surrogate must be willing to be inseminated by the sperm of a stranger, carry his baby for nine months, and then give the baby to the couple or the single man who contracted with her, usually for a fee. The commitment of a surrogate mother is substantial, both physically and emotionally. Moreover, the couple must rely totally on the good faith of the surrogate to keep her promise because they cannot be assured of any legal rights to the child.

In addition to these currently used techniques, substantially more revolutionary innovations are forthcoming. Egg fusion, or the combination of one mature egg with another, eliminates the need for male genetic material and always produces a female. In an extension of this technique, both eggs could be obtained from the same woman, thus producing a daughter who is totally hers genetically. Reproductive-aiding technologies also overlap with screening and selection technologies. Sperm separation techniques used in conjunction with AID and IVF now provide the means to maximize conception of a child of the desired sex. Increasingly precise genetic diagnosis using molecular probes of embryos prior to transfer will give us the capacity to identify and, perhaps, treat genetic disorders. Following discovery of a DNA probe for the Huntington's Disease gene in 1983, efforts have been initiated to identify possible genetic markers for Alzheimer's Disease, manic-depression, malignant melanoma, and a host of other conditions. In addition, considerable attention has been directed of late to the genetic bases of alcoholism, and work is proceeding at a rapid pace to provide techniques to identify persons who are susceptible to alcohol dependency. Eventually, genetic tests will allow scientists to identify not only the course of genetic abnormalities, but also traits that put certain individuals at higher risk for susceptibility to a host of environmental factors.[11]

POLICY ISSUES IN REPRODUCTIVE TECHNOLOGY

At the very least, these rapid advances in reproductive technology force us to reevaluate our beliefs concerning reproduction and the right of procreation. In a broader sense, they challenge traditional notions of parenthood. Now we must learn to distinguish among the genetic parents (who contribute the germ material), the biological mother (who carries the fetus to term) and the legal parents, one or both of whom might also be the genetic parents. Moreover, the extent to which these "artificial" methods of reproduction involve considerably more individuals (often third parties with a commercial interest) than the "natural" method means that procreation is no longer a private matter between a man and a woman.

Ironically, genetic intervention is especially controversial because of the rapid succession of advances in knowledge of human genetics and the shortened lead time between basic research and application. While fundamental values tend to change slowly across generations, the success of genetic technology threatens these values, but allows little opportunity for careful reflection. As a result, value conflicts are created within a very short time span and soon are elevated to the public policy arena.

In addition to challenging basic values, human genetics for many persons raises the spector of eugenics and social control. References to a Brave New World scenario, where human reproduction is a sophisticated manufacturing process and a "major instrument for social stability" are commonplace, as are aspersions to Nazi Germany.[12] Moreover, fears of human genetic engineering, itself often a pejorative term, are cast in terms of playing God or interfering with evolution. Not surprisingly, opposition to genetic and reproductive intervention in this context is frequently intense.

A complicating factor that heightens opposition to genetic intervention among some groups is the selective nature of genetic diseases. The success of genetic screening efforts often depends on the ability to isolate those groups which are at high risk. In targeting these groups, however, problems of stigmatization, due process, and privacy result. The early experience with sickle cell screening, for instance, led to perceived and real threats to the black community and raised severe criticisms of screening efforts. As DNA probes are used to identify individuals at heightened risk for alcoholism, personality disorders, and so forth, the issue of stigmatization is bound to reemerge, thus making any attempts to screen most controversial.

Until now, only what are generally perceived as disruptive effects of genetic intervention have been raised here. If this were the only side, there would be little debate. However, these same technologies promise vast benefits to many persons, in some cases their only hope. This accentuates the public debate and makes intervention a matter of public policy. Among the promises of benefits that accrue from genetic intervention are treatment or elimination of genetic disorders, overcoming infertility problems, and expanded control over the characteristics and destiny of future generations. Understandably, those individuals and groups who might benefit from these technologies are just as committed to their development and use as are those persons opposed.

Because of the intensity of these issues, technical specialization has multiplied the number of interest groups, each with its own specific goals and demands. These conflicting demands must be resolved through the political process. Very interesting alignments in opposition to many forms of reproductive intervention exist which cut across traditional liberal/conservative political lines. These include right-to-life, civil libertarian, minority, and feminist groups. Groups in favor of intervention generally include health professionals, representatives of commercial interests, and advocacy groups for more research and education on genetic disease. Complicating the dialogue is the fact that opposition interests focus attention on eugenic applications while those in favor of utilizing diagnostic and intervention innovations generally stress the clinical applications and minimize social control potentialities. One of the dilemmas raised by these technologies is that, depending on their specific application, they can be viewed as either extending procreative rights or constraining those same rights. Every genetic technology has a variety of clinical and eugenic applications, depending upon the motivation of the persons using it. Often this fact purposely is obscured by the rhetoric of both sides.

In an effort to make the analysis of policy issues in human genetics and reproduction more manageable, the issues are here grouped into three broad levels. The first level includes problems of regulation that are common to any endeavors that affect public health. As such, they most easily fit conventional models of governmental reaction to public problems. The second set of policy issues centers on problems of allocating scarce societal resources and of setting societal goals and priorities regarding their distribution. Again, although the intensity surrounding reproductive issues makes them formidable, clear policy precedents in other areas of biomedical technology exist. The third, and most difficult, set of policy issues pertains to the need to assess the impact of new intervention capabilities on basic societal values and structures and to make difficult policy choices in reaction to these innovations. Although the ethical dimensions of policymaking in regard to human reproductive intervention are present in all three sets of issues, they are most vivid in this last group.

ISSUES IN REGULATION

Current government reaction to dilemmas of human reproduction are piecemeal and often contradictory. Because of the inability and/or unwillingness of legislatures to take clear policy initiatives, in large part reproductive policy is being made through common law. One of the fastest growing areas of tort law centers on procreation, and although the courts largely are acting responsibly, they are incapable of making rational, consistent policy in an area as complex as human reproduction. State statutes, as they exist, result in a haphazard, inconsistent policy framework across the states. At a minimum, national regulatory guidelines are needed for the growing human genetics enterprise now being undertaken in the United States. Not surprisingly, countries with national health services have been more active in forming national guidelines.

One shared characteristic of all reproduction technologies from AID to gene therapy is that they introduce a third party into what has been a private matter between a man and a woman. The more complex the intervention, the more mediators are necessary. Embryologists, geneticists, and an array of other specialists become the new progenitors. Although these specialists' desire to help desperate patients may be genuine, their very presence takes control of procreation away from the couple. The willingness of many infertile couples to do (and pay) anything to have a child also encourages commercialization of procreation. The heightened demand raises the potential for exploitation of the consumers of these services. Third-party involvement raises critical questions as to who has access to the technologies. The danger, as in all health care, is a tiered system where the technologies serve primarily the upper middle class.

The shift of fertility services from the public sector to the private profit-making sector raises many questions concerning the necessity and applicability of government regulation of these businesses. I argue that the government has a crucial role in setting liability, safety, and confidentiality standards for these enterprises. Moreover, because of the huge potential profits and a hesitancy of the government to fund research in human reproduction, increasingly the development of these technologies is funded by the private sector. This eliminates both the government funding lever and peer review as control mechanisms over what directions we take. Furthermore, as consumer demand for reproductive technologies increases, the reproduction industry will become more competitive. This means that the lag time between basic research for a technique and its use is likely to be cut to a minimum, thus confusing the lines between therapy and experimentation. Finally, because of the trend toward commercialization of fertility services, the government must regulate their marketing and ensure the protection of potential consumers.

In addition to the need for a public policy to provide a regulatory context for human reproductive intervention, the potential for the mis-use of genetic data raises concerns regarding privacy and confidential-ity. As the technological capacity for establishing genetic profiles expands and genetic screening is more commonplace, pressure from insurance companies, employers, and other third parties for access to this data will increase. Congress must establish policies to protect the confidentiality of genetic data banks and preclude misuse of this infor-mation from third parties, including the government. Although the private sector has an important role to play here, only enlightened national awareness of the potential problems and systematic public safeguards will assure compliance, particularly from the government itself.

NATIONAL PRIORITIES AND THE ALLOCATION OF SCARCE RESOURCES

The second level of policy concern is the urgent need for a national dialogue over societal goals and priorities in human procreation. We must decide what research directions should take precedence and how we wish to allocate the limited resources available. Although the cost of a single procedure might be small compared to other medical interventions, cumulatively the costs of human genetic technologies is staggering. Also, any application represents trade-offs against other applications. For example, the current enthusiasm for reproductive mediating techniques, such as in vitro fertilization, clearly reflects a technological-fix orientation at the expense of a preventive approach. Money spent now to avert Chlamydia (a major cause of fallopian tube damage) would reduce the need for reparative treatment later. One policy task is the determination of how much of health resources should be directed toward human genetic and reproductive technologies.

Before adequate allocation decisions are made in human repro-duction, decisional criteria must be clarified and the political feasibil-ity of each option assessed. Policymakers must analyze what impact each allocation scheme would have on a variety of groups and individ-uals in society. Because of the sensitivity of human procreation, any government decision to encourage, discourage, prohibit, or mandate certain users of genetic intervention will raise issues of distributive justice. Particularly hard will be decisions that might deny allocation of public funds for the development and application of techniques deemed of a lesser priority. In addition to the need for Congress to monitor the allocation of resources into these technologies, the creation of a long-term, national, commission-type body to initiate a dialogue over societal priorities in human genetics and procreation is overdue.

INDIVIDUAL CHOICE AND SOCIAL VALUES

Although the policy issues in regulation and allocation are formidable, the most problematic set of policy issues are the less tangible ethical issues involving the way we view individuals and define their role in society. Unlike other Western democracies, in the United States these issues have been fought out primarily in the courts within a constitutional context. These issues deal with conflicts over individual choice, rights, and responsibilities. On the one hand, government intervention in this area is the most difficult to justify. Opponents argue that procreation must remain a private manner. Certainly the history of government involvement in reproduction is not encouraging, as is illustrated by compulsory sterilization laws and discriminatory policies aimed at women and minorities, especially the mentally retarded. On the other hand, I argue that because the new technical capacities to intervene will intensify conflicts among the rights of individuals (e.g., surrogate mother cases) the government must actively devise rational and fair means to clarify and resolve this conflict. Only the national government has the resources necessary to initiate a dialogue that forces consideration of the long-term impact of reproductive technologies on basic values. Because of their ramifications on how we view ourselves and others in society, several issues warrant special concern by policymakers.

Perceptions of Children. One cogent impact of the widespread use of the array of human genetic and reproductive intervention technologies that has substantial long-term implications for society is how they alter our perceptions of children. As couples (and singles) have fewer children, increasingly there is a demand for such technologies from parents who believe they can guarantee a "perfect child." According to many observers,[13] young couples are going to considerable lengths to ensure the birth of a near-perfect child, including selection of the sex of their progeny. Survey data indicate that many parents would consider termination of a pregnancy even for moderate defects in the unborn child, such as a heightened risk of early heart disease or criminal tendencies. Recent evidence of parents seeking human growth hormone "therapy" for their young children simply because estimates are that they will not reach their desired height attest to this quest for the "perfect child."

This emphasis on technological "perfection" raises questions concerning the purpose of children in this generation and tends to commodify them. It is not surprising that terms such as "quality control" over the reproductive process and children as "products" of particular techniques are commonplace. With the increased availability of sex and characteristic selection techniques, motivations for their application must be examined closely. There is a clear danger of viewing children as commodities.

Furthermore, it is probable that the availability of technologies for prenatal diagnosis, screening, and selection will heighten discrimination of children born with congenital or genetic disorders. Already there is a clear danger that acceptance of selective abortion reduces tolerance for the living affected. Leon Kass expresses concern for those abnormals who are viewed as having escaped the "net of detection and abortion," as attitudes toward such individuals are "progressively eroded."[14] In this atmosphere, increasingly such individuals will be viewed as unfit to be alive, as second class humans or lower, or as unnecessary persons who would not have been born if only someone had gotten to them in time. Parents are likely to resent such a child, especially if social pressures and stigma are directed against them. The "right to be born healthy," according to Murphy and associates, is misleading because it actually means that "only healthy persons have a right to be born."[15] For Alexander Capron, the recognition of an enforceable right to be born with a sound, normal mind and body would "open the door to judicially mediated genetic intervention of limitless dimensions."[16] The choice of those affected is not between a healthy and unhealthy existence, but rather between an unhealthy existence and none at all.

Reproductive Technologies and Reproductive Rights. No issue in recent decades has been more controversial among the American public than that of reproductive choice. The right to privacy in reproduction has been at the center of the women's movement for equal status in a society where their prime role in reproduction often has been used to deny them equality. The progression of Supreme Court decisions on procreative privacy beginning with *Skinner v. Oklahoma*,[17] continuing with *Griswold v. Connecticut*[18] and *Eisenstadt v. Baird*,[19] culminating in *Roe v. Wade*,[20] and reiterated by *City of Akron v. Akron Center for Reproductive Health*[21] has clearly enunciated a constitutional right of a woman *not* to conceive or bear a child if she so desires and thus to have access to contraception, sterilization, and abortion without state interference. Despite significant violation of this right in practice, as a concept the right to reproductive privacy is well established.

Although abortion continues to be a volatile issue, the complementary issue of whether all women (and men) have a corresponding right to have children is more problematic. If there is a right to have children, are there any limits that can be imposed as to the number or "quality" of those progeny?[22] For instance, is there a duty of carriers of genetic disease to refrain from having children from their own germ material and utilize "collaborative conception" technologies such as AID or embryo transfer?[23] Does a woman have a responsibility to avail herself of prenatal diagnostic techniques to identify "defective" fetuses and either abort or, if possible, treat the fetus? Women have been ordered by courts to undergo Caesarean sections against their wishes for the benefit of the fetus.[24] Should they, as a matter of public policy, also be required to have their body invaded to permit surgery on the fetus in utero? If so, who makes the policy and how is it implemented?

Until now, reproductive choice largely has been framed as a negative right which assures only that the choice cannot be constrained without a "compelling state interest." In the absence of a state interest that overrides the choice of the individual, she or he has a right to reproduce as long as the action does not harm a constitutionally defined person. The emergence of reproductive and genetic technologies drastically extends the potential scope of procreative choice, but ironically also threatens the rights to privacy in reproduction that have been gained by women in the last two decades.

Reproduction technologies raise the logical extension of reproductive autonomy as a positive right—a claim upon society to guarantee, through whatever means possible, the capacity to reproduce. If the right to procreation is interpreted as a positive one, then an infertile person might have a constitutional claim to these technologies. Under such circumstances, individuals who are unable to afford those treatments necessary to achieve reproductive capacity could expect society to guarantee access. A woman with blocked fallopian tubes would have a claim to corrective surgery or in vitro fertilization. An infertile man would be ensured access to artificial insemination or corrective surgery, if that is possible. Once procreative rights are stated as positive, however, drawing reasonable boundaries becomes difficult. Does a woman who is unable to carry a fetus to term because of the absence of a uterus or a high risk condition have a legitimate claim for a surrogate mother who would do so? Wherever the lines are drawn, some individuals are likely to have limited opportunity to have children. The advent of the new technologies of reproduction raises serious questions for procreative choice. Any shifts toward a positive-rights perspective will accentuate the already growing demand for these technologies, encourage entrepreneurs to provide a broad variety of these reproductive services, and, most importantly, put increasing pressures on the government to fund these services.

SUMMARY: HUMAN REPRODUCTIVE INTERVENTION

The technologies of human genetics and reproduction raise critical policy dilemmas that increasingly require public attention. On the one hand, these innovations promise to alleviate the individual and social costs of genetic disease and give us more control over the destiny of future generations. They allow us to alter the "givens" concerning what it means to be a human being. On the other hand, widespread use of these technologies expands considerably society's ability to label and categorize individuals according to precise genetic factors. There is the danger of altering our definition of humanhood so as to minimize the "human" aspects. This capacity to predetermine the sex of progeny, to select the frozen embryo that best meets one's expectation for a child, and to use prenatal diagnosis to eliminate fetuses with undesirable characteristics can easily dehumanize us despite giving the appearance of expanding individual choice. Clearly these technologies dramatize the ethical dimensions of any policy decisions made in this area.

In the early 1980s the President's Commission for the Study of Ethical Problems in Medicine and Biomedical and Biological Research, under strong pressure from religious organizations, studied the ethical dimensions of the issues of human genetic and reproductive technology. The commission issued two reports on this subject, one focusing on screening and counseling[25] and the other on genetic intervention.[26] There is a need for continuing governmental bodies, along the lines of this commission, to explicate the ethical aspects of the policy issues raised by these technologies.

Whether such mechanisms take the form of Milbrath's Council on Long Range Societal Guidance,[27] Abram and Wolf's temporary independent advisory commission,[28] Light's bipartisan commission model,[29] or one of many other innovative approaches, meaningful evaluation of reproductive technologies requires full attention to the broad range of issues they generate, including the difficult ethical ones. Furthermore, any efforts to manage these technologies must have a strong national component. Continued reliance on the states to set the agenda in human genetics and reproduction produces a haphazard and often contradictory policy context which largely obscures the broader ethical dimensions. Consistency and fairness necessitate a more vigorous role for the public through the national government. Although regulatory issues might continue to reside in the state agenda, only the national government has the resources to initiate a national dialogue on goals, priorities, and values raised earlier in this chapter.

CONCLUSIONS: BIOMEDICAL POLICY AND ETHICS

Innovations in biomedicine are creating policy issues that promise to become more problematical in the future. As the capacity of biomedical technologies expands, more complicated policy problems will emerge. Moreover, the rapid proliferation of advances in human genetics and reproduction demonstrate the inherent ethical dimensions of these issues. This chapter illustrates the impossibility of excluding from consideration the ethical ramifications of any policy regarding human intervention at these levels. Any policy that obscures the ethical factors is destined to fail.

Although the ethical aspects of public policy might be particularly vivid in the biomedical arena, in no area of technology policymaking can they be disregarded. To be successful, any technology policy evaluation must account for the ethical dimensions. All technologies have the potential to alter human values as well as social priorities. They solidify some values and threaten others. To effectively evaluate technology, therefore, we must explicitly acknowledge the complexity of the dilemmas they raise. This requires a thorough reexamination of traditional concepts such as individual rights and responsibility. It also necessitates a clarification of the evaluation criteria upon which public policy is made. These technologies offer tremendous opportunities but bring with them often difficult changes and costs. Because of the high stakes involved in biomedical technology, especially in human reproduction, these issues promise to be among the most difficult to resolve.

EVALUATING TECHNOLOGY THROUGH PUBLIC

PARTICIPATION: THE NUCLEAR WASTE

DISPOSAL CONTROVERSY

MICHAEL E. KRAFT

The disposal of radioactive waste from nuclear power plants has been on the back burner since the beginning of the nuclear age forty years ago. Long considered by an optimistic nuclear community to be an essentially technical job, and largely ignored as the nation increased its reliance on nuclear power, the waste issue has emerged in the 1980s as a profound test of our capacity to govern technology effectively and democratically. In 1982 the U.S. Congress enacted the Nuclear Waste Policy Act (NWPA), which initiated a comprehensive, long-term program for disposal of high-level nuclear waste in geologic repositories.[1] Since then the Department of Energy (DOE) has been struggling to implement the policy amid increasing public concern and opposition. In late 1987 Congress amended the act, but the policy's future remains in doubt. Resolution of the many disputes surrounding it raises important questions about how to decide what to do with this and comparable technologies.

If not disposed of safely, which requires isolation from the biosphere for tens of thousands of years, high-level nuclear wastes pose significant risks to both human health and environmental quality. But insuring that disposal goes well is a formidable managerial and political task, in part because of numerous uncertainties and disagreements over key aspects of the process. What kind of containment is best, and how safe will it be, especially hundreds or thousands of years into the future? What particular sites are most appropriate for long-term and safe isolation of wastes, and how should potential sites be evaluated? What kinds of procedures should be followed to insure that accurate information is available for government officials and the public at both the federal and state level? Who should decide, and how should they decide, where those waste repositories are placed?[2]

Langdon Winner argues in chapter 2 that technology shapes politics; it can establish a framework for public order (e.g., acceptance of powerful, centralized authority) that lasts for generations. But the inverse is also true; politics can affect technology in many ways, and the framework for public order is often at the center of disputes over how we should use technology. This is nowhere more evident than in the choices facing the United States and other nations in deciding how to deal with nuclear wastes. Some argue that the scale and complexity of the job require substantial reliance on the analytic and managerial expertise of centralized bureaucracies, such as the DOE, that are sufficiently experienced and able to perform and coordinate the manifold technical tasks involved. Others prefer that important policy decisions be made through a democratic political process that provides extended opportunities for consultation, debate, and interaction among interested parties, especially at the state and local level, thus promoting policy legitimation.

It is easy to say that both kinds of decisions are important and each should be made in an appropriate manner, but they may conflict with one another. The DOE, for example, is often accused of ignoring concerns expressed by the public and state officials; in turn, the nuclear community, including the DOE, has complained that involvement by an uninformed public creates delays and interferes with what they consider to be sound decision making. In fact, technical decisions cannot always be separated from policy decisions, and both may involve complex and difficult choices that will leave an enduring nuclear— and political—legacy. But it is not clear how those decisions should be made and what the consequences are.

In this chapter I examine how democratic politics, and especially public participation, can help evaluate technology and its attendant risks and thereby assist in making public policy choices. The case of nuclear waste disposal under the NWPA is used to explore that possibility. I turn first to some aspects of democratic theory and its relationship to the assessment of technology. In that light I discuss a number of approaches to public participation that might be appropriate for disposal of nuclear wastes and similar controversies. After reviewing the challenge of nuclear wastes, the specifications of the NWPA and

DOE's efforts to date to implement it, I return to the question of alternatives for public participation that might offer a more effective and responsive way to manage those wastes.

PUBLIC PARTICIPATION AND ASSESSMENT
OF RISKY TECHNOLOGIES

What is the best way to make governmental decisions that involve technology? The competing visions of optimal decision making range from technocratic to democratic, depending on the specific technology and circumstances. But especially when the question is determining the acceptability of risks associated with the introduction or extension of technology, the decisions are primarily normative or political. That is, they involve personal and social judgments (often implicit) about the risks we are willing to live with in exchange for the benefits we enjoy from use of that technology.[3] There are frequently intense disagreements over such judgments and how they are made which cannot be resolved through technical means. What is required is a process that allows clear articulation of the issues, dialogue between those who disagree, and negotiation and mutually acceptable settlement of disputes. In short, for this kind of evaluation of technology's risks we look to a variety of political processes for conflict resolution, whether at the federal, state, or local level or in legislative or executive institutions.

There are, to be sure, some methods of risk evaluation that technical personnel often use, which I discuss in chapter 9; these include natural standards (e.g., naturally occurring background radiation), implied preferences (what is implied by people's behavior), expressed preferences (what people indicate in opinion surveys), professional judgment (e.g., by nuclear engineers), and risk-cost-benefit analysis, all of which have been employed to assess nuclear power risks.[4] But applied to nuclear waste disposal and related technologies, these methods are limited by the intricacy of the problem being studied and the primitive nature of risk assessment and risk evaluation methods. Such evaluation also involves judgments about values and trade-offs between conflicting values that are extraordinarily difficult and arguably are best left to the public itself and its elected representatives.

For example, Walker, Gould, and Woodhouse delineate the "numerous value judgments" involved in nuclear waste decisions and argue for a value-oriented view instead of the predominant technically oriented view of waste management, in which many of the key decisions are made by technical experts in the bureaucracy and the nuclear industry. They refer specifically to value questions related to setting radiation standards; the use of various methods of storage, disposal, or reprocessing of nuclear waste; siting disposal facilities; and decontamination and decommissioning of nuclear power plants. But they also include the broader issues of national energy policy; for example, the extent to which nuclear power should be relied upon and the role the government assumes in encouraging or subsidizing various energy sources.[5]

Questions like these are what the National Research Council's Committee on Risk and Decision Making had in mind when, in a major report in 1982, it explicitly rejected the traditional emphasis on expertise in risk-related policymaking as "both unattainable and incompatible with democratic principles."[6] Expanding on the council's perspective, we might say that the case for democracy is especially compelling when the technology affects a large number of people, they hold intense opinions on the subject, and the risks associated with that technology are involuntary, long term, highly uncertain and possibly irreversible.

There are some complications, of course, to the simple notion that the public and its representatives should decide all important questions in using technology that involve conflicting values. One is that lay persons, including elected representatives, may not fully understand conflicts involving technically complex information and scientific uncertainties. Another is that the usual process of incremental or trial-and-error decision making, described by Woodhouse in chapter 10, may take too long to complete, yield inconclusive results, and rely too much on feedback (e.g., evidence of leakage) that may be detectable only in the long term.[7] A third complication is the problem of what to do about those who cannot be represented directly in any political process, namely future generations. Who should speak for them in risk-acceptance decisions? What standards or criteria are appropriate for comparing and balancing risks and benefits of present and future generations, especially for intergenerational equity?

A fourth issue especially likely to be important in nuclear waste disposal involves geographic distribution of risks. If the burden falls on a given region, state, or locality, which is likely in the NWPA case, what principles should inform the risk-acceptance decision (e.g., equity, desert, or need)? For example, to what extent should a state or locality be given authority to reject imposition of an unwanted risk like nuclear waste? Is doing so compatible with the national imperative of locating a disposal site? If such a risk must be imposed on a given population, should it be informed of potential hazards even when they are highly uncertain and such information may unduly slant its decision on whether to cooperate with or fight the federal government? Should the population be compensated, and in what way, for its willingness to accept the risk?[8]

One important conclusion from such considerations is that there is no easy way to put democratic principles into effect when dealing with nuclear wastes and related risks. Given the reservations about reliance on technical experts when value conflicts of this kind exist, how *can* we manage technological risks effectively? Can we do so democratically—with representation of all important interests and with sensitivity to appropriate value concerns? If so, how? Many different proposals have been advanced that may be suitable for resolving such value conflicts, including provisions for public education, public participation of both a conventional and innovative kind, various mediation proceedings, and technology tribunals. None promises a simple solution, but all are worth careful assessment.

Each of these approaches can be defended in terms of policy legitimation or political legitimacy. Policy legitimation refers to the legality of decisions (e.g., providing public notice, holding hearings, and maintaining records) as well as to representation of relevant publics in the decision process and whether it yields decisions broadly acceptable to them.[9] Political legitimacy concerns such basic matters as public trust and confidence in government. The DOE and the Nuclear Regulatory Commission (NRC) are especially vulnerable on that point because of a perceived failure over time to deal openly and competently with nuclear power and nuclear waste; a long history of false starts, mistakes, and suppression of critical information on the waste issue has clearly affected DOE's reputation.[10]

Despite their seeming attractiveness, there is little consensus on which of these approaches might work best and only modest empirical evidence to date on their advantages or disadvantages. But a review of different kinds of public participation as they apply to the problem of nuclear waste disposal can indicate at least some of the opportunities and limitations of each for evaluating this kind of technology.

PUBLIC EDUCATION

Strictly speaking, education is not a form of participation, but a closely allied activity. Creation of an informed public may be considered a prerequisite for effective participation and meaningful citizen judgment on the acceptability of technology. Educating the public for such ends is the ostensible purpose of many public "outreach" or information programs; they are one way of involving the public, even if only indirectly, in decision making on nuclear waste disposal and related issues. For these reasons, an assessment of education as a participation strategy is included here.

Public education is often suggested precisely because the public's fear of nuclear waste is so great. It is the single most feared risk among those commonly measured; moreover, a recent poll indicated that fully 67 percent of the American public is "very concerned" about nuclear waste disposal, the highest percentage for any radiation source people are likely to be exposed to, from nuclear power plants to medical X-rays.[11] Yet the public is not at all well informed about this or most other risks to health, safety, and environmental quality, and the nation's media do remarkably little to improve the situation; according to several studies, media coverage of nuclear issues is largely negative, which reinforces public preconceptions.[12] Given that situation, recommendations for public education are not hard to come by. For example, several authors in a report to DOE in 1982 described such basic approaches to "information dissemination and issue understanding" as direct mailing of brochures and reports to citizens in a local area; holding information seminars where interested parties come together in a face-to-face setting; informal group discussions involving citizens, community leaders, and agency officials; the "planned and systematic use of major media forums"; and the conduct of workshops as information review sessions open to a wide range of interested parties.[13]

As potentially useful as some of these techniques appear to be at first glance, there is evidence that provision of additional knowledge does not alter public attitudes, but rather is likely to reinforce existing beliefs. Consider, for example, the striking difference between supporters and opponents of nuclear power in their beliefs concerning whether nuclear waste can be disposed of safely: 67 percent of supporters believe it can be in contrast to only 12 percent of opponents.[14] How much is provision of new information likely to alter those beliefs? Skepticism about the impact of public education programs is consistent with the findings summarized in a recent review of technological risks and public reaction to them:

> Research has suggested that the primary correlates of public concern [over risks] are not mortality or morbidity rates, but characteristics such as potentially catastrophic effects, lack of familiarity and understanding, involuntariness, scientific uncertainty, lack of personal control by the individuals exposed, risks to future generations, unclear benefits, inequitable distribution of risks and benefits and potentially irreversible effects.[15]

Nuclear waste possesses precisely these characteristics, suggesting the obstacles facing those who attempt to alter the politics of nuclear waste, at least through conventional public education programs.

If there is any basis for optimism about the potential of public education efforts, it lies in the observation that one cannot predict precisely how the public will respond to nuclear power or nuclear waste. Much depends on how the issues are presented by the media, how they are defined in public debate, whether accidents or other salient events occur, and so on. Based on such considerations, for nuclear power to gain acceptance requires, according to one study, "an incontrovertible long-term safety record, a responsible agency that is respected and trusted, and a clear appreciation of benefit."[16] In a similar vein, a journalist who has covered the nuclear waste debate for years concluded that public trust in governmental efforts will be gained only "by building a record of sure, competent, open performance that gets good marks from independent peer reviewers and that shows a decent respect for the public's sensibilities and common sense."[17] Whether the DOE can meet such expectations is uncertain, but the recommendations are consistent with what we know about public attitudes toward risky technologies.

There is also evidence that technological risks are more easily accepted by the public if they are voluntary, controllable, known, familiar, and immediate. At least some of those characteristics may be affected by a properly designed siting and public participation process. Much of the recent emphasis on improving risk communication both in the media and in agency settings underscores the importance of improving public understanding of technical issues in this manner.[18] But by itself better risk communication does not eliminate the basis of public opposition to risks, which also reflects a lack of trust and confidence in government.

PUBLIC PARTICIPATION

There are many models of direct public participation in decision making. At one end of the spectrum are the conventional forms of political participation commonly cited in pluralist theory: those sufficiently concerned may organize and represent their interests through voting, lobbying legislators and administrators, litigation, and so forth. At the other end are the approaches favored by those partial to participatory democracy; these include making use of referenda and initiatives and creation of more innovative opportunities for direct participation, especially at the state and local level, for example, through citizen panels and workshops.

Some of the latter modes of participation may be particularly suitable for the issue of nuclear waste disposal. For example, Howell and Olsen offer a brief assessment of some twenty-one approaches to "Citizen/Government/Industry Interaction," including advocacy planning, citizen advisory committees, community forums, community planning councils, citizen assemblies, arbitrative planning, and citizen review boards.[19] What they have in common is creation of local forums where people can engage in public discourse about the community's interests. Few of these approaches have been used to any great extent, but there is considerable consensus emerging among citizen advocacy organizations that have been active on nuclear waste issues that such forms of participation are essential to building public confidence in any government siting process.[20]

Arguments for direct forms of public participation are also common in discussions of energy policy more generally, where their contribution is seen as quite positive. From this perspective, public participation is likely to broaden the concerns normally associated with energy policy (e.g., to include the optimal level of energy demand, comparison of different energy sources—especially sustainable versus conventional fossil fuel or nuclear sources—and questions of safety); that occurred in Sweden in 1974 when the government fostered study groups related to nuclear power.[21] Another argument is that participation promotes greater equity in the way the costs and benefits of energy policy are distributed and therefore can enhance social stability. A third is that public participation may be a countervailing influence that offsets various elite biases, promotes accountability, and prevents domination by special interests.[22]

There are also some good reasons to doubt that public participation will always make a positive contribution to resolving public problems. Most of these turn on the presumption that most of the time the general public is not very concerned with public affairs and especially not with intricate and remote issues of science and technology. People do not take the time to inform themselves on the issues or may be incapable of understanding many of them. As a consequence, they may misperceive risks and act on the basis of unwarranted fears. An agency that encourages participation without a sufficient attempt at public education is gambling against public prejudice and threatening the success of its program. Holding public hearings on the siting of a nuclear waste repository is seemingly such a gamble. Another concern is that hearings are a very limited form of public participation; generally few people attend them and they are not representative of the community, and the hearings rarely allow for meaningful communication and interaction between agency officials and the public. Nevertheless, how hearings are managed can make a significant difference, even in the case of nuclear waste disposal.[23]

MEDIATION

Mediation or dispute resolution processes include a variety of approaches that allow disputing parties to meet face to face to try to resolve the issues in a controversial situation in a mutually acceptable fashion. These are voluntary processes, and they usually involve consensus building, negotiation, and joint problem solving, all in a spirit of cooperation. They differ from litigation and administrative procedures where the overriding goal is not building consensus but gaining one's objectives at someone else's expense. Citizen groups have been represented in such proceedings along with government, industry, and other parties, and recent assessments of the record of mediation over the last decade are quite encouraging on their contribution to dispute resolution. Thus they seem to be worth considering for nuclear waste disposal and related siting controversies.[24]

In siting disputes interested parties would be provided with a forum to discuss safety, equity, compensation, and other issues. The mediation process also is flexible, encourages participation by those concerned, fosters a dialogue between parties that is often lacking in conventional public meetings or hearings, and can help to tailor policy to local needs. It may be a particularly helpful process when there is a good faith effort to find an acceptable solution, including consideration of compensation, which some writers believe to be essential for nuclear waste repository siting.[25]

The NWPA does authorize DOE to compensate local interests and encourages what Sigmon calls "a climate for meaningful negotiation between DOE and local interests." Yet as he notes in the case of the monitored, retrievable storage (MRS) proposal in Tennessee, there was local resistance even to enter into such negotiations; he concludes that negotiated compensation offers "no easy solution to the siting decision."[26] This is not to say, however, that there is not promise to mediation for many of the issues related to siting, particularly because some communities in New Mexico, Colorado, Washington, South Dakota, and elsewhere have in the past indicated that a nuclear waste facility might be acceptable to them.

There is also some evidence from surveys of public attitudes that casts doubt on the significance of the compensation issue. For example, one study indicated that nonmonetary incentives such as access to information, independent facility monitoring, representation on a governing body, and power to close down a repository may be more important than compensation for increasing public acceptance of a site.[27]

TECHNOLOGY TRIBUNALS

Technology tribunals, a variation on the idea of the "Science Court," have been suggested as a fourth way to involve the public in decisions on technology. Masters and Kantrowitz review an updated version of this as the Scientific Adversary Procedure in chapter 13. The earlier proposal of the technology tribunal was seen as a way to address both fact and value issues in technical controversies by providing a forum in which anywhere from several dozen to several thousand informed scientists and citizens would participate. There would be adversarial hearings similar to legal proceedings, where spokespersons for various competing perspectives could present their cases. Advocates would debate the issues, call and cross-examine witnesses, and defend specific policy recommendations. After reviewing the evidence and testimony, the tribunal would render a formal decision that attempts to create a rational balance among competing considerations implicit in policy alternatives. Thus some kind of democratic consensus would emerge and could then provide policymakers with a more refined and meaningful measure of public concerns and disagreements than is likely to be yielded by public opinion surveys, referenda, and other approaches that make little or no effort to educate the public or build public and expert consensus. Although there is some empirical evidence on the promise of this kind of approach, it is untested for most issues, including nuclear waste.

One conclusion from this review of possible mechanisms for public involvement in nuclear waste decisions is that simplistic prescriptions should be viewed skeptically, as should assertions of efficacy unaccompanied by empirical evidence. More positively, there are clearly many different ways in which people and organized interest groups may try to influence decisions about technology, from conventional forms of political participation such as voting, lobbying, and litigation to more unusual forms such as citizen panels and scientific tribunals for the review of technical disputes. Some are more suitable for a given purpose or time than others; thus mediation makes sense only when there are specific disputes to resolve, say between DOE and a state or community, and good faith efforts at consensus building. There is also much sense in seeking a mix of participation mechanisms, which may be more fruitful than reliance on any single approach. As will be evident below, the brief history of the NWPA suggests that experimentation with some of the more innovative kinds of participation promises important opportunities for the public to have a say in evaluating technology. It would also offer greater hope than present approaches for building public confidence in a waste disposal process.

THE NUCLEAR WASTE PROBLEM AND PUBLIC CONCERNS

The issue of nuclear waste is in some respects inseparable from the larger question of U.S. energy policy, that is, the kind of energy sources relied on and encouraged or subsidized by government. Some, and especially those in the nuclear industry, are concerned that a failure to deal effectively with the waste issue will in effect derail nuclear power as a major component of the nation's energy economy; thus they favor rapid construction of repositories. Opponents of nuclear power have argued that we should not move too quickly to construct storage or disposal facilities because to do so may further our reliance on nuclear power; they hope instead to begin a gradual phasing out of nuclear power plants, and they would like to make repository siting conditional upon such an agreement. Nuclear power is seemingly on its way out in the United States anyway, but largely for economic reasons; no new nuclear power plants have been proposed since 1978 because of sharply rising costs, various regulatory hurdles, and diminishing demand for additional power plants.

Despite all these concerns and ongoing debates, the United States remains committed to nuclear power as a significant source of energy for the next forty to fifty years. Currently it supplies more than 15 percent of the electricity produced in the United States, which is expected to increase to 20 percent in the 1990s.[28] Moreover, other sources of energy (especially coal) also pose major environmental risks which by some estimates rival if not exceed those associated with nuclear power. Even if no new nuclear power plants are built, however, high- and low-level wastes will accumulate for the next fifty years from the more than one hundred plants now in operation and the additional ones planned or under construction, and from military operations.

Estimates of the total amount of nuclear waste vary, but the stock of commercial spent fuel rods (the major component of civilian high-level waste) in 1982 totaled some 10,000 metric tons, and by 1985 was accumulating at the rate of about 3,000 tons per year. By the year 2000 the amount is expected to grow to about five times the 1985 total, and by the year 2020 reach some 130,000 metric tons.[29] The primary disposal site under the 1982 law is to be located in the West and is slated to hold no more than 70,000 metric tons, a figure that was selected by Congress to insure that no single state would become the nation's nuclear waste dump. Without expansion, the primary site will be insufficient much past the year 2000 if the present on-site, temporary storage facilities are phased out.

On the basis of volume, the accumulated military wastes greatly exceed wastes from commercial reactors, constituting some 90 percent of the total. But the number is misleading because the former are primarily in liquid form and the latter compacted into fuel rods. They are nearly equal in terms of the level of radioactivity, a more meaningful measure. Because commercially generated wastes are increasing much faster than military-related wastes, it is fair to say the long-term nuclear waste problem is essentially one of commercial wastes.[30]

High-level wastes have been accumulating in water-filled basins at those temporary surface storage sites for nearly forty years, which Gould (1983) notes "presents no technical or safety problems that have not already been encountered and dealt with fairly successfully," even if surface storage is more vulnerable than mined repositories and other permanent disposal techniques, may pose a greater risk to the biosphere, and is unsuitable for long-term storage (i.e., thousands of years).[31] Some of the nation's utilities have already essentially exhausted their on-site storage capacity (NRC has estimated that twenty-seven of the nation's operating reactors will have filled their spent fuel pools by 1990), and many more will have done so by the year 2000. That makes continued use of those facilities as an interim solution difficult. But it does not rule out construction of a proposed monitored, retrievable storage (MRS) facility to hold wastes temporarily until disputes over permanent disposal are settled.

Given what we know and the remaining uncertainties, is there something distinctive about this kind of technological risk that demands an unusual form of governmental management or of public involvement in those decisions? For many who have examined the case, the answer is clearly yes. Consider, for example, the following characteristics. The public, especially in a local community near a proposed site, is intensely concerned about the risk and strongly opposed. The Not-In-My-Back-Yard (NIMBY) reaction has occurred almost everywhere a potential site has been proposed, raising the distinct possibility that every prospective site will prove to be unacceptable to the local community or state; yet the waste must go somewhere. The risk posed by this waste is highly uncertain, but public perception of it is obviously negative, and no assurance of safety is likely to be believed. Further studies and use of improved methodologies of risk assessment and environmental impact assessment will surely help, but they will take time to complete and will likely be challenged both in scientific and governmental forums. The risk of leakage and eventual contamination of the biosphere is of a very long-term nature and no nation has successfully managed it before; that is, the proposed technology is untried and unproven.

These characteristics would seem to demand something other than business as usual if siting is to be successful. For example, there have been suggestions that a federal agency other than DOE, with greater credibility with the public, be given authority for the waste management program, that more direct forms of participation than hearings be instituted for the public in affected states, and that mediation and compensation be more fully employed. To date, however, the federal government under both the Carter and Reagan administrations has chosen to rely on a highly centralized siting process with conventional forms of public participation, and it has paid a price in failed policy implementation.

THE NWPA AND PUBLIC PARTICIPATION:
THE RECORD TO DATE

The NWPA grew out of an unusually comprehensive effort begun during the Carter administration to formulate the nation's first plan for nuclear waste disposal. Closely associated with Carter's national energy planning process, the Interagency Review Group (IRG) was composed of representatives from thirteen federal agencies and departments that worked together over a two-year period from 1977 to 1979 to devise its plan. In what the IRG knew would be a difficult bid for public support for the proposal, it circulated its draft report widely (some 15,000 copies were distributed and some 3,300 written comments were received), held public hearings on it in Washington and around the country, and arranged numerous meetings with relevant interest groups.[32] Finally, Carter sent his recommendations based on the IRG report to Congress in February 1980. The president's message gave particular attention to state, local, and public participation and public acceptance of the nuclear waste repository program, with some twenty-five references to these matters in his brief statement. But the precise nature of this public participation

—and the concomitant state role—was never made clear.

The U.S. Congress struggled with a number of different bills on both low-level and high-level waste over several years. In 1980 it approved the least controversial part of the Carter proposal as the Low-Level Radioactive Waste Policy Act, which gave states (through the formation of regional compacts) the responsibility for disposal of low-level waste produced by private industry. After another two years of intense controversy, centering on the authority of states to veto placement of a repository within their borders, in late 1982 Congress finally enacted the NWPA. Passage of the legislation should not be interpreted as evidence of a firm consensus in Congress or among the public on what to do about high-level nuclear waste disposal. Indeed, Congress waffled on some of the most contentious issues and left to the DOE the challenge of implementing the act with somewhat unclear guidelines on the nature, extent, and timing of state and public participation in siting decisions.

The NWPA in fact was a fragile combination of an elaborate, centralized, and technical process of site evaluation under the direction of the DOE and a democratic process of state consultation and public participation; a state veto provision was added at the last minute. Unfortunately, as is often the case with poorly conceived and hastily drafted legislative compromises, the combination has not worked well. Among other problems, the intensity of public and state opposition was severely underestimated.

Signed by President Reagan on January 7, 1983, the NWPA established a comprehensive national program for the permanent disposal of high-level commercial and military radioactive waste in mined geologic repositories. It created an Office of Civilian Radioactive Waste Management (OCRWM) within DOE to implement the program, and established a selection process for two disposal sites that included state and local involvement and a veto by a state or Indian tribe of the location of a repository within its jurisdiction; the veto can be overridden only by a majority vote in both houses of Congress.

A detailed schedule for the repository siting process was also set out in the act. The secretary of energy was required to study five potential sites for the first repository, conduct environmental assessments of them, and to recommend three of the sites to the president by January 1, 1985, to be followed by further site characterization. Five more potential sites, at least three of which were not in the first group, were to be studied and three of them recommended to the president by July 1, 1989, for a second repository. Other guidelines were set for DOE to follow in locating a site, including holding hearings in the vicinity of each site being considered.

The president was to make his recommendation to Congress on the first site by March 31, 1987, and on the second site by March 31, 1990; the deadlines could be extended for one year at the discretion of the president. A full environmental impact statement (EIS) is required once a site is selected by DOE for recommendation to the president as a repository, and the facility must be fully licensed by the NRC. In addition, judicial review is allowed for any final decision or action of the secretary of energy, the president, or the NRC in selecting a site for and constructing a repository. Finally, DOE is required to consult closely throughout the entire site selection process with states or Indian tribes that might be affected by the location of the repository; indeed, DOE must enter into binding, written agreements with the states the president recommends as candidate sites. As is evident in even this brief summary, there are many points of review, appeal, and potential delay built into the process.

PUBLIC AND STATE ROLES IN IMPLEMENTATION

Implementation of a complex policy is never easy. When intense public opposition exists, there is even less reason to expect achievement of a program's objectives. Unfortunately, from the perspective of effective implementation, the NWPA established a public review process that created a perfect forum for elected officials and the general public to give vent to their fears and concerns, and to denounce DOE's decision making on the siting process. The public hearing procedure, in particular, led to the classic NIMBY response to siting unwanted facilities which impose localized costs and risks while offering diffuse national benefits.

The DOE began the process well enough, at least from a managerial perspective. Following consultation with the Environmental Protection Agency (EPA), the U.S. Geological Survey, and other agencies, it issued draft siting guidelines amid complaints that it was moving too fast for sound scientific judgments to be made. By April 1984 DOE distributed the formal draft of its comprehensive Mission Plan, which contained its waste management plan and implementation program, essentially technical procedures, but also its intentions regarding state and public participation. Some 3,000 copies were circulated and 102 comments were received, most of them from state agencies and utility and nuclear industry organizations.[33] The public comment process seems to have been a quite limited effort that did not begin to tap the latent concern among relevant publics, yet DOE considered it to be a key component of its required consultation process. Much more intense public involvement (e.g., attendance at hearings) began the following year when the issues were far more salient.

On December 19, 1984, the siting process authorized under the NWPA began to come unglued. On that day DOE ranked nine candidate sites in six states and named the first three sites to be considered for the primary repository in the West: Deaf Smith County, Texas; Yucca Mountain, Nevada; and Hanford, Washington. In what was to become a predictable pattern, Nevada filed suit against DOE in federal court on December 14, three environmental groups filed on December 18, and Texas filed on December 19. Within six months of the first site nominations all three states were challenging the legality of the designation process.

Among the actions contested were DOE's environmental assessments (less thorough than an EIS), which critics charged were seriously flawed methodologically. For example, the director of Nevada's Radioactive Waste Project complained that the "process is rigged: It's prejudged, predetermined, and DOE is just filling in the data to fit."[34] There were enough objections that DOE revised its methodology for these assessments following a study by the National Academy of Sciences. But even in making that adjustment it further irritated the states when it denied them both access to the meetings and further time to review the revisions made. There were also allegations, which DOE denied, that it had destroyed key documents on the methodology used for the draft environmental assessments.[35]

In June 1985 DOE issued the final Mission Plan, and it was then prepared to move ahead on consideration of sites for the second repository. In contrast to the western states, the timetable at this stage allowed for considerable state involvement in the selection process. But by this time the issue of nuclear waste was also receiving far more attention in the press, and public concern was increasing sharply. DOE did not have an easy time here either. On January 16, 1986, the department announced that twenty locations in seven states, all in the Upper

Midwest or East, had been selected from an original list of 235 potential sites in seventeen states. The selection was said to be based on the siting guidelines, which called for the secondary site to be located in granite or other crystalline rocks, and which were to insure that the selection process was systematic, explicit, quantitative, and objective. Based on such criteria, DOE concluded that twelve of the locations were primary choices, and eight secondary. Public officials in the seven states (Minnesota, Wisconsin, Maine, New Hampshire, Virginia, North Carolina, and Georgia) immediately protested their inclusion on this select list and set the tone for the public hearings on DOE's draft Area Recommendation Report (ARR) that followed.

OCRWM conducted thirty-nine briefings and thirty-eight public hearings in fifteen states during a three-month period. All told some 18,000 people attended these sessions, and another 3,200 individuals and organizations provided written comments.[36] In a number of cases, for example in Maine and Wisconsin, the hearings and briefings in early 1986 were attended by thousands of impassioned citizens and state and local officials, with many of the latter actively encouraging public opposition to DOE's initial site characterization studies. These individuals were not as uninformed about the issues as is often assumed; a detailed analysis of the transcripts of hearings in Wisconsin indicates that a rather large percentage of those testifying were either familiar with the ARR or reasonably well acquainted with the technical aspects of nuclear waste disposal.[37]

Regardless of how well informed they were, there was little mistaking public sentiment on the issue, which in turn affected the extremely negative response of elected officials to DOE's siting process.[38] It was clear that acceptance by the general public was virtually impossible under the conditions that existed in 1986. The Chernobyl nuclear power plant accident in late April of 1986 did little to increase public confidence in either nuclear power or nuclear waste disposal, the risks of which are closely associated in the public's mind.

On May 27, 1986, DOE formally recommended the three western sites, and on May 28 President Reagan approved them. That designation meant moving on to the full site characterization in those states, a five-year effort estimated to cost some $1 billion per site. But other factors were to intervene at this time. Recognizing the inevitable political damage being created in an election year, the administration, overruling OCRWM's director, announced on the same day that it was "postponing indefinitely" the site selection process in the Midwest and East. The secretary of energy, John Herrington, added that no further evaluation at the second-round sites was expected until the mid-1990s, and that it would "go back to square one" if a secondary repository were shown to be needed at that time. Among the reasons offered for this dramatic change in the process was that new waste production calculations by DOE indicated that a second repository might not be needed until much later than previously thought, an assertion promptly challenged by others.[39] The secretary's announcement was greeted enthusiastically by public officials in the seven eastern and midwestern states, some of whom could not resist citing the reversal as evidence that "democracy works" and that "citizens can win the day on an issue when they are strongly united."[40]

As might be expected, officials in the three western states were not as happy with the outcome. They accused DOE of using political rather than technical criteria for site selection, and they filed suit once again, challenging DOE's legal authority to suspend the second-round process, among other actions.[41] In response to increased opposition, Congress cut the budget for the siting program and prohibited site-specific activities for fiscal year 1987; by July 1986 some two dozen lawsuits against DOE's siting decisions were pending.

Finally, on January 28, 1987, the Reagan administration proposed a five-year delay in opening the first repository site and repeated Secretary Herrington's earlier pledge to postpone any decision on a second site until the mid-1990s. These decisions required congressional approval of the Mission Plan Amendment DOE submitted to Congress in June 1987; failure to secure that approval, DOE warned Congress, would mean that the second-round siting process would resume in 1987. Under the proposed new timetable, the first site would not be opened until 2003, and the selection of possible second sites would not take place until 2007. DOE acknowledged that one reason for the extension was that "more time should be provided in the future for consultation and interaction with the states" and various Indian tribes.[42] Indeed, the only significant change included in the amendment was consistent with this alteration in the timetable: "The DOE therefore plans to increase its efforts to improve productive institutional relations and to negotiate formal C & C [consultation and cooperation] agreements."

CONCLUSIONS

One conclusion of this case study is inescapable. DOE failed to secure public acceptance for its proposed program for isolating high-level radioactive waste. In an early review of DOE activities in 1986, the General Accounting Office concluded that "in all cases, the problems that led to failure or delay stemmed primarily from public or political opposition."[43] Rejection of DOE's proposals was most striking in the Midwest and East, but it also faced renewed opposition in the West in large part because the Reagan administration decided to curtail further consideration of sites in the Midwest or East. In doing so it unraveled a key bargain struck in Congress over geographic distribution of the nuclear waste risk. Thus the NWPA needed congressional repair to resolve the continuing conflicts over the site selection process, and Congress responded with a major revision of the act in December 1987. The courts will also play a role as they consider the various pending lawsuits (as of late 1987 these numbered about forty). What else might be said, especially about public participation and the evaluation of technology?

By some accounts, particularly by well-informed scientists, the DOE Mission Plan of 1985 was a considerable improvement over earlier efforts to involve citizens in decisions on technology; there was much hope that these efforts would prove to be effective in siting a repository, depending on how DOE implemented the plan.[44] As written, the plan did indeed look quite promising, even if some of the more intensive and innovative forms of public involvement discussed above were not included. But in this case there is also a serious question about DOE's commitment to the public participation components of its plan. In short, the difficulty lies both in the initial policy design and in the way DOE carried it out.

The public participation element of the policy, as noted, was not as carefully considered by Congress as it might have been, given the negative public attitudes toward nuclear waste; however, this oversight does not distinguish the NWPA from other policies with a strong participation component.[45] Congress apparently assumed that through implementation of the act, the DOE could build public confidence in the siting process and promote eventual acceptance of a siting recommendation. This was an unreasonable assumption to make.

In retrospect, it is clear that the Washington DOE office did not sufficiently appreciate the need to gain public support through more than the usual hearing process. It fell back on conventional approaches when a break with convention was called for, and it tried to move ahead with implementation far too rapidly given the inevitable controversies and disruption that such a schedule would produce. It might have chosen a slower, more consultative process, and deemphasized the statutory deadlines for facility siting. That was the approach favored by environmentalists and nuclear critics. It was also the approach used by DOE's Crystalline Repository Project office in Illinois, which established much better working relations with the states than the Washington office had. But DOE chose instead to interpret the NWPA as requiring it to give a higher priority to meeting the deadlines than to conducting a comprehensive search process. Some evidence of that decision can be found in the department's timetables and operations charts in its Mission Plan, which focused almost exclusively on technical issues in waste management; they did not include methods, procedures, or schedules for public participation.

In defense of their actions several key officials in OCRWM placed much of the blame on Congress for putting unrealistic deadlines into the law: "One of the problems is that the law is on the books and we're bound to implement the law." They called attention to ambiguous congressional preferences, citing the sixteen committees and subcommittees with direct oversight over the waste disposal program and the varied signals received from Capitol Hill: "I think everyone here would say we'd like to get a clearer signal from Congress as to if they think we're doing something wrong. What do they think is right? Because a lot of people tell us what we're doing is wrong, but you get mixed messages as to what they think the solution for that is."[46] These officials believe OCRWM did all that it could reasonably be expected to do under those circumstances.

At an early stage in assessment of the western sites, DOE's adherence to the tight schedule caused further problems. According to some accounts, DOE encouraged field offices in the West to compete with each other to see which could complete its work most quickly; such behavior directly contributed to doubts about the quality of scientific data used in defense of specific sites and to general erosion of DOE's credibility, especially in the West.[47] Apparently this orientation continued after the public outcry in 1986; the department was still adhering to, and defensive of, its "aggressive" timetable.[48]

By the fall of 1987, however, a number of key officials in OCRWM seemed to appreciate the obstacles to rapid siting; several agreed that Congress was probably overly hasty and unwise in imposing, as one administrator put it, "a new level of C and C that had never been used before and [expecting] it to work the first time." He went on to note that the fact that the C and C compromise in 1982 "didn't work doesn't mean that it's not a solvable problem. Maybe that way of doing it was not quite the right way and maybe it was a little early."[49] Given that recognition, some officials were prepared to accept new approaches to gain public confidence. There was much talk of the possible contribution of negotiation, such as that provided in a bill authored by Representative Morris Udall, and of financial and other incentives included in a competing bill by Senator J. Bennett Johnston (discussed below).

Another explanation for policy failure is that the states also did not approach the consultation process seriously. They hoped to use their congressionally provided veto, confident that Congress would not override such action and impose so unwanted a technological risk on an unwilling state. Thus each state's officials believed they could pass the burden to others and then take political credit for battling against an unpopular federal agency.

A third explanation is that public opposition to nuclear waste disposal is so great that virtually no process of public education and involvement could have produced a different decision, at least in the short run; officials in the OCRWM clearly believed this even though they had "very, very little contact with Joe and Jane Public." Their interactions were chiefly with appointed and elected representatives of the states and Indian tribes, who regularly reiterated, according to one official, "their totally unalterable opposition and dedication to stopping us. That doesn't leave any room for negotiation. You can't get a negotiation going under those circumstances." But he admitted that "I'm sure that in back of all of this is the public's fear. . . . I think it's totally unwarranted, but I recognize that it's there."[50]

Many would add that by agreeing to the state consultation process and the state veto, Congress evaded the inevitable decision the federal government will have to make, and to some extent did make in 1987, which is imposing a waste repository on an unwilling state.

What might be said of the various suggestions for how best to site a repository in light of Congress's revision of the act in 1987? Critics of DOE's handling of the NWPA have advocated use of compensation and greater efforts at negotiation in dealing with potential host states (especially by a body other than DOE), increased public education and involvement in siting decisions, and construction of a temporary storage facility to postpone the decision on a permanent repository (and thus to allow time for public education and negotiation), among other actions. Many supporters of the agency continued to favor a fast-track approach regardless of how it might be designed. Congress addressed all of these issues as it considered some twenty different bills in 1987 in an effort to amend the NWPA. Two quite different proposals emerged from the pack, one in the Senate and one in the House. The Senate bill, sponsored by Johnston and Senator James McClure, concentrated on the compensation issue and greatly narrowed the field of candidate states to speed up the siting process. It would have eliminated the second site in the Midwest or East, called for a $100 million-a-year federal payment to the first state to accept a repository, and specified full evaluation of one western site at a time rather than all three, both to reduce the cost and accelerate the process. The House bill, initiated by Representative Udall, emphasized a fuller reconsideration of the process and negotiation independent of DOE. It would have put the whole selection process on hold for at least eighteen months to allow a special commission to study legislative solutions and a high-level negotiator (working out of the executive office of the president) to work with the states to find a willing recipient for the site; the negotiator would have had broad powers to bargain with the states over the terms for locating the repository within their borders.[51]

In late December Congress approved a package of amendments to the NWPA that directed the DOE to evaluate the Yucca Mountain site in Nevada, and to cease consideration of the other two western sites. It also canceled authorization for a second repository in the Midwest or East, nullified DOE's selection of Tennessee for an MRS facility, and authorized a special negotiator appointed by the president to seek a state or Indian tribe prepared to accept either the permanent repository or the temporary facility. The original proposal of $100 million a year was reduced to $20 million, and Congress authorized a temporary, surface facility, but not until construction of the permanent repository is licensed.[52] Although elements of both the Johnston and Udall bills were included, Senator Johnston clearly won on the most critical provisions.

The 1987 amendments constituted a politically expedient decision that let most members of Congress off the hook and may allow DOE to move ahead rapidly on the Nevada site. But controversy is likely to continue. For all that has been said about public involvement and negotiation with the states, in effect the repository was imposed on Nevada over its vigorous opposition, pending the outcome of DOE's elaborate site characterization. Many critics of Congress's action accused it of substituting a simple political solution for a complex technical problem.[53] Should the Nevada location prove to be technically unacceptable, the decision on how to proceed reverts again to Congress. Nevada also retains the right to legal challenge provided under the original NWPA, which one might expect it to use should negotiation fail to secure its cooperation or should doubts arise about the quality of the site evaluation itself.

The issues addressed in this essay remain important for the future of nuclear waste disposal. The federal government must still work with Nevada (or other states) on the particulars of the first repository site, and additional sites may be needed as the amount of high-level waste grows. Other nations are keenly interested in how the United States deals with this problem inasmuch as they face the same kinds of decisions. For all these reasons we need to examine more carefully the various alternative approaches to siting such hazardous facilities.

Our concern here has been the use of public participation for evaluating technology, particularly when the alternative is decision making dominated by bureaucratic experts. As discussed above, there are many approaches to public participation even if there is considerable uncertainty about their efficacy and consequences both in general and specifically on the nuclear waste question. One reason for the uncertainty is that there have been few studies of how participation plans are actually implemented; indeed, this case illustrates that one can have a promising approach on paper but not in reality. Further studies would help clarify what works and what does not. Similarly, experimental use of one or more of these alternatives to public involvement in several localities would at least provide some empirical evidence on *what difference* public participation makes for changing public attitudes, building support for government decisions, or setting long-term directions for energy policy. That kind of knowledge could help resolve the differences in what various authorities and informed observers have recommended on the nuclear waste issue in recent years.[54] The implications for other kinds of technological risk management are equally important.

The intensity of congressional debate over the 1987 mid-course correction to the NWPA is in large part attributable to the widespread citizen protest against the repository siting process. That Congress was able to revise the act at all is in many ways a hopeful sign for what Borgmann in chapter 3 calls a revival of democracy, a "public return to the substance of our lives." The reawakening of his "public conversation about the good life" may sound quite remote from policy battles over nuclear waste and related issues, but state and community reaction to DOE's nuclear waste plans can be seen as precisely what Borgmann has in mind. From that perspective, these citizen protests are as encouraging for democratic practice as they are seemingly out of step with the apathetic and conservative 1980s. A general conclusion from this case may be that when the effects of technology are perceived to affect people's "good life," their willingness to participate in collective decisions may increase dramatically. The challenge to democracy is then to provide appropriate forums or processes for public involvement that contribute to effective problem solving.

Nuclear waste is atypical of technology issues for reasons indicated above, and requires new approaches to politics to avoid the pitfalls of uninformed public involvement. But as unusual as this case is, it does illustrate the difficulties as well as the promise of public participation as an approach to evaluating technological risks. If we have, as Borgmann says, a crisis of democracy as well as a crisis of technology, there is hope in the invention of new forms of democratic participation that may reinvigorate the polity and citizens' involvement with it.

SCIENTIFIC ADVERSARY PROCEDURES:

THE SDI EXPERIMENTS AT DARTMOUTH

ROGER D. MASTERS AND ARTHUR R. KANTROWITZ

When scientific or technical facts become relevant to policy conflicts, the expected process of scientific inquiry is typically replaced by strident rhetoric and violent disagreement. In such controversies, although policymakers and the public alike would benefit from a more impartial assessment of scientific facts, institutionalized procedures to produce this assessment have not been developed. To meet the need for better communication between the scientific community and the public, the so-called Science Court was proposed over a decade ago.[1] In response to criticisms of the original proposal, a new and more effective alternative—now called "Scientific Adversary Procedures"—has been proposed and implemented in academic settings on an experimental basis.[2]

From the outset, the function of these processes was not to make a binding decision or even to recommend a decision. Their only purpose was to find the scientific facts which bear on political issues and governmental decisions. Because original proposals conjured images of a judicial verdict carrying legal authority, Scientific Adversary Procedures have been reconceptualized as an educational and informational experiment in a university setting. If public cross-examination by differing scientific or technical experts occurs in an academic context, it should be possible to institutionalize a more responsible dialogue between the public and specialists whose expertise may have been confounded with political passion or partisan preference.

Here, we report on the evolution of Scientific Adversary Procedures and the application of the most recent version of the concept to the scientific controversies surrounding President Reagan's Strategic Defense Initiative (whose popular name of "Star Wars" indicates clearly enough the nature of the technical and political debate). What is for its proponents the only chance to achieve lasting security is, for critics, a technically impossible threat to world peace. Political and strategic discussion on this issue has to an astounding degree focused on scientific and technical issues. If the experimental Scientific Adversary Procedures can contribute to better public policy, this area is surely a good place to begin.

THE PROBLEM: SCIENTIFIC EXPERTISE AND POLITICAL CONTROVERSY

The confusion of personal preferences and scientific expertise characterizes technical debates on many public policy issues in addition to SDI. No powerful constituency for the development of improved processes for getting at controversial technical information has yet appeared. We have many organizations which claim credibility because of who they are rather than how they proceed. Philip Handler, past president of the National Academy of Sciences, was quoted as saying, "if what we have to say is credible, the credibility rests on the distinction and prestige of the members."[3]

Although science itself rejects, in principle, the argument from authority, scientific and technological experts use this argument as soon as they enter the political arena. The Office of Technology Assessment is to be believed because it is an independent agency of the U.S. Congress. "Public interest" groups and regulatory agencies are to be believed because they exist only to protect the public interest. Industry is to be believed because of its expertise and experience.

Handler, in addressing the National Academy Bicentennial Symposium, reported the results as follows:

> to establish truth with respect to technical controversy relevant to matters of public policy, and to do so in full public view, has proved to be a surprisingly difficult challenge to the scientific community. To our simple code must be added one more canon: when describing technological risks to the non-scientific public, the scientist must be as honest, objective, and dispassionate as he knows he must be in the more conventional, time-honored, self-

policing scientific endeavor. This additional canon has not always been observed. Witness the chaos that has come with challenges to the use of nuclear power in several countries. Witness, in this country, the cacophony of charge and counter-charge concerning the safety of diverse food additives, pesticides, and drugs. We have learned that the scientist-advocate, on either side of such a debate, is likely to be more advocate than scientist, and this has unfavorably altered the public view of both the nature of the scientific endeavor and the personal attributes of scientists. In turn, that has given yet a greater sense of urgency to the public demand for assurance that the risks attendant upon the uses of technology be appraised and minimized. And what a huge task that is![4]

In no area is this "huge task" more evident than in the assessment of President Reagan's Strategic Defense Initiative. Ever since its original presentation to the public,[5] supporters have claimed that the technologies were both feasible and desirable. Because the strategic benefits of a total shield against strategic or long-range missiles were generally presumed to be self-evident, description of the proposal often focused on the technical means necessary for its implementation. Quite apart from strategic issues, it has been claimed that the means of implementing SDI would reinforce the development of other needed technologies, opening the way to radically improved computers, new generations of laser technology, and ultimately the colonization of space.

Critics have typically charged that SDI is dangerous because it is impossible on scientific or technical grounds. Interestingly enough, there has been virtually no discussion of whether permanent space colonies are a desirable goal which might be sought even if strategic defense itself turns out to be difficult or impossible to implement. One could imagine, for example, the argument that research on SDI should go forward precisely because the strategic defense systems themselves could never be functional, whereas the research effort involved would have positive technological or strategic effects. Conversely, it is possible to oppose SDI precisely *because* it is technically feasible, on the grounds that the process of research and development would have undesirable strategic or geopolitical effects that will not be mitigated by technological failure.

Because so much of the debate concerning SDI has focused on technological issues, competing scientific claims have tended to preempt the consideration of policy questions that might well have been joined. It is obvious that this is an unwise way to approach the formulation of public policies. On the one hand, politicians and administrators are tempted to abdicate their decision-making responsibilities by deferring to technical experts whose advice may be merely a covert form of policy or partisan preference; on the other, the judgments of the scientific community itself may be infected by the legitimate but conflicting concerns of its members acting in their role as citizens.

HISTORY: FROM THE SCIENCE COURT TO SCIENTIFIC ADVERSARY PROCEDURES

To begin what Handler called the "huge task" of establishing "truth with respect to technical controversy relevant to matters of public policy," we have been experimenting with a structured means by which to achieve higher credibility in the communication between the scientific community and the public. The credibility of the output would not depend entirely on the people involved, but rather on institutions incorporating some of society's wisdom in dealing with controversy. To paraphrase Handler, the intention was to create a structure in which the "scientist-advocate" would be more scientist than advocate. The scientific community has its traditions, which provide a kind of due process. What is needed is to extend the procedures normally accepted within scientific disciplines to provide information to the public in a way that both the policymaker and the scientist, not to mention the average citizen, will find credible.

To achieve this end, we propose the following ethical principle to be enforced by the scientific community:

> Any scientist who addresses the public or lay officials on scientific facts bearing on public policy matters should stand ready to answer publicly questions not only from the citizens and policymakers, but also from expert adversaries in the scientific community.

Two decades ago the "Science Court" was proposed as an experimental first step in the implementation of this ethical principle.[6] The experimental Scientific Adversary Procedures discussed here are a development of this idea, retaining the notion of open public cross-examination by differing scientific or technical experts, but adapted now to an academic setting. Whereas the original name falsely conjured images of a verdict carrying legal authority, the new name, Scientific Adversary Procedures, is designed to emphasize the role of a developing educational and informational process.

FROM A QUASI-JUDICIAL TO AN EDUCATIONAL MODEL

The adaptation of the Science Court to the academic setting involved several changes in basic thinking. First, there was the realization that while it was not hard to get endorsements of the idea from political candidates (e.g. Ford, Carter, and Reagan),[7] it was not easy to get elected officials to nurture a mechanism *intended* to reduce their power over public perception of scientific facts related to public policy. As long as Scientific Adversary Procedures were conceived as public institutions, akin to a court or a regulatory commission, their implementation would never be effective.

Second, for the university, Scientific Adversary Procedures can provide educational and research opportunities that benefit diverse constituencies. For the students and faculty of a university community, they provide an educational experience concerning the vital relationship between expertise and the making of public policy; for the general public, they synthesize the scientific information available while indicating uncertainties and areas of ignorance in specific controversies; for policymakers, they provide input from institutions with a vested interest in independence from partisanship. In this way universities could play a leadership role in improving the relationship between the scientific community and the public without depending on prior political or governmental initiative (as in contract research).

The experimental development of Scientific Adversary Procedures to a point of general utility is a substantial undertaking. Procedures need to be acceptable to all parties yet exhaustive, generating a statement of current knowledge sufficiently comprehensive to supply the needs of policymakers. Time and resources required would be comparable to those currently devoted to governmentally sponsored commissions of inquiry (like the one that investigated the Three Mile Island disaster). In the Scientific Adversary Procedures reported below, time and resource limitations prevented any attempt at full statements of current knowledge. It will also be necessary to develop the profession of scientist-advocate with a cadre of people skilled in the use of the procedure to exhibit the facts which support their point of view.

Hindsight makes it clear that nurturing and experimenting with the procedure in university settings will be much more successful than earlier proposals that involved quasi-judicial governmental institutions at the federal or state levels. Because the original title of a "Court" conjured images of a formal decision-making body, many scientists and experts rightly feared that it could become an agency of political control over the scientific community. By placing adversary procedures in an educational setting, cooperation of scientific advocates is more likely. To be sure, any single procedure is not likely to determine public opinion or establish policy. But repeated experiments with Scientific Adversary Procedures in different university settings with different participants could provide pluralism consistent with the norms of the scientific community and would add much to credibility. While the history of the first such experiments indicates how this process might work, the SDI procedures at Dartmouth are particularly important because they revealed unsuspected but important technical agreements that could possibly transform debate on a critical issue of public policy.

THE SCIENTIFIC ADVERSARY EXPERIMENTS AT BERKELEY

During the winter quarter of 1983, Frank Hurlbut and Arthur Kantrowitz conducted a workshop seminar at the Interdisciplinary Studies Center of the College of Engineering at the University of California, Berkeley. Three experimental "Micro Science Courts," characterized by progressively increasing realism, were conducted. The first concerned nuclear waste disposal, and the last two concerned the health hazards at Love Canal.

The selection of Love Canal as a topic was influenced by the possibility of finding scientists in the Berkeley community whose public statements had been diametrically opposed and who were emotionally involved in the Love Canal issue, but who were willing to answer publicly the questions of their expert adversary.

It was readily agreed that the rules of procedure would be those of a scientific meeting, not those of a court of law. No ad hominem remarks would be tolerated. The scientist-advocates would be expected to answer each others' scientific questions. Enforcement of these rules was the duty of the moderator, whose role was similar to that of the chair at a scientific meeting.

The scientist-advocates for the third Berkeley proceeding were Dr. Beverly Paigen, a geneticist who was the chief scientific advisor to the Love Canal homeowners, and Dr. William Havender, a biochemist who has written articles on Love Canal for the *American Spectator*. Dr. Paigen asserted that her results and the results of other studies "suggested" that health hazards still existed at Love Canal. Dr. Havender wrote that these researches were "unrelievedly abysmal," and that no defensible conclusions could be drawn from this work.

During the weeks which preceded the public cross-examination on February 24, 1983, Paigen and Havender determined their areas of agreement and disagreement in the course of many long meetings. They disagreed about the significance of Paigen's surveys of birth defects and about the significance of Dr. Picciano's studies of chromosome damage. These areas were dealt with in the public cross-examination session. During that session new extensions of their areas of agreement were identified, but complete agreement could not be reached. The enrolled students in the seminar, acting as reviewers, wrote opinions on the remaining disputed points.

In the Love Canal procedures major emphasis was placed on careful specification of arguable areas of scientific disagreement. Much less emphasis was placed on the specification of areas of agreement. Although the public session of February 24 was spirited and informative, it was clear that in the future more attention must be devoted to the negotiation of a useful list of agreed propositions.

THE SCIENTIFIC ADVERSARY
EXPERIMENTS AT DARTMOUTH

Experiments were conducted at Dartmouth in connection with a graduate engineering seminar on "Science, Engineering, and Public Policy" and a senior level policy studies course on "Policy Formation."[8] Three procedures were planned to deal with various aspects of President Reagan's Strategic Defense Initiative. This issue was chosen as a striking example of policymaking in the midst of vigorous controversy within the scientific community. Three opposed pairs of scientists prominent in the public debates were invited to spend a day at Dartmouth carrying out the procedures outlined below.

PROCEDURES AND SELECTION
OF THE SCIENTIST-ADVOCATES

Whereas in the Berkeley experiments the choice of topic was largely influenced by the availability of willing scientist-advocates, at Dartmouth we added an element of realism to the Scientific Adversary Experiment by first choosing the topic (SDI) and then seeking the scientist-advocates. Consequently the selection and recruitment of the scientist-advocates became much more difficult. We quickly confirmed Handler's conclusion that those deemed "scientists" in the public eye are often "more advocate than scientist"; many publicly known experts were much more comfortable with situations in which they were not committed to answer the questions of expert adversaries. Several of those prominent in the public debates declared that their positions were "centrist and unbiased," and simply refused to participate in an adversary procedure. Others had developed such animosity for their adversaries that they were unwilling to oppose them in an experimental Scientific Adversary Procedure. One of the three planned experiments had to be cancelled when a participant withdrew suddenly and unexpectedly. In the end, recruitment of scientist-advocates depended on finding participants in the SDI debate who already knew about and favored the earlier concept of a Science Court.

The following description of procedures was written and made available to the scientist-advocates prior to the actual sessions at Dartmouth:

> We will structure these sessions around specific scientific statements (propositions), e.g., How fast can a mirror be slewed? or: Can a booster be profitably decoyed? These will be statements of great importance to the feasibility of SDI, acceptable to one of the scientist-advocates, but which might be questioned by his adversary. We will search for informative propositions in 3 or more ways.
>
> 1. Groups of students in Engineering Science 200 will be assigned to study the published statements of each participant and to identify those scientific and technical propositions that are essential to his argument. The list of propositions concerning each participant's position will then be sent to him; any proposition he refuses to defend will be deleted and any additional statements he wishes to add will be added.
>
> 2. After each scientist-advocate has approved the list based on his

writings, it will be sent to his opponent and to other participants.

3. The scientist-advocates will be encouraged to offer statements which they are prepared to defend publicly in response to propositions offered by their adversary. Again, A might choose to suggest modifications or limitations to B's proposition so as to approach a mutually acceptable proposition. Alternatively it might be more informative to exhibit differences which would then be treated in an evening adversary session.

Propositions selected in these ways will be exchanged between the scientist-advocates to establish areas of agreement and areas of disagreement. During morning and afternoon sessions of each procedure, with the faculty committee and members of the participating classes present, an attempt will be made to widen the areas of agreement.

A list of agreed propositions will be prepared and made public at the evening sessions. An effort will be made to phrase these propositions so that they can be understood by as large an audience as possible.

It is anticipated that areas of essential disagreement will remain. During the daytime sessions we will also make another attempt to sharpen these areas of disagreement. We will seek two of the most important of these "challenged propositions," one advanced by each side, to be dealt with in a public adversary session in the evening at Rockefeller Center. In phrasing these challenged propositions, an effort will be made to avoid areas where classified information is essential.

The rules of the "adversary session" will be those of a scientific meeting, not those of a court of law. Thus no ad hominem remarks will be tolerated. The scientist-advocates will be expected to answer each other's scientific questions. Other procedural rules and details of the evening program (e.g., time to state the propositions and time for questions by adversaries, referees, etc.) will be worked out during the day.

These rules will be enforced by the moderator whose role will be similar to that of the chair at a scientific meeting.[9]

Reviewers, whose function is similar to that of peer reviewers for scientific journals, observed and participated in the adversary sessions. Members of the Dartmouth engineering and science faculty who had not taken public positions on the SDI were recruited for this function; we asked them to identify their private positions on SDI for the *Record*. After each Scientific Adversary Experiment was completed, the reviewers were asked to write a short statement summarizing areas of agreement and disagreement. These reviewers' statements are made public in the *Record*. At the end of each experimental procedure, suggestions for improvement were sought from all participants. In addition, evaluations were requested from scholars who had studied the role of scientific and technical information in the making of public policy.

THE FIRST DARTMOUTH SCIENTIFIC ADVERSARY EXPERIMENT:
THE COMPUTING ASPECTS OF SDI

The first Scientific Adversary Experiment, which formally took place on May 2, 1985, was focused on the computing aspects of SDI. Charles E. Hutchinson, dean of the Thayer School of Engineering at Dartmouth College and a consultant for the Institute for Defense Analyses, was scientist-advocate for the view favorable to SDI. Dr. Herbert Lin, postdoctoral research fellow, Arms Control and Defense Studies Program, Center for International Studies, MIT, represented the opposing view. The Union of Concerned Scientists (UCS) had used Dr. Lin as the chief source of information on which their criticism of the computing aspects of SDI was based.[10]

To arrive at a list of agreed propositions and two specific formulations of propositions in dispute, the scientist-advocates supplied us with their relevant writings, and the engineering students searched them for statements which might be challenged by their adversary; the resulting correspondence was itself useful. When Hutchinson and Lin met on May 2 during morning and afternoon sessions, with the faculty reviewers and the students from the two participating courses present, an attempt was made to widen the areas of agreement. To achieve clarity, it was necessary to record agreed *assumptions* which provided the basis of the other statements. This list, along with a list of agreed and disputed propositions (Hutchinson-Lin Statements), was prepared and made public at the final evening session. During the public session in the evening, after the agreed assumptions and propositions were presented, the scientific-advocates vigorously cross-examined each other.

The daytime sessions produced many significant agreed propositions, whereas there was general agreement that the two disputed propositions were too vague, and that the evening's cross-examination did little to dispel that vagueness. Three reviewers from the Dartmouth faculty were asked to witness only the evening cross-examination session, although it is not clear whether their presence would have changed the atmosphere of the daytime session during which the scientist-advocates worked out the areas of their agreement and disagreement.[11]

All the participants were surprised by the general agreement which was reached on the scientific facts, in view of the severely opposed policy positions of the scientist-advocates. Perhaps the vagueness of the evening cross-examination session was inevitable, since the areas of disagreement remaining were speculations concerning a system not yet invented. Some observers suggested, for example, that greater public involvement might be useful (although others wondered whether the presence of journalists and public attention might destroy the scientific character of the dialogue).

THE SECOND DARTMOUTH SCIENTIFIC ADVERSARY EXPERIMENT:
THE TECHNICAL ASPECTS OF SDI

In the second Scientific Adversary Procedure, which took place on May 23–24, 1985, the scientist-advocates were generally recognized leaders in the national debate on SDI. Dr. Richard Garwin, scientist-advocate for the view critical of SDI, was one of the authors of "The Fallacy of Star Wars," published by the Union of Concerned Scientists. Since 1950 he has been a technical consultant to the U.S. government and its contractors and has written and testified widely on SDI. Dr. Edward Gerry, who represented the view favorable to SDI, served on the Presidential Fletcher Commission on SDI as chief of the panel on boost phase defense. He has spent most of his career in scientific work related to SDI.

As in the first Dartmouth experiment, before the scientific advocates came to the campus, student review of Garwin's and Gerry's writings and correspondence helped to identify areas of agreement, and to a lesser degree areas of disagreement. Once this experimental procedure began, however, substantial difficulties were encountered during the private discussion intended to specify the lists of agreed and disputed propositions. It was difficult for the moderator to restrict discussion to matters of scientific fact. Compromise was achieved by entering statements of goals and recitations of political history into the Record. It is clear, for example, that several of the agreed propositions (e.g., #2) were, in fact, policy statements.

Although the reviewers in this second Dartmouth experiment were not present during the negotiation of the agreed propositions, they all found that these agreed propositions were by far the most important output of the procedure and should have been dealt with more fully in the public session.[12] The reviewers also found that each scientist-advocate could not prove a strongly contested assertion (Garwin's proposition that booster decoys could not be made cost-effective, and Gerry's insistence that they could) and suggested that some propositions were irrelevant or inappropriate (see Record).

Two external witnesses who evaluated the experiment made three useful observations.[13] First, a policymaker as comoderator could have helped to focus the discussion on policy-relevant scientific facts. Second, fundamental difficulties in dealing with classified information cannot be solved by Scientific Adversary Procedures, though this very fact may be useful in understanding some policy issues. Finally, but perhaps most important of all, it was observed that "more of value comes from isolating (and articulating) points of agreement from points of disagreement, even if the disagreements are never aired for judgment."

A record of the public hearing phase, which includes preliminary correspondence, agreed propositions, reviewers' comments, and analyses of the procedures, is available from Thayer School of Engineering.[14] This statement of scientific findings is significant in itself. But it is our hope that, if Scientific Adversary Procedures spread, it will become possible to develop more effective means for publishing the findings of such hearings at a variety of colleges and universities. Hence, over the long run, one could hope that developments arising from this mode of addressing policy-relevant scientific controversy would become institutionalized as a basic component of our educational system. This would not only have direct educational value, but would also make a significant contribution to the information base necessary for making public policy democratically.

Observers also noted that in the second experiment the open disagreement between the scientific adversaries was more evident (especially in the phase of negotiating agreed propositions). It is likely that well-known scientific adversaries are less disposed to enter into agreements due to their public commitments. While this probably explains the tendency of the public sessions to focus on disputed propositions, it further underlies the importance of the agreed-upon statements. Indeed, one observer suggested that the controversial public sessions might be the necessary cost for arriving at the more valuable—but more difficult to achieve—admission of a surprisingly broad degree of technical agreement among opposed scientist-advocates.

WHAT SCIENTIFIC ADVERSARY PROCEDURES
TAUGHT US ABOUT SDI

In both of the Dartmouth Scientific Adversary Procedures, observers and organizers were interested to note often-unstated but clearly agreed premises that have been missing from much public debate. Of particular interest was the agreement on the importance of cooperation with the Soviet Union. Whereas many political leaders have assumed that SDI is feasible as a unilateral endeavor and assessed it on this basis, both scientific advocates in the first experiment questioned the technical feasibility of computer software that could not be developed and verified in a cooperative manner. While the scientific adversaries were not totally in agreement on the extent of superpower cooperation needed, their consensus on this point illustrates a major benefit of the scientific adversary process. It may often be the case that opposed scientific advocates agree in questioning what is, for much of the political elite, a commonly shared but dubious assumption.

In the second experiment, the repeated agreement on the central importance of countermeasures was reinforced by the shared awareness that governmental secrecy made discussion of many technical aspects of this issue impossible. As in the first experiment, it was evident that cooperative development of SDI by the United States and USSR would be—from a technological point of view—more likely to succeed than a unilateral effort.

COMPUTING AND SDI

Agreed Propositions. The most striking result of the first Scientific Adversary Procedure was probably the large area of agreement between Hutchinson and Lin. It might not be surprising that they agreed readily on the goal of the Strategic Defense system ("to eliminate the threat of nuclear ballistic missiles") as well as on the area in which computing capabilities were at issue ("the primary computing issues arise in the battle management system [acquisition and tracking, classification, resource allocation, surveillance, rules of engagement, delegation, mutual defense, and situation assessment"]). These terms were taken from the Fletcher Commission Report and have not generally been a subject of controversy.

Much more important were the extensive areas of technical agreement. Hutchinson and Lin agreed on no less than ten specific statements during the day-long preparatory sessions. While there were additional areas of consensus noted by observers during the evening, the basic list of ten "agreed propositions" represent a major contribution to the narrowing of technical controversy about the feasibility of Star Wars defense.

First, the opposed experts agreed that hardware—at least at the "subsystem" level of components—would probably be able to meet the exacting standards required for the Strategic Defense Initiative. These hardware requirements were set at the capacity to handle "one billion operations per second, maintenance free for ten years, and hardened to radiation and shock." While not now in existence, Lin and Hutchinson agreed that they "will probably be developed within 5–10 years, based on continuation of current programs."

Second, the length of the software programs needed to operate the system was on the order of 50 million lines of code (i.e., the equivalent of 50 million lines of instructions for a home computer). As Hutchinson and Lin put it, "Given that estimates are ranging from ten million lines of code [the Fletcher Commission's figure] to a hundred million lines of code [the figure of some critics], a reasonable estimate is fifty million lines of code." It was agreed, moreover, that computer programs of this scale "will be an order of magnitude larger than anything developed to date."

Third, while James Fletcher, chair of the Fletcher Commission, has spoken of "error free" software, both experts agreed that "it is impossible to make a system . . . which is error free, but the requirement of absolute freedom of error is not necessary for SDI to succeed." That is, given the ubiquity of human error—as owners of home computers often discover—perfection is not likely to be achieved, but the existence of a glitch does not necessarily mean that a computer program will fail to do its job.

As will be evident at this stage, the opposed experts were each aware of the technical exaggerations of policy proponents who shared their conclusions. The general scope of the computing tasks is not at issue, nor is it likely that the principal difficulties will arise from the failure to improve the basic components of computer hardware. Were this all, however, one might dismiss the area of agreement as trivial —whereas in fact the consensus went much farther and has great relevance for the public policy debate.

Hutchinson and Lin agreed on a set of technical issues that will sound mysterious to the general public. These include the likelihood that communications would "not be limited by bandwidth considerations in the absence of Soviet countermeasures," that "parallel processing can achieve higher throughput on some significant problems (e.g., matrix manipulation)," and that "parallel processing may present a hardware problem" if there is need for "computation speed greater than 300 million operations per second." Similarly, the scientific adversaries accepted the Fletcher Commission's statement that "a demand for synchrony better than milliseconds could create great complications within the software."

Although these accepted propositions merely reveal a shared definition of the technical designs required for the Strategic Defense Initiative, other agreements touch more directly on matters that have been a focus of public discussion. Instead of speaking vaguely of a "robust" system, Lin and Hutchinson agreed that "the software system for SDI must be able to function without human intervention to correct real-time hardware and software failures and to function in environments unanticipated by system planners." Equally important for public discussion was the consensus that these requirements are more extensive than the computer programs needed for offensive weapons systems. In plain terms this means that even a supporter of Star Wars recognizes that the computer software must be able to compensate for hardware failure as well as software malfunction, that humans cannot be counted upon for such tasks, that the system must be so designed as to withstand extensive and unplanned environmental shocks, and that all these requirements for a defensive system go beyond what is required for offensive missiles.

During our day-long session Dr. Lin and Dean Hutchinson therefore focused their technical disagreement on two propositions. Hutchinson claimed that "advances in programming techniques for developing large software systems can be reasonably expected to make the software issues . . . tractable in a ten year time frame"; Dr. Lin rejected this view. Hence the first controversial area concerns the extent to which new techniques of computer programs will be able to solve problems not now feasible.

The second issue concerned testing. Lin asserted that "thorough testing, both before and after deployment, including full-scale operational tests, will be required. Complete cooperation with the Soviets for the duration of BMD [battlefield management design] significance and mutual trust is necessary but far from sufficient to achieve adequate testing." Hutchinson would accept only a narrower statement that "thorough testing will be required. Cooperation with Soviets is necessary to achieve adequate testing."

As will be evident, there was an important overlap in the second of these propositions—an agreement that in fact is of the greatest possible significance in the determination of public policy. In the discussion and cross-examination during the evening, we found that the sharpening of disagreement actually revealed further precision about the technical questions that could greatly change the popular understanding of Star Wars. In addition, however, the procedure itself clearly indicated that scientists addressing each other are capable of separating those areas that are most likely to be technically controversial from the matters no longer in scientific dispute (even where, as with some of the above propositions, presidential commissions and well-known technical spokesmen have exaggerated for political effect).

Disputed Propositions. On both the requirements for producing the required computer software and the needs for testing, Lin and Hutchinson engaged in lively—and civil—discussion. Shared standards of scientific evidence meant that each addressed the arguments of the other, unlike those political debates in which the rivals seek merely to impress the audience. The area of disagreement remained, however, very large. Hutchinson insisted that radically new computer languages and methods for managing software development would increase the productivity of computer programmers by an order of magnitude; Lin insisted that the practical difficulties facing such a task would be insuperable. The testing requirements outlined by Lin appeared, to Hutchinson, unreasonable and unnecessary.

We concluded from this element of the procedure that there is indeed an area of scientific and technical controversy concerning the ability to develop the computer software for the SDI. When these disputes were narrowed to very specific questions, however, we discovered that there were additional elements of agreement—and that these elements might transform the public debate.

First, let us look at the issue of software development. Dean Hutchinson listed five characteristics of new programming techniques that could increase productivity to permit the solution of SDI problems: reusability of program code, configuration management, design reduction, optimizing compilers, and automatic programming. Both adversaries agree that the first three would be critical, since without them the required software would not be produced.

One need not understand the technicalities of these new techniques to realize the nature of the issue. Dr. Lin believes that it will be simply impossible to organize the number of computer programmers necessary, to train them in the use of radically new techniques, and to integrate their work in a coherent system. Dean Hutchinson believes that the next generation of computer software will resolve all of these issues. In short, problems of human social organization—which for Dr. Lin implied limits on conceivable software development—were treated by Dean Hutchinson as soluble by computer techniques.

Politicians on either side of the Star Wars debate might take comfort in this disagreement, since each can cite a favorable expert and neither must confront a consensus of the scientific community. The same cannot be said, however, for some—though by no means all—of the problems associated with testing. On this point, as we discovered, computer software may have some unsuspected political implications.

Testing and Cooperation with the Russians. The second major area of dispute concerned the extent of testing that would be required to meet the agreed-upon standards of reliability. On this issue, the disagreement revealed several paradoxes of the greatest importance. The first was the amount of agreement hidden in the disagreement.

As noted above, Dean Hutchinson agreed that "thorough testing will be required"—though he was unwilling to go as far as to assert that "full-scale operational tests" were necessary, as Dr. Lin asserted. This measure of agreement has political consequences, since Dean Hutchinson also agreed with Dr. Lin that "cooperation with the Soviets is necessary to achieve adequate testing." The area of dispute was how far or "complete" that cooperation would have to be.

During the evening cross-examination, both scientific adversaries agreed that it would not be necessary to share the computer programs themselves with the Russians. The disagreement concerned a different problem, namely the nature of the tests of an integrated system (as distinct from preliminary tests of components of the software, with or without actual peripheral devices being monitored or controlled). In other words, the question was how much "field testing" would be required, using the computers to monitor, locate, and destroy real missiles in flight.

Computer owners know that software systems have to be "debugged"—and that some real users are needed to test a system before it goes on the market. Before the country "buys" Star Wars, the question here concerns how much testing will be needed. More specifically, how closely must the Soviet Union cooperate in giving the computer software the minimal testing necessary for the system to be reliable?

Dr. Lin claimed that between twenty and twenty-five tests, each of which requires the firing of up to 300 simultaneous missiles, would be needed to verify the complex computer systems envisaged for the Strategic Defense Initiative. He cited, as an example, the first test of the Aegis air defense system, in which six of sixteen targets were not shot down due to faulty hardware. Overall, Lin claimed that there could be as many as 50 million discrete tests—perhaps taking as much as fifty years to complete and including numerous full-scale launches of masses of missiles. Since the Soviet Union would have to be assured that none of these missiles was an armed weapon aimed at the USSR and hidden in the testing, Lin concluded that an extraordinary degree of mutual confidence between the superpowers would be necessary to test the complex computer control systems.

Dean Hutchinson considered this estimate exaggerated, since testing might not require more than a few launches of two or three missiles each. Hutchinson claimed, moreover, that many of the tests described by Dr. Lin could be simultaneous, greatly reducing the time needed to put the system in place. But on a central political point, Dean Hutchinson was convinced that closer cooperation between the superpowers would be required than Dr. Lin had assumed necessary.

Whereas Lin spoke of the need to reassure the Russians during a test of a large number of American missiles, Dean Hutchinson concluded that at least some tests would be required with *Soviet* missiles. Perhaps we could convince the Soviets that a test of American missiles was honest by allowing them to inspect our missiles before the salvo was fired or providing other evidence that none had warheads that could threaten the USSR. But can one picture the attitude of the U.S. Senate on hearing that several Russian missiles—supposedly without warheads—were to be fired in order to test the SDI computers? Is it likely that the Russians would allow our experts to satisfy themselves that the missiles were indeed unarmed?

It is hard to know which of our two scientific adversaries—Dr. Lin, who opposes SDI, or Dean Hutchinson, who favors it—actually posed a greater challenge to the political feasibility of Star Wars. Of course, President Reagan has spoken of sharing the technology with the Soviet Union. But a test salvo, whether comprised of 200 to 300 American missiles or merely 2 or 3 Russian ones, requires more than sharing the technology after the fact—it requires a substantial degree of confidence during the developmental phase of the technology.

Conclusions on Computing and SDI. The Scientific Adversary Procedures illuminated both the process by which technical experts disagree about public policy and the specific requirements of the computing capability needed for President Reagan's SDI. Both the wide area of technical agreement and the specific issues on which debate could not be resolved were reassuring. Opposed scientists can narrow the area of technical uncertainty without abandoning their policy preferences, and thereby contribute to a sharper understanding of just what the issues underlying a policy really are.

In the present case, we found that neither the technical capacity of hardware nor the scale of needed software are at issue. On the one hand, there remains disagreement on the extent to which new programming languages and techniques will provide productivity increases that permit the development of computer systems at least ten times larger than any known to date; on the other, experts disagree on the extent to which full-scale or operational tests would be required. This latter disagreement was, however, less extensive than might first appear, since both scientific adversaries agreed on the need for far greater cooperation with the USSR than has been generally assumed.

As Dean Hutchinson and Dr. Lin put this element of their agreement, not only is "the technology conceived under the research program planned for SDI . . . to be shared with the Soviets, thereby reassuring the Soviets about American intentions," but "without Soviet cooperation, the SDI program is most unlikely to achieve its goal." That is, not only must we be willing to cooperate with the Russians; they must be willing to cooperate with us.

The testing of computer software of hitherto unknown complexity is, for Dr. Lin and Dean Hutchinson, a matter that will be required for the success of SDI. It is, moreover, agreed that the computer technology required is far more extensive than that of offensive weapons, suggesting that the test phase cannot be considered as something separate and distinct from design: some elements of testing a system against actual missile launches would apparently be required merely to insure that the computers were functioning (not to mention to test other components of the system). Since these tests cannot be conducted without the active cooperation of the USSR, the assumptions of many critics and supporters alike need to be reexamined.

COUNTERMEASURES AND SECURITY

The second experimental Scientific Adversary Procedure was, in some ways, less satisfactory than the first. Perhaps because the scientific advocates were both nationally known and perhaps because they sought to cover the entire range of the debate, the day-long negotiating session was more difficult and the public session in the evening more controversial. Even here, however, the range of agreed propositions was extraordinary and the nature of the dialogue useful.

Policy Divergence. Perhaps as the "admission price" to the negotiation of agreed propositions, Garwin and Gerry began by stating their contradictory policy positions in a technical form. Garwin wanted to be on record as formally stating the following specific policy objective: "The goal of continued avoidance of nuclear war is better achieved *within* the ABM treaty (which prohibits significant defense against strategic ballistic missiles and does *not* require ever-increasing forces). It could be accomplished stably with 2,000 warheads on each side if: both sides abandon the goal of destroying the strategic retaliatory force of the other side, and as is the purpose of the ABM treaty, both sides abandon defense against the strategic retaliatory force of the other side."[15]

Gerry formulated a different policy objective: "The goal of the SDI program is to determine whether it is feasible to improve the security of the US and its allies, while reducing the number and power of offensive nuclear weapons via a transition to defensive systems as the primary basis for continued deterrence of nuclear war.''[16] Garwin also inserted a formal statement that "there has been no study within the government as to *whether* the US should pursue the research" outlined by President Reagan. Finally, it was agreed that the critical area of "countermeasure effectiveness" could not be debated because "Gerry feels that official secrecy precludes his participation"; all that could be asserted on this point was that "Garwin states that countermeasures will defeat high performance systems while Gerry believes that solutions can be developed." As the tone of these statements indicates, the scientific advocates clearly sought to insure, from the outset, that their positions would not be misinterpreted.

Agreed Propositions. Given the broad divergence in goals, the range of agreement on technical matters was surprisingly great. The agreed propositions reveal an extensive consensus that has important lessons both in the specific matter of SDI and in demonstrating the utility of Scientific Adversary Procedures (for the text, see the appendix at the end of the chapter). While some propositions seem to have been covert ways of inserting policy preferences—Garwin's doubts about the number of lasers needed (Agreed Proposition #11) and Gerry's belief that these limits can be overcome by increased laser brightness (Agreed Proposition #12)—the agreed propositions are significant.

Two points in particular stand out. First, the development of effective countermeasures is absolutely critical to the *deployment* of a unilateral SDI system as well as to its effective *survival*. Decoys, space mines, modifications of delivery vehicles, and ability to neutralize space-based systems could all easily negate any system. And second, some goals of SDI could be met without such a system, whereas the possibility of abandoning totally all "capability for nuclear retaliation" that is claimed by some politicians was agreed to be impossible even with such a system (Agreed Proposition #15).

Of these two points, the first is by far the more critical. Considering the entire range of agreed propositions concerning countermeasures, it becomes obvious that serious public discussion of the likelihood of achieving the stated goals of SDI (Agreed Proposition #1) is rendered virtually impossible by governmental secrecy. There is no way that an informed citizen or political leader could assess whether agreed Proposition #14 means that the exploration of "solutions to all of the countermeasures issues" will actually provide such solutions. Indeed, the inability of Gerry to enter into detailed discussion on this point only confirmed the importance of secrecy.

By definition, moreover, the countermeasure issue is symmetrical for the two superpowers. Neither the Soviet Union nor the United States could avoid the danger of its rival using countermeasures that might nullify the entire investment in an SDI system. Conversely, development of countermeasures (or of systems that would induce a superpower to consider countermeasure design) becomes a critical defense against the possibility that the other superpower might embark on deployment of a potentially effective system. In short, this logic leads to the paradoxical conclusion that perhaps deployment could be prevented by sufficiently vigorous, imaginative, and adequately publicized research and development by both superpowers.

As in the first experiment, therefore, many of the popular assumptions behind the SDI debate seem to be challenged by the agreed propositions. For critics, the consequence of the agreed propositions is that ending research and development would create the risk of inviting a Soviet system for which the United States would be ill-prepared (because of a lack of development of effective countermeasures). For supporters, however, the agreed propositions imply that a unilateral system can never be effectively deployed by the United States as long as the Soviets are presumed to be developing countermeasures—and, if the Soviets are not so doing, their lack of hostile intent seemingly nullifies the logic of the entire SDI effort. Arguments for research and development may need to be separated entirely from discussion of deployment, and both topics related more directly to the possibility of cooperative development of SDI systems by both superpowers as a means of increasing stability in a world of nuclear proliferation.

Disputed Propositions. Given the saliency of debate on technical issues concerning SDI, the disagreements were hardly surprising. Indeed, the tendency of the two scientist-advocates to dispute technical matters seemed so pervasive that the specification of detailed points of disagreement was not pursued as far as in the first experiment. Several points were asserted as detailed matters of *scientific* disagreement. For example, Gerry stated that "boosters have a very large infrared radiation which cannot be decoyed in a cost-effective way," whereas Garwin proposed the statement that "a gradual reduction of the probability of war can lead to a *finite* hazard of nuclear war to eternity."

The first of these propositions illustrates the critical role of countermeasures—and the impossibility of making assessments about their feasibility without knowledge that is often in part or entirely classified. The second reflects the way policy issues and assessments are often stated in ways that, to rival experts, seem to be beyond scientific disconfirmation and hence essentially polemic. In both cases, however, the disputed propositions provide a needed way for scientific experts to express their carefully balanced assessment of the net costs and benefits of alternatives. Hence even though the disputed propositions may provide a limited contribution to the policy debate about SDI, their presence in the Scientific Adversary Process may be the condition for outlining agreed propositions that are a genuine contribution to the policymaking process.

CONCLUSIONS

Scientific Adversary Procedures—and particularly the Dartmouth experiments concerning SDI—show that new methods can be created to improve the technical and scientific information provided to policymakers. When scientist-advocates appear in public today, they are usually questioned—if at all—by nontechnical policymakers (such as legislators and legislative aides, administrators, and journalists). The experimental approach described here provides an alternative, in which opposed scientist-advocates confront each other.

Such a procedure can have significant advantages as a means of enhancing our society's control over rapidly changing technologies. Although a lay person may ask intelligent questions concerning a scientist's expertise, it is becoming increasingly difficult for nonspecialists to challenge that expertise itself or to elicit unspoken technical information that is highly germane to intelligent public policy. When opposed scientist-advocates seek to define with precision the area of their agreement as well as disagreement, the results can be a sharper understanding of technical information than is otherwise likely to occur. Where experts with opposed policy preferences agree, the statement of their area of consensus should become a basis for further policy debate; where they disagree, the statement of the technical issues should indicate areas on which scientific expertise may be biased by the policy preferences of the experts themselves.

In exploring the benefits of both agreement and disagreement between scientist-advocates, the Berkeley and the Dartmouth experiments were complementary. The former emphasized the disputed propositions, which were carefully negotiated. The cross-examination session at Berkeley was indeed useful. On the other hand, no recorded agreed propositions were negotiated, and the opportunity to inform policymaking with such agreements was lost.

The Dartmouth experiments emphasized the agreed propositions; all the participants found these agreements informative. The degree to which opposed scientists can narrow the area of technical uncertainty without abandoning their policy preferences was striking. There were suggestions that, in the public sessions, there should have been more time devoted to a detailed explanation of the meaning and the importance of these agreements to help achieve a sharper understanding of the issues underlying policy.

It may be difficult to gain both of these benefits in the same procedure. In the Dartmouth experiments, for example, too little time was made available for formulation of suitable disputed propositions, and the cross-examination sessions were "anticlimactic," "vague," and much less exciting than the Berkeley session. One of the outside evaluators (Professor Mazur) suggested that the second SDI experiment could have been simplified by eliminating the cross-examination sessions altogether. It is hard to know, however, whether as much agreement could be reached if the scientist-advocates did not feel the pressure of the forthcoming cross-examination, especially since publicly answering questions from expert adversaries is a vital part of the traditional methodology of science. Future experiments are needed to see if it is possible to achieve a better balance between agreed and disputed propositions by slight modifications, such as interposing a recess of several weeks between the negotiation of agreements and the cross-examination procedures.

The educational potential of these experiments is considerable. The Love Canal experiments attracted a great deal of interest in the Berkeley community. There was general agreement that the cross-examination session shed valuable light on the available scientific knowledge of the health hazards at Love Canal and on the serious obstacles to objective research imposed by politicians in conflict. At Dartmouth, we increased the awareness of the campus community of what is known and what is not known concerning President Reagan's Strategic Defense Initiative.

For the students and observers who participated in these experiments, the procedures gave particularly useful insight into the nature of the current dialogue between science and society. For example, in the experiments on SDI, it was anticipated that important areas would be excluded because of secrecy, and indeed this was the case. Secrecy inevitably limits democratic control of technology. For the participants in the Dartmouth experiments, the Scientific Adversary Procedures had the advantage of making this limitation on informed public assessment of policy alternatives more explicit.

Above all, however, the spread of Scientific Adversary Procedures and dissemination of their findings could provide welcome information to the general public as well as to legislators and administrators. One of the principal benefits of dialogue and cross-examination between equally qualified experts could be the unanticipated reconceptualization of policy debates that have become ideological rather than pragmatic. When rival scientific advocates agree—or specify the area of their disagreement in technical terms—the result can shed new light on old controversies.

It is easy to illustrate this last point from the Scientific Adversary Procedures devoted to SDI. The technical consensus that testing of computer systems would be a more important constraint than hardware or the scale of software led to an awareness of the needs for cooperation between the United States and the USSR as an integral part of research and development. The same conclusion could be derived from the agreement on the importance of decoys and other countermeasures. Both of the Dartmouth procedures thus raised a profound question about the technical feasibility of unilateral development and deployment of SDI.

This conclusion is, paradoxically, *not* tantamount to an argument against SDI. Quite the contrary, for one can readily imagine both strategic interests and military motives leading the two superpowers to cooperate to test and deploy a strategic defence system jointly. Among other policy goals, a condominium—providing the superpowers a jointly operated shield against missile threats from secondary or third-ranking powers—might well be attractive even if it did not completely rid either the United States or the USSR of the need to maintain deterrent forces against the other.

The irony, of course, is that this way of conceptualizing the policy issues would totally reverse the prevailing ideological debate. Those in favor of détente would see SDI as a means of sharing technological information between the superpowers as a means of building trust and reducing the risks of accidental war. Those who fear the Soviet Union would have reasons to prefer other approaches to military strategy if it becomes apparent that SDI requires cooperation between the super-powers. As was noted above, discovery of the technological require-ments of a public policy is not the same thing as advocacy for or against it.

APPENDIX

AGREED PROPOSITIONS—
FIRST DARTMOUTH SCIENTIFIC ADVERSARY PROCEDURE

1. The subsystem-level hardware computing issue for SDI can be parameterized as follows:

a. one billion operations per second
b. maintenance free for ten years
c. hardened to radiation and shock

These hardware capabilities will probably be developed within 5–10 years, based on continuation of current programs.

2. The Fletcher Commission reports that the software computing issue for SDI will require ten million lines of code.

Given that estimates range from ten million to a hundred million lines of code, a reasonable estimate is fifty million lines of code, which will be used below. (There is such a wide range because of the double uncertainty of both unspecified requirements and design.)

3. James Fletcher, director of the Fletcher Commission, said that the software for SDI must be "error free." It is impossible to make a system of the magnitude described in proposition #2 which is error free, but the requirement of absolute freedom of error is not necessary for SDI to succeed.

4. The communications issues will not be limited by bandwidth considerations, in the absence of Soviet countermeasures. In the pres-ence of Soviet countermeasures, bandwidth considerations may or may not limit communications. In this case, official secrecy inhibits serious public discussion.

5. Parallel processing can achieve higher throughput on some (e.g., matrix manipulation) of the significant problems we forsee, with-out presenting insurmountable computing issues.

6. Other significant problems may not be amenable to solution through parallel processing. This may present a hardware problem if such a problem requires computation speed greater than 300 million operations per second.

7. Distributed processing tasks (e.g., database management) require synchrony. "A demand for synchrony better than milliseconds could create complications within the software."[17]

8. Based on the lines of code as a metric of complexity, the software system for SDI will be an order of magnitude larger than anything developed to date.

9. The software system for SDI must be able to function without human intervention to correct real time hardware and software failures and to function in environments unanticipated by system planners.

10. Our ability to verify and validate the computing performance needed in a comprehensive BMD is not as high as our ability to do so for our unopposed offensive systems.

AGREED PROPOSITIONS—
SECOND DARTMOUTH SCIENTIFIC ADVERSARY PROCEDURE

1. No system has been publicly presented which satisfies the twin requirements of the administration as presented by Paul Nitze on February 20, 1985—to be survivable and to be cost-effective.

2. No viable defensive system can allow space mines to be placed within lethal range of space assets.

3. The utility of pop-up for boost phase intercept can be negated by fast-burn boosters.

4. If rail guns are to be used for ballistic missile defense, they must propel homing kill vehicles.

5. Energy efficiency considerations favor chemically propelling homing kill vehicles over rail guns up to an added velocity given by [an agreed upon] equation. Under assumptions of an electrical generation efficiency of 30 percent, rail gun efficiency of 30 percent, chemical rocket specific impulse of 300 seconds and stage-mass fraction of 90 percent, and reasonable number of stages, this velocity is approximately 14km/sec. [A detailed table of calculations was agreed as well as the basic equation—see the full record.]

6. Close-spaced decoys multiply greatly the number of HKVs

[homing kill vehicles] needed for mid-course intercept unless they can be discriminated and designated.

7. Space-based kinetic energy weapons are fundamentally limited in effective range by their velocity and the time available for flyout to the target after launch. (Agreement on this point was considered trivial.)

8. In the context of an effective surveillance, acquisition, tracking, and designating system, HKVs would be effective in boost phase against the current class and deployment of Soviet ICBMs and SLBMs, and would have continuing effectiveness against reentry vehicles in mid-course and in defense of space-based assets, providing the space-based systems can survive, and Soviet countermeasures aren't effective. (Gerry believes that the system can survive and be effective against counter-measures, Garwin dissents.)

9. In the continuing context of deterrence of nuclear war by threat of retaliation, technologies already exist to solve the problem of strategic force vulnerability sooner and at lower cost than via layered defense with space components.

10. Within the context of continuing deterrence of nuclear war by threat of retaliation, existing technology involving nuclear intercepts in space could be employed to handle a few rogue nation ICBMs. A cooperative system could handle accidental lauch of one or a few Soviet ICBMs.

11. Equation 13 of Garwin's "How Many Orbiting Lasers for Boost Phase Intercept?" provides a good estimate of the number of laser battle stations of a given brightness and retarget time to counter a prescribed threat.[18] [A table of results of the calculation was also inserted into the record.]

12. There is no known fundamental limit to laser power or brightness that can be achieved other than cost.

13. Countermeasures are a fundamental problem to the success of a high-performance strategic defense.

14. The SDI program is exploring possible solutions to all of the countermeasures issues which have been raised publicly and more.

15. So long as the Soviets can reliably deliver by *any* means (e.g., aircraft, cruise missiles, suitcase bombs) numbers of nuclear weapons causing catastrophic national damage, capability for nuclear retaliation against the Soviets will still be required for deterrence.

14

CONCLUSION

NORMAN J. VIG AND MICHAEL E. KRAFT

Four themes stand out in this volume. The first is that technology is inevitably a social, and therefore political, phenomenon. The second is that our present political institutions and processes are not well suited to the governance of technology. The third is that the methods and procedures currently used for assessing and regulating technological risks need to be reconsidered and made more responsive to both public concerns and economic needs. The fourth is that we need to explore alternative ways to evaluate—in open and democratic fashion —both the technical feasibility and the social and moral consequences of technological change if we are to legitimize governmental decision making and improve the chances for resolving technological controversies in the future.

TECHNOLOGY AS A POLITICAL PHENOMENON

The thesis of the first section of the book is that technology is not simply a useful tool or instrument for achieving human ends, but a distinctive way of understanding and dealing with both material and social reality and, consequently, of defining human character and purpose. Technology entails an epistemology of instrumental rationality and problem solving that brings to center stage man's quest for ever higher levels of material comfort, power, and efficiency. Insofar as those who live in a technologically saturated culture cannot avoid the influence of technological thought and artifacts in their daily lives, technology can be said to assume a profound ontological dimension.

The extent to which technology determines, or is determined by, social structure and culture is at the heart of philosophical debate on technology, and this question inevitably carries over into politics.

Philosophers such as Langdon Winner and Albert Borgmann fear that mankind is abdicating moral responsibility by allowing technological opportunism and "drift" to define human ends by default. In their view, the essential political and ethical questions that ought to be the *subject* of democratic discussion and debate are obscured by the technological devices and commodities that become the *object* of politics in contemporary society. Consequently they believe that the development of technology tends to displace ethical and political judgment by arbitrarily "legislating" new social rules and relationships.

On a second level, the political process itself is altered by technology. As Norman Vig points out in chapter 1, technology increasingly defines the opportunity structure within which democratic political competition is conducted. Mass communication technologies such as television influence the content as well as the style of political discourse. TV has turned electoral campaigns into public relations exercises for the marketing of candidates rather than occasions for serious debate and reflection on issues. Computerized marketing techniques also allow organized interest groups to identify and target specific audiences and constituencies likely to support their cause, encouraging "single interest" politics and intensifying inequalities of representation. Political leaders inevitably become preoccupied with the public image of their actions that is instantaneously conveyed by the telecommunications media.

Third, technology is political in the sense that government makes decisions on the development of certain technologies in a highly politicized institutional environment. Chapter 4 by W. Henry Lambright and Dianne Rahm and chapter 6 by Roger Noll and Linda Cohen emphasize the political incentives that motivate presidents and other public officials in making decisions on large technology projects. Politics inevitably plays a major role in the design and implementation of such projects since they affect the allocation and expenditure of huge sums of money, the creation of thousands of jobs, and consequently the economic health of whole communities and industries. The government bureaucracies and corporations that plan and manage such projects also have large political and economic stakes in their perpetuation. In short, once government undertakes technology projects they are often subject to the same kinds of political pressures as other programs.

A fourth sense in which technology is political is that it requires public regulation. Technologies produce negative as well as positive externalities and can pose substantial risks to health and the environment; hence societal judgments are needed on *which* technologies to regulate, to *what extent* to regulate them, and *how* to regulate them. The definition of acceptable social risk or "how safe is safe enough?" is an intensely political matter. As Harvey Brooks points out in his essay, there has been something of a regulatory revolution due to increased awareness of hazards and capabilities for monitoring them. We now have numerous laws and regulatory agencies for assessing and controlling the social and ecological impacts of technology. Yet there is little consensus on the costs and benefits of regulation or on the appropriate methodologies for assessing them. As Michael Kraft explains in his chapter on risk assessment, there is no truly "objective" or "scientific" way of choosing one methodology over another or of evaluating results, given the inherent uncertainties of environmental and health impacts; yet the selection and use of analytical methods often determines the outcome. Regulatory agencies are also heavily lobbied by elected officials and interest groups and are frequently challenged in court. Hence the public administrators and technical experts charged with regulating technology cannot avoid making political judgments either.

Finally, technology has become a leading issue in international politics. The accelerated transfer and diffusion of technology has created new economic superpowers, new global markets and trading patterns, and new threats to political and ecological stability. Although largely beyond the scope of this volume, it is clear that the new international economic competition is increasingly influencing national priorities and policies for technology. Pressures to protect both new and outmoded national technologies are likely to mount in the United States and other Western countries, giving rise to new internal conflicts and straining alliance relations. At the same time, however, nations will be forced to seek new forms of international cooperation in areas of rapidly developing technology, such as telecommunications, and in controlling threats to the global ecosystem ranging from acid rain to nuclear war. Whether cooperation or conflict predominates may obviously determine the future viability of the planet.

PROBLEMS OF GOVERNANCE

The idea of governing technology suggests an impossibility because almost everything involves technology. Furthermore, most technology is generated in the private sector of the economy, and no one (at least in this volume) is talking about nationalizing the economy. We are concerned with a narrower range of activities that involve government promotion, regulation, and management of certain technologies in the national interest. All nations, regardless of political and ideological orientation, engage in such activities with greater or lesser success. The success of our own government in this regard is no longer assured and, indeed, a consensus seems to be growing that we lack effective institutional means for making technology policies.

Much of the institutional problem lies in the constitutional and political structure itself. With power so fragmented and dispersed, without a powerful and respected permanent civil service, and without strong leadership from either the White House or Congress, we can hardly expect coherent national policies. But technology presents special problems because it is both ubiquitous and subordinated instrumentally to the specific interests and missions of particular agencies and their clienteles. Priorities have been determined in an ad hoc manner by program commitments, and there has been little overall effort to coordinate technological activities. The Department of Defense, the nuclear programs of the Department of Energy, and the military components of NASA's space programs presently account for some three-quarters of all federal R&D spending. Unfortunately, no executive agency or congressional committee has authority to define an overall national strategy for technological development, nor is there an effective advisory apparatus at the presidential level with a broader view of national needs. The result is a national "nonpolicy" for technology.

The lack of planning and foresight is manifested in various ways. Although the Office of Technology Assessment can do long-term studies for the Congress, the policymaking apparatus in both branches is overwhelmingly geared toward short-term solutions and crisis management. The frequent change of administrations, noted by several authors, contributes to the short time horizons and lack of commitment to strategic projects over extended periods. Noll and Cohen have a strong point in arguing that immediate political payoffs have too large an influence on the selection, timing, and administration of R&D

programs, and that long-term economic investment criteria play too small a role.

Regulatory administration suffers from many of the same problems. The efforts of the president and his political appointees (and sometimes members of Congress) to intervene in the details of regulatory policymaking frequently undermine professional competence and expertise and can produce major disruptions in policy implementation.[1] Methodologies such as cost-benefit and risk-benefit analysis are controversial enough without being manipulated for partisan advantage. On the other hand, the press and television media often overdramatize accidents and other risks to the public, as Allan Mazur points out in his critique. Administrators are often caught in the middle of such controversies. It is partly for this reason that Brooks would like to place greater reliance on expert regulatory bodies such as those in Europe that are more insulated from politics and the public. Other contributors, including Michael Kraft and Edward Woodhouse, disagree and would put more emphasis on public participation and pluralistic approaches to risk assessment, as discussed further below.

The point here is not simply that government promotion and management of technology is political—for as we have argued above, technology *is* a political phenomenon and *ought to be debated more widely*—but rather that our governance system does not facilitate an orderly and democratic process of policymaking on the public purposes of technology and means for attaining them. The broader implications of technology are rarely on the political agenda, nor is the allocation of resources to different fields of technology. Policy formulation and implementation is episodic, fragmented, and inconsistent, as Lambright and Rahm bring out so starkly in their chapter, and regulation is beset with conflicts over economic interests, scientific uncertainties, and public distrust and apprehension. Many of these conflicts are inevitable in a pluralistic democracy, but improvements can be made in at least two areas: risk assessment and regulation, and public participation in resolving technological disputes.

IMPROVING RISK ASSESSMENT AND REGULATION

Regulation has been much criticized in the 1980s, with arguments made from both the right and the left on the need to make governmental efforts more efficient and effective. One need not be enamored of the various techniques and methods of regulatory control proffered to recognize that there is a clear need to set policy priorities more carefully (e.g., to give adequate attention to the most severe risks facing the nation) and to improve the procedures used in the regulation of technology's varied risks. The authors of part III and the more general commentary on risks and regulation focus on both the methods used in these tasks and the processes of decision making within the agencies charged with these responsibilities.

Woodhouse and Kraft, in particular, express concern with the inherent limitations of technology assessment and risk assessment and call for both careful use of these methods and serious consideration of how they might be improved. Certainly much can be done over time to improve the data bases used by regulators and to refine the techniques of measurement. Risks can also be communicated more clearly to policymakers and the public at large. Dealing with the great degree of uncertainty that surrounds many estimates of risk, particularly those involving low probability of potentially severe accidents and those phenomena (such as depletion of the ozone layer) at the outer limits of scientific knowledge, is more problematic. Here, as Woodhouse suggests, we need the additional precautions offered by a change in the procedures of decision making.

We need to improve decision making in a number of ways. One is to adopt procedures that encourage institutional caution in making risk estimates, particularly where the risks can be catastrophic or irreversible. Another is to facilitate learning within various institutional settings so that decision processes can be quickly changed to take account of experience and new evidence, some of which might come from modest experiments to test the nature of a risk and appropriate control techniques. A third is to improve the overall capacity of government to identify and assess technological risks; this means a greater investment of resources in risk assessment, and particularly more emphasis on forecasting the changing global conditions that pose serious long-term risks to public health and environmental quality.

Other changes involve the way in which agencies judge the acceptability of risk—that is, how they set safety levels. Although science and politics are often thoroughly intertwined in such decisions, we could improve the credibility of the judgments made by insuring that the decisions take place in an open, pluralistic, and accountable process. Where possible, public involvement in such decisions should be encouraged and efforts made to improve public knowledge of the facts and issues. While public participation in decisions on technical and complex regulatory problems is by no means easy, its support can pay many dividends. It might well improve the quality of the decisions made to subject them to intense scrutiny and encourage dialogue on critical aspects of policy choices such as the appropriate level of safety to be required. It might also help to counteract a natural bureaucratic tendency to be overly responsive to well-established but narrow constituency interests. Over time it could also improve public trust and confidence in governmental regulation, which has suffered of late. In short, it should be possible not only to improve the effectiveness of governmental regulation but to make it more sensitive to public preferences and to a variety of needs at the same time.

IMPROVING THE EVALUATION OF TECHNOLOGY

Along with improvement in the methods and procedures of risk assessment, we need to develop new and better ways to evaluate technology, and particularly to involve a wider range of participants, including the public, in such evaluation. Roger Masters and Arthur Kantrowitz offer a promising approach to assessing the factual components of technological developments through their Scientific Advisory Procedures. Public debates between experts and other citizen-oriented technology policy hearings can, if they are carefully planned and focused, help to separate factual assertions from value judgments and thereby contribute to productive dialogue over the best course of action to take.

As Robert Blank reminds us, though, we need to address more fully and more explicitly the ethical issues often ignored or downplayed in policy dialogues that concentrate on scientific developments and techniques. There is no approach that can guarantee that such issues are faced up to by policymakers and the public. But policy analysts and planners can help by incorporating ethical questions into their assessments and reports and thereby enhancing the visibility of these issues. They can improve their own capacity to speak to such issues with as much professional ability as they typically apply to assessing the economic costs and benefits of technologies.

Public involvement in the evaluation of technology is a third need. Too often decisions about the development and use of technology have been left to the private sector or to experts in government bureaucracies. A more diverse set of participants may enhance the legitimacy of the decisions by bringing additional perspectives to bear on the issues and creating a forum for discussion of the technology and its consequences. Public participation is not without substantial risks if handled poorly. But there are many ways to increase public involvement that would yield more positive results (as explained in Kraft's chapter on nuclear waste disposal). More research on the results of past experience with public participation programs is urgently needed to identify the most fruitful approaches. Further experimentation might also tell us which approaches work best in particular situations.

THE CHALLENGE OF THE FUTURE

Many of the challenges posed by technology are of very recent origin and we are only beginning to learn how to assess and cope with them. Our experience to date has been largely with older mechanical and chemical systems of industrial technology and their by-products (e.g., steel mills, automobiles, oil spills, and toxic substances). Increasingly we are facing quite different technologies based on the generation and communication of information (e.g., genetic engineering and networking of large computer data banks). Some of the effects of newer technologies, as well as the older ones, may not be felt for decades or generations. Hence we need to radically improve our ability to envision and anticipate technology's consequences *before* the effects are manifested, and to consciously design institutions and processes for choosing those courses of development that truly serve the humanistic ends we all desire.

The task may seem impossibly difficult, but there is reason for hope. We understand much more today than we did twenty or thirty years ago, and it is not unreasonable to expect that our social learning processes will improve more rapidly than in the past. With sufficient attention, foresight, and care, we can create a sustainable, environmentally sound, and humane society both in the United States and the world. But this will not come about spontaneously. To a great extent the future will be created by human choice and action, much of it through politics and government. We need to begin by making technology the subject as well as the object of politics.

NOTES

INTRODUCTION TO PART I

1 Lynn T. White, *Medieval Technology and Social Change* (London: Oxford University Press, 1964).
2 See J. David Bolter, *Turing's Man: Western Culture in the Computer Age* (Chapel Hill: University of North Carolina Press, 1984).
3 There has also been more resistance to technological change in the past than is generally recognized; see Witold Rybczynski, *Taming the Tiger: The Struggle to Control Technology* (New York: Viking Press, 1983).
4 For two contrasting statements on this point, cf. Julian L. Simon and Herman Kahn, eds., *The Resourceful Earth* (New York: Blackwell, 1984), and Joseph Agassi, *Technology: Philosophical and Social Aspects* (Dordrecht, Holland: D. Reidel, 1985).
5 See Samuel C. Florman, *Blaming Technology* (New York: St. Martin's Press, 1981), chapter 2.
6 See Stewart Brand, *The Media Lab: Inventing the Future at MIT* (New York: Viking Press, 1987), esp. p. 11.
7 Ithiel de Sola Pool, *Technologies of Freedom* (Cambridge, Mass.: Belknap Press, 1983).
8 Sherry Turkle, *The Second Self: Computers and the Human Spirit* (New York: Simon and Schuster, 1984).
9 See, e.g., Harley Shaiken, *Work Transformed: Automation and Labor in the Computer Age* (New York: Holt, Rinehart and Winston, 1985); and Robert Howard, *Brave New Workplace* (New York: Viking Press, 1985).
10 Florman, *Blaming Technology*, chapter 9.

CHAPTER 1

1 See, e.g., Melvin Kranzberg, "Technology and Human Values," in Larry Hickman and Azizah al-Hibri, eds., *Technology and Human Affairs* (St. Louis: C. V. Mosby, 1981), pp. 393–99. But the idea of technological progress has undergone significant

change over time; see Leo Marx, *The Machine in the Garden* (New York: Oxford University Press, 1964); and Howard P. Segal, *Technological Utopianism in American Culture* (Chicago: University of Chicago Press, 1985).

2 Jacques Ellul, *The Technological Society* (New York: Random House, 1964); Herbert Marcuse, *One-Dimensional Man: Studies in the Ideology of Advanced Industrial Society* (Boston: Beacon Press, 1964).

3 E. F. Schumacher, *Small Is Beautiful: Economics as if People Mattered* (New York: Harper and Row, 1973).

4 See Carl Mitcham and Robert Mackey, eds., *Philosophy and Technology: Readings in the Philosophical Problems of Technology* (New York: Free Press, 1972, 1983); and Paul T. Durbin, ed., *Research in Philosophy and Technology* (Greenwich, Conn.: JAI Press, annual). For a brief overview of the origins and development of the field, see Carl Mitcham, "What Is the Philosophy of Technology?" *International Philosophical Quarterly* 25 (March 1985), pp. 73–88.

5 See James K. Feibleman, "Pure Science, Applied Science, and Technology: An Attempt at Definitions," in Mitcham and Mackey, *Philosophy and Technology*, pp. 33–41; John M. Staudenmaier, S.J., *Technology's Storytellers: Reweaving the Human Fabric* (Cambridge, Mass.: MIT Press, 1985), chapter 3; Jacques Ellul, *The Technological System* (New York: Continuum, 1980); and Arnold Pacey, *The Culture of Technology* (Cambridge, Mass.: MIT Press, 1983).

One of the important themes in the new literature on technology is that technology contributes as much to the advancement of science as vice versa:

> Where science and technology are connected, as they increasingly have been in this century, it is mistaken to see the connection between them as one in which technology is one-sidedly dependent on science. Technology has arguably contributed as much to science as vice versa—think of the great dependence of science on the computer, without which some modern scientific specialties could scarcely have come into existence. Most importantly, where technology does draw on science the nature of that relation is not one of technologists obediently working out the "implications" of a scientific advance. Technologists use science. They seek from science resources to help them solve the problems they have, to achieve the goals toward which they are working. These problems are at least as important in explaining what they do as the science that is available for them to use.

Donald MacKenzie and Judy Wajcman, eds., *The Social Shaping of Technology* (Milton Keynes and Philadelphia: Open University Press, 1985), p. 9.

6 Webster F. Hood, "The Aristotelian Versus the Heideggerian Approach to the Problem of Technology," in Mitcham and Mackey, *Philosophy and Technology*, pp. 347–63.

7 Martin Heidegger, *The Question Concerning Technology and Other Essays*, trans. William Lovitt (New York: Harper and Row, 1977). Useful interpretations can be found in Mitcham, "What Is the Philosophy of Technology?"; and Leo Marx, "On Heidegger's Conception of 'Technology' and its Historical Validity," *The Massachusetts Review* 25 (Winter 1984), pp. 638–52.

8 Hans Jonas, *The Imperative of Responsibility: In Search of an Ethics for the Tech-*

nological Age (Chicago: University of Chicago Press, 1984), pp. 9, 18.

9   Langdon Winner, *The Whale and the Reactor: A Search for Limits in an Age of High Technology* (Chicago: University of Chicago Press, 1986), p. 12.

10   Manfred Stanley, "Technology and Its Critics," in Philip L. Bereano, ed., *Technology as a Social and Political Phenomenon* (New York: John Wiley & Sons, 1976), pp. 20–24, and *The Technological Conscience: Survival and Dignity in an Age of Expertise* (New York: Free Press, 1978).

11   Jonas, *Imperative of Responsibility*, chapter 5. See also Paul T. Durbin, ed., *Technology and Responsibility*, vol. 3 of *Philosophy and Technology* (Dordrecht, Holland: D. Reidel, 1987); and Joseph Agassi, *Technology: Philosophical and Social Aspects*, vol. 11 of *Episteme* (Dordrecht, Holland: D. Reidel, 1985).

12   Emmanuel G. Mesthene, *Technological Change: Its Impact on Man and Society* (New York: New American Library, 1970), p. 60.

13   David F. Noble, *America by Design: Science, Technology, and the Rise of Corporate Capitalism* (New York: Knopf, 1977).

14   See, e.g., Peter F. Drucker, "New Technology: Predicting Its Impact," in Albert H. Teich, ed., *Technology and the Future*, 4th ed. (New York: St. Martin's Press, 1986).

15   Staudenmaier, *Technology's Storytellers*, p. 165.

16   Many examples, including the mechanical clocks, are discussed in Arnold Pacey, *The Maze of Ingenuity: Ideas and Idealism in the Development of Technology* (Cambridge, Mass.: MIT Press, 1976). See also Ruth Schwartz Cowan, *More Work for Mother: The Ironies of Household Technology from the Open Hearth to the Microwave* (New York: Basic Books, 1983), esp. pp. 142–45; Michael Goldhaber, *Reinventing Technology: Policies for Democratic Values* (New York: Routledge and Kegan Paul, 1986); MacKenzie and Wajcman, *The Social Shaping of Technology*; and Wiebe E. Bijker et al., eds., *The Social Construction of Technological Systems* (Cambridge, Mass.: MIT Press, 1987).

It should be pointed out that this position does not imply that the individual inventor or innovator is necessarily motivated by the values that influence the deployment and use of a technology in the sense that, for example, Henry Ford was. The Apple computer is a case in point. Steve Wozniak, cofounder of the Apple company, is reported to have designed the original Apple computer "in his spare time for his own pleasure and to excite his friends at the Homebrew Computer Club" (Stewart Brand, *The Media Lab: Inventing the Future at MIT* [New York: Viking Press, 1987], p. 175). The history of technology is replete with similar examples of brilliant "tinkering," but that does not explain the social application of technologies. Of course the same technology can also have quite different social consequences in different cultures and social settings; e.g., computers can either centralize or decentralize authority depending on their organizational context and functional use. See James N. Danziger and Kenneth L. Kraemer, *People and Computers: The Impacts of Computing on End Users in Organizations* (New York: Columbia University Press, 1986).

17   See Donald MacKenzie, "Marx and the Machine," *Technology and Culture* 25 (July 1984), pp. 473–502; Erik P. Hoffmann and Robbin F. Laird, *Technocratic Socialism: The Soviet Union in the Advanced Industrial Era* (Durham, N.C.: Duke University Press, 1985); and Bruce Parrott, *Politics and Technology in the Soviet Union* (Cam-

bridge, Mass.: MIT Press, 1985). For a neo-Marxist interpretation, see Bernard Gendron, *Technology and the Human Condition* (New York: St. Martin's Press, 1977).

18 Economists tend to eschew cultural and sociological explanations in favor of universalistic theories. They have traditionally explained different levels of economic and technological development in terms of relative factor endowments or differential cost structures, which in turn produce intercountry variations in "comparative advantage." More recently they have come to see comparative advantage as a dynamic rather than static factor, as nations have learned to "engineer" national competitive advantage through rapid introduction and application of advanced technologies and adoption of export-oriented trade policies. See, e.g., Paul R. Krugman, ed., *Strategic Trade Policy and the New International Economics* (Cambridge, Mass.: MIT Press, 1986).

19 Lewis Mumford, *The Myth of the Machine: Technics and Human Development* (New York: Harcourt, Brace and World, 1967); Marcuse, *One-Dimensional Man*; Schumacher, *Small Is Beautiful*. Popular best-selling books critical of technology included Theodore Roszak, *The Making of a Counter-Culture: Reflections on the Technocratic Society and Its Youthful Opposition* (Garden City, N.Y.: Doubleday, 1969); Charles A. Reich, *The Greening of America* (New York: Random House, 1970); and Barry Commoner, *The Closing Circle* (New York: Knopf, 1971).

20 Ellul, *Technological Society*, p. 98.

21 This point is made in Melvin Kranzberg, "Technology and History: 'Kranzberg's Laws,'" *Technology and Culture* 27 (July 1986), p. 546. See also Ian G. Barbour, *Technology, Environment, and Human Values* (New York: Praeger, 1980).

22 Langdon Winner, *Autonomous Technology: Technics-out-of-Control as a Theme in Political Thought* (Cambridge, Mass.: MIT Press, 1977), pp. 317–25. See also Richard E. Sclove, "The Nuts and Bolts of Democracy: Democratic Theory and Technological Design" (Paper prepared for delivery at the 1987 Annual Meeting of the American Political Science Association, Chicago, September 1987).

23 Winner, *Autonomous Technology*, chapter 2, and *Whale and the Reactor*, chapter 1.

24 Albert Borgmann, *Technology and the Character of Contemporary Life* (Chicago: University of Chicago Press, 1984), pp. 104–5.

25 Daniel J. Boorstin, *The Republic of Technology: Reflections on Our Future Community* (New York: Harper and Row, 1978).

26 C. B. Macpherson, "Democratic Theory: Ontology and Technology," in Mitcham and Mackey, *Philosophy and Technology*, pp. 161–70.

27 The Office of Technology Assessment of the U.S. Congress is currently completing a study on "Science, Technology and the Constitution in the Information Age," which covers these and other areas. See also Kenneth L. Kraemer and John L. King, "Computers and the Constitution: A Helpful, Harmful or Harmless Relationship?" *Public Administration Review* 47 (January–February 1987), pp. 93–105; and Ithiel de Sola Pool, *Technologies of Freedom* (Cambridge, Mass.: Belknap Press, 1983).

28 See, e.g., Daniel Callahan, "How Technology is Reframing the Abortion Debate," *Hastings Center Report* (February 1986), pp. 33–42; Ira H. Carmen, *Cloning and the Constitution: An Inquiry into Governmental Policy Making and Genetic Engineering* (Madison: University of Wisconsin Press, 1985); and Robert Howard, *Brave New*

Workplace (New York: Viking Press, 1985).

29 Lester C. Thurow, "A Surge in Inequality," *Scientific American* (May 1987), pp. 30–37.

30 A classic study of totalitarianism concluded that "totalitarian societies appear to be merely exaggerations, but nonetheless logical exaggerations, of the technological state of modern society." Carl J. Friedrich and Zbigniew K. Brzezinski, *Totalitarian Dictatorship and Autocracy*, rev. ed. (New York: Praeger, 1964), p. 24.

31 Winner, *Autonomous Technology*, chapter 4. For the origin of the term, see Daniel Bell, *The Coming of Post-Industrial Society* (New York: Basic Books, 1973), p. 349, n. 8.

32 Galbraith, *The New Industrial State* (Boston: Houghton Mifflin, 1967), esp. chapter Bell, *Coming of Post-Industrial Society*, p. 348. Bell argued, however, that politics would dominate technocracy in the foreseeable future (ibid., pp. 364–65).

33 Brooks, quoted in Mesthene, *Technological Change*, p. 79.

34 Ibid., p. 65.

35 Victor C. Ferkiss, *Technological Man: The Myth and the Reality* (New York: New American Library, 1970), chapter 7; and Charles A. Thrall and Jerold M. Starr, eds., *Technology, Power, and Social Change* (Lexington, Mass.: Lexington Books, 1972). For interesting recent discussions of the centralizing or decentralizing potentials of computer technology, cf. Kraemer and King, "Computers and the Constitution"; and Richard L. Harris, "The Impact of the Micro-electronics Revolution on the Basic Structure of Modern Organizations," *Science, Technology, & Human Values* 11 (Fall 1986), pp. 31–44.

36 Don K. Price, *The Scientific Estate* (New York: Oxford University Press, 1965). For a careful discussion, see also Sanford A. Lakoff, "Scientists, Technologists and Political Power," in Ina Spiegel-Rosing and Derek de Solla Price, eds., *Science, Technology and Society: A Cross-Disciplinary Perspective* (London and Beverly Hills: Sage Publications, 1977), pp. 355–91.

37 Patrick W. Hamlett, "Understanding Technological Development: A Decisionmaking Approach," *Science, Technology, & Human Values* 9 (Summer 1984), pp. 33–46. See also Richard Barke, *Science, Technology, and Public Policy* (Washington, D.C.: Congressional Quarterly Press, 1986); and Malcolm L. Goggin, ed., *Governing Science and Technology in a Democracy* (Knoxville: University of Tennessee Press, 1986).

38 See Harold P. Green and Alan Rosenthal, *Government of the Atom: The Integration of Powers* (New York: Atherton Press, 1963); and Steven L. Del Sesto, *Science, Politics, and Controversy: Civilian Nuclear Power in the United States, 1946–1974* (Boulder, Colo.: Westview Press, 1979).

39 Hamlett, "Understanding Technological Development," pp. 43–44.

40 David Dickson, *The New Politics of Science* (New York: Pantheon, 1984).

41 Nathan Rotenstreich, "Technology and Politics," in Mitcham and Mackey, *Philosophy and Technology*, p. 157. See also Jarol B. Manheim, "Can Democracy Survive Television?" in Doris A. Graber, ed., *Media Power in Politics* (Washington, D.C.: Congressional Quarterly Press, 1984), pp. 131–37.

42 Rotenstreich, "Technology and Politics," p. 157. Cf. Ferkiss, *Technological Man*,

pp. 153–55.

43   The literature on this point is huge. See Gerald Benjamin, ed., *The Communications Revolution in Politics* (New York: Academy of Political Science, 1982); Austin Ranney, *Channels of Power: The Impact of Television on American Politics* (New York: Basic Books, 1983), pp. 76–86; David C. Hammack, "Technology and the Transformation of the American Party System," in Joel Colton and Stuart Bruchey, eds., *Technology, The Economy, and Society* (New York: Columbia University Press, 1987), pp. 126–49; Tim Luke, "Televisual Democracy and the Politics of Charisma," *Telos* 70 (Winter 1986–87), pp. 59–79; Doris A. Graber, *Mass Media and American Politics*, 2nd ed. (Washington, D.C.: Congressional Quarterly Press, 1984), chapter 6; and Ronald Berkman and Laura W. Kitch, *Politics in the Media Age* (New York: McGraw-Hill, 1986), pp. 135–140.

44   Edwin Diamond and Stephen Bates, *The Spot: The Rise of Political Advertising on Television* (Cambridge, Mass.: MIT Press, 1984); Larry J. Sabato, *The Rise of Political Consultants* (New York: Basic Books, 1981); Berkman and Kitch, *Politics in the Media Age*, chapter 6; Ranney, *Channels of Power*, chapter 4.

45   Ranney, *Channels of Power*, chapter 5. For some striking recent evidence on the impact of television news on public opinion, see Benjamin I. Page, Robert Y. Shapiro, and Glenn R. Dempsey, "What Moves Public Opinion?" *American Political Science Review* 81 (March 1987), pp. 23–43; and Shanto Iyengar and Donald R. Kinder, *News That Matters: Television and American Opinion* (Chicago: University of Chicago Press, 1987).

46   For a thoughtful evaluation of these experiments, see F. Christopher Arterton, *Teledemocracy: Can Technology Protect Democracy?* (Newbury Park, Calif.: Sage Publications, 1987).

47   Walter A. McDougall, . . . *The Heavens and the Earth: A Political History of the Space Age* (New York: Basic Books, 1985), pp. 6–7.

48   See, e.g., National Academy of Sciences, National Research Council, *The Race for the New Frontier: International Competition in Advanced Technology—Decisions for America* (New York: Simon and Schuster, 1984); *OECD Science and Technology Indicators, No. 2, R&D, Invention and Competitiveness* (Paris: Organisation for Economic Co-operation and Development, 1986); C. A. Tisdell, *Science and Technology Policy: Priorities of Governments* (London: Chapman and Hall, 1981).

49   McDougall, *Heavens and the Earth*, pp. 71–72, 76–79; J. Stefan Dupre and Sanford A. Lakoff, *Science and the Nation* (Englewood Cliffs, N.J.: Prentice-Hall, 1962); and Daniel J. Kevles, *The Physicists* (New York: Random House, 1971). On the other hand, the military played an important role in the development and diffusion of technology throughout the nineteenth and twentieth centuries; see Merritt Roe Smith, *Military Enterprise and Technological Change: Perspectives on the American Experience* (Cambridge, Mass.: MIT Press, 1985).

50   Quoted in Joseph J. Trento, *Prescription for Disaster* (New York: Crown Publishers, 1987), p. 36.

51   Robert B. Reich, "The Rise of Techno-Nationalism," *The Atlantic* (May 1987), pp. 63–69.

52   Commoner, *The Closing Circle*, chapter 9.

53   See Kenneth Flamm, *Creating the Computer: Government, Industry, and High Tech-*

nology (Washington, D.C.: Brookings Institution, 1987).

54   See W. Henry Lambright, *Governing Science and Technology* (New York: Oxford University Press, 1976); and William A. Blanpied and Rachelle D. Hollander, "The Political Non-Politics of U.S. Science Policy," and Leon E. Trachtman, "Science and Technology: Who Governs?" in Goggin, *Governing Science and Technology in a Democracy*.

55   These and other examples are discussed in James Everett Katz, *Presidential Politics and Science Policy* (New York: Praeger, 1978); and Joel Primack and Frank von Hippel, *Advice and Dissent: Scientists in the Political Arena* (New York: Basic Books, 1974).

56   On the synfuels program, see Richard H. K. Vietor, *Energy Policy in America Since 1945: A Study of Business-Government Relations* (Cambridge: Cambridge University Press, 1984), pp. 324–44.

57   Hans A. Bethe and John Bardeen, "Back to Science Advisers," *New York Times*, May 17, 1986, p. 19. See also William J. Broad, *Star Warriors* (New York: Simon and Schuster, 1985), p. 122; and Will Lepkowski, "New Presidential Science Adviser Will Face Complex Issues," *Chemical & Engineering News*, July 7, 1986, pp. 23–26.

58   See, e.g., Strobe Talbott, *Deadly Gambits* (New York: Alfred A. Knopf, 1984), pp. 317–18.

59   At this writing, a Technology Policy Task Force of the House Committee on Science, Space, and Technology is preparing a comprehensive report on U.S. technology policy. On the organization and role of Congress, see Barke, *Science, Technology, and Public Policy*, chapter 2.

60   On the concept of technology assessment, see articles by Harvey Brooks and Raymond Bowers, Hugh Folk, Joseph Coates, David Kiefer, and Michael Baram, in Albert H. Teich, ed., *Technology and Man's Future*, 2d ed. (New York: St. Martin's Press, 1977). See also David M. O'Brien and Donald A. Marchand, *The Politics of Technology Assessment: Institutions, Processes, and Policy Disputes* (Lexington, Mass.: Lexington Books, 1982); and David Whiteman, "The Fate of Policy Analysis in Congressional Decision Making: Three Types of Use in Committees," *Western Political Quarterly* 38 (June 1985), pp. 294–311.

61   Norman J. Vig and Patrick J. Bruer, "The Courts and Risk Assessment," *Policy Studies Review* 1 (May 1982), pp. 716–27.

62   Richard N. Perle, "Technology Security, National Security, and U.S. Competitiveness," *Issues in Science and Technology* 3 (Fall 1986), pp. 106–14; Bruce Stokes, "Fighting Separate Wars," *National Journal* (March 14, 1987), 602–7; Carol Matlack, "Signing Up Science," *National Journal* (May 23, 1987), pp. 1348–53.

63   Norman J. Vig and Michael E. Kraft, eds., *Environmental Policy in the 1980s: Reagan's New Agenda* (Washington, D.C.: Congressional Quarterly Press, 1984).

64   Some of the flavor of such competition is captured in David H. Brandin and Michael A. Harrison, *The Technology War: A Case for Competitiveness* (New York: Wiley, 1987).

65   See Edwin Wenk, Jr., *Tradeoffs: Imperatives of Choice in a High-Tech World* (Baltimore: Johns Hopkins University Press, 1986), esp. chapter 10, for some constructive suggestions.

CHAPTER 2

1 Lewis Mumford, "Authoritarian and Democratic Technics," *Technology and Culture* 5 (1964), pp. 1–8.

2 Denis Hayes, *Rays of Hope: The Transition to a Post-Petroleum World* (New York: W. W. Norton, 1977), pp. 71, 159.

3 David Lillienthal, *T.V.A.: Democracy on the March* (New York: Harper and Brothers, 1944), pp. 72–83.

4 Daniel J. Boorstin, *The Republic of Technology* (New York: Harper and Row, 1978), p. 7.

5 Langdon Winner, *Autonomous Technology: Technics-Out-of-Control as a Theme in Political Thought* (Cambridge, Mass.: MIT Press, 1977).

6 The meaning of "technology" I employ in this essay does not encompass some of the broader definitions of that concept found in contemporary literature, for example, the notion of "technique" in the writings of Jacques Ellul. My purposes here are more limited. For a discussion of the difficulties that arise in attempts to define "technology," see *Autonomous Technology*, pp. 8–12.

7 Robert A. Caro, *The Power Broker: Robert Moses and the Fall of New York* (New York: Random House, 1974), pp. 318, 481, 514, 546, 951–58.

8 Robert Ozanne, *A Century of Labor-Management Relations at McCormick and International Harvester* (Madison: University of Wisconsin Press, 1967), p. 20.

9 The early history of the tomato harvester is told in Wayne D. Rasmussen, "Advances in American Agriculture: The Mechanical Tomato Harvester as a Case Study," *Technology and Culture* 9 (1968), pp. 531–43.

10 Andrew Schmitz and David Seckler, "Mechanized Agriculture and Social Welfare: The Case of the Tomato Harvester," *American Journal of Agricultural Economics* 52 (1970), pp. 569–77.

11 William H. Friedland and Amy Barton, "Tomato Technology," *Society* 13 (September–October 1976), p. 6. See also William H. Friedland, *Social Sleepwalkers: Scientific and Technological Research in California Agriculture*, University of California, Davis, Department of Applied Behavioral Sciences, Research Monograph no. 13, 1974.

12 *University of California Clip Sheet* 54 (May 1, 1979), p. 36.

13 "Tomato Technology."

14 A history and critical analysis of agricultural research in the land-grant colleges is given in James Hightower, *Hard Tomatoes, Hard Times* (Cambridge, Mass.: Schenkman, 1978).

15 David F. Noble, *Forces of Production: A Social History of Machine Tool Automation* (New York: Knopf, 1984).

16 Friedrich Engels, "On Authority," in *The Marx-Engels Reader*, Robert Tucker, ed. (New York: W. W. Norton, 1978), p. 731.

17 Ibid.

18 Ibid., pp. 732, 731.

19 Karl Marx, *Capital*, vol. 1, trans. Samuel Moore and Edward Aveling (New York: Modern Library, 1906), p. 530.

20 Jerry Mander, *Four Arguments for the Elimination of Television* (New York: William

Morrow, 1978), p. 44.

21   See, for example, Robert Argue, Barbara Emanuel, and Stephen Graham, *The Sun Builders: A People's Guide to Solar, Wind and Wood Energy in Canada* (Toronto: Renewable Energy in Canada, 1978). "We think decentralization is an implicit component of renewable energy; this implies the decentralization of energy systems, communities and of power. Renewable energy doesn't require mammoth generation sources of disruptive transmission corridors. Our cities and towns, which have been dependent on centralized energy supplies, may be able to achieve some degree of autonomy, thereby controlling and administering their own energy needs." (p. 16)

22   Alfred D. Chandler, Jr., *The Visible Hand: The Managerial Revolution in American Business* (Cambridge, Mass.: Belknap, 1977), p. 244.

23   Ibid.

24   Ibid., p. 500.

25   Leonard Silk and David Vogel, *Ethics and Profits: The Crisis of Confidence in American Business* (New York: Simon and Schuster, 1976), p. 191.

26   Russell W. Ayres, "Policing Plutonium: The Civil Liberties Fallout," *Harvard Civil Rights—Civil Liberties Law Review* 10 (1975), pp. 443, 413–14, 374.

CHAPTER 3

1   Cf. Robert L. Heilbroner, *An Inquiry into the Human Prospect: Updated and Reconsidered for the 1980s* (New York, 1980); and Samuel P. Huntington, "The United States," in *The Crisis of Democracy*, by Michel Crozier, Huntington, and Joji Watanuki (New York, 1975), pp. 59–118.

2   See Heilbroner and Huntington as cited in the preceding note. This was also the thrust of President Jimmy Carter's speeches on April 18 and 20, 1977, in which he outlined his energy policy.

3   "Liberalism" has been used and studied in the broadest and most ambitious sense by Roberto Mangabeira Unger in *Knowledge and Politics* (New York, 1975). Cf. also Paul N. Goldstene, *The Collapse of Liberal Empire* (Novato, Calif., 1980), and the references below.

4   John Stuart Mill, *On Liberty*, ed. Currin V. Shields (Indianapolis, 1956), title page of the treatise.

5   See Mill's *Autobiography* (New York, 1944), pp. 178–80. Cf. C. B. Macpherson, "Democratic Theory: Ontology and Technology," *Philosophy and Technology*, ed. Carl Mitcham and Robert Mackey (New York, 1972), p. 166.

6   C. B. Macpherson, *The Life and Times of Liberal Democracy* (Oxford, 1977), p. 1.

7   Ibid.

8   Ibid., p. 2.

9   Ronald Dworkin, "Liberalism," *Public and Private Morality*, ed. Stuart Hampshire (New York, 1978), pp. 130–33.

10   Macpherson, *The Life and Times*, p. 47.

11   Ibid., p. 99.

12   Ronald Dworkin, "Liberalism," p. 127. An elaboration of Dworkin's position can be found in Bruce A. Ackerman, *Social Justice in the Liberal State* (New Haven, Conn., 1980). For a broader background of the liberal agnosticism with regard to

human goods see Manfred Stanley, *The Technological Conscience* (New York, 1978), pp. 2–74, pp. 21–24 in particular.

13 Ronald Dworkin, p. 127.

14 Ibid., p. 142.

15 See Gerald Dworkin, "Paternalism," *Morality and the Law*, ed. Richard A. Wasserstrom (Belmont, Calif., 1971), pp. 107–26.

16 Cf. Christopher Jencks, *Who Gets Ahead? The Determinants of Economic Success in America* (New York, 1979).

17 E.g., Eugene S. Ferguson, "The American-ness of American Technology," *Technology and Culture* 20 (1979): 3–24; Bertrand de Jouvenel, "Technology as a Means," in K. Baier and N. Rescher, eds., *Values and the Future* (New York, 1969), pp. 217–32; and Daniel J. Boorstin, "Tomorrow: The Republic of Technology," *Time*, January 17, 1977, pp. 36–38. Scandinavia and Western Europe are better examples of universal if unequal prosperity than the United States.

18 Gerald Dworkin, "Paternalism," p. 118.

19 Ibid., pp. 123, 124.

20 See Carl Mitcham, "Types of Technology," *Research in Philosophy and Technology*, vol. 1 (1978), pp. 229–94.

21 Francis Bacon, *The New Organon and Related Writings*, ed. Fulton H. Anderson (Indianapolis, 1960), p. 16; René Descartes, *Discourse on Method*, trans. Laurence J. Lafleur (Indianapolis, 1956), pp. 39–40.

22 See Karl Polanyi, *The Great Transformation* (New York, 1944).

23 See Ferguson, "American-ness of American Technology," p. 16.

24 See Hugo A. Meier, "Technology and Democracy," *Mississippi Historical Review* 43 (1957): 618–40; and Leo Marx, *The Machine in the Garden* (Oxford, 1964), pp. 181–242.

25 *Wall Street Journal*, April 13, 1976, p. 11. The promise of technology takes its commonest, but also its vaguest and most confusing, form in the notion of scientific and technological progress.

26 *Passages*, November 1979, p. 111.

27 *New York Times Magazine*, November 4, 1979, p. 69.

28 *Frontier*, May/June 1978, p. 1.

29 *Wall Street Journal*, April 13, 1976, p. 11. Ferguson's faith in technology (taken broadly) is not unqualified either. See "American-ness of American Technology," pp. 23–24.

30 *Wall Street Journal*, April 13, 1976, p. 11.

31 Ibid. Wiesner gives a longer and more qualified statement of his view on technology in "Technology Is for Mankind," *Technology Review* 75 (May 1973): 10–13.

32 *Consumer Reports* 37 (1972): 746.

33 See Georges Friedmann, "Leisure and Technological Civilization," *International Social Science Journal* 12 (1960): 509–21.

34 Staffan B. Linder makes this distinction of periods in regard to economic growth in *The Harried Leisure Class* (New York, 1970), pp. 129–46.

35 See Heilbroner, *Inquiry into the Human Prospect*, p. 13, and Christopher Lasch, *Haven in a Heartless World*, pp. xiv–xv and passim.

36 For a description of the device paradigm see my "Orientation in Technology,"

Philosophy Today 16 (1972), pp. 135–47.

37   Jürgen Habermas, *Legitimation Crisis*, trans. Thomas McCarthy (Boston, 1975), pp. 60, 61, 135.

38   Aldous Huxley, *Brave New World* (New York, 1953 [first published 1932]); Stanley, *The Technological Conscience*, pp. 39–42.

39   Cf. Todd LaPorte and David Metlay, "Public Attitudes toward Present and Future Technologies," *Social Studies of Science* 5 (1975), pp. 373–98, p. 382 in particular.

40   Norman H. Nie, Sidney Verba, and John R. Petrocik, *The Changing American Voter* (Cambridge, Mass., 1976).

41   See Arthur T. Hadley, *The Empty Polling Booth* (Englewood Cliffs, N.J., 1978), pp. 15–26.

42   They constitute 35 percent of those who refrain from voting; the poor and uneducated represent 13 percent; the alienated 22 percent.

43   See Donald J. Devine, *The Attentive Public: Polyarchical Democracy* (Chicago, 1970); and LaPorte and Metlay, "Technology Observed," *Science* 188 (April 11, 1975), p. 125.

44   The force of the democratic call for equality makes itself felt in cycles, as Huntington has pointed out in *The Crisis of Democracy*, pp. 59–118, p. 112 in particular.

45   Immanuel Kant, *Foundations of the Metaphysics of Morals*, trans. Lewis White Beck (Indianapolis, 1959), pp. 51–53. Cf. Andrew Hacker, "Creating American Inequality," *New York Review of Books*, 27, no. 4 (March 20, 1980), pp. 20, 26–28.

46   See Lester C. Thurow, "Tax Wealth, Not Income," *New York Times Magazine*, April 11, 1976, pp. 32–33, 102–9.

47   See Richard A. Posner, "Economic Justice and the Economist," *The Public Interest* 33 (Fall 1973), pp. 116–18.

48   Equality has equal rights as necessary or formal conditions. But the substantive degree (or the sufficiency of the conditions) of equality is measured by income (or wealth).

49   Cf. Thurow, "Toward a Definition of Economic Justice," *The Public Interest* 31 (Spring 1973), pp. 56–63; and Posner, "Economic Justice," pp. 114–16.

50   See Thurow, "Toward a Definition," p. 77.

51   See Hacker, "Creating American Inequality," p. 21. The families whose income is $50,000 or higher constitute, as said before, 3.6 percent.

52   See Peter Laslett, *The World We Have Lost* (New York, 1965); Macpherson, *The Life and Times of Liberal Democracy*, pp. 9–43; Thurow, "Toward a Definition," pp. 68–69.

53   See Hacker, "Creating American Inequality," p. 21; and Thurow, "Tax Wealth, Not Income," p. 32.

54   Cf. Thurow's puzzlement, ibid., pp. 102–3.

55   On the obstacles to a new solution see Thurow, *The Zero-Sum Society* (New York, 1980).

56   Cf. Jacques Ellul, *The Technological Society*, trans. John Wilkinson (New York, 1964), pp. 229–318.

57   See Sabastian de Grazia, *Of Time, Work, and Leisure* (Garden City, N.Y., 1964); John P. Robinson, *How Americans Use Time* (New York, 1977); E. Louis Davis and Albert B. Cherns, eds., *The Quality of Working Life*, 2 vols. (New York, 1975). Work satis-

faction, to be sure, is a controversial topic; cf. William H. Form, "Auto Workers and Their Machines: A Study of Work, Factory, and Job Satisfaction in Four Countries," *Social Forces* 52 (1973), pp. 1–15.

58   Walter Kerr, *The Decline of Pleasure* (New York, 1962); Tibor Scitovsky, *The Joyless Economy* (Oxford, 1976). In the same vein, if less indicative in their titles, are August Heckscher, *The Public Happiness* (New York, 1962); and Fred Hirsch, *Social Limits to Growth* (Cambridge, Mass., 1976).

59   The following suggestions, due to their brevity, may appear ambiguous or unrealistic. I have supplied a more explicit theoretical framework, a consideration of the major objections, and a survey of the pertinent empirical evidence in a longer study which I have just now completed.

60   Cf. Lowdon Wingo, "The Quality of Life: Toward a Microeconomic Definition," *Urban Studies* 10 (1973), pp. 3–18.

INTRODUCTION TO PART II

1   Malcolm L. Goggin, ed., *Governing Science and Technology in a Democracy* (Knoxville: University of Tennessee Press, 1986).

2   See especially W. Henry Lambright, *Governing Science and Technology* (New York: Oxford University Press, 1976); and Richard Barke, *Science, Technology, and Public Policy* (Washington, D.C.: Congressional Quarterly Press, 1986).

3   Joel Primack and Frank von Hippel, *Advice and Dissent: Scientists in the Political Arena* (New York: Basic Books, 1974).

4   Frank Press, "Science and Technology in the White House, 1977–1980," Parts I and II, *Science* (January 9 and 16, 1981).

5   Will Lepkowski, "New Presidential Science Adviser Will Face Complex Issues," *Chemical and Engineering News*, July 7, 1986.

6   Twentieth Century Fund, *Science in the Streets* (New York: Priority Press, 1984); William Colglazier, Jr., and Michael Rice, "Media Coverage of Complex Technological Issues," in Dorothy S. Zinberg, ed., *Uncertain Power: The Struggle for a National Energy Policy* (New York: Pergamon Press, 1983).

7   See John Rees, ed., *Technology, Regions, and Policy* (Totowa, N.J.: Rowman and Allanheld, 1986).

8   C. A. Tisdell, *Science and Technology Policy: Priorities of Governments* (London: Chapman and Hall, 1981); and John Irvine and Ben R. Martin, *Foresight in Science: Picking the Winners* (London: Frances Pinter, 1984).

9   For examples of specific sectors, see Margaret Sharp, ed., *Europe and the New Technologies* (Ithaca, N.Y.: Cornell University Press, 1986).

10   Deborah Shapley and Rustum Roy, *Lost at the Frontier: U.S. Science and Technology Policy Adrift* (Philadelphia: ISI Press, 1985).

CHAPTER 4

1   Thomas E. Cronin, *The State of the Presidency* (Boston and Toronto: Little, Brown, 1975), pp. 13–16.

2   W. Henry Lambright, *Governing Science and Technology* (New York, London,

Toronto: Oxford University Press, 1976).

3   Daniel Lerner and Harold D. Lasswell, eds., *The Policy Sciences* (Stanford: Stanford University Press, 1951). Also see Gary D. Brewer, "The Policy Sciences Emerge: To Nurture and Structure a Discipline," Rand Paper P–5206, April 1974; and Charles O. Jones, *An Introduction to the Study of Public Policy* (Monterey, Calif.: Brooks/ Cole, 1984).

4   W. Henry Lambright, *Presidential Management of Technology: The Johnson Presidency* (Austin: University of Texas Press, 1985).

5   W. Henry Lambright and James A. Heckley, "Policy Making for Emerging Technologies: The Case of Earthquake Prediction," *Policy Sciences* 18 (1985), pp. 227–40.

6   Paul C. Light, *The Presidential Agenda: Domestic Policy Choice From Kennedy to Carter (With Notes on Ronald Reagan)* (Baltimore and London: Johns Hopkins University Press, 1982).

7   W. Henry Lambright and Harvey Sapolsky, "Terminating Federal Research and Development Programs," *Policy Sciences* 7 (June 1976).

8   John Logsdon, *The Decision To Go to the Moon* (Cambridge, Mass.: MIT Press, 1970), pp. 56–57. See also NASA, *Preliminary History of the National Aeronautics and Space Administration during the Administration of President Lyndon B. Johnson* (Washington, D.C.: NASA, 1969); Arnold S. Levine, *Managing NASA in the Apollo Era* (Washington, D.C.: NASA, 1982); Robert Rosholt, *An Administrative History of NASA* (Washington, D.C.: NASA, 1966); and C. G. Brooks et al., *Chariots for Apollo* (Washington, D.C.: NASA, 1979).

9   Robert Gillette, "Space Shuttle: A Giant Step for NASA and the Military?" *Science* 171 (March 12, 1971), pp. 991–93.

10 John Logsdon, "The Space Shuttle Program: A Policy Failure?" *Science* 232 (May 30, 1986), pp. 1099–1105.

11 Claude E. Barfield, "Science Report/Nuclear Establishment Wins Commitment to Speed Development of Breeder Reactor," *National Journal* (July 17, 1971), pp. 1495–97.

12 *New York Times*, March 25, 1983, p. 1.

13 "Address to the Nation on Defense and National Security" (March 23, 1983), in *Public Papers of the Presidents of the United States: Ronald Reagan, 1983* (Washington, D.C.: Government Printing Office, 1984), pp. 437–43.

14 Gary L. Guertner and Donald M. Snow, *The Last Frontier: An Analysis of the Strategic Defense Initiative* (Lexington, Mass.: Lexington Books, 1986), p. 20.

15 *Washington Post*, March 25, 1983, p. A1. Also see *New York Times*, March 25, 1983, p. 8.

16 *New York Times*, March 27, 1983, p. I14. Also see *Washington Post*, March 27, 1983, p. A14.

17 Lambright, *Governing Science and Technology*, p. 55.

18 Barfield, "Science Report/Nuclear Establishment Wins Commitment," p. 1502.

19 Deborah Shapley, "Plutonium: Reactor Proliferation Threatens a Nuclear Black Market," *Science* 172 (April 9, 1971), pp. 143–46.

20 "Special Message to the Congress on Energy Resources" (June 4, 1971), in *Public Papers of the Presidents of the United States: Richard Nixon, 1971* (Washington, D.C.: Government Printing Office, 1972), p. 706.

21 "Address to the Nation on Defense and National Security" (March 23, 1983), p. 443.
22 Robert Scheer, *With Enough Shovels: Reagan, Bush, and Nuclear War* (New York: Random House, 1982), p. 31.
23 "Address to the Nation on Defense and National Security" (March 23, 1983), p. 441.
24 Ibid., p. 443.
25 W. Henry Lambright, "James Webb and the Uses of Administrative Power," in J. Doig and E. Hargrove, eds., *Leadership and Innovation: A Biographical Perspective on Entrepreneurs in Government* (Baltimore: Johns Hopkins University Press, forthcoming).
26 Robert Gillette, "Space Shuttle: Studies Open Cost-Benefit Conflict," *Science* 172 (June 11, 1971), p. 1112.
27 Logsdon, "The Space Shuttle Program," p. 1104.
28 Robert Gillette, "Energy: President Asks $3 Billion for Breeder Reactor, Fuel Studies," *Science* 172 (June 11, 1971), pp. 1114–16.
29 Barfield, "Science Report/Nuclear Establishment Wins Commitment," p. 1494. Also see Claude E. Barfield, "Science Report/ Nuclear Breeder-Reactor Program Delayed by Court Decision, Contract Disputes," *National Journal* (June 30, 1973), p. 956.
30 *New York Times*, June 30, 1973, p. 20.
31 *New York Times*, June 13, 1973, p. 15.
32 *Washington Post*, May 7, 1974, p. A6.
33 Guertner and Snow, *The Last Frontier*, pp. 21–22.
34 *New York Times*, October 13, 1986, p. 1.
35 R. Jeffrey Smith, "Weapons Bureaucracy Spurns Star Wars Goal," *Science* 224 (April 6, 1984), pp. 32–34.
36 *New York Times*, April 5, 1983, p. 7. Also see *New York Times*, July 20, 1983, p. 20; November 16, 1983, p. 8; and March 29, 1985, p. 20.
37 *Christian Science Monitor*, April 26, 1984, p. 2.
38 *New York Times*, May 29, 1984, p. III–1.
39 R. Jeffrey Smith, "Star War Panel Highlights Uncertainties," *Science* 224 (April 4, 1984), p. 33.
40 *New York Times*, May 10, 1984, p. 15.
41 *New York Times*, December 23, 1984, p. 1.
42 *New York Times*, December 24, 1984, p. 7.
43 *New York Times*, June 21, 1985, p. 1.
44 "Star War's Chief Takes Aim at Critics," *Science* 225 (August 10, 1984), p. 600. Also see Paul Mann, "Congress, Pentagon Clash on Report Citing SDI Technical Problems," *Aviation Week and Space Technology* 124 (April 7, 1986), p. 27.
45 Strobe Talbott, "A Shield against Arms Control," *Time*, February 2, 1987, p. 25.
46 "Star Wars Grants Attract Universities," *Science* 228 (April 19, 1985), p. 304. Also see "Ten Companies, Teams Win Strategic Defense Studies," *Aviation Week and Space Technology* 122 (January 7, 1985), p. 27. Also see Herbert J. Coleman, "SDI Subcontracting Opens Door for Small Business Research," *Aviation Week and Space Technology* (January 27, 1986), pp. 20–21.
47 W. Henry Lambright, *Presidential Management of Science and Technology: The Johnson Presidency* (Austin: University of Texas Press, 1985), pp. 104–8.
48 *Wall Street Journal*, June 2, 1975, p. 26.

49 *New York Times*, August 3, 1975, p. 28.
50 "Special Message to the Congress Urging Enactment of Proposed Energy Legisla-
    tion" (February 26, 1976), in *Public Papers of the Presidents of the United States:
    Gerald R. Ford, 1976* (Washington, D.C.: Government Printing Office, 1979), p. 140.
51 "Statement on Nuclear Policy" (October 28, 1976), in *Public Papers of the Presi-
    dents of the United States: Gerald R. Ford, 1976* (Washington, D.C.: Government
    Printing Office, 1979), pp. 2763ff.
52 "Carter vs. Plutonium: The Battle is Joined," *Nuclear News* (May 1977), pp. 21,
    33–38.
53 *New York Times*, April 22, 1977, p. II–7.
54 "Veto of Department of Energy Authorization Bill: Message to the Senate Returning
    S. 1811 Without Approval," (November 5, 1977), in *Public Papers of the Presidents
    of the United States: Jimmy Carter, 1977* (Washington, D.C.: Government Printing
    Office, 1978), p. 1972.
55 *New York Times*, March 10, 1981, p. III–1.
56 William J. Lanouette, "Clinch River Breeder Project Draws Opposition of Strange
    Bedfellows," *National Journal* (October 2, 1982), p. 1679.
57 "Last of a Breed," *Industry Week* (November 14, 1983), p. 21.
58 Joseph Trento, *Prescription for Disaster* (New York: Crown Publishers, 1987), pp.
    169–70.
59 *Report of the Presidential Commission on the Space Shuttle Challenger Accident*
    (Washington, D.C.: Government Printing Office, 1986), p. 82.

CHAPTER 5

1 Yi-Fu Tuan, "Our Treatment of the Environment in Ideal and Actuality," *American
   Scientist* 58 (1970), p. 244.
2 Sophocles, "Antigone," in Moses Hadas, ed., *Greek Drama* (New York: Bantam
   Books, 1962).
3 Plato, "Critias," in Edith Hamilton and Huntington Cairns, eds., *Plato: The Collected Dialogues* (Princeton, N.J.: Princeton University Press, 1962).
4 Barry Commoner, *The Closing Circle* (New York: Knopf, 1970).
5 Garret Hardin, "The Tragedy of the Commons," *Science* 62 (1968), p. 1243.
6 Niccolo Machiavelli, *The Prince*, George Bull, trans. (Baltimore: Penguin Classics,
   1961).
7 "Science and Space—Technology Seers," *Newsweek*, March 6, 1972.
8 Senator Edward M. Kennedy, Statement Before the Subcommittee on Computer
   Services of the Committee on Rules and Administration, United States Senate, on
   S.230 and H.10243, March 2, 1972.
9 Kenneth R. Hammond, Jeryl Mumpower, Robin L. Dennis, Samuel Fitch, and Wilson Crumpacker, "Fundamental Obstacles to the Use of Scientific Information in
   Public Policy Making," *Technological Forecasting and Social Change* 24 (1983), pp.
   287–97.
10 Richard L. Garwin, "Presidential Science Advising," *Technology In Society* 2 (1980),
    pp. 115–28.
11 Harvey Brooks, "The Resolution of Technically Intensive Public Policy Disputes,"

Science, Technology, and Human Values 9:1 (Winter 1984), pp. 39–50.

12   "Faith in Science," QQ (Report from the Center for Philosophy and Public Policy) 51, no. 2 (Spring 1985).

13   William Ophuls, *Ecology and the Politics of Scarcity* (San Francisco: W. H. Freeman, 1977).

14   Committee on Public Engineering Policy, *A Study of Technology Assessment* (Washington, D.C.: National Academy of Engineering, 1969).

15   Panel on Technology Assessment, *Technology: Process of Assessment and Choice* (Washington, D.C.: National Academy of Sciences, 1969).

16   Public Law 91-484, 92nd Congress, October 13, 1972.

17   Legislative History: House Reports no. 92-469 (Committee on Science and Astronautics) and no. 92-1436 (Conference Committee); Senate Report no. 92-1123 (Committee on Rules and Administration); Congressional Record, vol. 18 (1972) (February 8—considered and passed the House; September 14—considered and passed the Senate, amended; September 22—Senate agreed to conference report; October 4—House agreed to conference report).

18   Lewis Gray, "On 'Complete' OTA Reports," *Technological Forecasting and Social Change* 22 (1982), pp. 299–319.

19   John H. Gibbons, "Technology Assessment for the Congress," *The Bridge* (Summer 1984). The sections on the assessment process and timing of reports also draw from this article.

20   Charles A. Mosher, "The Office of Technology Assessment—Personal Observation," *Journal of the International Society for Technology Assessment* (June 1975).

21   Fred B. Wood, "The Status of Technology Assessment: A View from the Congressional Office of Technology Assessment," *Technological Forecasting and Social Change* 22 (1982), pp. 211–22; and OTA Proposed Guidelines, approved by TAB in April 1977.

22   Philip Handler, "On Reports," *The National Research Council in 1978* (Washington, D.C.: National Academy of Sciences, 1979).

23   John H. Gibbons, "Technology Assessment and Governance in a Technological Age: The Role of the Congressional Office of Technology Assessment," *Conference Papers: U.S.–China Conference on Science Policy*, January 9–12, 1983 (Washington, D.C.: National Academy Press, 1985).

24   A Bill on the formation of a parliamentary committee to be called the Parliamentary Office for the Evaluation of Scientific and Technological Options, no. 422, National Assembly, Constitution of October 4, 1958, 7th Legislature, 2nd Regular Session of 1982–83, France.

25   Vary T. Coates and Thecla Fabian, "Technology Assessment in Europe and Japan," *Technological Forecasting and Social Change* 22 (1982), pp. 343–62.

26   Ian Lloyd, Member of Parliament, personal communication, May 5, 1985.

27   Robert H. Randolph and Bruch Koppel, "Technology Assessment in Asia: Status and Prospects," *Technological Forecasting and Social Change* 22 (1982), pp. 263–384.

28   John W. Gardner, "Toward a Pluralistic But Coherent Society," Aspen Institute for Humanistic Studies, no. 0-89843-025-9 (1980).

29   John G. Kemeny, "Saving American Democracy: The Lessons of Three Mile Island," *Technology Review* 83 (June–July 1980), p. 65.

CHAPTER 6

1   Morris P. Fiorina, *Retrospective Voting in American National Elections* (New Haven, Conn.: Yale University Press, 1981).
2   Morris P. Fiorina and Roger G. Noll, "Majority Rule Models and Legislative Elections," *Journal of Politics* 42 (1979), pp. 1081–1104.
3   Barry R. Weingast, Kenneth A. Shepsle, and Christopher Johnson, "The Political Economy of Benefits and Costs," *Journal of Political Economy* 89 (1981), pp. 642–64.
4   Linda R. Cohen and Roger G. Noll, "The Electoral Connection to Intertemporal Policy Evaluation by a Legislator," Stanford University, Center for Economic Policy Research Publication no. 36, September 1984.
5   See Jeffrey Banks, "The Space Shuttle," and Linda R. Cohen and Roger G. Noll, "The Clinch River Breeder Reactor," which will appear in Cohen and Noll, *The Technology Pork Barrel* (forthcoming).
6   Linda R. Cohen and Roger G. Noll, "The Political Economy of Government Research: The Communications Satellite Program" (Presented at the Annual Meeting of the American Political Science Association, 1984), and "Government R&D Programs for Commercializing Space," *American Economic Review*, 76 (1986), pp. 269–72.
7   Barbara Goody Katz and Almarin Phillips, "The Computer Industry," and Richard Levin, "The Semiconductor Industry," in *Government and Technical Progress*, Richard R. Nelson, ed. (New York: Pergamon Press, 1982).

CHAPTER 7

1   Sharon Dunwoody, "The Science Writing Inner Club," *Science, Technology, and Human Values* 5 (Winter 1980), pp. 14–22.
2   Jon Swan, "Uncovering Love Canal," *Columbia Journalism Review* 17 (January–February 1979), p. 50.
3   Allan Mazur, "The Journalists and Technology: Reporting about Love Canal and Three Mile Island," *Minerva* 22 (Spring 1984), pp. 45–66.
4   Donald McNeil, Jr., "Upstate Waste Site May Endanger Lives," *New York Times*, August 2, 1978, p. 1.
5   Adeline Levine, *Love Canal: Science, Politics, and People* (Lexington, Mass.: Lexington Books, 1982), pp. 39–45.
6   *Love Canal: Public Health Time Bomb* (Albany: New York State Department of Health, 1978).
7   Lois Gibbs, *Love Canal: My Story* (Albany: State University of New York Press, 1982).
8   Irvin Molotsky, "Damage to Chromosomes Found in Love Canal Tests," *New York Times*, May 17, 1980, p. 1.
9   Gina Kolata, "Love Canal: False Alarm Caused by Botched Study," *Science* 208 (June 13, 1980), pp. 1239–42.

10   Philip Boffey, "New Love Canal Study Finds No Links to Genetic Diseases," *New York Times*, May 18, 1983, p. A1.

11   Associated Press, "Chromosome Damage Possible," *Syracuse Herald-Journal*, May 17, 1980, p. 1.

12   Gibbs, *Love Canal*, pp. 142–55.

13   Peter Sandman and Mary Paden, "At Three Mile Island," *Columbia Journalism Review* 18 (July–August 1979), pp. 43–58.

14   See Mazur, "The Journalists and Technology," for methodological details of all figures presented here.

15   Elliot Marshall, "The Salem Case," *Science* 210 (April 15, 1983), pp. 280–82.

16   Michael Brown, *Laying Waste: The Poisoning of America by Toxic Chemicals* (New York: Pantheon Books, 1979).

17   Frank Gibney and Richard Pope, *Catastrophe! When Man Loses Control* (New York: Bantam/Britannica Books, 1979).

18   Walter Cronkite, "CBS Evening News with Walter Cronkite," television broadcast, Columbia Broadcasting System, New York, March 30, 1979.

19   President's Commission on the Accident at Three Mile Island, *Report of the Public's Right to Information Task Force* (Washington, D.C.: U.S. Government Printing Office, 1979). Hereinafter cited as President's Commission.

20   Ibid., pp. 143–65.

21   Mazur, "The Journalists and Technology," pp. 56–57.

22   Stanley Rothman and S. Lichter, "The Nuclear Energy Debate: Scientists, the Media and the Public," *Public Opinion* 5 (August–September 1982), pp. 47–52.

23   Sandman and Paden, "At Three Mile Island," pp. 57–58.

24   Ed Magnuson, "A Nuclear Nightmare," *Time* 113 (April 9, 1979), pp. 8–17; M. Sheils et al., "Nuclear Accident," *Newsweek* 94 (April 9, 1979), p. 26.

25   Oliphant, editorial cartoon in *Washington Star*, reprinted in *Science* 204 (April 13, 1979), p. 153.

26   McNeil, "Upstate Waste Site."

27   L. Thomas et al., *Report of the Governor's Panel to Review Scientific Studies and the Development of Public Policy on Problems Resulting from Hazardous Wastes* (New York: Memorial Sloan-Kettering Cancer Center, 1980). See Levine, *Love Canal*, pp. 157–64, for a critique of this report.

28   *Love Canal* (Albany: New York State Department of Health, 1983); D. Janerich et al., "Cancer Incidence in the Love Canal Area," *Science* 212 (June 19, 1981), pp. 1404–7; N. Vianna and A. Polan, "Incidence of Low Birth Weight among Love Canal Residents," *Science* 226 (December 7, 1984), pp. 1217–19; Boffey, "New Love Canal Study."

29   Rae Goodell, "The Role of the Mass Media in Scientific Controversies," in H. Engelhardt, Jr., and A. Caplan, *Scientific Controversies* (New York: Cambridge University Press, 1987), pp. 585–97.

30   Allan Mazur, *The Dynamics of Technical Controversy* (Washington, D.C.: Communications Press, 1981), pp. 99–110.

31   Gibbs, *Love Canal*.

INTRODUCTION TO PART III

1 See Charles A. Walker, Leroy C. Gould, and Edward J. Woodhouse, eds., *Too Hot to Handle? Social and Policy Issues in the Management of Radioactive Waste* (New Haven, Conn.: Yale University Press, 1983); and Walter A. Rosenbaum, *Energy, Politics, and Public Policy*, 2nd ed. (Washington, D.C.: Congressional Quarterly Press, 1987).

2 See Michael D. Reagan, *Regulation: The Politics of Policy* (Boston: Little, Brown, 1987); and Kenneth J. Meier, *Regulation: Politics, Bureaucracy, and Economics* (New York: St. Martin's Press, 1985).

3 See, e.g., Eugene Bardach and Robert A. Kagan, *Going by the Book: The Problem of Regulatory Unreasonableness* (Philadelphia: Temple University Press, 1982); Robert E. Litan and William D. Nordhaus, *Reforming Federal Regulation* (New Haven, Conn.: Yale University Press, 1983); and Lester B. Lave, *The Strategy of Social Regulation* (Washington, D.C.: Brookings Institution, 1981).

4 One of the best volumes on the use of these methods is Vincent T. Covello, Joshua Menkes, and Jeryl Mumpower, eds., *Risk Evaluation and Management* (New York: Plenum Press, 1986).

5 For an argument critical of an overly protective stance on regulation of technology, see Mary Douglas and Aaron Wildavsky, *Risk and Culture* (Berkeley: University of California Press, 1982). A discussion of the ethical issues involved in making regulatory decisions about technological risk can be found in Albert Flores and Michael E. Kraft, "Determining the Acceptability of Risk in Regulatory Policy: Ethics, Politics, and Risk Analysis," in James S. Bowman and Frederick A. Elliston, eds., *Ethics, Government, and Public Policy* (Westport, Conn.: Greenwood Press, 1988).

6 See, e.g., Susan G. Hadden, ed., "Symposium on Public Policy Toward Risk," *Policy Studies Review* 1, no. 4 (May 1982), pp. 651–747; Mark E. Rushefsky, *Making Cancer Policy* (Albany: State University of New York Press, 1986); and Gary C. Bryner, *Bureaucratic Discretion: Law and Policy in Federal Regulatory Agencies* (New York: Pergamon Press, 1987).

7 For example, see Sheldon Krimsky and Alonzo Plough, eds., "Symposium on Risk Communication," *Science, Technology and Human Values*, vol. 12, issues 3 and 4 (Summer/Fall 1987).

8 A fuller discussion of this perspective can be found in Joseph G. Morone and Edward J. Woodhouse, *Averting Catastrophe: Strategies for Regulating Risky Technologies* (Berkeley: University of California Press, 1986).

CHAPTER 8

1 Nathan Rosenberg and L. E. Birdzell, Jr., *How the West Grew Rich: The Economic Transformation of the Industrial World* (New York: Basic Books, 1986), p. 33.

2 Ibid., p. 259.

3 Interview with Max Geldens, "Towards Fuller Employment: We Have Been Here Before," *The Economist* (July 28, 1984), pp. 12–22.

4 Bruce Williams, "Long-Term Trends of Working Time and the Goal of Full Employ-

ment," Directorate for Social Affairs, Manpower and Education, OECD draft working paper (SME/SC/83.12), December 22, 1983.

5 William H. Friedland and Amy Barton, *Destalking the Wily Tomato: A Case Study in Social Consequences in California Agricultural Research*, Research Monograph no. 15 (Davis: University of California, Department of Applied Behavioral Sciences, 1975); Jim Hightower, *Hard Tomatoes, Hard Times: The Failure of the Land Grant Colleges Complex* (Cambridge, Mass.: Schenkman, 1978).

6 Harvey Brooks, "Technology Assessment and Environmental Impact Assessment," in U.S.-China Conference on Science Policy, January 9–12, 1983, *Conference Papers, Committee on Scholarly Communication with the People's Republic of China* (Washington, D.C.: National Academy Press, 1985).

7 Rachel Carson, *Silent Spring* (Boston: Houghton Mifflin, 1962).

8 Kenneth S. Davis, "The Deadly Dust: The Unhappy History of DDT," *American Heritage* 22, no. 2 (February 1971), pp. 44–47, 92–93.

9 Harvey Brooks, "The Typology of Surprises in Technology, Institutions and Development," chapter 11, in William C. Clark and R. E. Munn, eds., *Sustainable Development of the Biosphere* (New York: Cambridge University Press, 1986), pp. 325–50.

10 Statement of J. E. McDonald, Hearings before a Subcommittee of the Committee on Appropriations, U.S. House of Representatives, Civil Supersonic Aircraft Development, 1971.

11 William W. Lowrance, *Of Acceptable Risk: Science and the Determination of Safety* (Los Altos, Calif.: William W. Kaufmann, 1976), p. 23; News and Comment, "Pollution and Public Health: Taconite Case Poses Major Challenge," *Science* 186 (1974), pp. 31–36.

12 Howard Kunreuther, Joanne Linnerooth, and Rhoda Starnes, eds., *Liquified Energy Gases Facility Siting: International Comparisons* (Laxenburg, Austria: International Institute for Applied Systems Analysis, 1982); Wolf Hafele, "Hypotheticality and the New Challenges: The Pathfinder Role of Nuclear Energy," *Minerva* 12 (1974), pp. 303–22.

13 A. K. Ahmed, D. F. McLeod, and J. Carmody, "Control for Asbestos," *Environment* 14, no. 10 (December 1982); Bruce Porter, "An Asbestos Town Struggles With a Killer," *Saturday Review* (February 26, 1973), pp. 26–31.

14 Harvey Brooks and Chester L. Cooper, eds., *Science for Public Policy* (Oxford: Pergamon Press, 1987).

15 Sheila Jasanoff, *Risk Management and Political Culture, Social Research Perspectives*, Occasional Reports on Current Topics No. 12 (New York: Russell Sage Foundation, 1986).

16 Howard C. Kunreuther and Eryl V. Ley, eds., *The Risk Analysis Controversy: An Institutional Perspective* (New York: Springer-Verlag, 1982); Kunreuther, Linnerooth, and Starnes, *Liquified Energy Gases*.

17 Ronald Brickman, Sheila Jasanoff, and Thomas Ilgen, *Controlling Chemicals: The Politics of Regulation in Europe and the United States* (Ithaca, N.Y.: Cornell University Press, 1985); Dorothy Nelkin, ed., *Controversy*, 2nd edition (Beverly Hills: Sage Publications, 1984).

18 Lowrance, *Of Acceptable Risk*, pp. 82–84; U.S. Code of Federal Regulations 409

(c)(3)(A) (1958).

19   Cf., for example, Bruce Ames, "Dietary Carcinogens and Anticarcinogens," *Science*
     221 (1983), pp. 1249–64.

20   Cf., for example, Thomas M. Gerusky, "Pennsylvania: Protecting the Home Front,"
     Environment 29, no. 1 (January/February 1987), pp. 12, 14, 16, 35–37.

21   Jasanoff, *Risk Management*, p. 57.

22   T. J. Allen, J. M. Utterback et al., "Government Influence on the Process of Innovation
     in Europe and Japan," *Policy Research* 7, no. 2 (April 1978), pp. 124–49.

23   Philip Harter, "Negotiating Regulations: A Cure for the Malaise, *Environmental
     Impact Assessment Review* 3, (1982), pp. 75–92.

24   G. Majone, Comments on the Internationalization of Regulatory Science in Relation
     to H. Brooks, "The Role of International Institutions," chapter 11 in Brooks and
     Cooper, *Science for Public Policy*.

CHAPTER 9

1   See, for example, Norman J. Vig and Michael E. Kraft, eds., *Environmental Policy
    in the 1980s: Reagan's New Agenda* (Washington, D.C.: Congressional Quar-
    terly Press, 1984); and Kenneth J. Meier, *Regulation: Politics, Bureaucracy, and
    Economics* (New York: St. Martin's Press, 1985).

2   See Lester Lave, ed., *Quantitative Risk Assessment in Regulation* (Washington,
    D.C.: Brookings Institution, 1982); National Research Council, *Risk Assessment in
    the Federal Government: Managing the Process* (Washington, D.C.: National Acad-
    emy Press, 1983); and Richard C. Schwing and Walter A. Albers, Jr., eds., *Societal
    Risk Assessment: How Safe Is Safe Enough?* (New York: Plenum, 1980).

3   See Vincent T. Covello and Jeryl Mumpower, "Risk Analysis and Risk Management:
    A Historical Perspective," in Vincent T. Covello, Joshua Menkes, and Jeryl
    Mumpower, eds., *Risk Evaluation and Management* (New York: Plenum, 1986),
    reprinted from *Risk Analysis* 5, no. 2 (1985). See also William W. Lowrance, *Of
    Acceptable Risk: Science and the Determination of Safety* (Los Altos, Calif.: Wil-
    liam Kaufman, 1976), pp. 1–7.

4   See Mary Douglas and Aaron Wildavsky, *Risk and Culture* (Berkeley: University of
    California Press, 1982); Julian Simon and Herman Kahn, "Introduction," in Simon
    and Kahn, eds., *The Resourceful Earth: A Response to Global 2000* (New York:
    Basil Blackwell, 1984); and chapter 8 by Harvey Brooks in this volume.

5   See "How Much Risk? An Evaluation of Public Attitudes," *Public Opinion* (February/
    March 1986), pp. 21–30.

6   Covello and Mumpower, "Risk Analysis," p. 535.

7   Paul Slovic, "Perception of Risk," *Science* 236 (April 17, 1987), pp. 280–85.

8   See Douglas and Wildavsky, *Risk and Culture*; and Sheila Jasanoff, *Risk Manage-
    ment and Political Culture* (New York: Russell Sage Foundation, 1986).

9   Covello and Mumpower, "Risk Analysis," pp. 535–37.

10   Lowrance, *Of Acceptable Risk*, p. 8.

11   Chauncey Starr, "Social Benefit Versus Technological Risk: What Is Our Society
     Willing to Pay for Safety," *Science* 165 (1969), pp. 1232–38.

12   Norman C. Rasmussen et al., "Reactor Safety Study: An Assessment of Accident

Risks in U.S. Commercial Nuclear Power Plants" (Washington, D.C.: Nuclear Regulatory Commission, WASH-1400, NUREG-75/014, 1975). For a current review of NRC safety goals, see David Okrent, "The Safety Goals of the U.S. Nuclear Regulatory Commission," *Science* 236 (April 17, 1987), pp. 296–300.

13 See Harvey Brooks, "Technology Assessment and Environmental Impact Assessment," in *U.S.-China Conference on Science Policy* (Washington, D.C.: National Academy Press, 1985).

14 See, e.g., Robert Field, "Statutory Language and Risk Management," Report to the Committee on Risk and Decision-Making of the National Academy of Sciences (Washington, D.C.: National Academy of Sciences, 1981); and Arthur A. Atkisson, Michael E. Kraft, and Lloyd L. Philipson, *Risk Analysis Methods and Their Employment in Governmental Risk Management*, Final Report to the National Science Foundation (Redondo Beach, Calif.: J. H. Wiggins, February 1985), esp. pp. 98–110.

15 Committee on Environmental Decision Making, National Research Council, *Decision Making in the Environmental Protection Agency*, vol. 2 (Washington, D.C.: National Academy of Sciences, 1977).

16 For example, see Peter Huber, "Exorcists Vs. Gatekeepers in Risk Regulation," *Regulation* (November/December 1983); and Aaron Wildavsky, "Richer is Safer," *The Public Interest* (Summer 1980), pp. 23–39. It is a rare issue of *Regulation* that does not contain several articles, news items, or letters critical of regulating risks.

17 See Norman J. Vig and Patrick J. Bruer, "The Courts and Risk Assessment," *Policy Studies Review* 1, no. 4 (May 1982), pp. 716–27. In the first case, *Industrial Union Department, AFL-CIO v. American Petroleum Institute* (1980), the Supreme Court criticized OSHA for not demonstrating that a proposed regulation would result in appreciable health benefits. In the second case, *American Textile Manufacturers Institute v. Donovan* (1981), the Court ruled that OSHA was not required to provide a full cost-benefit analysis to justify its regulation. Thus depending on statutory specifications, agencies must demonstrate benefits (reduced risk) of regulation even if they need not use a complete cost-benefit analysis. Doubtless the courts will clarify expectations more fully in the future.

18 See Covello and Mumpower, "Risk Analysis," p. 535; and Covello, Menkes, and Mumpower, *Risk Evaluation and Management*. The new literature is too extensive to cite here, but see the bibliography compiled by V. Covello and M. Abernathy, "Risk Analysis and Technological Hazards: A Policy-Related Bibliography," in P. Ricci, L. Sagan, and C. Whipple, eds., *Technological Risk Assessment* (Boston: Martinus Nijhoff, 1984). The leading journal for this new field is *Risk Analysis*, published by the Society for Risk Analysis.

19 William Ruckelshaus, "Science, Risk, and Public Policy," *Science* 221 (1983), pp. 1026–28.

20 Lowrance, *Of Acceptable Risk*; and National Research Council, *Risk Assessment in the Federal Government*.

21 Ruckelshaus, "Science, Risk, and Public Policy," p. 1026.

22 See, e.g., Lave, "Methods of Risk Assessment," in Lave, ed., *Quantitative Risk Assessment in Regulation*; and Mark E. Rushefsky, *Making Cancer Policy* (Albany: State University of New York Press, 1986).

23 See, e.g., Richard Wilson and E. A. C. Crouch, "Risk Assessment and Comparisons:

An Introduction," *Science* 236 (April 17, 1987), pp. 267–70; and William J. Petak and Arthur A. Atkisson, *Natural Hazard Risk Assessment and Public Policy: Anticipating the Unexpected* (New York: Springer-Verlag, 1982).

24 National Research Council, *Risk Assessment in the Federal Government*, pp. 3, 17–50.

25 See Rushefsky, *Making Cancer Policy*; and Judith Havemann, "How Do You Estimate Cancer Risk? OMB Thinks It's Got a Better Way," *Washington Post National Weekly Edition*, July 28, 1986, p. 31.

26 National Research Council, *Risk and Decision Making: Perspectives and Research* (Washington, D.C.: National Academy Press, 1982), p. 33.

27 Lowrance, *Of Acceptable Risk*, chapter 3.

28 For an overview of these and other methods, see Baruch Fischhoff, Sarah Lichtenstein, Paul Slovic, Stephen L. Derby, and Ralph L. Keeney, *Acceptable Risk* (New York: Cambridge University Press, 1981).

29 Cited in Fischhoff et al., *Acceptable Risk*, p. 81. See also Wilson and Crouch, "Risk Assessment."

30 John F. Morrall III, "A Review of the Record," *Regulation* (November/December 1986), pp. 25–34, esp. table 4, "The Cost of Various Risk-Reducing Regulations Per Life Saved."

31 See Slovic, "Perception of Risk."

32 Slovic, "Perception of Risk," p. 285. For a recent compilation of public opinion poll data on public attitudes toward risk, see "How Much Risk? An Examination of Public Attitudes."

33 For an attempt to compare forty-four proposed, final, or rejected federal regulations in terms of risks, costs, and benefits, see Morrall, "A Review of the Record"; see also Albert L. Nichols and Richard J. Zeckhauser, "The Perils of Prudence: How Conservative Risk Assessments Distort Regulation," *Regulation* (November/December 1986), pp. 13–24.

34 Executive Order 12291, February 17, 1981.

35 See John D. Graham and James W. Vaupel, "The Value of a Life: Does It Make a Difference," *Risk Analysis* 1 (1982), pp. 89–95. For a fuller review of the methods, see Lester B. Lave, *The Strategy of Social Regulation* (Washington, D.C.: Brookings Institution, 1981). For a discussion of the advantages and disadvantages of using such methods, see Daniel Swartzman, Richard A. Liroff, and Kevin G. Croke, eds., *Cost-Benefit Analysis and Environmental Regulations: Politics, Ethics, and Methods* (Washington, D.C.: Conservation Foundation, 1982).

36 See William R. Greer, "Value of One Life? From $8.37 to $10 Million," *New York Times*, June 26, 1985, p. 1.

37 See, e.g., Lowrance, *Of Acceptable Risk*; Lave, *Quantitative Risk Assessment in Regulation*; and Fischhoff et al., *Acceptable Risk*.

38 See, e.g., Lave, *Quantitative Risk Assessment in Regulation* and *The Strategy of Social Regulation*.

39 See, e.g., Michael E. Baram, "Cost-Benefit Analysis: An Inadequate Basis for Health, Safety, and Environmental Regulatory Decision-Making," *Ecology Law Quarterly* 8 (1980), pp. 473–531; Kenneth T. Bogen, "Public Policy and Technological Risk," *Idea: The Journal of Law and Technology* 21 (1980), pp. 37–74; and U.S. Congress,

Risk/Benefit Analysis in the Legislative Process, Summary of a Congress/Science Joint Forum (Washington, D.C.: Government Printing Office, 1980).

40   Langdon Winner, *The Whale and the Reactor* (Chicago: University of Chicago Press, 1986), chapter 8.

41   Kristin Shrader-Frechette, *Risk Analysis and Scientific Method: Methodological and Ethical Problems with Evaluating Societal Hazards* (Boston: D. Reidel, 1985); and Rosemarie Tong, *Ethics in Policy Analysis* (Englewood Cliffs, N.J.: Prentice-Hall, 1986), chapter 2. See also Albert Flores and Michael E. Kraft, "Determining the Acceptability of Risk in Regulatory Policy: Ethics, Politics, and Risk Analysis," in James S. Bowman and Frederick A. Elliston, eds., *Ethics, Government, and Public Policy* (Westport, Conn.: Greenwood Press, 1988).

42   E.g., Rushefsky, *Making Cancer Policy.*

43   Michael E. Kraft, "The Use of Risk Analysis in Federal Regulatory Agencies: An Exploration," *Policy Studies Review* 1, no. 4 (May 1982), pp. 666–75. The research was supported by a grant from the National Science Foundation, Division of Policy Research and Analysis, NSF PRA 800 7228.

44   See George C. Eads and Michael Fix, eds., *Relief or Reform? Reagan's Regulatory Dilemma* (Washington, D.C.: Urban Institute, 1984), esp. chapter 6; V. Kerry Smith, ed., *Environmental Policy under Reagan's Executive Order: The Role of Benefit-Cost Analysis* (Chapel Hill: University of North Carolina Press, 1984); and James L. Regens, Thomas M. Dietz, and Robert W. Rycroft, "Risk Assessment in the Policy-Making Process: Environmental Health and Safety Protection," *Public Administration Review* 43 (March/April 1983), pp. 137–45.

45   See Havemann, "How Do You Estimate Cancer Risks." See also Rochelle E. Stanfield, "Environmental Focus: Reducing Risk?" *National Journal*, August 16, 1986, p. 2032; and Margaret E. Kriz, "Kibitzer with Clout," *National Journal*, May 30, 1987, pp. 1404–8. For a balanced assessment of OMB in light of these criticisms, see "Presidential Management of Rulemaking in Regulatory Agencies," Report by a Panel of the National Academy of Public Administration (Washington, D.C.: National Academy of Public Administration, 1987).

46   See, e.g., Robert V. Bartlett, "The Budgetary Process and Environmental Policy," in Vig and Kraft, *Environmental Policy in the 1980s.*

47   Morris S. Ogul, *Congress Oversees the Bureaucracy: Studies in Legislative Supervision* (Pittsburgh: University of Pittsburgh Press, 1976); and Joel D. Aberbach, "Changes in Congressional Oversight," *American Behavioral Scientist* 22, pp. 493–515.

48   See Vig and Kraft, "*Environmental Policy in the 1980s*; and Joseph A. Davis, "RCRA Rewrite Strengthens Hazardous Waste Protections," *Congressional Quarterly Weekly Report*, October 6, 1984, pp. 2453–55.

49   See Flores and Kraft, "Determining the Acceptability of Risk."

50   A special issue of the journal *Science, Technology and Human Values*, vol. 12, issues 3 and 4 (Summer/Fall 1987) was devoted to risk communication.

51   See Sherry Arnstein, "A Ladder of Citizen Participation," *Journal of the American Institute of Planners* 35, no. 4 (July 1969), pp. 216–24; and Edward J. Woodhouse, "The Politics of Nuclear Waste Management," in Charles A. Walker, Leroy C. Gould, and Edward J. Woodhouse, eds., *Too Hot to Handle? Social and Policy Issues in the*

Management of Radioactive Wastes (New Haven, Conn.: Yale University Press, 1983), esp. pp. 173–79.

52 See Vig and Bruer, "The Courts and Risk Assessment."

53 See Joseph G. Morone and Edward J. Woodhouse, *Averting Catastrophe: Strategies for Regulating Risky Technologies* (Berkeley: University of California Press, 1986), chapter 8.

54 U.S. EPA, *Unfinished Business: A Comparative Assessment of Environmental Problems* (Washington, D.C.: EPA, Office of Policy Analysis, February 1987).

CHAPTER 10

1 Senator John O. Pastore, in U.S. Congress, Joint Committee on Atomic Energy, hearings on "The Status of Nuclear Reactor Safety," 1973.

2 David Collingridge and Colin Reeve, *Science Speaks to Power: The Role of Experts in Policy Making* (London: Frances Pinter, 1986), quote from p. 36. More generally, the section on lead is based largely on this work.

3 Collingridge and Reeve, *Science Speaks to Power*, pp. 42, 43, 44.

4 Ibid., p. 45.

5 For further details on the greenhouse threat, see Morone and Woodhouse, *Averting Catastrophe: Strategies for Regulating Risky Technologies* (Berkeley: University of California Press, 1986), chapter six.

6 Concerning the ongoing technical debate over smoking and lung cancer, see Collingridge and Reeve, *Science Speaks to Power*, chapter 10.

7 Among other recent works raising such ethical conundrums, see Anne L. Hiskes and Richard P. Hiskes, *Science, Technology, and Policy Decisions* (Boulder, Colo.: Westview, 1986); Deborah G. Johnson, *Computer Ethics* (Englewood Cliffs, N.J.: Prentice-Hall, 1985); and K. S. Shrader-Frechette, *Nuclear Power and Public Policy: The Social and Ethical Problems of Fission Technology*, second ed. (Boston: D. Reidel, 1983).

8 Peter F. Drucker, "New Technology: Predicting Its Impact," *New York Times*, April 8, 1973, reprinted in Albert H. Teich, ed., *Technology and the Future*, fourth ed. (New York: St. Martin's Press, 1986), pp. 214–18, quote from p. 214.

9 John Jewkes, David Sawers, and Richard Stillerman, *The Sources of Invention*, 2d ed. (New York: W. W. Norton, 1969), p. 11.

10 On the multitude of problems that make many kinds of forecasting a thankless task, see William Ascher, *Forecasting: An Analysis for Policy-Makers and Planners* (Baltimore: Johns Hopkins University Press, 1978).

11 Such is the conclusion, albeit a reluctant one for some theorists, of the contemporary literature on decision theory in political science, economics, and psychology. The classic arguments include Charles E. Lindblom, "The Science of Muddling Through," *Public Administration Review* 19 (1959), pp. 79–88; "Still Muddling, Not Yet Through," *Public Administration Review* 39 (1979), pp. 517–26; and, with David Braybrooke, *A Strategy of Decision* (New York: Free Press, 1963); Herbert A. Simon, "A Behavioral Model of Rational Choice," in *Models of Man* (New York: Wiley, 1957); and, with James G. March, *Organizations* (New York: Wiley, 1958).

Efforts to reduce reliance on trial and error, and increase reliance on analytic inputs, include Amitai Etzioni, "Mixed-Scanning: A 'Third' Approach to Decision-Making," *Public Administration Review* 27 (1967), pp. 385–92; and Yehezkel Dror, *Ventures in Policy Sciences* (New York: American Elsevier, 1971).

From decision theory in behavioral science, see Neil McK. Agnew and John L. Brown, "Bounded Rationality: Fallible Decisions in Unbounded Decision Space," *Behavioral Science* 31 (1986), pp. 148–61. From psychology, Amos Tversky and Daniel Kahneman, "Judgment under Uncertainty: Heuristics and Biases," *Science* 185 (1974), pp. 1124–31.

12   U.S. Congress, Senate, *Toxic Substances Control Act, Report of the Senate Committee on Commerce on S. 3149*, Senate Report 94-698, March 16, 1976.

13   On the privileged position of business in many kinds of decision making, see Charles E. Lindblom, *Politics and Markets: The World's Political-Economic Systems* (New York: Basic Books, 1977).

14   For further discussion of the ozone issue, see Morone and Woodhouse, *Averting Catastrophe*, chapter 5.

15   Baruch Fischhoff, Paul Slovic, and Sarah Lichtenstein, "Which Risks Are Acceptable?" *Environment* 21 (May 1979), pp. 17–20, 32–38, quote from p. 35.

16   David Collingridge, *Technology in the Policy Process: Controlling Nuclear Power* (London: Frances Pinter, 1983), p. 236.

17   Pertti J. Pelto, *The Snowmobile Revolution: Technology and Social Change in the Arctic* (Menlo Park, Calif.: Cummings, 1973).

18   David A. Mayhew, *Congress: The Electoral Connection* (New Haven, Conn.: Yale University Press, 1974).

19   Graham T. Allison, *Essence of Decision: Explaining the Cuban Missile Crisis* (Boston: Little, Brown, 1971); Jeffrey L. Pressman and Aaron B. Wildavsky, *Implementation* (Berkeley: University of California Press, 1973).

20   Tversky and Kahneman, "Judgment under Uncertainty"; Lloyd S. Etheredge, *Can Governments Learn? American Foreign Policy and Central American Revolutions* (New York: Pergamon Press, 1985).

21   E. E. Schattschneider, *The Semi-Sovereign People: A Realist's View of Democracy in America* (New York: Holt, Rinehart and Winston, 1960). Kay Lehman Schlozman and John T. Tierney, *Organized Interests and American Democracy* (New York: Harper and Row, 1986).

22   James L. Sundquist, *Constitutional Reform and Effective Government* (Washington, D.C.: Brookings Institution, 1986), p. 16.

23   For unclear reasons, much of the literature relies on relatively correctable errors; flagging sales in a basically healthy corporation is one of the key examples in Richard Cyert and James March, *A Behavioral Theory of the Firm*, 1963. Lindblom, "Science of Muddling Through," and "Still Muddling," refers to interest rates. John Steinbruner, in contrast, deals with tougher cases in *A Cybernetic Theory of Decision* (Princeton, N.J.: Princeton University Press, 1974).

24   For further discussion of the nongovernmental system for technological decision making, see Edward J. Woodhouse, "Decision Theory and the Private Governance of Technology," *Teaching Political Science: Politics in Perspective* 14 (Summer 1987).

25   *Wall Street Journal*, January 19, 1978, p. 38.

26 For a brief review of the accident and references to the applicable studies, see Morone and Woodhouse, *Averting Catastrophe*, chapter three.

27 On the Interagency Testing Committee and other aspects of the Toxic Substances Control Act, see Edward J. Woodhouse, "External Influences on Productivity: EPA's Implementation of TSCA," *Policy Studies Review* 4 (1985), pp. 497–503.

28 See Sheldon Krimsky, *Genetic Alchemy: The Social History of the Recombinant DNA Controversy* (Cambridge, Mass.: MIT Press, 1982), for a scholar-participant's reflections on the recombinant DNA regulatory process. For a later analysis, see Morone and Woodhouse, *Averting Catastrophe*, chapter four.

29 Early discussions of the idea include Harvey Brooks and Raymond Bowers, "Technology: Processes of Assessment and Choice," 1972, reprinted in Albert H. Teich, ed., *Technology and Man's Future*, 2d ed. (New York: St. Martin's Press, 1976), pp. 229–42; Hugh Folk, "The Role of Technology Assessment in Public Policy" (Presented at the 1969 meeting of the American Association for the Advancement of Science), reprinted in Teich, *Technology and Man's Future*, pp. 243–51.

30 Joseph F. Coates, "Technology Assessment," pp. 65–74, in *McGraw-Hill Yearbook of Science and Technology* (New York: McGraw-Hill, 1974), reprinted in Teich, *Technology and Man's Future*, pp. 251–69, quote from p. 260.

31 See chapter 5 in this volume for further discussion of OTA. Recent studies include U.S. Office of Technology Assessment, "Commercial Biotechnology: An International Analysis," pp. 360–85, in Albert H. Teich, ed., *Technology and the Future*, fourth ed.; U.S. Office of Technology Assessment, *Serious Reduction of Hazardous Waste: For Pollution Prevention and Industrial Efficiency* (Washington, D.C., 1986).

32 Lester B. Lave, *The Strategy of Social Regulation: Decision Frameworks for Policy* (Washington, D.C.: Brookings Institution, 1981), pp. 18–19.

33 Ibid., pp. 24–25.

34 Daniel Swartzman, Richard A. Liroff, and Kevin G. Croke, eds., *Cost-Benefit Analysis and Environmental Regulations: Politics, Ethics, and Methods* (Washington, D.C.: Conservation Foundation, 1982), p. 175.

35 Langdon Winner eloquently critiques the absurdity of failing to govern the full range of technological design; see chapter 2 in this volume, as well as *The Whale and the Reactor: The Search for Limits in an Age of High Technology* (Chicago: University of Chicago Press, 1986).

INTRODUCTION TO PART IV

1 See, e.g., Malcolm L. Goggin, ed., *Governing Science and Technology in a Democracy* (Knoxville: University of Tennessee Press, 1986), and the broad discussion of these issues in chapter 1 in this volume.

2 For discussion of these points see Richard Barke, *Science, Technology and Public Policy* (Washington, D.C.: Congressional Quarterly Press, 1986); and Dorothy Nelkin, ed., *Controversy: Politics of Technical Decisions*, 2d ed. (Beverly Hills, Calif.: Sage Publications, 1984).

3 For a review of the general limitations and potential contributions of case studies in the study of politics, see Harry Eckstein, "Case Study and Theory in Political Science," in Fred I. Greenstein and Nelson W. Polsby, eds., *The Handbook of Politi-*

cal Science, vol. 7, *Strategies of Inquiry* (Reading, Mass.: Addison-Wesley, 1975).

4 For a comparison of U.S., European, and Japanese approaches to nuclear waste disposal, see Luther J. Carter, *Nuclear Imperatives and Public Trust: Dealing with Radioactive Waste* (Washington, D.C.: Resources for the Future, 1987).

5 See Barry M. Casper, "Technology Policy and Democracy: Is the Proposed Science Court What We Need?" *Science* 194 (October 1, 1976), pp. 29–35.

6 See, e.g., Charles W. Anderson, "The Place of Principles in Policy Analysis," *American Political Science Review*" 73 (September 1979), pp. 711–23; and James S. Bowman and Frederick A. Elliston, eds., *Ethics, Government, and Public Policy* (Westport, Conn.: Greenwood Press, 1988).

CHAPTER 11

1 Amitai Etzioni, *Genetic Fix: The Next Technological Revolution* (New York: Harper and Row, 1973).

2 Robert J. Blendon, "Health Policy Choices for the 1990s," *Issues in Science and Technology* 2, no. 4 (1986), p. 67.

3 Robert H. Blank, *Rationing Medicine* (New York: Columbia University Press, forthcoming).

4 William A. Knaus, "Rationing, Justice and the American Physician," *Journal of the American Medical Association* 255, no. 9 (1986), pp. 1176–77.

5 David M. Freeman, *Technology and Society: Issues in Assessment, Conflict and Choice* (Chicago: Rand McNally, 1974), p. 29.

6 Henry J. Aaron and William B. Schwartz, *The Painful Prescription: Rationing Hospital Care* (Washington, D.C.: The Brookings Institution, 1984).

7 William P. Brandon, "Health-Related Tax Subsidies: Government Handouts for the Affluent," *New England Journal of Medicine* 305, no. 15 (1982), pp. 947–50.

8 Office of Technology Assessment, *OTA Proposal: Infertility Prevention and Treatment* (Washington, D.C.: OTA, 1987), p. 1.

9 Laurene Mascola and Mary E. Guinan, "Screening to Reduce Transmission of Sexually Transmitted Diseases in Semen Used for Artificial Insemination," *New England Journal of Medicine* 314, no. 21 (1986), pp. 1354–59.

10 National Academy of Sciences, *Assessing Biomedical Technologies: An Inquiry into the Nature of the Process* (Washington, D.C.: Natural Science Foundation, 1975).

11 Gina Kolata, "Genetic Screening Raises Questions for Employers and Insurers," *Science* 232 (April 18, 1986), pp. 317–19.

12 Ted Howard and Jeremy Rifkin, *Who Should Play God?* (New York: Dell, 1977).

13 Jerry E. Bishop and Michael Waldholz, "The Search for a Perfect Child," *Wall Street Journal*, March 19, 1986.

14 Leon R. Kass, "Implications of Prenatal Diagnosis for the Human Right to Life," in J. M. Humber and R. F. Almeder, eds., *Biomedical Ethics and the Law* (New York: Plenum Press, 1976), p. 317.

15 E. A. Murphy, G. Chase, and A. Rodriguez, "Genetic Intervention: Some Social, Psychological, and Philosophical Aspects," in Bernard H. Cohen, ed., *Genetic Issues in Public Health and Medicine* (Springfield, Ill.: Charles C Thomas, 1978), p. 358.

16   Alexander A. Capron, "Tort Liability in Genetic Counseling," *Columbia Law Review* 79 (1979), p. 681.
17   316 U.S. 535 (1942).
18   381 U.S. 479 (1965).
19   405 U.S. 438 (1972).
20   410 U.S. 113 (1973).
21   51 L.W. 4767 (1983).
22   L. M. Purdy, "Genetic Diseases: Can Having Children Be Immoral?" in J. J. Buckley, ed., *Genetics Now: Ethical Issues in Genetic Research* (Washington, D.C.: University Press of America, 1978).
23   Robert H. Blank, "Emerging Notions of Women's Rights and Responsibilities During Gestation," *Journal of Legal Medicine* 7, no. 4 (December 1986), p. 459.
24   Ibid., pp. 464–68.
25   President's Commission for the Study of Ethical Problems in Medicine . . . , *Screening and Counseling for Genetic Conditions* (Washington, D.C.: Government Printing Office, 1983).
26   President's Commission for the Study of Ethical Problems in Medicine . . . , *Splicing Life* (Washington, D.C.: Government Printing Office, 1982).
27   Lester W. Milbrath, "A Governance Structure Designed to Help a Society Learn to Become Sustainable" (Paper presented at the annual meeting of the American Political Science Association, Washington, D.C., August 30, 1986).
28   Morris B. Abram and Susan M. Wolf, "Public Involvement in Medical Ethics: A Model for Government Action," *New England Journal of Medicine* 310, no. 10 (1984), pp. 627–32.
29   Paul Light, *The Politics of Social Security Reform* (New York: Random House, 1985).

CHAPTER 12

1   The NWPA is Public Law 97-425, signed by the president on January 7, 1983. See 96 STAT. 2201-63. High-level waste refers to intensely radioactive nuclear waste, consisting chiefly of spent fuel rods from nuclear power plants. Low-level waste, in contrast, consists of a variety of less hazardous material such as irradiated glassware and plastic, power plant piping, and hospital waste from radiotherapy, with relatively short-lived isotopes.
2   On the range of technical tasks, see Office of Civilian Radioactive Waste Management, *Mission Plan for the Civilian Radioactive Waste Management Program*, Final report, DOE/RW-0005, 3 vols. (Washington, D.C.: Department of Energy, June 1985); and Office of Technology Assessment, *Managing the Nation's Commercial High-Level Radioactive Waste* (Washington, D.C.: U.S. Congress, Office of Technology Assessment, OTA-O-171, March 1985). On the more political tasks, see National Academy of Sciences, *Social and Economic Aspects of Radioactive Waste Disposal: Considerations for Institutional Management* (Washington, D.C.: National Academy Press, 1984); Charles A. Walker, Leroy C. Gould, and Edward J. Woodhouse, eds., *Too Hot to Handle? Social and Policy Issues in the Management of Radioactive Wastes* (New Haven, Conn.: Yale University Press, 1983); and E. William

Colglazier, Jr., ed., *The Politics of Nuclear Waste* (New York: Pergamon, 1982).

3   See William W. Lowrance, *Of Acceptable Risk: Science and the Determination of Safety* (Los Altos, Calif.: William Kaufman, 1976). The risk of concern here is the product of the probability of accidental release of radiation (e.g., from transportation or disposal) times the adverse health or environmental effects of the release.

4   See, e.g., Baruch Fischhoff, Sarah Lichtenstein, Paul Slovic, Steven L. Derby, and Ralph L. Keeney, *Acceptable Risk* (New York: Cambridge University Press, 1981); and Baruch Fischhoff, "'Acceptable Risk': The Case of Nuclear Power," *Journal of Policy Analysis and Management* 2, no. 4 (1983), pp. 559–75.

5   Charles A. Walker, Leroy C. Gould, and Edward J. Woodhouse, "Value Issues in Radioactive Waste Management," in Walker, Gould, and Woodhouse, eds., *Too Hot to Handle?*

6   Committee on Risk and Decision Making, National Research Council, *Risk and Decision Making: Perspectives and Research* (Washington, D.C.: National Academy Press, 1982), p. 28. See also Rosemarie Tong, *Ethics in Policy Analysis* (Englewood Cliffs, N.J.: Prentice-Hall, 1986), especially chapters 2–3.

7   See especially Todd R. La Porte, "Managing Nuclear Waste," *Society* (July/August 1981), pp. 57–65.

8   On ethics in risk evaluation, see Albert Flores and Michael E. Kraft, "Determining the Acceptability of Risk in Regulatory Policy: Ethics, Politics, and Risk Analysis," in James S. Bowman and Frederick A. Elliston, eds., *Ethics, Government, and Public Policy* (Westport, Conn.: Greenwood Press, 1988).

9   See Charles O. Jones, *An Introduction to the Study of Public Policy*, 3d ed. (Monterey, Calif.: Brooks/Cole, 1984), chapter 6.

10   See, e.g., David F. Salisbury, "Storing Nuclear Waste," *Christian Science Monitor*, June 24–28, 1985; and John Abbotts, "Radioactive Waste: A Technical Solution?" *Bulletin of the Atomic Scientist* (October 1979), pp. 11–18.

11   Paul Slovic and Baruch Fischhoff, "How Safe Is Safe Enough? Determinants of Perceived and Acceptable Risk," in Walker, Gould, and Woodhouse, *Too Hot to Handle?* The recent Roper Poll results are reported in *National Journal*, November 8, 1986, p. 2734.

12   Stanley Rothman and S. Robert Lichter, "The Nuclear Energy Debate: Scientists, the Media and the Public," *Public Opinion* (August/September 1982), pp. 47–52.

13   Robert E. Howell and Darryll Olsen, *Citizen Participation in Nuclear Waste Repository Siting* (Columbus, Ohio: Battelle Memorial Institute, ONWI-267, 1982).

14   Barry Sussman, "Nuclear Energy: Skepticism Rises," *Washington Post National Weekly Edition*, June 9, 1986, p. 37.

15   Vincent T. Covello and Jeryl Mumpower, "Risk Analysis and Risk Management: A Historical Perspective," in Vincent T. Covello, Joshua Menkes, and Jeryl Mumpower, eds., *Risk Evaluation and Management* (New York: Plenum, 1986), p. 536.

16   Slovic and Fischhoff, "How Safe Is Safe Enough?," p. 127.

17   Luther J. Carter, "Nuclear Imperatives and Public Trust: Dealing with Radioactive Waste," *Issues in Science and Technology* (Winter 1987), pp. 46–61. A fuller discussion of these issues can be found in Carter's book, *Nuclear Imperatives and Public Trust: Dealing with Radioactive Waste* (Washington, D.C.: Resources for the Future, 1987).

18 See, e.g., Twentieth Century Fund, *Science in the Streets*, Report of the Twentieth Century Fund Task Force on the Communication of Scientific Risk (New York: Priority Press, 1984); and Roger E. Kasperson, "Six Propositions on Public Participation and their Relevance for Risk Communication," *Risk Analysis* 6 (1986), pp. 275–81. See also Sheldon Krimsky and Alonzo Plough, eds., "The Technical and Ethical Aspects of Risk Communication," *Science, Technology, and Human Values*, vol. 12, issues 3 and 4 (Summer/Fall 1987).

19 Howell and Olsen, *Citizen Participation in Nuclear Waste Repository Siting*.

20 See, for example, "Public Participation in Developing National Plans for Radioactive Waste Management: Summary Report of the Second Keystone Conference on Public Participation in Radioactive Waste Management Decision Making" (Keystone, Colo.: Keystone Center for Continuing Education, October 1980); and Office of Technology Assessment, *Managing the Nation's Commercial High-Level Radioactive Waste*, chapter 8.

21 See Dorothy Nelkin and Michael Pollak, "The Politics of Participation and the Nuclear Debate in Sweden, The Netherlands, and Austria," *Public Policy* 25 (Summer 1977), pp. 333–57. See also Dorothy Nelkin, *Technological Decisions and Democracy: European Experiments in Public Participation* (Beverly Hills, Calif.: Sage Publications, 1977); and Amory B. Lovins, *Soft Energy Paths: Toward a Durable Peace* (Cambridge, Mass.: Ballinger, 1977).

22 See David W. Orr, "U.S. Energy Policy and the Political Economy of Participation," *Journal of Politics* 41 (November 1979), pp. 1027–56.

23 See Sherry Arnstein, "A Ladder of Citizen Participation," *Journal of the American Institute of Planners* 35, no. 4 (July 1969), pp. 216–24. Some findings along this line from our own research are reported in Michael E. Kraft, Bruce B. Clary, and Jame Schaefer, "Politics, Planning and Technological Risks: State and Citizen Participation in Nuclear Waste Management" (Paper presented at the annual meeting of the American Political Science Association, Chicago, September 1987).

24 See Gail Bingham, *Resolving Environmental Disputes: A Decade of Experience* (Washington, D.C.: Conservation Foundation, 1986).

25 See Margaret Kettles Boryczka, "Intergovernmental Policy Implementation and Nuclear Waste Disposal," in Helen M. Ingram and R. Kenneth Godwin, eds., *Public Policy and the Natural Environment* (Greenwich, Conn.: JAI Press, 1985); and Barry D. Solomon and Diane M. Cameron, "Nuclear Waste Repository Siting: An Alternative Approach," *Energy Policy* 13, no. 6 (December 1985), pp. 564–80.

26 E. Brent Sigmon, "Achieving a Negotiated Compensation Agreement in Siting: The MRS Case," *Journal of Policy Analysis and Management* 6 (Winter 1987), pp. 170–79.

27 See Sam A. Carnes et al., "Incentives and Nuclear Waste Siting: Prospects and Constraints," *Energy Systems and Policy* 7, no. 4 (1983), pp. 335–37.

28 Council on Environmental Quality, *Environmental Quality 1984* (Washington, D.C.: Government Printing Office, 1986), p. 353.

29 Ibid., p. 354.

30 See Charles A. Walker, "Science and Technology of the Sources and Management of Radioactive Wastes," in Walker, Gould, and Woodhouse, *Too Hot to Handle?* p. 46.

31 Leroy C. Gould, "The Radioactive Waste Management Problem," in Walker, Gould, and Woodhouse, *Too Hot to Handle?*

32   See Ted Greenwood, "Nuclear Waste Management in the United States," in Colglazier, ed., *Politics of Nuclear Waste*.

33   U.S. Department of Energy, Office of Civilian Radioactive Waste Management, *Record of Responses to Public Comments on the Draft Mission Plan for the Civilian Radioactive Waste Management Program*, vol. 2 (Washington, D.C.: Department of Energy, June 1985), p. 5; see also OTA, *Managing the Nation's Commercial High-Level Radioactive Waste*, which was written in response to the draft Mission Plan and offered suggestions for improvement.

34   Cited in Salisbury, "Storing Nuclear Waste."

35   See Carter, "Nuclear Imperatives and Public Trust," p. 49; the excellent series by Salisbury, "Storing Nuclear Waste"; James B. Martin, "Review of *Managing the Nation's Commercial High-Level Radioactive Waste*," *Environment* 27, no. 6 (July/August 1985), pp. 25–29; General Accounting Office, *Nuclear Waste: Quarterly Report on DOE's Nuclear Waste Program as of March 31, 1986* (Washington, D.C.: General Accounting Office, GAO/RCED-86-154FS, April 1986); and *Environment Reporter*, July 18, 1986, p. 430, and October 31, 1986, pp. 1022–23.

36   U.S. Department of Energy, Office of Civilian Radioactive Waste Management, *Annual Report to Congress* (Washington, D.C.: Department of Energy, April 1987), p. 2.

37   Kraft, Clary, and Schaefer, "Politics, Planning and Technological Risks." A fuller report on our content analysis of the public hearings will be prepared in spring 1988.

38   For a discussion of public opposition, the reasons for it, and the consequences, see Carter, "Nuclear Imperatives and Public Trust"; Joyce Maynard, "The Story of a Town," *New York Times Magazine*, May 11, 1986; and Matthew L. Wald, "Maine Saying No to U.S. Nuclear Waste Plan," *New York Times*, March 26, 1986, pp. 1, 10.

39   Joseph A. Davis, "Nuclear Waste: An Issue That Won't Stay Buried," *Congressional Quarterly Weekly Report*, March 14, 1987, pp. 451–56; and *Environment Reporter*, May 30, 1986, p. 110.

40   Robert D. Hershey, "U.S. Suspends Plan for Nuclear Waste Dump in East or Midwest," *New York Times*, May 29, 1986, pp. 1, 10.

41   *New York Times*, "Nuclear Waste Plan Leads Western States to File Suit," June 8, 1986, p. 21. The Comptroller General ruled on September 12, 1986, that the DOE decision to suspend the second-round search was illegal. See *Environment Reporter*, September 19, 1986, pp. 739–40.

42   Robert D. Hershey, "U.S. Proposes 5-Year Delay in Opening of Nuclear Waste Site," *New York Times*, January 29, 1987, p. 10. See also U.S. Department of Energy, OCRWM *Mission Plan Amendment* (Washington, D.C.: Department of Energy, June 1987), pp. 6–11. Curiously, there were few written comments submitted on the Mission Plan Amendment, a total of only fifty-eight.

43   *Environment Reporter*, June 13, 1986, p. 174.

44   Charles A. Walker, "Review of DOE Mission Plan for the Civilian Radioactive Waste Management Program," *American Scientist* 74, no. 1 (January–February 1986), pp. 79–80.

45   For example, see Advisory Commission on Intergovernmental Relations, *Citizen Participation in the American Federal System* (Washington, D.C.: ACIR, A-73, 1979).

46   Personal interviews in the Office of Civilian Radioactive Waste Management (OCRWM),

October 21, 1987. The interviews were tape-recorded with a guarantee of confidentiality; thus the names of the officials are not included here.

47 See Salisbury, "Storing Nuclear Waste."

48 See Rochelle L. Stanfield, "Nuclear Waste Politics," *National Journal*, October 4, 1986, pp. 2371–73; and DOE *Mission Plan Amendment*, p. 6. DOE described its siting schedule as "aggressive and success oriented."

49 Personal interview in OCRWM, October 21, 1987.

50 Personal interview in OCRWM, October 22, 1987.

51 "Atomic Waste Plan Pointing to Nevada Voted by the Senate," *New York Times*, November 13, 1987, p. 9; and Joseph A. Davis, "Udall Urges New Study of Nuclear-Waste Issue," *Congressional Quarterly Weekly Report*, October 10, 1987, pp. 2478–79, and "Congress Tries to Shy Away from Nuclear-Waste Decision," *Congressional Quarterly Weekly Report*, October 24, 1987, pp. 2605–6.

52 Joseph A. Davis, "Nevada to Get Nuclear Waste; Everyone Else 'Off the Hook,'" *Congressional Quarterly Weekly Report*, December 19, 1987, pp. 3136–38.

53 Rochelle L. Stanfield, "How Nevada Was Dealt a Losing Hand," *National Journal*, January 16, 1988, pp. 146–47.

54 For example, compare the position taken by Walker, Gould, and Woodhouse to that of Luther Carter. The former favor "genuine" consultation and public involvement, including use of "a randomly selected cross-section of the public in hearings and workshops, paying expenses and honoraria to encourage widespread and representative involvement, and employing professionals who are capable of translating complex issues of nuclear waste management into simpler terms." See "Value Issues in Radioactive Waste Management." In contrast, Carter places his faith in a pluralistic and representative, but fairly conventional, political process not unlike what Congress provided in 1987, where a "new, clearer, and broader consensus" may emerge from the participation of "importantly affected interests that were not much heard from in 1982." See Carter, "Nuclear Imperatives and Public Trust." The strong emphasis on participatory democracy in Walker, Gould, and Woodhouse closely resembles the position favored by several democratic theorists in recent works. See Benjamin R. Barber, *Strong Democracy* (Berkeley: University of California Press, 1984); and Jane J. Mansbridge, *Beyond Adversary Democracy* (Chicago: University of Chicago Press, 1983), original edition published by Basic Books in 1980.

CHAPTER 13

1 Arthur Kantrowitz, "Proposal for an Institution for Scientific Judgement," *Science* 156 (May 12, 1967), pp. 763–64; Presidential Task Force on the Science Court (A. Kantrowitz et al.), "The Science Court Experiment: An Interim Report," *Science* 193 (August 20, 1976), pp. 653–56.

2 Arthur Kantrowitz and Roger Masters, "Scientific Adversary Experiments," *Directions* (Thayer School of Engineering, Dartmouth College, Hanover, N.H.) (Fall 1986), pp. 14–21.

3 P. Handler, "National Academy of Sciences: Entering the Energy Debate," in "Washington Report," *EPRI Journal* 5 (April 1980), pp. 32–36.

4   P. Handler, "Science and Hope," in *Science: A Resource for Humankind, Proceedings of the National Academy of Sciences Bicentennial Symposium* (Washington, D.C., 1976), pp. 12–24.

5   Steven R. Weisman, "Reagan Proposes U.S. Seek New Way to Block Missiles," *New York Times*, March 24, 1983, pp. A1 (A21); Transcript of Reagan's speech on p. A20.

6   In addition to references in notes 1 and 2, see A. Mazur, A. Marino, and R. Becker. "Airing Technical Disputes: A Case Study" (presented at the annual meeting of the American Association for the Advancement of Science, Washington, D.C., February 13, 1977), in A. Mazur, *The Dynamics of Technical Controversy* (Washington, D.C.: Communications Press, 1981), pp. 34–42; Division of Magnetic Fusion Energy, U.S. Energy Research and Development Administration, *An Evaluation of Alternate Magnetic Fusion Concepts* (Washington, D.C.: U.S. Department of Energy, 1977); *Proceedings*, Colloquium on the Science Court, PB-261 305 (Washington, D.C.: U.S. Department of Commerce, 1977), available from the National Technical Information Service, Washington, D.C.

7   See endorsements of the Science Court by Presidents Ford and Carter in *Chemical and Engineering News* 54 (October 18, 1976), p. 28. For Reagan's endorsement, see *Physics Today* 33 (October 1980), pp. 49–52.

8   The Scientific Adversary Experiments were originally planned by Arthur Kantrowitz and Roger Masters under the aegis of the John Sloan Dickey Third Century Professorship and were supported by grants from the Rockefeller Center for the Social Sciences and the Mellon Grant to Dartmouth College. The program was managed by a faculty committee consisting of Jonathan N. Brownell (Environmental and Policy Studies), Arthur R. Kantrowitz (Thayer School), Roger D. Masters (Government), and Douglas Yates, Jr. (Policy Studies).

9   *Record: The Dartmouth Scientific Adversary Procedures*, vol. 1, *The Computing Aspects of the Strategic Defense Initiative*, vol. 2, *The Technical Aspects of the Strategic Defense Initiative*, available from Thayer School of Engineering, Dartmouth College, Hanover, N.H. 03755. $5.00 (two vols).

10   It is a pleasure to acknowledge the assistance of Henry Kendall, chair of the UCS, who was very helpful in referring us to Dr. Lin. For the curriculum vitae of the scientist-advocates, see *Record*.

11   The reviewers were Professors Thomas E. Kurtz (Mathematics and Computer Science), Elisha R. Huggins (Physics), and William F. Joyce (Tuck School). Professor Gene Lyons (Department of Government) evaluated the process and wrote his conclusions for the *Record*.

12   Again, three reviewers were drawn from the Dartmouth faculty: Professors Bengt U. O. Sonnerup (Thayer School), Walter H. Stockmayer (Chemistry), and John W. Strohbehn (Thayer School).

13   The second experiment was evaluated by Ambassador Robert L. Barry (John Sloan Dickey Fellow, Dartmouth College, 1984–85, U.S. Ambassador to Bulgaria, 1981–84), and by Professor Allan Mazur (professor of sociology, Syracuse University).

14   *Record*.

15   *Record*.

16 *Record.*
17 Fletcher Commission, "Strategic Defense Initiative: Defensive Technology Study" (Washington, D.C.: U.S. Department of Defense, March 1984), p. 23.
18 R. L. Garwin, "How Many Orbiting Lasers for Boost Phase Intercept?" *Nature* 315 (May 23, 1985), pp. 286–90.

CONCLUSION

1 For a more detailed discussion on this point, see Michael E. Kraft and Norman J. Vig, "Environmental Policy in the Reagan Presidency," *Political Science Quarterly* 99 (Fall 1984), pp. 415–39.

INDEX

ABOUT THE EDITORS AND CONTRIBUTORS

Robert H. Blank is professor of political science at Northern Illinois University and is affiliated with its Program for Biosocial Research. He is the author of *The Political Implications of Human Genetic Technology* and coeditor of *Biological Differences and Social Equality: Implications for Social Policy.*

Albert Borgmann is professor of philosophy at the University of Montana. He has written extensively on philosophical issues raised by technology and is the author of *Technology and the Character of Contemporary Life: A Philosophical Inquiry.*

Harvey Brooks is professor of technology and public policy at the Kennedy School of Government and former dean of engineering and applied science at Harvard University. He has written and lectured widely on science and technology policy, is the author of *The Government of Science*, and is coauthor of *Energy and American Values.*

Linda Cohen is a visiting member of the economics faculty at the University of Washington. Previously she taught at the Kennedy School of Government at Harvard University and served on the staff of the Brookings Institution and the Rand Corporation. She and Roger Noll are the coauthors of the forthcoming *The Technology Pork Barrel.*

John H. Gibbons is director of the congressional Office of Technology Assessment. Previously he spent nineteen years with the Oak Ridge National Laboratory, where he was director of the Environmental Program. He was also director of the Energy, Environment, and Resources Center, University of Tennessee.

Holly L. Gwin is an attorney and management analyst at the congressional Office of Technology Assessment. Her publications include articles on energy and security and environmental regulations.

Arthur Kantrowitz is professor of electrical engineering in the Thayer School of Engineering, Dartmouth College. He is a member of the National Academy of Sciences and the National Academy of Engineering. He was the originator and chief proponent of the Science Court proposal and served as chairman of the Presidential Task Force on the Science Court in 1975–76.

Michael E. Kraft is professor of political science at the University of Wisconsin–Green Bay and currently occupies the Herbert Fisk Johnson Professorship in Environmental Studies. He has taught previously at Vassar College, Oberlin College, and the University of Wisconsin–Madison's La Follette Institute of Public Affairs. He is coeditor with Norman Vig of *Environmental Policy in the 1980s: Reagan's New Agenda* and has written extensively on environmental policy and politics.

W. Henry Lambright is professor of political science in the Maxwell School at Syracuse University and author of *Governing Science and Technology* and *Presidential Management of Science and Technology Policy: The Johnson Presidency.*

Roger D. Masters is professor and chairman of the department of government at Dartmouth College. He is the author of numerous articles on human ethology and sociobiology and coeditor of *Ostracism: A Social and Biological Phenomenon.* From 1979 to 1984 he held the John Sloan Dickey Third Century Professorship in the Social Sciences at Dartmouth.

Allan Mazur is a former aerospace engineer who is professor of sociology at Syracuse University. He is the author of *The Dynamics of Technical Controversy* and numerous articles on social behavior and technology.

Roger G. Noll is professor of economics and political science at Stanford University, where he is also director of the Public Policy Program. Previously he taught at the California Institute of Technology and was a staff member at the Brookings Institution and the President's Council of Economic Advisors. He is the coauthor of *The Political Economy of Deregulation: Interest Groups in the Regulatory Process* and editor of *Regulatory Policy and the Social Sciences.*

Dianne Rahm is a research associate in the Technology and Information Policy Program of Syracuse University's Maxwell School of Citizenship and Public Affairs. She is completing her doctoral degree in public administration at the Maxwell School, with a specialty in science, technology, and public policy.

Norman J. Vig is professor of political science and director of the Science, Technology, and Public Policy Program at Carleton College. He is the author of *Science and Technology in British Politics,* coeditor of *Political Economy in Western Democracies,* and coeditor with Michael Kraft of *Environmental Policy in the 1980s.*

Langdon Winner is associate professor of political science in the department of science and technology studies at Rensselaer Polytechnic Institute. He has also taught at the University of California, Santa Cruz, and the Massachusetts Institute of Technology. He is author of *Autonomous Technology* and *The Whale and the Reactor: A Search for Limits in an Age of High Technology.*

Edward J. Woodhouse is assistant professor of political science in the department of science and technology studies, Rensselaer Polytechnic Institute. He is coauthor of *Averting Catastrophe: Strategies for Regulating Risky Technologies* and coeditor of *Too Hot to Handle? Social and Policy Issues in the Management of Radioactive Waste.*

Library of Congress Cataloging-in-Publication Data
Technology and Politics.
Bibliography: p.
Includes index.
1. Technology—Social aspects. 2. Technology and
state. I. Kraft, Michael E. II. Vig, Norman J.
T14.5T44163 1988   303.4'83 88-3841
ISBN 0-8223-0846-0
ISBN 0-8223-0838-X (pbk.)